I0591521

JOHN CLARE: THE CRITICAL HERITAGE

THE CRITICAL HERITAGE SERIES

General Editor: B. C. Southam

The Critical Heritage series collects together a large body of criticism on major figures in literature. Each volume presents the contemporary responses to a particular writer, enabling the student to follow the formation of critical attitudes to the writer's work and its place within a literary tradition.

The carefully selected sources range from landmark essays in the history of criticism to fragments of contemporary opinion and little published documentary material, such as letters and diaries.

Significant pieces of criticism from later periods are also included in order to demonstrate fluctuations in reputation following the writer's death.

JOHN CLARE

THE CRITICAL HERITAGE

Edited by

MARK STOREY

Routledge
Taylor & Francis Group

LONDON AND NEW YORK

First Published in 1973
Reprinted in 1995 by Routledge

2 Park Square, Milton Park, Abingdon, Oxfordshire OX14 4RN
&
711 Third Avenue, New York, NY 10017

Transferred to Digital Printing 2007

First issued in paperback 2013

Routledge is an imprint of the Taylor & Francis Group, an informa business

Compilation, introduction, notes and index © 1973 Mark Storey

All rights reserved. No part of this book may be reprinted or reproduced
or utilized in any form or by any electronic, mechanical, or other means,
now known or hereafter invented, including photocopying and recording,
or in any information storage or retrieval system, without permission in
writing from the publishers.

British Library Cataloguing in Publication Data

ISBN 13: 978-0-415-13449-1 (hbk)
ISBN 13: 978-0-415-86734-4 (pbk)
ISBN 13: 978-0-415-13469-9 (set)

Publisher's Note
The publisher has gone to great lengths to ensure the quality of this reprint
but points out that some imperfections in the original may be apparent

General Editor's Preface

The reception given to a writer by his contemporaries and near-contemporaries is evidence of considerable value to the student of literature. On one side we learn a great deal about the state of criticism at large and in particular about the development of critical attitudes towards a single writer; at the same time, through private comments in letters, journals or marginalia, we gain an insight upon the tastes and literary thought of individual readers of the period. Evidence of this kind helps us to understand the writer's historical situation, the nature of his immediate reading-public, and his response to these pressures.

The separate volumes in the *Critical Heritage Series* present a record of this early criticism. Clearly, for many of the highly productive and lengthily reviewed nineteenth- and twentieth-century writers, there exists an enormous body of material; and in these cases the volume editors have made a selection of the most important views, significant for their intrinsic critical worth or for their representative quality—perhaps even registering incomprehension!

For earlier writers, notably pre-eighteenth century, the materials are much scarcer and the historical period has been extended, sometimes far beyond the writer's lifetime, in order to show the inception and growth of critical views which were initially slow to appear.

In each volume the documents are headed by an Introduction, discussing the material assembled and relating the early stages of the author's reception to what we have come to identify as the critical tradition. The volumes will make available much material which would otherwise be difficult of access and it is hoped that the modern reader will be thereby helped towards an informed understanding of the ways in which literature has been read and judged.

B.C.S.

Contents

CONTENTS

Preface

This volume contains most of the reviews and notices of Clare's work that appeared in his lifetime, except those that were entirely biographical. Many of these early reviews were written by uninspired, journeymen critics, now anonymous; but they still have their value. Some make points that have always been important in discussions about Clare, others reflect the particular concerns of the time. The assumptions and contradictions lurking behind all these accounts are interesting in themselves, for the light they throw on reactions to other poets of the period, as well as for what they show of the response to Clare.

The numerous letters written to Clare are well represented, as they constituted a powerful form of encouragement and persuasion. In the extracts from letters from Mrs Emmerson, Octavius Gilchrist, Edward Drury, Taylor and Hessey, we can see something of individual readers' responses which qualify and enlarge upon the more formal reactions of the reviews. Extracts from Clare's own letters help to show what effect these pressures had on him.

For the period after Clare's death, the documents are necessarily of a different kind, and rather more selective. Each document has its own special interest—historical, critical, or even biographical (as this affects critical attitudes). Although most of the important responses are represented, there is nothing from the standard biographies by J. W. and Anne Tibble. These two works have played a crucial part in the revival and maintaining of interest in Clare this century, and some reactions to them are recorded here; but it would have been a travesty of their scope and intentions to pick and choose passages from them.

Documents are arranged chronologically. In one or two instances, however, a particular issue or theme is followed through, under one heading, so that, for example, the various views on a particular poem are gathered together, as are the differing opinions on matters of indelicacy, within a particular period. The general scheme is further broken up by a focusing of each of the early sections upon a particular volume. Therefore the critical reactions to *Poems Descriptive of Rural Life and Scenery* are to be found in sequence, and a separate section charts comments (usually from letters) on the growth of what was to become *The Village Minstrel*, even though this results in some chrono-logical overlapping between sections. Each volume of Clare's poems, published in his lifetime, is treated in the same way; I hope the greater pattern and order that results does not entirely eliminate the sense of a series of gropings towards some kind of critical truth.

Acknowledgments

I should like to thank the following for permission to reprint copyright material:

G. Bell and Sons, Ltd for C. H. Herford, *The Age of Wordsworth*; Basil Blackwell and Mott Ltd for an article by Alan Porter in *Oxford Outlook*; Mr Edmund Blunden for *Votive Tablets*; Cambridge University Press for Hugh Walker, *The Literature of the Victorian Era*; the Clarendon Press, Oxford for C. C. Abbott, ed., *The Life and Letters of George Darley*, for an article by Leslie Stephen in *Dictionary of National Biography*, for Arthur Symons, the Introduction to *Selected Poems of John Clare*, and for an article by J. W. R. Purser in *Review of English Studies*; Cornell University Press for Harold Bloom, *The Visionary Company: A Reading of English Romantic Poetry*; the *Daily Telegraph and Morning Post* for an article by Edmund Blunden; J. M. Dent and Sons Ltd for E. V. Lucas, ed., *The Letters of Charles and Mary Lamb*; Mr Geoffrey Grigson for the Introduction to *Selected Poems of John Clare*; William Heinemann Ltd for Maurice Hewlett, *Last Essays*, and for Edmund Gosse, *Silhouettes*; the *Hudson Review* for an article by Robert Graves (from the *Hudson Review*, vol. viii, no. 1, spring 1955); Mr Thomas Moult for an article in the *English Review*; the *New Statesman* for articles by H. J. Massingham, Robert Lynd, Percy Lubbock, Naomi Lewis, and Donald Davie in the *Athenaeum, Nation, Nation and Athenaeum,* and the *New Statesman*; the Northamptonshire Record Society, Sir Gyles Isham, and the author for an article by Robert Shaw in *Northamptonshire Past and Present*; the *Observer* and Mr Raglan Squire for an article by J. C. Squire; Oxford University Press for R. George Thomas, ed., *Letters from Edward Thomas to Gordon Bottomley*; A. D. Peters and Company, and the author, for Edmund Blunden, *Nature in English Literature*, and for Maurice Hewlett, *Wiltshire Essays*; Routledge & Kegan Paul Ltd for W. K. Richmond, *Poetry and the People*, and for J. W. and Anne Tibble, eds, *The Letters of John Clare* (and Barnes & Noble Inc.); the Poetry Society for an article by Samuel Looker in the *Poetry Review*; the Society of Authors as the literary representative of the Estate of John Middleton Murry for *John Clare and Other Studies*, and as the literary representative of the Estate of H. J. Massingham for an article in the *Athenaeum*, and for *The English Countryman*; the *Spectator* for an article by Alan Porter; Mr John Speirs for an article in *Scrutiny*; the *Sunday Times* for an article by Edmund Gosse; *The Times Literary Supplement* for two articles.

The British Museum, Northampton Central Library, and Peterborough Corporation kindly allowed me to transcribe from manuscripts in their possession; through the benevolence of the Meyerstein Fund, of the English Faculty at the University of Oxford, I have been able to make use of a microfilm of the letters to Clare in the British Museum; the Queen's University of Belfast has been generous with grants to cover the cost of travel and photocopying.

Abbreviations

The following abbreviations have been used:

Eg. British Museum MS. Egerton 2245–50.

NMS. Northampton MS., in the John Clare Collection of Northampton Public Library.

PMS. Peterborough MS., in Peterborough Museum.

Poems *The Poems of John Clare*, ed. J. W. Tibble, 1935.

Life J. W. and Anne Tibble, *John Clare: A Life*, 1932.

LJC *The Letters of John Clare*, ed. J. W. and Anne Tibble, 1951.

Introduction

John Clare has always been something of a problem for readers and
critics; this volume charts their successive attempts to come to terms
with him. Behind many of the confident assertions lies a perplexity
which springs ultimately from the confusion between the poet's life
and his work. Biographies of Clare abound, but nobody has given a
coherent critical account of the poetry in all its detail and abundance.
A similar uncertainty and reluctance coloured most of the contemporary
comment: it was the phenomenon of Clare, the Northamptonshire
Peasant Poet, which was attractive, rather than the poetry itself. Those
who espoused Clare's cause could count on a certain amount of
fashionable appeal, but they had to contend with the inevitable reaction
against peasant poets and their ilk. Consequently John Taylor, his
publisher, Mrs Emmerson, Clare's indefatigable London correspondent,
Lord Radstock and his wealthy friends—all these enthusiasts found
themselves putting forward their claims for this latest country bumpkin
with some bewilderment, in which extravagant praise was balanced
uneasily by cautious reserve. For some, it was rather a question of
getting Clare financial security, than of actively encouraging him as a
poet: he was just another person to be fed and then forgotten.

Many of the early reviews contented themselves with lengthy
extracts from Taylor's Introductions to *Poems Descriptive of Rural Life
and Scenery* (1820) and *The Village Minstrel* (1821). Praise or blame was
carefully hedged about with placatory qualifications. The hesitation
was understandable, in that the first volume in particular was not an
outstanding success, and we ought perhaps to applaud the tenacity of
those who could see the potential qualities of the new poet, rather than
censure those who threw him only a casual glance. None of these early
reviews is particularly long, and the quality of comment is not usually
high. Clare does not at any stage in his life attract the really big guns:
by the majority of critics and poets alike he is ignored. There are
passing comments by Byron and Keats (No. 36); Lamb (No. 64) and
De Quincey (No. 100) put in a word for him, but there is nothing
approaching a sustained interest amongst any of them. Although Clare
visited London, attending the dinner parties held by John Taylor for

his authors, it was essentially as an outsider, fascinated and repelled by the metropolis, ill at ease and obviously happier with a mug of beer in his hand. There was no dialogue between the two worlds. For all the lionizing, Clare was undoubtedly in his own day a minor figure.

The sentimentality which had initially attended Clare's cause came out again when his incarceration, first at High Beech, and then in the asylum at Northampton, captured the public imagination. As Clare began to write a new type of poetry, some of it dribbled into various newspapers and journals, thanks to men like Cyrus Redding, Thomas Inskip, and William Knight. After his death in 1864, Martin's *Life* (1865), as also Cherry's, of 1873, reawakened interest. Clare was now not only the peasant poet, but also the mad poet of genius.

Considered critical reactions emerged slowly. Towards the end of the century Clare tended to be read in a spuriously moralistic way, and it was not until Arthur Symons's selection of poems (1908) that the criticism of Clare attained its maturity. From this point onwards it is possible to see the swing towards a preference for the asylum poetry, a preference that has continued for much of this century. Critics have been able to trace development in the poetry, to see the asylum verse as a culmination of all that preceded it. But the arguments as to Clare's stature, and to the relative merits of the early and the late work, have never been resolved, and the convenient solution has been to make Clare an anthology poet.

The terminal date for this volume is 1964, the centenary of Clare's death, an appropriate occasion for reconsidering Clare's place in the poetic hierarchy. In many respects the critical interest in Clare is a development of this century, and the 'critical heritage' has its special significance in this wider context; whatever the problems Clare poses, at least we ought now to take him seriously and without condescension.

1820 TO 1835

Poems Descriptive of Rural Life and Scenery (1820)
Clare's early success owed much to Edward Drury, a Stamford book-seller and cousin of the London publisher John Taylor. Drury had an astute eye for business, and was quick to wrest Clare's affairs out of the hands of another bookseller, J. B. Henson, who was doing his utmost to persuade Clare to publish. It was due to Henson that the Prospectus was printed; the 'Address to the Public' (No. 2) makes no great claims for the work, but the promise evinced by 'The Setting Sun', the poem

included in the Prospectus, was sufficient to arouse Drury's interest. In no time at all Drury had persuaded Clare 'not to have anything to do with Henson'.[1] Clare submitted to Drury, and Drury soon found himself having to submit to his cousin.

At this stage, critical comment from any quarter was slight. But it is from Drury that we first learn something about this protégé:[2]

Clare cannot *reason*: he writes & can give no reason for using a fine expression, or a beautiful idea: if you read poetry to him, he'll exclaim at each delicate expression 'beautiful! fine!' but can give no reason: Yet is *always* correct and just in his remarks. He is low in stature—long visage—light hair—coarse features—ungaitly—awkward—is a fiddler—loves ale—likes the *girls*—somewhat idle—hates work.

Here are the germs of the myth that was soon to accumulate around the Peasant Poet. Personal details about the poet are as important as anything about the poetry. Drury told Taylor of Clare's 'ambitious views, his propensities to *licentiousness* or rather *sensuality*, and his weak reasoning powers';[3] and in January 1820 was warning Taylor: 'It is to be greatly feared that the man will be inflicted with insanity if his talent continues to be forced as it has been these 4 months past; he has no other mode of easing the fever that oppresses him after a tremendous fit of rhyming except by getting tipsy.'[4] A month after this he was complaining that Clare's drunkenness was a cause of great inconvenience, of a 'very disgusting nature'.[5] There is almost a sound of relief in his announcement of 30 May 1820 that he is now promoting a 'young Scotchman'.[6] But Drury had been candid about his motives when he told Taylor, 'I acknowledge, dear Cousin, that I desire to secure to myself some merit in bringing this rustic genius into notice',[7] and he was reluctant to see the likelihood of such glorification slipping away as Taylor wielded his superior influence. For all his disgust at Clare's drinking habits, he clung on doggedly to the manuscripts, even though it had been agreed in May 1819 that Taylor was to take charge.

The pressures on Clare, at the centre of intrigue and backbiting, were formidable, and it is scarcely surprising that the uncertainty and lack of confidence which consumed him—anticipating the puzzlement of many of the reviewers—were reflected in the poetry. Whereas later in life (Nos. 79, 91) he was to say that he wanted to be judged on criteria that ignored his peasant origins, initially he was actutely aware of his deficiencies, and the sort of public response his poems were likely to meet with. Drury wrote to Taylor on 5 May 1819 that Clare's envy

3

and anguish at other people's education and opportunities were such that he made himself really sick and ill,[8] and Drury was determined, paradoxically, that Clare should not achieve the success for which he craved: 'Though his day dreams picture the most exaggerated success, & though his hopes are preposterous to excess, I do not fear with careful management his pride & ambition will be checked.'[9] The strength of his ambition, closely connected with his sense of inferiority, comes out in several of the early poems, and a distinction needs to be made between Clare's gaucheness and the tone of someone like John Atkin, a joiner, who wrote to Clare on 19 January 1820, self-consciously announcing, 'I am an Ardent Admirer of rural Poetry, and have myself composed a few *pieces*, perhaps to *blush unseen*. . . .'[10] Clare's sense of purpose, feeling as he did so much more acutely his place in society, was infinitely greater, although he constantly felt obliged to temper it. He intended, for example, in February 1820, to append to the second edition of *Poems Descriptive* an address to the public, beginning: 'Gratitude induces the unletterd author in this the second Edit of his trifles to come forward in an artless self address artless it will be & nothing else will be expected as the generous public are aware of his uncultvated [sic] pen. . . .'[11] Clare had originally written 'second Edit of his *poems*'.

A sense of gratitude was expected of Clare from all quarters: Mrs Emmerson, Lord Radstock, the reviewers, clergymen. Taylor was more prepared to side with Clare against Radstock, certainly over the business of excisions on grounds of 'radical' sentiments (No. 11); his partner Hessey acted as go-between, putting the reasoned view that usually prevailed. The forces of conservatism and moral rectitude represented by Lord Radstock had to be acknowledged. Similarly the interest shown by Mrs Emmerson sprang from an infinite compassion for Clare's predicament; but having cajoled Lord Radstock into taking an active part in Clare's patronage, she would not let Clare forget this. It was the moral fibre of Clare's poetry which she especially applauded, and consequently she expected of him the necessary humility and gratitude. Several reviewers were much more concerned with Clare's 'good character' than with the poetry (the same had been true of Bloomfield), and the image of the wholesome, righteous, upstanding peasant continued, in spite of talk of drink and women, after his death, as for example in S. T. Hall's *Book of Memories* (1871). A typical contemporary response (February 1820), which nods at the man and his poetry simultaneously, is from Captain M. E. Sherwill: 'I have been made acquainted with your situation, your purity of heart, & your simple though chaste imagery by your Poems & Sonnets lately published.'[12] Sherwill continued to stress in his letters the importance of Clare's *'refined* purity of *thought'*. Taylor's exasperation at the demands for gratitude is keenly expressed in a letter of 29 December 1820:[13]

After being *required* to feel grateful, and being told that you never can make an adequate Return, this consciousness of having nobody but God to thank, is a thousand fold sweeter than ever. When L.R.'s voracious Appetite is satisfied, you will feel independent, but I fear he will not be content till he is acknowledged your supreme Friend, & pre-eminent Patron.

Clare's self-consciousness reflected his social position. John Taylor, and the reviewers, tended accordingly to emphasize the peasant in Clare, encouraged by a general desire to fall at the feet of another Robert Bloomfield (or to pat him on the head, depending on individual reactions). Taylor's introduction was a model of tact, putting up a case for the poetry, but with honesty and caution (No. 7). Whilst being remarkably fair in his critical comments, Taylor managed to get Clare into four editions within the year. He was wise not to make too many claims for the poetry, and to emphasize the appalling conditions under which most of the poems had been written. Drury had in fact implored Taylor not to claim indulgence for Clare's situation, but was clearly very much aware of it himself, as an earlier letter to Taylor shows: '. . . he must keep in his station; and the notice he receives should tend to improve his condition rather as a gardener than as a poet'.[14] (Similarly Hannah More had said of Ann Yearsley, the Bristol milkwoman-poet, 'It is not fame, but bread, which I am anxious to secure to her.'[15] But Taylor on the whole avoided the condescension which coloured several of the reviews.

The first account of Clare had appeared, before *Poems Descriptive* was published, in the first volume of John Scott's *London Magazine*, in January 1820 (No. 6), and it is doubtful whether this account, by Octavius Gilchrist, was of much service to the cause. For all its surface charm, there is an uneasiness which suggests Gilchrist's inability to accept Clare on his own terms; although shrugging off any critical commitment, the article combines sentimentality, pomposity, and facetiousness. There is a wariness of tone oddly at variance with the prevailing cocksureness, as though Gilchrist feels the need to score off Clare, his own urbane wit set against Clare's quaint rusticity. Many of the reviews were equally uncertain of their ground. There was generally heavy reliance on Taylor's Introduction, which had virtually forestalled criticism, and nobody seems to have minded very much: the issues raised by Gilchrist and Taylor were those raised by the reviewers. In all fairness it ought to be said that several of these issues were interesting and important, and they recurred throughout the century; but there was rarely any real depth of response.

The question of Clare's 'genius' was an inevitable talking-point: here was an ideal example of one of nature's untutored children, an incarnation of Beattie's Edwin. The *Northampton Mercury* was able to refer to Clare as 'that extraordinary genius' without appearing absurd,[16] and it is no surprise to find the *New Times* (No. 8) putting out the same feelers as Taylor, and stating the dilemma of the too-cultivated man, at one remove both from the natural world, and from his inner self, out of touch with the sources of emotion and expression, overcluttered with the trappings of a literary heritage which he cannot properly assimilate. This suggests a reason for Clare's importance, in that he is unburdened by such artificial, literary restraints. It is an overstated argument, ignoring the strong literary influence on Clare's poetry; but it is helpful in acknowledging the difficulties of writing a particular sort of poetry: 'It is seldom that we can see the impression of loveliness of nature on a man of vivid perception and strong feeling. . . . Such a man is Clare.' These qualities Clare had, valuable at a time when poetic confusion was rife, when integrity seemed increasingly difficult to achieve. (It is ironical that Clare's initial acceptance was partly due to the current tolerance of the second-rate. In a society less kindly disposed towards outsiders, peasant-poets, and beginners, he would have had much less chance of recognition or success.) But in spite of its apparent enlightenment on this point, the *New Times*, whilst accepting Clare's provincialisms, declares that in the long run it matters little: 'There is little danger of his being quoted as an authority for alterations or innovations.' Clare is crushed at one blow.

A more discriminating attitude showed itself in John Scott's review, in the *London Magazine* (No. 17). Even the quotations from the Introduction are chosen to support an argument, and the peasant in Clare is brought out for slightly better reasons: Clare is contrasted with Burns, not assimilated into some easy formula. The emphasis has subtly altered, the facts are accepted for what they are, and sentimentality and condescension have receded. Astonishment may be expressed at the emergence of such a poet from such unlikely circumstances (even allowing for precedents), but it is a positive astonishment, working towards a fairer assessment of the poetry. The *New Monthly* (No. 14) took an indulgent, but not uncritical line; Clare was not yet ready to be judged *in vacuo*. What is refreshing about the *New Monthly*'s attitude is the importance attached to Clare's accuracy of observation, which is regarded as a virtue; the poetry is looked at more closely than usual, without recourse to notions of 'genius'. The *Eclectic Review*, on the other hand, spoke warmly of the uncommon genius that characterized the volume (No. 23); the common distinction between genius and talent was brought into play to Clare's advantage.[17] Whilst stressing the social aspect of the problem, the reviewer was clearly trying to make some claims for Clare, over and above the circumstances. It was perhaps inevitable that this review, favourable for the most part, should conclude in equivocation: it was impossible to predict Clare's development. The review in the *Quarterly Review* (No. 25) was of comparable length and seriousness. Apparently the joint effort of Gilchrist and William Gifford, it was much fairer than Gilchrist's previous piece. It realised the crucial connection between the poet and nature, the personal, spiritual element which most others failed to grasp. A similar perspicuity enabled Gilchrist and Gifford, in appreciating the relationship between 'external objects and internal sensations', to distinguish between Clare and Bloomfield.

The formula of critical reserve was repeated in the *Antijacobin* (No. 29), where emphasis was again placed on natural genius, and on the quality of 'honest simplicity'. This was to become a fairly common phrase, although nobody seemed to be sure of its implications. The *Antijacobin* was not sure, adding that Clare had neither Bloomfield's polish, nor Burns's wild energy: this was a more sophisticated version of the argument found in Gilchrist's original article. J. G. Lockhart in *Blackwood's Edinburgh Magazine* (No. 27) was rather more impatient about the claims being made for Clare, and dissident voices had been raised by the *Guardian* (No. 26), the *Monthly Review* (No. 15), and the *Monthly Magazine* (No. 16); the latter agreed that the poems were remarkable as the products of a labourer, but they could 'not stand the test of a trial by themselves'. This was the sort of reaction that Taylor had hoped to avoid by disarming the critics in his introduction. What the *Monthly Magazine* said frankly and cruelly, other journals thought in less strong terms. Their lack of conviction about how to receive Clare was the pale reflection of the *Monthly Magazine*'s conviction of his essential unimportance.

The progression of attitudes in this first year of public attention may be summarized. First there is the fact of Clare's peasant background; he is a quaint figure, perhaps unique, but with some general precedents (Duck, Burns, Bloomfield), unlettered, hardly influenced by literary sources. This leads to a more intelligent appraisal of the possibilities for poetry in this situation. There is a growing realization that Clare is initially a nature poet; there is modification of this when it becomes clear that nature is in some way related to the poet's personality and sense of suffering. There is an acknowledgment of Clare's difficulty in writing poetry, and his coming to terms with this problem. Although unlettered, he may be a real poet. All these suggestions lurk beneath the surface, but no one is sure enough to bring them out into the open. It is not an ecstatic welcome.

The Village Minstrel (1821)

As soon as the first volume was published, Clare was busily working on another, encouraged by all his London friends. He became more confident, and whilst still relying on Taylor's judgment, was not afraid to disagree. Taylor and Hessey thought that this second collection would be an improvement on the first, and this was the general opinion of other readers, as well as the reviewers. Taylor gave no such positive lead, as he had done the year before, in his Introduction to The Village Minstrel (1821): it was a much shorter piece, written in great haste and only after several promptings from Clare (No. 52). In acknowledging the reception given to Poems Descriptive, Taylor had cause to be thankful; he was running a risk, and the publication of The Village Minstrel was an even greater risk: the delays seem to reflect his doubts. He had to tread warily; nevertheless, he had some discreetly harsh things to say about the relation of poets to critics, and about the present 'illiberal state of criticism'. He knew the potential damage the critics could inflict: he had seen Keats savaged. How much more vulnerable was this poet from the fields of Northamptonshire. Taylor tried to put squarely the difficulties of criticism when faced with Clare; it was not a matter of public sympathy for an impoverished poet (that was another side of the issue, and Taylor had already made his position clear) but rather of a sympathetic approach to a poet who had not yet found his true voice, who went from good to bad without seeming to know the difference.

In June 1821 the British Critic (No. 35) reviewed Vicissitude, a poem by Robert Millhouse, corporal of the Staff of the Royal Sherwood Foresters. It was scornful of the current trend for peasant verse, pointing out with some truth: 'Nothing is more easy than for any person, of moderate talents, be his situation what it may, who can read and write, and is in possession of Thomson's Seasons and Beattie's Minstrel, and one or two other poems of that class, to cultivate a talent for making verses.' This was a fair attitude: it was such people who contributed to the magazines their proud trifles. But it was not fair to Clare. Yet even the critics who had praised him had often done so on these terms. Both the *British Critic* and the *Monthly Magazine* realized the dilemma of their age, but in seeking a remedy they were too ruthless to accommodate Clare. Their attitude was increasingly common: the indiscriminate passion for peasant poetry which had brought Clare to the public notice was answered by the indiscriminate distaste for anything that smacked of the countryside.

These were the extremes between which the more moderate magazines moved in their gentlemanly fashion. The *Literary Chronicle*'s first concern seemed to be with Clare's financial circumstances, and the *Gentleman's Magazine* was equally pleased with what it regarded as Clare's very comfortable position.[18] Letters to the *Morning Post* stressed his newfound 'comforts and enjoyments', all those 'which a man, in his situation of life, could with reason hope for'.[19] None the less the *Chronicle* (No. 55a) saw the superiority of this second collection, and was judicious in its criticisms. An interesting warning was delivered to Clare in a letter in the *Chronicle* two weeks later; Clare should beware the effects of too much reading, as it would only lead to imitation (No. 55b). The *European Magazine* cribbed the *Literary Gazette*'s observation that Clare was a 'genuine poet, and richly entitled to the fostering smiles of the liberal and enlightened' (No. 58). But side by side with gratification that Clare was comfortably placed went the realization of Clare's place in nature, 'seen with a Poet's eye, and depicted in a Poet's language'. The *Monthly Magazine* (No. 56), in a vigorous review, saw no reason substantially to alter its opinion of a year before, but the *New Monthly Magazine* (No. 59) was much kinder, with talk of 'carping criticism and chilling ridicule'; inclined to favour Clare's poetry, it could see the differences between Clare, Bloomfield, and Burns, without regarding this as damaging to Clare. But even here there was disconcerting mention of 'pure and virtuous feelings' and 'the heavenly gift of genius'. John Taylor's account of his visit to Clare, in the *London Magazine* (No. 57), took the place of a review, and contained an extremely sympathetic portrayal of Clare in his natural surroundings, furthering the notion that interest in his poetry necessitated interest in the man, but at the same time demonstrating the power whereby Clare had transformed the dull countryside of North-amptonshire into poetry. The *Eclectic Review* (No. 60), a staunch supporter of Clare throughout his life, contained a careful review, with the emphasis on Clare's spontaneity as opposed to the contrived artificialities of much contemporary verse: 'Such a poet as John Clare, education could not have made, nor could adversity destroy.' In general, the reviews of *The Village Minstrel* were fairer and more usefully critical than those of *Poems Descriptive*. There was not quite the same concern for his origins, his poverty, the burden of his ailing parents. He was beginning to be accepted as a poet.

The Shepherd's Calendar (1827)
During the years (1821–6) in which Clare was busy preparing *The Shepherd's Calendar*, there was frequent discussion between him and his correspondents as to the particular merits of his poetry. Mrs Emmerson and Taylor were united in their praise of 'Superstition's Dream'; the attempt at sublimity was all that Eliza could have desired (No. 68). It was characteristic of the prevailing poetic climate that Taylor should encourage Clare to write sonnets of a quasi-metaphysical, bombastic strain, rather than stick to the 'purely descriptive' style. This was the real bone of contention throughout this period. As early as April 1820 Taylor had characterized the particular sort of description in which Clare excelled: 'The putting of passion into inanimate nature';[20] when Clare sent a specimen of his *Summer Walks* (which later became *The Shepherd's Calendar*) to H. F. Cary, the translator of Dante, Cary was sure that the new poem would 'be as faithful to nature and as much elevated by reflection, as your poems have hitherto generally been'.[21] But there was little agreement as to what this really meant in practice.

The problem was not peculiar to Clare: as detail in poetry increased, as nature poetry became more tied to the countryside as it really was, the balance between description and the imagination became more important for the theorists, and harder to achieve in practice. Even John Aikin warned against Dutchification: Crabbe became the butt of Wordsworth, Coleridge, and Hazlitt.[22] The attack on Crabbe was symptomatic of the revulsion felt by the Romantic writers at the introduction of low life, mere facts, into poetry.[23] Few people had the discrimination of Jeffrey; for a distinction had to be made between Crabbe, and the absurd efforts of Erasmus Darwin, or even Thomas Gisborne.[24]

Something of the confusion that remained may be seen in the advice meted out to Clare in his formative years. In 1820 Captain Sherwill was telling Clare that 'the present public taste is decidely in favor of rural & pastoral poetry'.[25] But two years later Drury announced that the public was tiring of 'simple naked nature. Some refinement is now necessary on purely rustic manners & scenery.'[26] *The Forest Minstrel*, by the industrious William and Mary Howitt, was greeted with scorn by the *Literary Gazette* in 1823;[27] and it was a similar impatience with trifling, botanical detail that led the *Edinburgh Magazine* to give a backhanded compliment to Darwin, and the 'Darwinian school of poetry', in observing that whilst for them description constituted poetry, with no need for any superadded or inherent emotion, none the less, Darwin 'in the mechanical structure of verse, and the powers of description . . . has few superiors within the range of British poetry'.[28] Mrs Emmerson saw more than detail in Clare's poetry: in April 1820 she declared that Clare excelled in 'animated descriptions of *Nature!* Heightened by the finer Sensibilities of the Soul!' and a month later reminded him that he was best in 'the simple scenes of pastoral nature, the pathetically descriptive, and the sublime!'[29] Mrs Emmerson realized the wrongheadedness of the supposition that description necessarily excluded the truly poetical.

Although Hessey assured Clare in February 1823 that 'you are generally right in your estimate of your Poems',[30] he was not happy with the batch of poems he received later that year. Taylor had told Clare 'to elevate his views', and Hessey advised him to introduce narrative interest;[31] the following year he pointed out, 'there is Poetry & Philosophy and Religion too to be found in the Works of Nature as we call them, but it is not everyone who can discover them'.[32] Clare refused to comply with these prescriptions: although the dangers of sameness and repetition were real, the proposed remedy was uncongenial to Clare, who could not forget what he could do best. Taylor and Hessey became increasingly impatient as Clare continued to send up manuscripts full of 'descriptive poetry', and when 'July' was received, Taylor exploded: hardly anything in it was worth keeping.[33] But Mrs Emmerson told Clare just before the book was published, that 'as a whole this Volume is much *richer* in *language, thought*, and *imagery* —than either of your preceding ones'.[34]

Tempers were badly frayed by the time *The Shepherd's Calendar* appeared in 1827, and the general sense of frustration must have been made worse by the *ennui* that afflicted the reading public. Taylor bemoaned the decline of interest in poetry:[35] it was an extremely ironic comment on his own procrastination. In the age of keepsakes and annuals and poetical gems (to which Clare had to contribute) there was no chance of a repetition of the phenomenal success of *Poems Descriptive*; even the so-called second edition of *The Village Minstrel* had merely been another issue of a thousand unbound copies of the original edition, with a new frontispiece added to the second volume.

Although those close to Clare recognized a noticeably firmer grasp of his potentialities, very few reviews took much notice. As usual the *Eclectic Review*, through Josiah Conder, spoke out strongly in support of Clare (No. 81); the tone adopted was one of affection and understatement. By deliberately seeming to make no great claims for the poetry, and by admitting partiality, Conder managed to suggest something of the inherent strength of the work, whilst at the same time relating it to a healthy and growing tradition. Put in the context of this tradition, Clare was vindicated. The *Literary Chronicle* (No. 83) could hardly say enough in praise of the new volume (like the *Eclectic Review*, eagerly noting the difference between Clare and contemporary versifiers), but the *Literary Gazette* (No. 80) was slightly less ardent, qualifying the stature of the volume in a way that must have irritated Clare: 'There is a great deal of sweet poetry in this little volume,—snatches of song springing like wildflowers on the heath, or in the green lanes.' Significantly the *Gazette* did not approve of the narrative sections. A more equivocal notice appeared in the *London Weekly Review* (No. 82), showing how Clare could still 'provoke spleen'. A short notice like this, with its unformulated response, illustrates the difficulties posed by Clare for mediocre critics. The *Literary Magnet* was content to avoid argument, by observing that Clare maintained the standard of his earlier productions.[36]

The Rural Muse (1835)
Clare's final volume, *The Rural Muse*, edited by Taylor and Mrs Emmerson, was published in 1835. Clare's gardening friend Henderson wrote in August, referring to 'the favourable and well deserved reception which your poems have met with'.[37] But the volume sold poorly, and made little impression. Of the reviewers, John Wilson ('Christopher North') in *Blackwood's Edinburgh Magazine* was the most ardent and discriminating admirer (No. 96), and what he and the *New Monthly* (No. 98) had to say in its favour was offset by the flippancy of the *Literary Gazette* (No. 95), and the weary neglect of the other journals.

Mrs Emmerson seemed to expect a generous review from Henry Coleridge in the *Quarterly Review*, but her hopes were disappointed.[38] The *Athenaeum* signalled its approval (No. 94), but gave itself room for little more than the usual nod at genius combating disadvantages. The *New Monthly*'s brief account agreed with the *Athenaeum* in noticing further improvement, but this in itself suggests the failings of the contemporary response. There was a general obligation to notice improvement; it is disturbing to see Clare's muse characterized as 'chaste and elegant', and in the applause for the 'far superior finish' we can surely detect a blindness to the real power of Clare's poetry. *The Rural Muse* was a mixed volume, and on the whole less impressive than *The Shepherd's Calendar*. No one who reviewed it was prepared to admit this. Wilson, in his long review, is interesting because he shows a genuine feeling for the poetry, and conveys his excitement at discovering a real poet; in his strictures on *The Rural Muse* he appears to realize where Clare is at his best, and urges him to return to the themes most congenial to him. It is consequently a surprise to find Wilson comparing Clare unfavourably with Bloomfield, and Taylor was rightly indignant. None the less Wilson emphasized the originality of Clare's mind at a time when others were losing interest.

THE ASYLUM YEARS 1837–64

Although most people had forgotten about Clare by the time he went to High Beech in 1837, the curiosity of the few still dogged him. It became his fate, yet again, to be held up as a classic instance of something, this time of the romantic, visionary, mad poet; the myth was given a further boost by the cruel truth. The first substantial news to reach the outside world came in May 1841, when Cyrus Redding published an account of his visit to Clare, in his newly started *English Journal* (No. 101). It is an extremely sympathetic account, with a lengthy and impassioned plea for financial support, lack of which he blames for Clare's mental disturbance. He goes on to draw a parallel with Christopher Smart, and prints some of the asylum poems, which, he says, 'show nothing of his mental complaint, as if the strength of the poetic feeling were beyond the reach of a common cause to disarrange'. Open enough to admit his own perplexity, Redding does not go so far as to suggest that the asylum poems are better than the earlier work; in a second article he rests his case on Clare's achievement in sanity, and as Redding states it, it is an impressive case.

In 1841 Clare escaped from High Beech, but by December was again in an asylum, this time permanently, at Northampton. The sympathetic steward, William Knight, transcribed hundreds of his poems; there was talk of a possible publication. Knight wrote from Birmingham in May 1850 to Charles Clare that 'I have many pieces that are very choice and do think would be appreciated by the world'.[39] But nothing ever came of it. Mary Russell Mitford, in 1852, sounded a warning note: 'Let us beware of indulging ourselves by encouraging the class of pseudo-peasant poets.'[40] The remedy was to 'let our peasants become as intelligent as our artisans, and we shall have no more prodigies, no more martyrs'. However, some poems seeped into local newspapers. One of those instrumental was Thomas Inskip, whom Clare had known since 1824. Inskip makes one or two interesting comments on the poetry: he sees the merit of some of the asylum poems, and his judgment offsets Thomas Prichard's doleful note of 1843 that Clare used to write good pieces, though rarely finished, whereas 'he now writes but little and in a coarse style, very unlike his former compositions'.[41] Inskip casts a retrospective glance at *The Village Minstrel*, which he judges 'a bundle of very commonplace Rhyme where Poetry cometh not'; he sees *The Rural Muse* as superior to it, but, more importantly, sees many asylum poems as better than most of *The Rural Muse*. He realizes that poetry requires an audience: it cannot exist in a vacuum (hence so much feeble versifying in the asylum). And yet Inskip is not altogether reliable; of 'Invite to Eternity' he writes: it 'is a splendid piece of Poetry although it means nothing, it is however as pretty none the worse for that.' In the same breath he says 'there is nothing in all his writings has lifted his genius so high in my estimation as this little poem'.[42] Already we are beginning to get here the muddled response to visionary poetry: Inskip was not alone in this.

Then in 1851 appeared Edwin Paxton Hood's volume, *The Literature of Labour* (No. 102), in which a whole chapter was devoted to Clare. It is a remarkably sustained performance, cleverly combining the biographical and the critical, the asylum and the pre-asylum poetry. Although using Clare to make a point, he never exploits him. Hood, a Congregational minister, tends to take a lofty tone, innocently rejoicing that Clare 'never went to the Public House', and has an unduly optimistic view of the poor; he does not, at this stage, seem to have appreciated the tragic quality of Clare's life and vision. None the less he refuses to categorize him as 'merely a rustic Poet, or a rural Bard', recognizing the essential dignity of Clare's world. He sees him as a reflective writer, able to accept what he sees literally, and to transform it into a poetry that is not merely passive. Hood glimpses 'the eternal growth and eternal mystery' behind Clare's vision of nature, and works towards an awareness of Clare's poetry as an expression of that vision. No one before Hood had explored the full implications of this.

OBITUARIES AND LIVES 1864–73

The *Northampton Mercury* reported on 21 May 1864: 'Poor John Clare, the Northamptonshire poet, died yesterday afternoon in the North-ampton Asylum, of which he has been many years an inmate.' The following issue contained an obituary (No. 106). From now on, people began to take stock of Clare, trying to sort out where his importance lay. This particular obituary did no more than restate the now accepted attitudes, with references to 'pleasant verses' and 'the simple and thoroughly rural nature of the Poet'. But about the asylum verses there was much less certainty, and John Askham in the same number (No. 107) preferred to limit his remarks to the earlier verse, declaring 'he is almost purely a descriptive poet'. The Kettering poet John Plummer, who had visited Clare in the asylum, wrote in similar vein in *St. James's Magazine* (No. 108).

Within a year Frederick Martin's *Life* had appeared. This is an extraordinary work. For all its romanticizing it is a valuable document; but for some it was too sympathetic, too biased against the London literary world. In an angry review the *Examiner* attacked the 'bastard picturesque' of Martin;[43] Dickens was incensed: 'Did you ever see such preposterous exaggeration of small claims? And isn't it expressive, the perpetual prating of him in the book as the *Poet*?'[44] It was easy enough to scoff at Martin's stylistic oddities (for some of course the romantic strain was only too tempting to copy). But for immediacy and breadth his work was without precedent; although there is scarcely any specific critical comment in the whole book, Martin manages to convince his reader of the unique quality of Clare, both as man and poet.

J. L. Cherry's *Life and Remains* (1873) was in some ways a more reliable work, quoting directly from letters, and less inclined to soar into the fanciful; its chief interest lay in the number of asylum poems it printed. The image of a peasant poet was being very radically altered. Whereas Spencer T. Hall (No. 109) had declared 'The Rural Muse and his long insanity were, in my opinion, about the two best friends under a merciful Heaven by which John Clare was ever visited', Cherry pointed the theme of the 'disastrous gift of the poetic faculty' (No. 112). Clare's tragedy was, not to be poor, or a peasant, but to be a poet. Practically every provincial newspaper had something to say about Cherry's volume, and some of their comments indicate the general movements of opinion. The *Staffordshire Advertiser* (8 February 1873) saw how necessary it was for the health of the poetical climate to turn from 'the brilliant white lights of Tennyson's canvas' 'to the grey and softer tones of John Clare': 'We shall never reduce our contemporary poets to their proper dimensions so long as we neglect the simple aspects of nature which Clare so exquisitely portrays.' If the emphasis is on the nature poetry, at least an attempt is made to relate Clare to a later generation of poets. The *Birmingham Morning News* (4 February 1873) boldly declared 'Clare may be classed among the very best of our rural poets'. The *Pall Mall Gazette* was doubtful about the asylum poems: 'There is room, we think, for a careful selection of the best poems produced by this genuine rural poet previous to 1837, but we should not recommend the editor to overweight the volume with any of the asylum poems.'[45] The *Potteries Examiner* (22 February 1873) repeated the classification of Burns and Clare as 'peasant poets'. The *Chester Chronicle* (8 February 1873) registered the impression of Clare as a past phenomenon, pointing out that 'more than a generation has passed since the name of Clare was familiar to magazine readers and to offer to the public any *résumé* of his life or works now seems as much like delving into the past as it would be to issue a memoir of Byron or Kirke White'. The *Chester Chronicle* was also emphatic in its praise of the asylum poetry, which showed 'that the poet was not dead even when the main current of his life was tinged with imbecility'. The *Manchester Guardian* (No. 113) had a fuller critique, and was inclined to place Clare fairly low down the ladder of perfection; but it clearly preferred the pathos of the asylum poems. The *Nonconformist* (No. 113) was also able to see merit here, but refused to call Clare a great poet. In its context, this denial of greatness comes as a surprise, and suggests a new line of development, for this was something that no one had really considered. Cherry's *Life and Remains* had prompted a few pertinent questions, even if the answers were not forthcoming.

1873 TO 1920

Towards the end of the century, Clare was in as unfortunate a position as he was when he first appeared. The debate on what constituted poetry continued, and so-called rural poetry was increasingly despised. In his *Studies in English Literature* (1876) John Dennis provided a chapter on 'English Rural Poetry', in which he set out to redefine the term. Refusing to allow 'rural' to be synonymous with 'pastoral', Dennis dismisses the 'grotesque' poetry written by men of the city without any knowledge of the countryside. Descriptive accuracy is a necessary starting-point, and Thomson's value, significantly, is that he proves 'that poetic thought can gain some of its richest sentiment from natural objects' (p. 373). Bloomfield is described as a 'small rural poet' who 'chirped feebly of the countryside' (p. 376). Dennis then shows his hand: 'Of rural poetry—which, if the bull may be excused, is not poetry—the last century produced a load large enough, if a man were doomed to read it all, to make him loathe the very thought of verse' (p. 377). In this dreary context Cowper's strength stands out, as against Crabbe, who has no sense of beauty. Finally the inevitable comparison is made with Wordsworth: 'It is not to men who are essentially rural poets that we must look for the best rural poetry; not to Clare, truthful as his descriptions are, so much as to Wordsworth . . .' (p. 382). Clare is caught on the wrong side of Dennis's redefined boundary. J. C. Shairp's *On Poetic Interpretation of Nature* (1877) moved in the same direction. Without mentioning Clare, he was anxious to establish Wordsworth's supremacy; he demolished, on the way, the poet-painter analogy that had so hindered criticism of descriptive poetry in the nineteenth century: 'There are no doubt poets who are mainly taken up with the forms and colours of things, and yet no poet can rest wholly in them, for this, if for no other reason, that in the power of rendering them his art necessarily falls so far below that of the painter' (p. 68). Although Francis Palgrave reverted to the analogy in 1897 (in *Landscape in Poetry*), he was trying to see the effect in terms of verbal artistry. However, he could do no more than invoke the *je ne sais quoi*; of Clare's poetry he wrote, 'It is pure landscape painting, like that of Keats in youth, though beneath that in power . . . by inborn gift only, not labour ever so strenuous can this be effected.' Palgrave seems happier with the asylum verse: 'No poetry known to me has a sadness more absolute than Clare's asylum songs, reverting with what pathetic yearning to the village scenes of his hard-worked youth' (p. 207).

Some letters in the *Literary World*, at the time of the centenary celebrations in 1893, indicate the continuing confusion and lack of critical bearings. A lengthy letter from C. Ernest Smith suggests that Clare's poetry is chiefly remarkable for its unobtrusive skill, and the pictorial effect is 'heightened by the poet's attention to details'. Smith is sure that Clare is not a great poet, but 'he may most fitly be called the poet of homely human nature'.[46] This tepid commendation is paralleled by the bewilderment of Jesse Hall (a visitor to Clare in 1848) over the 'Invite to Eternity': this is 'weird and mysterious, and it requires an effort to grasp its full meaning'.[47] John Clare appeared in *The Poets and Poetry of the Century* (ed. Alfred H. Miles) in 1892. Roden Noel was sufficiently perceptive to see 'the very distinctive value' of the early poetry, the advantages of Clare's 'homespun racy diction' over conventional poetic vocabulary, and the grace of the asylum verse. But Noel confused criticism with sentimentality: 'Does not the gentle insanity . . . give a savour of wildness, and a certain etherial tone to the last poems, so as to render them treasures of quite singular value?' (iii, 81).

It was left to Arthur Symons, in his selection of 1908 (No. 117) to inaugurate a new way of looking at Clare, that was both sensitive and coherent. His sense was a salutary corrective to the effusiveness of, for example, Norman Gale (No. 116). When we remember that Symons did not know of much of the poetry that has since come to light, his perspicacity is even more remarkable. For the first time in the history of criticism of Clare there was no hedging, no feeble reliance on 'sweet' and 'charming' as the appropriate epithets. Symons can say outright that in the early poetry, 'there is more reality than poetry'; he can indicate without being vague, Clare's intimacy with his subject; he can dismiss Bloomfield with authority. He appreciates the paradox of Clare's development: torn up from the native soil that was his whole life, Clare achieved, in the asylum, poetry 'of a rarer and finer quality than any of the verse written while he was at liberty and at home'. Any later assessment of Clare has had to face this paradox. Symons's view of Clare is exhilarating in its discernment, its awareness of the multiplicity of Clare's verse, the complex wholeness of the man. We even begin to get a responsible attitude to the text of the poems (one of the chief bugbears in Clare studies). Symons does not concern himself with the question of greatness, but contents himself with pointing to the distinguishing characteristics. It is only after Symons that the critical heritage begins to cohere.

1920 TO 1964

Edmund Blunden and Alan Porter prompted a new appraisal of Clare in 1920, with *Poems Chiefly from Manuscript*, followed four years later by *Madrigals and Chronicles*. Both editors had a passionate commit-ment: indeed, judging by a rather tart correspondence in the *Athenaeum*, they clearly differed in their estimates of Clare.[48] Porter's outburst in *Oxford Outlook* (No. 121) may now seem strident (it was certainly in-accurate in points of detail), but it was a clear signal for battle to commence. In the taking of sides that ensued, Edmund Gosse (No. 127) represented the camp of scepticism. He could not see what the fuss was about, and refused to be swayed by appeals to a sense of outrage: Clare 'had no gifts except his dreamy sweetness of character, his childlike simplicity, and his redundant flow of verses'. There was little to be said in Clare's favour; his range was limited, he was repetitious, monotonous, diluted, his talent 'stunted and ineffective'. Gosse was impatient with Clare's 'extraordinary keenness and accuracy' of observation: for him it was 'exquisite', but 'prolonged beyond measure', and 'relieved by no reflection'. He elaborated on this theme in a review of *Madrigals and Chronicles* (No. 134), weighing his remarks in the light of what had been said by Blunden and Porter, and John Middleton Murry. Accord-ing to Gosse, Clare views only from the outside; there is no 'organic sensibility' as there is in Wordsworth. Gosse writes persuasively and passionately; but several critics saw the flaws in his argument, and took up the challenge.

Thomas Moult (No. 128), agreeing with Gosse that Clare 'observed too much', none the less was aware that Clare was moving towards the imaginative world of Keats and Wordsworth. Robert Lynd (No. 126) was not so certain. He was not prepared to put Clare on the shelf with Keats or Shelley or Burns or Collins or Blake: W. H. Hudson would be a more apposite companion. H. J. Massingham was asking a similar question in the *Athenaeum* (No. 124): 'How does Clare fit into the map of his own poetic period?' The answer was that Clare was unique. Accepting Clare's development as the crucial factor, Massingham felt able to say that Clare 'cannot any longer be handled as a minor poet'. Murry (No. 125) was so enthusiastic that he had to draw himself up, reminding us that Wordsworth and Keats (although in some ways inferior to Clare) were great poets, whereas Clare was not. What was lacking was the sense of inner growth. Whilst this is reminiscent of Gosse's criticism, the tone and the direction are completely different. Murry accepts Clare's limitations, and then surrenders. Clare is 'the love poet of nature'; description is no longer the operative word. Murry further shifted the emphasis when in 1924, whilst pointing to Clare's weakness of poetic thought, he asserted: 'Clare's faculty of sheer vision is unique in English poetry: not only is it purer than Wordsworth's; it is purer even than Shakespeare's.' The paradox was that his vision was too perfect, and Clare remained a child.

J. W. Tibble's edition of the *Poems* (1935) hardly brought about a convincing reconsideration of positions. The *Times Literary Supplement* (No. 136) was grateful: 'John Clare's place is secure among the poets.' But not everyone agreed. John Speirs in *Scrutiny* (No. 137) was doubtful if anything was added to Clare's reputation as it stood in 1920: the danger was that Clare's limitations would be emphasized, as would the lack of development of what really mattered. Speirs saw Clare's characteristic and best work as belonging (rather like Crabbe's) to the eighteenth century, and compared with this earlier work, the asylum verse was unsatisfactory. Blunden disagreed, but had no room to show why.[49] Claude Colleer Abbott agreed with Speirs that 'the appeal of Clare is strengthened rather than fundamentally altered by this edition'. Abbott fell back on the old peasant poet image: 'In his own field, as interpreter and chronicler, he stands alone.'[50]

An interesting examination of Clare as peasant was made by W. K. Richmond in 1947 (No. 139). Richmond talks of the plodders, 'the dull fellows rather than the shining ones'; Crabbe, Burns, Wordsworth, and Clare belong to this band, and they are the poets to watch, in spite of the fact that 'they trudged rather than soared. They were often long-winded, uneven, rarely at their best.' But their humility and seriousness of concern distinguish them from the Romantic high-fliers. (It is worth noticing that Edward Thomas's reference (No. 120) to Clare's 'pedestrian muse' is not derogatory.) Richmond, however, pursues his argument to the point at which he pronounces Clare a failure: Clare apparently ceases to be a peasant poet when he goes in upon himself, he becomes one of the 'lost' when he should have been a 'seeker'. It is an involved and rather wayward argument, leading Richmond to say of 'I am' that Clare 'understood only too well the essential ghastliness of his failure'. But the failure hinted at is not one of literary convention; Geoffrey Grigson (No. 140) was more correct to say that 'there was no failure of nerve, no concealment of such failure under the rhetoric of a false optimism'.

Richmond was not alone in attending in a more helpful way to the origins of Clare. John Heath-Stubbs and Rayner Unwin both put Clare in a context of rural poetic tradition.[51] But the visionary element began to predominate. Middleton Murry 'revisited' Clare in 1956 (in *Un-*

professional Essays), answering Richmond by observing that it is when Clare is faced with the threat of the 'disintegration of personality' that he emerges as a true poet. The emphasis on the visionary led several critics to characterize Clare's gifts as essentially lyrical, although they found it hard to reach beyond the notion of the pure note of song. J. W. R. Purser's abortive attempt (No. 144) to tackle the problem of lyrical simplicity underlines the critical difficulties.

One person who was clear in his own mind about Clare was Geoffrey Grigson (No. 140). His *Poems of John Clare's Madness* (1949), and the *Selected Poems* (1950) contain, in their Introductions, essential perceptions on the poetry. He was able to elaborate on Clare's originality, and to demonstrate convincingly, both by what he presented in his selections, and by argument, that Clare 'was rather more than the lyric poet writing in answer to an intermittency of impulse'. *The Times Literary Supplement* (No. 142) in a strong review of the *Life and Poetry*, by J. W. and Anne Tibble (1956), challenged the literary world to accept Clare into the canon, awkward intruder (like Hopkins) that he was. Clare became, in a dozen or so poems, a momentous poet, and the charge of imperfections was thrown back at the accusers: 'Faced with Clare's imperfections, we still have to ask who is perfect.' Robert Graves (No. 141) thought along similar lines; and in 1962 Harold Bloom felt able to include Clare in a study of the Romantic vision (No. 145). Yet the following year Ian Jack, in the *Oxford History of English Literature*, plumped for putting Clare in with the minor poets (the *Cambridge Bibliography* made him a major poet in 1940), and had second thoughts about his praise of *The Shepherd's Calendar*. An embarrassed *corrigendum* revealed a failure of nerve that must give any critic of Clare pause for thought.[52]

CENTENARY COMMENTS

The centenary of Clare's death was celebrated by several publications, notably *The Shepherd's Calendar* and *The Later Poems*, both edited by Eric Robinson and Geoffrey Summerfield. Clare was at last receiving serious textual attention. Exhibitions were held, talks and readings given. But critically little new emerged. Anne Tibble, in a letter to the *Listener*, thought we must give Clare time, for his true stature to reveal itself.[53] *The Times* was generous in its praise,[54] and Grigson observed how 'woefully' Clare was underestimated, pointing again to the asylum poems for his vindication.[55] *The Times Literary Supplement* could not see why 'nature poetry' need be invoked at all; no longer could Clare be

called a minor romantic, and the epithet 'simple' was strongly challenged, with reference to *The Shepherd's Calendar*: 'if we call this kind of
writing "simple" it is because our own sophistication blinds us to the
quality of true poetry and the true poet.'[56] Sophistication was scoffed
at also by Donald Davie (No. 146c) who emphatically preferred the
early poetry to that of the asylum.

This preference has asserted itself elsewhere: Eric Robinson and
Geoffrey Summerfield have suggested that we should not place too
much emphasis on the asylum poems, at the expense of the early work;[57]
an essay by Ian Jack was deliberately entitled 'Poems of John Clare's
Sanity';[58] Elaine Feinstein in her introduction to a selection of the poems
thought the 'mad poetry' had 'won disproportionate praise'.[59] Certainly, the hopeless banality of so many of the Knight Transcripts should
make us aware of the extremely precarious success that Clare achieved
in the asylum. Elaine Feinstein was quite right to point to Clare's 'sense
of the solidity of "the real world"' as one of his great strengths, and
she was correct in realizing that this is not a quality of many of the
asylum poems. We must agree with Robinson and Summerfield that
Clare's published work, by the time he first entered the asylum in 1837,
was a remarkable achievement. None the less, any balanced and truly
sane view of Clare must include an acknowledgment that the asylum
poetry represents the culmination and fulfilment of that achievement.

AMERICAN AND CONTINENTAL RESPONSES

Clare's appeal on the Continent and in America has never been very
great (although several important manuscripts have made their way to
America). Harold Bloom's discussion in 1962 (No. 145) was the first
really important assessment of Clare in America, apart from the
occasional thesis. Most contemporary comment had been confined to
biographical details; poems were sometimes reprinted in journals and
magazines, together with extracts culled from reviews in English
journals.[60] Of the major American poets, only Emerson seems to have
known (or cared) about Clare: he quoted part of the 'Address to Plenty'
in his journal for 1841-4.[61] When comment was independent, it was
rarely illuminating or distinctive. Some of the visitors to the asylum at
Northampton were American: one was a writer called Dean Dudley,
who was carried away by the pathetic history of this 'unfortunate son
of Apollo', but had no critical insights to offer.[62] The pious approach of
Harper's New Monthly Magazine in 1869 (No. 111) hardly allowed

criticism to flourish. The journalist Benjamin Avery wrote about Clare in the *Overland Monthly* for 1873, in response to Cherry's *Life*, and in order to introduce some poems brought over to America by his painter-friend J. B. Wandesforde, who had visited Clare.[63] Although this article was sympathetic, it continued to romanticize. When the poet Richard Henry Stoddard took a look at the poetry in 1893 (No. 115b), it was only to discount the possibility of criticism; the best he could say about Clare's poetry was that it was 'winsome and charming'. It is significant that something of this attitude has survived in a standard work, the *Literary History of England*, edited by Albert C. Baugh (1948): this declares that Clare has 'of late been overpraised for his sensitive descriptions of the small sights and sounds of the natural world'. As for the asylum poems, they possess a 'childlike charm' for those ignorant of the circumstances in which they were written, a 'painful interest' for those who know the details.

The European response has been practically non-existent. Louis Cazamian complained, in the *History of English Literature* which he wrote with Emile Legouis (1927; revised edition 1964), that Clare's 'remarkably spontaneous feeling for nature' was marred by 'a form that is unfortunately less fresh'. (It is not clear whether it is Donald Davie or Pierre Legouis, responsible for the Bibliographies, who confuses Clare with James Hogg, the Ettrick Shepherd, on page 1064.) The rest, including Taine's monumental *Histoire de la Littérature anglaise* (1863–4), appears to be silence.

NOTE ON THE SALES FIGURES OF CLARE'S POETRY

Clare's first volume, *Poems Descriptive of Rural Life and Scenery* (1820), appeared at just the right time from a commercial point of view: poetry was a saleable commodity. However, whilst it is instructive to know how many copies of his work were printed, and how many sold, it has to be remembered that there was often little relation between such figures and poetic merit. Taylor lamented that it was a struggle to get rid of 500 copies of Keats's volume of 1820, and Wordsworth's *Excursion* (1814) sold even more poorly (though with more justification). On the other hand, Byron and Scott, Campbell and Moore (and even Crabbe) were making vast sums from sales and copyrights. Against their successes we must set the gloomy account of Clare's affairs that he received from his publishers in 1829 (after much prodding): he had apparently (Clare disputed it) made no profit at all, but lost £140. Yet there had been three editions (of 1,000 copies each) of *Poems Descriptive* all sold out, and a fourth, of which 616 copies were sold; all four editions were published by 1821. *The Village Minstrel* (1821) had sold, by 1829, 1,250 copies; Taylor had had 2,000 copies printed for the first edition, of which 800 were sold in the first three months, from September to December 1821. The 'second edition' of 1823 consisted of the second thousand copies of the first edition, which had not been bound in 1821. *The Shepherd's Calendar* (1827) had sold only 425 copies by 1829, and *The Rural Muse* (1835) showed no signs of being anything like sold out by the end of the year in which it was published. Although Clare earned £40 from the copyright, the book could not claim to be a financial success: his new publisher Whittaker had hoped that a second edition might be called for, but these hopes were unfounded.[64]

NOTES

1 Drury to Clare, 24 December 1818: Eg. 2245, fol. 10.
2 Drury to Taylor, 20 April 1819: NMS. 43 (2).
3 ibid.
4 Drury to Taylor, 2 January 1820: NMS. 43 (11).
5 Drury to Taylor, 5 February 1820: NMS. 43 (14).
6 Drury to Taylor: NMS. 43 (24).
7 NMS. 43 (2).
8 NMS. 43 (3).
9 Drury to Taylor, 3 June 1819: NMS. 43 (4).
10 Eg. 2245, fol. 23.
11 NMS. 32 (18).
12 Sherwill to Clare, 7 February 1820: PMS. F1, p. 22.
13 Eg. 2245, fol. 261.
14 NMS. 43 (4) and (3).
15 Quoted in Rayner Unwin, *The Rural Muse*, 1954, p. 77; cf. Stephen Duck's prophecy: 'Thus shall tradition keep my Fame alive;/The *Bard* may die, the *Thresher* still survive.'
16 *Northampton Mercury*, 29 January 1820, vol. 99.
17 See Logan Pearsall Smith, *Four Words: Romantic, Originality, Creative, Genius* (S.P.E. Tract no. xvii), 1924.
18 *Gentleman's Magazine*, October 1821, xci, 344–7.
19 *Morning Post*, 19 May 1820: from 'A friend to the deserving'.
20 Taylor to Clare, 27 April 1820: Eg. 2245, fol. 104ᵛ.
21 1 September 1822: Eg. 2246, fol. 101ᵛ.
22 John Aikin, *Letters to a Young Lady on a Course of English Poetry*, 1804, pp.

155, 291. But see *An Essay on the Application of Natural History to Poetry*, Warrington 1777, pp. 58, 71; Coleridge, *Biographia Literaria*, ed. J. Shawcross, Oxford 1907, ii, 101–2; *Coleridge's Shakespearean Criticism*, ed. T. M. Raysor, Oxford 1930, ii, 174; Coleridge, *Table Talk and Omniana*, 1917, p. 293; Hazlitt, *Complete Works*, ed. P. P. Howe, 1930, v, 87, xi, 165; *The Critical Opinions of William Wordsworth*, ed. Markham L. Peacock, Jr., Baltimore 1950, p. 235.

23 See Walter E. Broman, 'Factors in Crabbe's eminence in the early nineteenth century', *Modern Philology*, August 1953, li, 42–9.

24 For Gisborne's manifesto, see *Walks in a Forest*, 1794; cf. John Scott's Preface to *Amoebean Eclogues*, 1768, quoted in Varley Lang, 'Crabbe and the Eighteenth Century', *ELH*, 1938, v, 311.

25 12 February 1820: PMS. F1, p. 20.

26 3 August 1822: Eg. 2246, fol. 90.

27 *Literary Gazette*, 27 September 1823, no. 349, 611.

28 *Edinburgh Magazine*, April 1818, ii, 316.

29 25 April 1820: Eg. 2245, foll. 96ᵛ–97, and 8 May 1820: Eg. 2245, foll. 112ᵛ–113.

30 5 February 1823: Eg. 2246, fol. 154.

31 Taylor to Clare, 18 February 1822: Eg. 2246, fol. 43ᵛ. Hessey to Clare, 13 October 1823: Eg. 2246, fol. 245ᵛ, and 26 December 1823: Eg. 2246, fol. 268ᵛ.

32 7 September 1824: Eg. 2246, fol. 377.

33 28 January 1826: Eg. 2247, fol. 133.

34 15 December 1826: Eg. 2247, fol. 240ᵛ.

35 3 August 1827: Eg. 2247, fol. 322.

36 *Literary Magnet*, 1827, n.s. iii, 58.

37 5 August 1835: Eg. 2249, fol. 297.

38 Mrs Emmerson to Clare, 26 July 1835: Eg. 2249, fol. 293.

39 25 May 1850: Eg. 2250, fol. 40ᵛ.

40 *Recollections of a Literary Life*, 2nd ed. 1858, p. 161.

41 10 November 1843: Eg. 2250, fol. 32.

42 23 July 1847: NMS. 52 (17, 38).

43 *Examiner*, 5 August, no. 3001; this was a carefully written attack on the *Life*, often convincing in its questioning of the facts.

44 Dickens to John Forster, 15 August 1865; *Nonesuch Edition*, iii, 433.

45 *Pall Mall Gazette*, 19 March 1873, xvii, 12.

46 *Literary World*, 15 September 1893, n.s. xlviii, 189.

47 *Literary World*, 8 September 1893, n.s. xlviii, 173.

48 *Athenaeum*, 12 March 1920, no. 4689, 350; 19 March 1920, no. 4690, 379–80.

49 *Fortnightly Review*, April 1935, 143, 497–8.

50 *Sunday Times*, 3 March 1935, no. 5838, 12.

51 John Heath-Stubbs, *The Darkling Plain*, 1950: 'John Clare and the Peasant

Tradition' first appeared in 1947 in *Penguin New Writing*; Rayner Unwin, *The Rural Muse*, 1954.

52 Clare had appeared in several histories of literature before this, but always as a minor or incidental figure.

53 *Listener*, 9 July 1964, lxxii, 58.

54 *The Times*, 21 May 1964, no. 56017, 15.

55 *Observer*, 17 May 1964, no. 9020, 27.

56 *The Times Literary Supplement*, 14 May 1964, no. 3246, 416.

57 *Clare, Selected Poems and Prose*, ed. Eric Robinson and Geoffrey Summerfield, 1966, p. 38.

58 In *Some British Romantics*, ed. James V. Logan et al., Ohio State University Press 1966, pp. 191–232.

59 *John Clare, Selected Poems*, ed. Elaine Feinstein, 1968, p. 25.

60 See David Bonnell Green, 'Three Early American Admirers of John Clare', *Bulletin of the John Rylands Library*, spring 1968, 50, 365–86. But see also Mark Storey, 'Edwin Paxton Hood (Not the Reverend Romeo Elton) and John Clare', *Notes and Queries*, October 1971, ccxvi, 386–7.

61 *The Journals and Miscellaneous Notebooks of Ralph Waldo Emerson*, ed. William H. Gilman and J. E. Parsons, Cambridge Mass. 1970, viii, 207–8.

62 *Pictures of Life in England and America*, Boston 1851.

63 *Overland Monthly*, February 1873, x, 134–41.

64 The financial details of Clare's transactions with his publishers can be found in the two standard biographies of Clare, by J. W. and Anne Tibble.

Note on the Text

The documents are of two sorts: manuscript material—mainly letters to and from Clare—and printed comments, reviews, notices, essays, and articles. Manuscript material has been transcribed as accurately as possible, and no attempt has been made to regularize spelling, punctuation, or capitalization. Editorial additions are within square brackets, except for the completion of words and phrases (lost when the paper has been torn), where the convention < > has been used. As virtually all the manuscript documents included are extracts from letters, it was not necessary to indicate, separately for each item, that it was an extract, and only omissions within the extracts are indicated. Where dates of letters differ from those given in *Letters of John Clare*, ed. J. W. and Anne Tibble, 1951, reference may be made to my 'Letters of John Clare, 1821: Revised Datings', *Notes and Queries*, February 1969, ccxiv, 58–64. For printed material, the original texts have been followed, but certain punctuation and spelling have been regularized. Biographical details, so common a feature of many reviews, have been omitted, except in a few interesting cases. The innumerable quotations from the poems have usually been omitted, with a brief indication of the poems or lines involved; references are to *The Poems of John Clare*, ed. J. W. Tibble, 1935. But when a quotation from a poem is included, the text has been left as it appeared in that particular document: it will not necessarily be the text to be found in *The Poems of John Clare*, or other more recent editions, where Clare's manuscripts have been followed more scrupulously than they were by his own publishers.

Editorial footnotes, which have been kept to a minimum, are numbered, while original footnotes are indicated by asterisks (*), daggers (†), etc.

THE EARLY DAYS

1818–20

1. John Clare apologizes

?1818

From an undated and unfinished note in NMS. 1, p. 9. This manuscript ('A Rustic's Pastime') contained many of Clare's early poems.

As the ensuing Trifles are nothing but the simple productions of an Unlettered Rustic their faults & Imperfections will undoubtedly be nothing more than what might be expected—as correct composition & Gramatical accuracy can never be lookd for from one whose mental facculties (such as they were) being continually overburthend & depressd by hard labour which fate ordained to be his constant employ-ment—It is hoped the unnoticd Imitation should any occur (being unknown to the author) will not be deem'd as Plagarisms as the humble station of life in which providence has placed him has ever debarred him from Reaping that advantage of extending his knowledge by reading of Books the small catalogue he has seen might easily be enumerated a Thompson & a Milton when a school boy was the constant companions of his leisure hours—The first of which still continues to be his favourite author—

> whos mildly pleasing song
> he hums in rapture as he strolls along

The imitations if any he may be proud of as boasting thoughts similar to those of his superiors

therefore resting in the humble hopes. . . .

2. John Clare addresses the public

1818

From the Prospectus, printed by J. B. Henson of Market Deeping, in an attempt to gain subscribers to the projected volume of poems. A sonnet ('The Setting Sun') was included as a specimen of Clare's powers, but only a handful of people showed any interest, before Edward Drury saw it.

The public are requested to observe, that the Trifles humbly offered for their candid perusal can lay no claim to eloquence of composition, (whoever thinks so will be deceived,) the greater part of them being *Juvenile* productions; and those of a later date offsprings of those leisure intervals which the short remittance from hard and manual labour sparingly afforded to compose them. It is hoped that the humble situation which distinguishes their author will be some excuse in their favour, and serve to make an atonement for the many inaccuracies and imperfections that will be found in them. The least touch from the iron hand of *Criticism* is able to crush them to nothing, and sink them at once to utter oblivion. May they be allowed to live their little day, and give satisfaction to those who may choose to honour them with a perusal, they will gain the end for which they were designed, and their author's wishes will be gratified. Meeting with this encouragement, it will induce him to publish a similar collection, of which this is offered as a specimen.

3. John Clare on his hopes of success

1818

From a letter to J. B. Henson, copied by Henson and sent back to Clare two years later (31 March 1820) as a reminder of their former relationship (see Introduction, p. 2), Eg. 2245, fol. 75. Henson was the bookseller who undertook to publish Clare's proposals for a subscription, and who was now pressing Clare to let him publish his next volume. John Taylor (see No. 5) thought Henson was treated too favourably in Octavius Gilchrist's account, in the *Quarterly Review*, of the publishing history of *Poems Descriptive* (see No. 25).

I send you some of the principal subscribers which I have procured lately, the first of which is a Baronet!!! who speaks very highly of my 'Sonnet' in the prospectus—good God, how great are my Expectations, what hopes do I cherish! as great as the unfortunate Chattertons were on his first entrance into London which is now pictured in my Mind— & undoubtedly like him I may be building 'Castles in the Air' but Time will prove it.

4. The problem of the 'Dedication' to *Poems Descriptive*

1818

This episode neatly illustrates the conflicting interests involved in the publication of *Poems Descriptive of Rural Life and Scenery*, 1820. In the event, no dedication appeared. Edward Drury, cousin of the London publisher, John Taylor, was an astute bookseller from Stamford (Henson's rival), anxious to have a hand in Clare's concerns, and reluctant to part with MSS. Great ill-feeling developed, as Drury realized he was being ousted: nobody comes out of the protracted affair with much dignity (see Introduction, p. 3). For Taylor, see No. 5; for Gilchrist, No. 6.

(a) Clare to Taylor, dated by Taylor 24 November 1818 (the postmark is too faint to help), *LJC* (NMS. 32), p. 27:

I was very pleased with the dedication which Mr. Gilchrist wrote for me on Sunday but after a little Consideration percieved it was too Refined & Elegant to flow from the pen of a Clown & as such Unsuitable for the Book altogether. Therefore I have done one in my own way above which your Taste will model in shape most Suitable.

This letter included the following Dedication:

To the Right Honourable Charles William Lord Viscount Milton These artless Rural Delineations are most humbly & unostentasiously inscribed with the gratitude of the Northamptonshire Peasant who feeling the blessings of his Lordships benevolence to an helpless & afflicted Parent thus dares to declare his admiration & thankfulness.

(b) Drury to Taylor, NMS. 32, written on the back of the above letter, but with no date:

I think John Clare's [sic] has a very good idea of a dedication, although the specimen on the other side is none of the happiest; however you judge it best to have what he writes without aid, & so you have this;—I earnestly beg you politely to decline Mr. G.'s proffered dedication.—I am almost jealous of that gentleman, because I think he would not willingly miss being thought one of Clare's early patrons;—if he can possibly effect his name, or his writing, being in the book, he *will*. But as he took no trouble in the matter when Clare was mentioned to him some months ago, I think it not fair he should have any credit for the labour of others. . . . Pray excuse my apparently unkind comment on your friend; I perhaps know too little or too much of him. I make no disguise with *you*, so you must excuse my ill-nature if it be as bad, and don't let it hurt me in your opinion.—I must say I felt pained at the *little* time you contrived to spare for consultation—scarcely ¼ of an hour! I wanted to make many inquiries vivâ voce which on paper may appear to my discredit, therefore I will not now communicate my thoughts.

5. Words of warning

1820

John Taylor (1781–1864), the publisher of Keats, had by now taken over from his cousin Drury the task of fostering Clare's talent. Extract (b) is one of the first of innumerable letters he sent to Clare, often with detailed suggestions as to what Clare should do. For all his faults, Taylor was an indispensable ally.

(a) Drury to Taylor, 2 January 1820, NMS. 43:

It is to be greatly feared that the man will be afflicted with insanity if his talent continues to be forced as it has been these 4 months past; he has no other mode of easing the fever that oppresses him after a tremendous fit of rhyming except by getting tipsy.

The same letter quotes Clare as saying that he wants copies of Chaucer and other 'old poets': '"I must have Poetry to read otherwise I cannot rhyme; & these Wordsworth's, Bowles &c that Mr Gilchrist lends do me no good."'

(b) Taylor to Clare, 13 January 1820, Eg. 2245, fol. 21, with a copy of Chaucer:

I hope you will like the Work now it is finished, and if you can make presents or otherwise dispose of 12 Copies, they are yours. . . . But let me beg of you to be more patient in the attempt to write, whatever you may do with Respect to reading.—Your best Pieces are those which you were the longest Time over, & to succeed in others you must not hurry.—Nevertheless whenever you have anything else to send me, I shall be most happy to give you my Opinion of it.

6. Octavius Gilchrist introduces Clare to the literary world

1820

'Some Account of John Clare, an Agricultural Labourer and Poet', *London Magazine*, January 1820, i, 7–11.

Octavius Gilchrist (1779–1823) a Stamford grocer, poet, critic and journalist (editor of *Drakard's Stamford News*), formed, through Taylor, a warm friendship with Clare. He was also an antiquary, an expert on Ford and Jonson, and a friend of William Gifford, editor of the *Quarterly Review* (see No. 25); he became involved in the Bowles-Byron controversy over Pope, with his *Letter to the Rev. William Bowles*, 1820. After Gilchrist's death in 1823, his widow continued to correspond fairly regularly with Clare. Gilchrist was rather apologetic about this introductory article: he wrote on 14 January 1820, 'In the article in the Magazine I thought it expedient to praise as little as might be, because people don't like to have their judgment anticipated, and those who know anything of the world know how to contrive their best' (Eg. 2245, fol. 19). But a week later (21 January) he reported that he had received a 'satisfactory letter from Taylor,—satisfactory inasmuch as he thinks my article calculated to be of essential service in promoting the sale of the Poems' (Eg. 2245, fol. 27). But Drury was more critical: he noted, in an undated letter to Taylor, that 'Mr. G. has *picturesqued* finely in the London Mag.' (NMS. 43); and, hearing that Gilchrist was contemplating another article (see No. 22), he hoped (31 January 1820) that his 'forthcoming comments will be less far-fetched and less laboured than his former favour—because it looks as if he wrote per force and not voluntarily' (NMS. 43). See Introduction, p. 5.

Song was his favourite and first pursuit:
His infant muse, though artless, was not mute;

Of elegance as yet he took no care,
For this of time and culture is the fruit:
Perhaps he gained at last this fruit so rare,
For so in future verse we purpose to declare.   BEATTIE.

'A HAPPY new year,' and the first number of a publication which has
for its object to extend the influence of letters, and to aid the inquiries of
science, may not be inaptly employed in introducing to the world a
name, hitherto altogether unknown to literature, but which, if our
estimate of genius be not more than commonly inaccurate, seems to
merit a considerable portion of regard, while, at the same time, it stands
in need of popular encouragement, and even protection. The time has
not long passed—

And pity 'tis, so good a time had wings
To fly away—

when an aspiration, merely, toward loftier pursuits, among those to
whom fortune has been sparing of her indulgence, has been fostered
and encouraged by liberal natures, to whom the same fickle lady has
been lavish of her bounties. The subsiding of the surprise which the
appearance of extraordinary abilities in most unpromising situations
had excited, and the failure of some pretensions not very judiciously
countenanced, have, it is to be feared, engendered a feeling unfriendly,
and somewhat obstinate, toward candidates better qualified. And yet it
may be reasonably questioned, if the instances were collected and produced, of energies misapplied and talents ill-understood from a hasty
belief of their competence to better things, whether the examples of
those who have been generously and judiciously aided and encouraged
in those more exalted pursuits for which the inexplicable gift of nature
seemed to have designed them, would not considerably out-number the
amount of failures. It requires no great exercise of the memory to call
to mind the names of various claimants to poetic fame, whom unaided
genius has, by her stirring influence alone, placed in a station of no
inferior rank in literature; a station from which neither the sneers of
envy nor the caprices of fashion are likely ever to displace them.
Whether the *novus hospes*[1] whose claims it is the purpose of the present
essayist to present, shall hereafter be of that honoured tribe, it would be
presumptuous and unjust to decide before his pretensions be examined.
These claims, it must be candidly acknowledged, the recent and imperfect acquaintance of the present writer with his subject disqualifies

[1] 'new guest'; see Virgil, *Aeneid*, iv, 10.

him from satisfactorily submitting. The evidences, however, will not be long withheld: in the mean time, we shall content ourselves with a slight endeavour to excite that curiosity which we have, as yet, neither the means, nor, indeed, the inclination to fully satisfy.

In a conversation on literary subjects, during the spring of the present year, with my excellent friend Mr. Taylor, of Fleet Street, he inquired of me if I knew any thing of John Clare, an agricultural labourer in the neighbourhood of Stamford, of whose talent for poetical composition he then possessed a considerable number of specimens, transmitted to him by Mr. Drury, a bookseller at Stamford. The name was wholly unknown to me, and,—to drop the style royal and critical, and speak in the first person,—I cannot account for, nor excuse the indifference, by which the subject was afterwards permitted to escape altogether from my regard. Returning, a few days since, from the North of England, Mr. Taylor became my guest for a day or two; and, the name of Clare being repeated, I expressed a wish to see the person of whose abilities my friend's correct judgment pronounced so favourably. Mr. Taylor had seen Clare, for the first time, in the morning, and he doubted much if our invitation would be accepted by the rustic poet, who had now just returned from his daily labour, shy, and reserved, and disarrayed, as he was. In a few minutes, however, Clare announced his arrival by a hesitating knock at the door,—'between a single and a double rap,'— and immediately upon his introduction he dropped into a chair. Nothing could exceed the meekness, and simplicity, and diffidence with which he answered the various inquiries concerning his life and habits, which we mingled with subjects calculated or designed to put him much at his ease. Nothing, certainly, could less resemble splendour than the room into which Clare was shown; but there was a carpet, upon which it is likely he never previously set foot; and wine, of which assuredly he had never tasted before. Of music he expressed himself passionately fond, and had learned to play a little on the violin, in the humble hope of obtaining a trifle at the annual feasts in the neighbourhood, and at Christmas. The piano-forte he had heard, or supposed it must be *that* he heard, passing the house of a family, whose name I am not authorised to mention, and for whom, if I did name them, I should feel it difficult to express the affection that I feel. No plaudit could equal the acknowledgment paid to her voice, while the tear stole silently down the cheek of the rustic poet, as one of our little party sung the pathetic ballad of *Auld Robin Gray*. His account of his birth is melancholy enough. Nothing can be conceived much humbler than the origin of John Clare, poetry herself does not supply a more lowly descent. His father, who still resides, where the poet was born, at Helpstone (a village in Northamptonshire, seven miles distant from Stamford) while health and strength were his possession, was a daily labourer, but decrepitude has now reduced him to the parish for subsistence. His son, when of sufficient age, assisted his father in thrashing, and other agricultural labours;—at intervals, sometimes of great distance, attending a little school in the adjoining village of Glinton, where he learned to read and to write. Having there, also, attained the rudiments of arithmetic, his attention became riveted to figures, and, without assistance, he mastered the first eight problems of Ward's Algebra, stimulated by the laudable but humble ambition of qualifying himself for the office of usher in a village school. The intricacies of mathematics, however, without a guide, at length subdued the zeal of the youth, while the excitement of fancy seduced him from the study of Bonnycastle and Fenning. But to labour was the destiny of John Clare, and gardening being considered by his parents an occupation better fitted than the plough for a frame of no sturdy structure, he was sent for instruction to work in the gardens of the Marquis of Exeter, at Burghley; and, though the brutal disposition and dissolute habits of his teacher compelled him to relinquish his instructions at the end of nine months, it is to the use of the spade that Clare has ever since been indebted for his precarious and narrow subsistence; and, when the writer of this narrative first saw the poet, he had just quitted an engagement in the vicinity of Stamford, because his employer had reduced his stipend from eighteen to fourteen pence *per diem*! Under the circumstances here disclosed, it will not be supposed that Clare had ever much time for study, or even the means for study, if leisure had not been wanting. Beyond his Bible he had read nothing but a few odd volumes, the very titles of some of which he had forgotten, and others, which he remembered, were so utterly worthless, that I should shame to mention the names. A single volume of Pope, however, with the *Wild Flowers* of Bloomfield, and the writings of Burns, were sufficient to stimulate his innate genius for poetry.

From the early age of twelve, Clare amused his leisure minutes—for much beyond this the claims of needful industry did not afford him,—with short poetical efforts, which were regularly deposited in a chink in the wall,—*fissus erat rimâ*,[1] as in that which parted Pyramus and

[1] Cf. Ovid, *Metamorphoses*, iv, 65, 'fissus erat tenui rima', 'the wall had been split by a fine crack'.

Thisbe; whence, by a fate far more destructive than that which accompanied the manuscript of Alma, they were daily and duly subtracted by his mother to boil the morning's kettle. Let no scornful wag inquire if the dame thought her son's poetry *wanted fire*? Grave Bodley himself felt not more contempt than the good woman for all 'baggage books,' and—

> —————————idle poetry,—
> That fruitless and unprofitable art,
> Good unto none, but least to the professors,

but which her son, perhaps, like young Knowell, 'thought the mistress of all knowledge.' To a question if he had preserved no copies of these earliest compositions, he calmly answered, 'they were, he dared to say, good for nothing.' The zeal of the young enthusiast was not to be subdued by the untoward fate of his poetical offspring; and, while, like the eggs of the ostrich scattered on the sands, some were ripened by the sun, while others were destroyed, amid much that perished by heedlessness, a few early compositions have still escaped. To form a fair judgment as to what is accomplished in poetry, it seems but common candour to take natural advantages and impediments into the estimate; and fancy, surely, can scarcely suggest scenery less fitted for the excitement of picturesque and vivid description, than the dank copses and sedgy margin of the fens: yet,—

> (Nostra nec erubuit sylvas habitare Thalia.)

even in this unpromising situation there are objects out of which an acute observer of nature, aided by genius, can find fit motive for the muse, and such is the subject of the following sonnet, written at the age of sixteen.

TO A PRIMROSE.

> Welcome, pale primrose, starting up between
> Dead matted leaves of oak, and ash, that strew
> The every lawn, the wood, and spinney through,
> Mid creeping moss, and ivy's darker green.
> How much thy presence beautifies the ground;
> How sweet thy modest, unaffected pride
> Glows on the sunny bank and wood's warm side:
> And where thy fairy flow'rs in groups are found,
> The school-boy roams enchantedly along,
> Plucking the fairest with a rude delight;

---

1 'My muse Thalia was not ashamed to live in the woods', Virgil, *Eclogues*, vi, 2.

While the meek shepherd stops his simple song,
　To gaze a moment on the pleasing sight;—
O'erjoy'd to see the flow'rs that truly bring
　The welcome news of sweet returning spring.

It would be presumptuous in me, having seen but two or three short poems, to pronounce that Clare's genius is not framed for sustained or lofty flights; it is enough for me to acknowledge, that the few little pieces which I have seen want the proofs of his capacity for such: but the most fastidious critic will allow, that the above little poem evinces minute observation of nature, delicacy of feeling, and fidelity of description; and that poetry affords few trifles of greater promise composed at so early an age and under equal disadvantages. The following, which combines these qualities with a strong moral and religious feeling, will be perused by some readers with still greater interest, though somewhat more incorrect in language, and answering less strictly to the legitimate structure of the sonnet, of which, it is pretty certain, the unlettered author knew nothing.

THE SETTING SUN.

This scene, how beauteous to the musing mind,
　That now swift slides from my enchanted view!
The sun, sweet setting yon far hill behind,
　In other worlds his visit to renew.

What spangling glories all around him shine,
　What nameless colours, cloudless and serene!
A heavenly prospect, brightest in decline,
　Attends his exit from this lovely scene.

So sets the Christian's sun in glories clear;
So shines his soul at his departure here;
　No cloudy doubts nor misty fears arise
To dim hope's golden rays of being forgiven,
　His sun, sweet setting in the clearest skies,
In meek assurance wings the soul to heaven.

It is always interesting, though somewhat painful, to trace the difficulties with which the poet of humble life has to contend. In the conversation with Clare of which I have already spoken, I gathered that these suggestions of the imagination were written, at intervals stolen from his hasty meals, with a pencil, upon small slips of paper laid on the crown of his hat. At night they were duly deposited in the chasm on the wall, as before related, like the bequest of the celebrated Noy to his son, 'to be dispersed and wasted, for he hoped no better.' *Pulchrorum Autumnus pulcher*,[1] seems the universal feeling of poets, and I learned that the fall of the leaf was the season of Clare's poetical activity. Though remarked among his neighbours for his sequestered habits and poetical accomplishments, I was surprised to find that his talents had excited no interest in his behalf, and had consequently obtained him no efficient friend. He told me, indeed, that Mr. Holland, a Calvinistic preacher in an adjoining hamlet, had paid him some attention, but his means of aiding the needy youth was small, whatever might have been his wish, and he has now quitted his charge. I inquired if Clare frequented Mr. Holland's meeting-house? He had never heard him preach. 'My father was brought up in the communion of the Church of England,' he said, 'and I have found no cause to withdraw myself from it.' His modest demeanour and decent habits are every way creditable to the faith he has thus conscientiously adopted and adhered to.

As the person who has generously undertaken the charge of giving a selection of Clare's poems to the press, will most probably accompany the volume with some particulars of the author's life and habits, it were impertinent on my part to extend this paper, even if I were furnished with materials; I shall therefore only add one other to the two specimens already adduced as examples of his poetical talents. The former are of a *sombre* and chastened description, according but too well with the cheerless condition of his present situation; the one I am about to offer is of a more lively character, and, while it evinces the susceptibility of his feelings and the promptness of his fancy, it proves also that nothing but a little friendly countenance and a more consoling prospect are wanting, to give animation, variety, and cheerfulness to his muse.

Our interview with Clare lasted about two hours; during the whole of which it was evident, nothwithstanding our endeavours, that he was little at his ease, and was, perhaps, not sorry at being relieved from restraint: he had not parted from us more than ten minutes, when his sensations were thrown into verse, and sent to us in the shape of a poem which he called—

THE INVITATION.[2]

A witch or wizard, God knows what,
　　Rallied at Drury's door like thunder,
(Or riding beesom—stick, or not)
　　Her message struck a lout with wonder:

[1] 'Autumn, beautiful in its beauties'.
[2] This poem is not included in *Poems*.

She ask'd for Johnny,—'aye, for what?'
  His muse had made him known, God speed her,—
He hobbled up, put on his hat,
  And hung like ass behind his leader.

The door was shown—he gave a tap—
  His fingers 'neath the knocker trembled;
A lady hasten'd to the rap,
  She welcom'd in, *He* bow'd and mumbled.

The finery dazzled a'e his sight,
  Rooms far too fine for clowns to bide in,
He blinkt, like owls at candle-light,
  And vainly wish'd a hole to hide in.

He sat him down most prim the night—
  His head might itch, he dare not scratch it;
Each flea had liberty to bite,
  He could not wave a finger at it.

But soon he prov'd his notions wrong,
  For each good friend, tho' finely 'pearing,
Did put clown's language on his tongue,
  As suited well the Rustic's hearing.

He felt the gentry's kindness much,
  The Muse, she whisper'd 'pen a sonnet,'
'Ye can't gi'e less return for such,
  'So instantly begin upon it!'

So, after gazing round about,
  And musing o'er his undertaking,
Right glad was he to shamble out,
  With little ceremony making.

POEMS DESCRIPTIVE OF RURAL LIFE AND SCENERY

January 1820

7. John Taylor, Introduction to *Poems Descriptive*

Taylor's careful Introduction determined, to a large extent, the immediate critical response, and also provided the relevant biographical details which became inextricably linked to any critical comment (see Introduction, p. 5).

The following Poems will probably attract some notice by their intrinsic merit; but they are also entitled to attention from the circumstances under which they were written. They are the genuine productions of a young Peasant, a day-labourer in husbandry, who has had no advantages of education beyond others of his class; and though Poets in this country have seldom been fortunate men, yet he is, perhaps, the least favoured by circumstances, and the most destitute of friends, of any that ever existed.

JOHN CLARE, the author of this Volume, was born at Helpstone, near Peterborough, Northamptonshire, on the 13th of July, 1793. He is the only son of Parker and Ann Clare, who are also natives of the same village, where they have always resided in extreme poverty; nor are they aware that any of their ancestors have been in better circumstances. Parker Clare is a farmer's labourer, and latterly he was employed in threshing; but violent colds brought on the rheumatism to such a degree that he was at length unable to work, or even to move without assistance. By the kind liberality of Lord Milton he was then sent to the Sea-bathing Infirmary at Scarborough, where he found great relief; but returning home part of the way on foot, from a desire to save expenses, his exertions and exposure to the weather brought on the pain again, and reduced him to a more deplorable state than ever. He is now a helpless cripple, and a pauper, receiving an allowance of five shillings a week from the parish.

JOHN CLARE has always lived with his parents at Helpstone, except for those short periods when the distance to which he was obliged to go for work prevented his return every evening. At his own home, therefore, he saw Poverty in all its most affecting shapes, and when he speaks of it, as in the Address to Plenty,

> Oh, sad sons of Poverty!
> Victims doom'd to misery;
> Who can paint what pain prevails
> O'er that heart which want assails?
> Modest Shame the pain conceals:
> No one knows, but he who feels—

And again:

> Toiling in the naked fields,
> Where no bush a shelter yields,
> Needy Labour dithering stands,
> Beats and blows his numbing hands;
> And upon the crumping snows
> Stamps, in vain, to warm his toes—

he utters 'no idly-feign'd poetic pains:' it is a picture of what he has constantly witnessed and felt. One of our poets has gained great credit by his exterior delineations of what the poor man suffers; but in the reality of wretchedness, when 'the iron enters into the soul,' there is a tone which cannot be imitated. CLARE has here an unhappy advantage over other poets. The most miserable of them were not always wretched. Penury and disease were not constantly at their heels, nor was pauperism their only prospect. But he has no other, for the lot which has befallen his father, may, with too much reason, be looked forward to as the portion of his own old age. In the 'annals of the poor' want occupies a part of every page, except the last, where the scene changes to the work-house, but then the burthen which is taken from the body is laid upon the spirit: at least it would be so with CLARE; for though the contemplation of parochial relief may administer to some minds a thankless, hopeless sort of consolation, under the pressure of extreme distress, yet to the writer of the following lines it must be the highest aggravation of affliction:—

44

> Oh, may I die, before I'm doom'd to seek
>   That last resource of hope, but ill supplied;
> To claim the humble pittance once a week,
>   Which justice forces from disdainful pride!

While such was the destitute condition of his parents, it may seem extraordinary that CLARE should have found the means to acquire any learning whatever, but by extra work as a ploughboy, and by helping his father morning and evening at threshing, he earned the money which paid for his education. From the labour of eight weeks he generally acquired as many pence as would pay for a month's schooling; and thus in the course of three years he received, at different times, so much instruction that he could read very well in the Bible. He considers himself to have derived much benefit from the judicious encouragement of his schoolmaster, Mr. Seaton, of Glinton, an adjoining parish, from whom he sometimes obtained threepence a week in rewards, and who once gave him sixpence for repeating, from memory, the third chapter of Job. With these little sums he bought a few books.

When he had learned to read toleraby well, he borrowed from one of his companions that universal favourite, Robinson Crusoe, and in the perusal of this he greatly increased his stock of knowledge and his desire for reading. He was thirteen years of age when another boy shewed him Thomson's Seasons. They were out in the fields together, and during the day CLARE had a good opportunity of looking at the book. It called forth all the passion of his soul for poetry. He was determined to possess the work himself; and as soon as he had saved a shilling to buy it with, he set off for Stamford at so early an hour, that none of the shops were open when he got there. It was a fine Spring morning; and after he had made his purchase, he was returning through the beautiful scenery of Burghley Park, when he composed his first piece of poetry, which he called 'The Morning Walk.' This was soon followed by the 'Evening Walk,' and some other little pieces.

But the first expression of his fondness for Poetry was before he had learnt to read. He was tired one day with looking at the pictures in a volume of poems, which he thinks were Pomfret's, when his father read him one piece in the book to amuse him. The delight he felt, at hearing this read, still warms him when he thinks of the circumstance; but though he distinctly recollects the vivid pleasure which thrilled through him then, he has lost all trace of the incidents as well as of the language, nor can he find any poem of Pomfret's at all answering the faint conception he retains of it. It is possible that his chief gratification was in the harmony of the numbers, and that he had thoughts of his own floating onward with the verse very different from those which the same words would now suggest. The various melody of the earliest of his own compositions is some argument in favour of this opinion.

His love of Poetry, however, would soon have spent itself in compositions as little to be remembered as that which has just been mentioned, had it not been for the kindness of Mr. John Turnill, late of Helpstone, now in the Excise, who was indeed a benefactor to him. From his instruction CLARE, though he knew a little of the rudiments before, learnt Writing and Arithmetic; and to this friend he must, therefore, consider himself indebted for whatever good may accrue to him from the exercise of those powers of mind with which he is naturally endowed. For it is very probable, that, without the means of recording his productions on paper, CLARE would not only have lost the advantage he may derive from the publication of his works, but that also in himself he would not have been the Poet he is; that, without writing down his thoughts, he could not have evolved them from his mind; and that his vocabulary would have been too scanty to express even what his imagination had strength enough to conceive. Besides, if he did succeed in partial instances, the aggregate amount of them could not have been collected and estimated. A few detached songs or short passages might be, perhaps, treasured in the memory of his companions for a short period, but they would soon perish, leaving his name and fame without a record.

In the 'Dawnings of Genius,' CLARE describes the condition of a man, whose education has been too contracted to allow him to utter the thoughts of which he is conscious:—

> Thus pausing wild on all he saunters by,
> He feels enraptur'd though he knows not why;
> And hums and mutters o'er his joys in vain,
> And dwells on something which he can't explain.
> The bursts of thought, with which his soul's perplex'd,
> Are bred one moment, and are gone the next;
> Yet still the heart will kindling sparks retain,
> And thoughts will rise, and Fancy strive again.

There is, perhaps, no feeling so distressing to the individual, as that of Genius thus struggling in vain for sounds to convey an idea of its almost intolerable sensations,

> Till by successless sallies wearied quite,
> The Memory fails, and Fancy takes her flight;

46

The wick confin'd within the socket dies,
Borne down and smother'd in a thousand sighs.

that this would have been CLARE's fate, unless he had been taught to
write, cannot be doubted; and a perusal of his Poems will convince any
one, that something of this kind he still feels, from his inability to find
those words which can fully declare his meaning. From the want of a
due supply of these, and from his ignorance of grammar, he seems to
labour under great disadvantages. On the other hand, his want forces
him to an extraordinary exertion of his native powers, in order to supply
the deficiency. He employs the language under his command with great
effect, in those unusual and unprecedented combinations of words which
must be made, even by the learned, when they attempt to describe
perfectly something which they have never seen or heard expressed
before. And in this respect CLARE's deficiencies are the cause of many
beauties,—for though he must, of course, innovate, that he may succeed
in his purpose, yet he does it according to that rational mode of
procedure, by which all languages have been formed and perfected.
Thus he frequently makes verbs of substantives, as in the lines,

Dark and darker *glooms* the sky——
To *pint* it just at my desire——

Or verbs of adjectives, as in the following,

Spring's pencil *pinks* thee in thy flushy stain.

But in this he has done no more than the man who first employed
crimson as a verb: and as we had no word that would in such brief
compass supply so clearly the sense of this, he was justified no doubt in
taking it. Some future writers may, perhaps, feel thankful for the
precedent. But there is no innovation in such cases as these. Inseparably
connected with the use of speech is the privilege to abbreviate; and
those new ideas, which in one age are obliged to be communicated
paraphrastically, have generally in the next some definite term assigned
them: so legitimate, however, is the process of this, by reason of certain
laws of analogy which are inherent in the mind of man, and universally
attended to in the formation of new words, that no confusion can arise;
for the word thus introduced into a language always contains its meaning in its derivation and composition, except it be such mere cant as is
not meant to live beyond the day; and further, the correspondent word
to it may always be found in other more perfect languages, if the people

who spoke that language were alike conversant with the idea, and equally under the temptation of employing some word to signify it.

But a very great number of those words which are generally called new, are, in fact, some of the oldest in our language: many of them are extant in the works of our earliest authors; and a still greater number float on the popular voice, preserved only by tradition, till the same things to which they were originally applied again attract notice, and some writer, in want of the word, either ignorantly or wisely, but in either case happily, restores it to its proper place. Many of the provincial expressions, to which CLARE has been forced to have recourse, are of this description, forming part of a large number which may be called the unwritten language of England. They were once, perhaps, as current throughout the land, and are still many of them as well-sounding and significant, as any that are sanctioned by the press. In the midland counties they are readily understood without a glossary; but, for the use of those who are unaccustomed to them, all such as are not to be found in Johnson's Dictionary will be printed at the end, with explanations.

Another peculiarity in CLARE's writing, which may be the occasion of some misunderstanding in those who are critically nice in the construction of a sentence, is the indifference with which he regards words as governing each other; but this defect, which arises from his evident ignorance of grammar, is never so great as to give any real embarrassment to the reader*. An example occurs at p. 41:—

> Just so 'twill fare with me in Autumn's Life,

instead of 'the Autumn of Life,' but who can doubt the sense? And it may be worth while to mention here another line, which for the same reason may be objected to by some persons:—

> But still Hope's smiles unpoint the thorns of Care——

as if he had intended to say 'Hope smiling;' yet as the passage now stands it has also great propriety, and the Poet's conception of the effect of those smiles may have been, that they could blunt the thorns of care. But CLARE, as well as many other poets, does not regard language in the same way that a logician does. He considers it collectively rather than in detail, and paints up to his mind's original by mingling words, as a painter mixes his colours. And without this method, it would be

---

* The irregularity here mentioned was, from the same cause, practised by Shakespeare. —See Ritson's note, Shaks. vol. xi. p. 106. Edit. 21 vols, 1813.

impossible to convey to the understanding of the reader an adequate notion of some things, and especially of the effects of nature, seen under certain influences of time, circumstance, and colour. In Prose these things are never attempted, unless with great circumlocution; but Poetry is always straining after them concisely, as they increase her power of giving pleasure; and much allowance ought to be made if her efforts in this way are not always successful. Instances of the free grouping of words occur in the Sonnet to the Glow-worm:—

> Tasteful Illumination of the night!
> Bright, scatter'd, twinkling star of spangled earth, &c.

And in the following lines:—

> Aside the green hill's steepy brow,
> Where shades the oak its darksome bough.
> So have I mark'd the dying embers light,——
> With glimmering glow oft redden up again,
> And sparks crack'd brightening into life, in vain.

> Brisk winds the lighten'd branches shake,
>   By pattering, plashing drops confess'd;
> And, where oaks dripping shade the lake,
>   Print crimpling dimples on its breast.

Examples of the use of Colour may be seen in the Sonnets—To the Primrose, The Gipsy's Evening Blaze, A Scene, and in the following verse:—

> First sunbeam, calling night away,
>   To see how sweet thy summons seems,
> Split by the willow's wavy grey,
>   And sweetly dancing on the streams.

The whole of the Sonnet to the river Gwash is an instance of it, down to the line

> And moss and ivy speckling on my eye.

A dry critic would call the former passages redundant in epithets; and the word *speckling* would excite, perhaps, his spleen in the latter: but ask the question, and you will probably find that this critic himself has no eye for colour,—that the light, and shade, and mezzotint of a landscape, have no charms for him,—that 'his eye indeed is open, but its sense is shut;' and then, what dependance can be placed upon his judgment in these matters?

CLARE, it is evident, is susceptible of extreme pleasure from the

49

varied hues, forms, and combinations in nature, and what he most enjoys, he endeavours to pourtray for the gratification of others. He is most thoroughly the Poet as well as the Child of Nature; and, according to his opportunities, no poet has more completely devoted himself to her service, studied her more closely, or exhibited so many sketches of her under new and interesting appearances. There is some merit in all this, for Wordsworth asserts, 'that, excepting a passage or two in the Windsor Forest of Pope, and some delightful pictures in the Poems of Lady Winchelsea, the Poetry of the period intervening between the publication of the Paradise Lost, and the Seasons [60 years], does not contain a single new image of external nature.' But CLARE has no idea of excelling others in doing this. He loves the fields, the flowers, 'the common air, the sun, the skies;' and, therefore, he writes about them. He is happier in the presence of Nature than elsewhere. He looks as anxiously on her face as if she were a living friend, whom he might lose; and hence he has learnt to notice every change in her countenance, and to delineate all the delicate varieties of her character. Most of his poems were composed under the immediate impression of this feeling, in the fields, or on the road-sides. He could not trust his memory, and therefore he wrote them down with a pencil on the spot, his hat serving him for a desk; and if it happened that he had no opportunity soon after of transcribing these imperfect memorials, he could seldom decypher them, or recover his first thoughts. From this cause several of his poems are quite lost, and others exist only in fragments. Of those which he had committed to writing, especially his earlier pieces, many were destroyed from another circumstance, which shews how little he expected to please others with them: from a hole in the wall of his room, where he stuffed his manuscripts, a piece of paper was often taken to hold the kettle with, or light the fire.

It is now thirteen years since CLARE composed his first poem: in all that time he has gone on secretly cultivating his taste and talent for poetry, without one word of encouragement, or the most distant prospect of reward. That passion must have been originally very strong and pure, which could sustain itself, for so many years, through want, and toil, and hopeless misery. His labour in the fields through all seasons, it might be thought, would have disgusted him with those objects which he so much admired at first; and his taste might have altered with his age: but the foundation of his regard was too deeply laid in truth to be shaken. On the contrary, he found delight in scenes which no other poet has thought of celebrating. 'The swampy falls of pasture ground, and rushy spreading greens,' 'plashy streams,' and 'weed-beds wild and rank,' give him as much real transport as common minds feel at what are called the most romantic prospects. And if there were any question as to the intensity or sincerity of his feeling for Poetry and Nature, the commendation of these simple, unthought of, and generally despised objects would decide it.

Of the poems which form the present collection some few were among CLARE's earliest efforts. The Fate of Amy was begun when he was fourteen; Helpstone, The Gipsy's Evening Blaze, Reflection in Autumn, The Robin, Noon, The Universal Epitaph, and some others, were written before he was seventeen. The rest bear various dates, but the greater number are of recent origin. The Village Funeral was written in 1815; The Address to Plenty, in December 1817; The Elegy on the Ruins of Pickworth, in 1818. To describe the occupations of CLARE, we must not say that Labour and the Muse went hand in hand: they rather kept alternate watch, and when Labour was exhausted with fatigue, she 'cheer'd his needy toilings with a song.' In a note on this poem, CLARE says, 'The Elegy on the Ruins of Pickworth was written one Sunday morning, after I had been helping to dig the hole for a lime-kiln, where the many fragments of mortality and perished ruins inspired me with thoughts of other times, and warmed me into song.'

In the last two years he has written, What is Life? The Fountain, My Mary, To a Rosebud, Effusion to Poesy, The Summer Evening, Summer Morning, First of May, The Dawnings of Genius, The Contrast, Dolly's Mistake, Harvest Morning, The Poet's Wish, Crazy Nell, and several other pieces, with almost all the Sonnets. One of the last productions of CLARE's fancy is the following Song, which, as it came too late to be inserted in its proper place in this volume, may as well appear here, where it fitly closes the chronicle of his Poems.

THE MEETING.[1]

> Here we meet, too soon to part,
> Here to leave will raise a smart,
> Here I'll press thee to my heart,
>   Where none have place above thee:
> Here I vow to love thee well,
> And could words unseal the spell,
> Had but language strength to tell,
>   I'd say how much I love thee.

[1] This poem is not included in *Poems*.

Here, the rose that decks thy door,
Here, the thorn that speads thy bow'r,
Here, the willow on the moor,
   The birds at rest above thee,
Had they light of life to see,
Sense of soul like thee and me,
Soon might each a witness be
   How doatingly I love thee.

By the night-sky's purple ether,
And by even's sweetest weather,
That oft has blest us both together,—
   The moon that shines above thee,
And shews thy beauteous cheek so blooming,
And by pale age's winter coming,
The charms, and casualties of woman,
   I will for ever love thee.

This song is written nearly in the metre of one by Burns, 'O were I on Parnassus' Hill,' and the subject is the same, but in the execution they are quite different. CLARE has a great delight in trying to run races with other men, and unluckily this cannot always be attempted without subjecting him to the charge of imitating; but he will be found free from this imputation in all the best parts of his poetry, and in the present instance it may be worth while comparing him with his prototype, to see how little he stands in need of such assistance. The propensity to emulate another is a youthful emotion, and in his friendless state it afforded him an obvious, and, perhaps, the only mode of endeavouring to ascertain what kind and degree of ability he possessed as a Poet.

This song, 'The Meeting,' was written at Helpstone, where CLARE is again residing with his parents, working for any one who will employ him, but without any regular occupation. He had an engagement during the greater part of the year with Mr. Wilders, of Bridge-Casterton, two miles north of Stamford; where the river Gwash, which crosses the road, gave him a subject for one of his Sonnets. His wages were nine shillings a week, and his food; out of which he had to pay one shilling and sixpence a week for a bed, it being impossible that he could return every night to Helpstone, a distance of nine miles: but at the beginning of November, his employer proposed to allow him only seven shillings a week; on which, he quitted his service and returned home.

It was an accident which led to the publication of these Poems. In

December 1818, Mr. Edward Drury, Bookseller, of Stamford, met by
chance with the Sonnet to the Setting Sun, written on a piece of paper
in which a letter had been wrapped up, and signed J. C. Having
ascertained the name and residence of the writer, he went to Helpstone,
where he saw some other poems with which he was much pleased. At
his request, CLARE made a collection of the pieces he had written, and
added some others to them. They were then sent to London, for the
opinion of the publishers, and they selected those which form the
present volume. They have been printed with the usual corrections
only of orthography and grammar, in such instances as allowed of its
being done without changing the words: the proofs were then revised
by CLARE, and a few alterations were made at his desire. The original
MSS. may be seen at Messrs. Taylor and Hessey's.

The Author and his Poems are now before the public; and its
decision will speedily fix the fate of the one, and, ultimately, that of the
other: but whatever be the result to either, this will at least be granted,
that no Poet of our country has shewn greater ability, under circumstances so hostile to its developement. And all this is found here without
any of those distressing and revolting alloys, which too often debase
the native worth of genius, and make him who was gifted with powers
to command admiration, live to be the object of contempt or pity. The
lower the condition of its possessor, the more unfavourable, generally,
has been the effect of genius on his life. That this has not been the case
with CLARE may, perhaps, be imputed to the absolute depression of his
fortune. It is certain that he has not had the opportunity hitherto of
being injured by prosperity; and that he may escape in future, it is
hoped that those persons who intend to shew him kindness, will not do
it suddenly or partially, but so as it will yield him permanent benefit.
Yet when we hear the consciousness of possessing talent, and the natural
irritability of the poetic temperament, pleaded in extenuation of the
follies and vices of men in high life, let it be accounted no mean praise
to such a man as CLARE, that, with all the excitements of *their* sensibility
in *his* station, he has preserved a fair character, amid dangers which presumption did not create, and difficulties which discretion could not
avoid. In the real troubles of life, when they are not brought on by the
misconduct of the individual, a strong mind acquires the power of
righting itself after each attack, and this philosophy, not to call it by a
better name, CLARE possesses. If the expectations of 'better life,' which
he cannot help indulging, should all be disappointed, by the coldness
with which this volume may be received, he can

———put up with distress, and be content.

In one of his letters he says, 'If my hopes don't succeed, the hazard is not of much consequence: if I fall, I am advanced at no great distance from my low condition: if I sink for want of friends, my old friend Necessity is ready to help me, as before. It was never my fortune as yet to meet advancement from friendship: my fate has ever been hard labour among the most vulgar and lowest conditions of men; and very small is the pittance hard labour allows me, though I always toiled even beyond my strength to obtain it.'—To see a man of talent struggling under great adversity with such a spirit, must surely excite in every generous heart the wish to befriend him. But if it be otherwise, and he should be doomed to remediless misery,

> Why let the stricken deer go weep,
>   The hart ungalled play;
> For some must watch, while some must sleep,—
>   Thus runs the world away.

8. From an unsigned review, *New Times*

21 January 1820

This review was reprinted in the *Gentleman's Magazine*, February 1820, xc, 146–9. The *New Times* had, on 4 January, promptly taken Gilchrist's 'Account' straight out of the *London Magazine* (see No. 6). See Introduction, pp. 5-6.

The efforts of the uncultivated mind—the outpourings of genius un-moulded by scholastic system and unimbued with scholastic lore must ever be interesting to the lover of literature, and the observer of human nature. Few men whose reading has been extensive, and whose taste has been refined by an acquaintance with the classical productions of ancient and of modern times venture to lay before the world their real meditations. They dare not speak 'as they ruminate', unless supported by the consciousness of powerful genius. They become readers and critics, but seldom soar into the regions of poetry, where such alarming competition awaits them. We have seldom an opportunity of learning the unmixed and unadulterated impression of the loveliness of nature on a man of vivid perception and strong feeling, equally unacquainted with the arts and reserve of the world, and with the riches, rules, and prejudices of literature. Such a man is Clare. In moments snatched from the labour by which he earned a scanty subsistence, with no other writing apparatus than his hat, a scrap of paper, and a pencil, he eagerly endeavoured to express the thoughts which crowded upon his mind, or to describe the objects around him which delighted his fancy. How difficult a task this must have been to an untaught peasant, ignorant even of grammar, will be conceived by every one who has a spark of poetic feeling. There is scarcely a man breathing, however education may have assisted him, who has not at times found how inadequate words are to the expression of the workings of an active imagination, how far passion expressed falls short of passion felt. Clare himself complains of the painful consciousness of his inability to utter

The bursts of thought with which his soul's perplexed.

This poverty of his vocabulary obliged him frequently to coin words and to use provincialisms. In some instances he is fortunate: those in which he is not so, we are willing to pass over without particular censure; there is little danger of his being quoted as an authority for alterations or innovations. Many expressions which are considered vulgar and provincial, are forcible and not unpoetical: but in making the selection of those which may be adopted, much care and discrimination should be exercised.

9. Octavius Gilchrist on *Poems Descriptive*

1820

Gilchrist to Clare, 21 January 1820, Eg. 2245, fol. 27.

Gilchrist wrote on 25 January that he was sure of the success of the new volume (Eg. 2245, fol. 30).

And this brings me to the Poems themselves, which I have at length seen, and I must tell you candidly, and without a compliment, they have disappointed me:—they have disappointed me agreeably, for they are still better than I looked to find them. Tenderness and feeling and a mind awake to the beauties of nature I expected to find,—but there is occasionally a grasp of thought and strength of expression,—as in 'What is Life?'—which I was not quite prepared for. I know not what the MSS. where [sic] in the gross, but from the selection I should think you are much indebted to Mr Taylor's judgment. By the way, Taylor is fearful that you are exciting your mind too much in composition, and he urges me to use my influence in dissuading you from that course: this I should very strenuously do, if I thought his fears were well founded, which I trust they are not. . . .

A very worthy friend of mine the Rev. Mr Bonney of Normanton, arrived this morning from London, and he also says that the article has been read with considerable interest in the circles that he has visited in London, so that at least the poems will have had sufficient recommendation to get them into fair circulation, and I have little doubt of their success.

10. Tributes in verse

1820, 1821

(a) Eliza Louisa Emmerson. Mrs Emmerson (1782–1847), the wife of a London picture importer, became Clare's most frequent, tireless, and tiresome correspondent. Her poem to Clare, dated in manuscript 30 January 1820 (Eg. 2245, fol. 33), was published in the *Morning Post*, 8 February 1820, entitled 'Lines written by a Lady, and Presented with a volume of "Clare's Poems" to a Noble Friend.' The noble friend was none other than Admiral Lord Radstock (1753–1825), who rewarded Clare with a copy of Blair's *Sermons*. Mrs Emmerson, signing herself 'A Constant Reader', urged the *Morning Post* to insert specimens of *Poems Descriptive* in order to induce 'the liberal encouragers of genius to snatch from impending misery this wonderful Child of Nature! so, that by degrees, he might be raised from the lowly and lost situation in which he now stands; not only for himself, but indeed, I may almost say, still more so for the world'. The poem's final line is taken from the end of Clare's poem, 'Helpstone'.

> Oh! take this little volume to thy care—
> And be the friend of Genius—and of 'Clare!'
> There Nature's dictates, unadorn'd by art,
> She sweetly tells; and powerful, doth impart
> Those moral precepts—in such simple strain
> We read—we wonder—and respect the swain.
> Hail! native genius! bred in lowly vale,
> May'st thou be cherish'd by a fostering gale.
> Ye friends to genius! early succour yield
> And pluck this wild flower from the common field—
> Transplant it to a soil more genial, warm,
> Where by fond culture it each sense may charm;
> Oh! nurse this minstrel! Nature's simple child
> 'That he may sing his wood-notes sweet and wild,'
> To charm the ear, to glad the feeling heart,
> And to the mind, new beauties to impart;

Let not such talent pine in shades away—
Oh, call the labourer forth to brighter day!
But should alas! such succour not be lent
'He'll put up with distress—and be content'.

(b) J. Harper (a journeyman printer, who wrote to Clare sending his poem), 'Sonnet to Mr. John Clare', Eg. 2250, fol. 208. The poem is undated.

> What was it moved thee, say, friend Clare,
> When nipping winds made Nature bare,
> To woo the smiling Maids of Song,
> And dare on Pegasus to trot along?
> Bold Child of Nature! thus to steer
> Safe thro' the wide Poesian sphere,
> And gather from the Muses' bower
> Full many a sweetly-scented flower!
>> Yes—thou hast formed the rosy wreath,
>> Which braves the wintry blast of death.
>> Thy thoughts on Virtue's pinions fly,
>> Round Nature's vast immensity!
>> Mild be the sun of life to thee,
>> The Child of rural Minstrelsy.

(c) Chauncy Hare Townsend (1798–1868), a recent visitor from Cambridge, wrote his 'Sonnet' to Clare on 18 April 1820. It was published in the *Morning Post*, 15 May; Clare spotted that a line was missing, and urged Taylor to 'get it reprinted in some other paper' (20 May, *LJC*, p. 50). It accordingly appeared in the *New Times* on 24 May, with the same heading: 'This Gentleman's rare poetic talents have been long known to the world; consequently, such an Address, from such a person, cannot but be highly flattering to the young Poet.' Clare acknowledged the poem, sent to him by Townsend (Eg. 2245, fol. 88), with thanks, 'Tho I doubt your fine Sonnet flatters me too much be as it may I have vanity to be proud of such notice who would not' (*LJC*, p. 40; for obvious reasons this letter cannot be dated March, as *LJC* suggests: it must be April). But in telling Gilchrist of Townsend's visit, Clare wrote, 'Flattering verses teems in upon me fast inspired with £1 notes these are pieces you know I must praise & I intend not to be sparing of it' (April 1820; *LJC*, p. 39).

There is a vivid lightning of the breast,
Flash'd from a spark of kindred poesy,
Which poets only know, when rapt they see
Some hidden thought, some feeling unexprest
Upon the pages of the Bard imprest
In all the warmth of Nature's energy.
O Clare, such answering electricity
Darts, from thy numbers to my soul addrest!
Thou hast read Nature with a Poet's eye,
Thou hast felt Nature with a Poet's heart,
Not the broad page, which all expansed descry,
But the fine secrets, which poetic art
Alone unravels,—can alone impart,
And to which none but Poets' souls reply.

(d) 'A Poetical Tribute of Respect to John Clare, the Northampton-shire Poet', dated 28 March 1821, Eg. 2245, fol. 306. The author is not known.

Hail! Pleasing Poet; though distrest, and poor,
Thy richer Genius Nature can display;
And though unskill'd in deep and classick lore,
Her varied Beauties faithfully portray.

Creation's Wonders, though minute and small,
Are open to thy fond research and view;
With miscroscopic eye thou scann'st them all,
And giv'st thy praises, where the praise is due.

Whene'er, to leave this earth thy warning's giv'n,
(Her pure, rich joys, thy still exhaustless mine;)
O may the purer, richer joys of Heav'n,
Through all Eternity, O Clare, be thine.

11. Advice on alterations and omissions: trouble with the native

1820

In the first edition of *Poems Descriptive* there were several poems and lines offensive to Clare's patrons. This section charts some of the fluctuations of opinion, and Clare's obduracy (see Introduction, pp. 3–4). But the bibliographica lfacts are·eloquent: 'The Country Girl' was omitted from the second edition, 'My Mary' and 'Dolly's Mistake' from the third. The fourth edition lost, in addition to these poems, 'Friend Lubin', the offending line from 'Dawnings of Genius' and part of 'Helpstone'.

(a) Taylor to Clare, 12 February 1820, Eg. 2245, fol. 37ᵛ. The poem in question is 'My Mary'.

If you have no objection we will insert *unfit* in the following Line, when the next Edition comes—

> 'Who when the Baby's all unfit' . . .

As it stands the Blank is objected to as much almost as the other Word would be, & Lord Radstock wishes that this Poem & Dolly's Mistake shoᵈ both be omitted next Time—So have several other Persons— For my own part I am not so fastidious.—Has any one said anything to you about them?

(b) Drury to Taylor, 13 February 1820, NMS. 43. Drury thinks 'My Mary' an 'index of a mind above commonplace', and would retain it, whilst reflecting that in this day and age it perhaps will not do. He suggests that it is not sufficiently humorous and concludes, 'It is more disgusting than otherwise'. But on 20 February he adduces Burns as an example of someone who 'gets away with it', and reports to Taylor, 'He [Clare] has a great notion of "My Mary" and the dirty verse he *prizes*!'

(c) Gilchrist to Clare, 21 March 1820, Eg. 2245, fol. 68. The sort of rumour mentioned here was common, and gave rise to great ill-will in the 1830s.

. . . I have seen the second edition of the poems at Drakard's; nothing is omitted. Taylor's word 'unfit' is substituted for the one which shocked the delicate sensibilities of Portland Place; and instead of 'safe assurance',—a tautological phrase, in the first sonnet, he has printed 'Faith's assurance', which to me sounds very harsh. It is *rumoured* here that Lord Milton is building a cottage for you: is the fact so, or is this only the breath of one of the Lady Fame's many tongues?

(d) Eliza Emmerson to Clare, 11 May 1820, Eg. 2245, foll. 118–120ᵛ. Mrs Emmerson has had an irate letter from Lord Radstock, from which she gives copious extracts:

If you are determined to serve poor Clare—you *must do your duty*! you must tell him—to expunge certain highly objectionable passages in his 1st Volume—before the 3rd Edition appears—passages, wherein, his then depressed state hurried him not only into error, but into the most flagrant acts of injustice; by accusing those of pride, cruelty, vices, and ill-directed passions—who, are the very persons, by whose truly generous and noble exertions he has been raised from misery and despondency. . . . It has been my anxious desire of late, to establish our poets character, as that, of an honest and upright man—as a man feeling the strongest sense of gratitude for the encouragement he has received—but how is it possible I can continue to do this if he suffers another Edition of his poems to appear with those vile, unjust, and now would be ungrateful passages in them?—no, he must cut them out; or I cannot be satisfied that Clare is really as honest & upright as I could wish him!—tell Clare if he has still a recollection of what I have done, and am still doing for him, he must give me unquestionable *proofs*, of being that man I would have him to be—he *must expunge*!

Mrs. Emmerson supported this plea:

Let me now entreat you, as a true friend—as a sister—to write immediately to Mr. Taylor, and desire him *from yourself*, to expunge the objectionable lines—you have them *marked* in the Volume I sent you— for alas! they were named to me but too soon after your poems were published—as conveying '*Radical* and *ungrateful* sentiments', & I in consequence ventured to *note* them so pointedly in the margin, hoping

you would withdraw them of your own accord, after the 1st Edition:—
It is *not* now too late, to undo all the mischief. . . . There are 10 lines
in the 'Helpstone' beginning with 'Accursed wealth'—and also one
sadly disliked in your beautiful poem on 'Genius'—'That necessary tool
to wealth and pride'. I ventured to write a line in the margin to substitute this— & I thought it connected the subject very well—if you will
indulge me by adopting this line, no person can ever know it, or indeed
any other alteration I presumed to suggest in my marginal notes. . . .
And now let me tell you, that I have ventured to *pledge myself* to our
noble friend!—that *you* will *readily* make the *alterations required*—Oh
yes, you have a *just* and noble soul! you cannot deny that to others,
which you have so often sighed for yourself—*Injustice*! Ask your heart,
your understanding—your Genius, and they will all exclaim! *Gratitude*
should be now your theme. . . .

(e) Clare to Taylor, 16 May 1820, *LJC*, p. 49:

Being very much bothered latley I must trouble you to leave out the
8 lines in 'Helpstone' beginning 'Accursed wealth' and two under 'when
ease and plenty'—and one in 'Dawnings of Genius' 'That nessesary
tool' leave it out and put ★ ★ ★ ★ ★ to fill up the blank this will let em
see I do it as negligent as possible D-n that canting way of being forced
to please I say—I cant abide it and one day or other I will show my
Independence more strongly then ever you know who's the promoter
of the scheme I dare say—I have told you to order and therefore the
fault rests not with me while you are left to act as you please.

(f) Eliza Emmerson to Clare, 24 May 1820, Eg. 2245, fol. 130. For the
offending line in 'Dawnings of Genius' she wants to substitute 'With
Nature! simple Nature! for his guide': '. . . but I am informed of the
impossibility of any alteration being made in the 3rd Edition. . . .'
Taylor has told her that the fourth edition might have such parts
removed, and Lord Radstock is pleased that Clare has agreed to the
alterations. But Taylor was telling Clare on 6 June (Eg. 2245, fol.
140ᵛ), 'A strong attempt is made to get those Passages expunged from
the next Edition, which you left it to me to do as I pleased about; but
I am inclined to remain obstinate, and if any Objection is made to my
judgment for so doing I am willing to abide the Consequences. . . .'

(g) Clare to James Hessey, July 1820, *LJC*, pp. 58–9. Hessey was
Taylor's partner until 1825.

I have seen the third Edition I am cursed mad about it the Judgement of T. is a button hole lower in my opinion—it is good—but too subject to be tainted by medlars *false delicasy* damn it I hate it beyond everything those frumpt up misses brought up in those seminaries of mysterious wickedness (Boarding Schools) what will please em? why we well know—but while their heart and soul loves to extravagance (what we dare not mention) false delicasy's seriousness muscles up the mouth and condemns it—what in the name of delicasy doth poor Dolly say to incur such malice as to have her artless lamentations shut out—they blush to read what they go nightly to balls for and love to practice alas false delicasy—I fear thou art worse then Dolly say nothing to T.—he is left to do as he likes you know—and if we controul him he will give us up—but I think I shall soon be qualified to be my own editor. . . . I have felt long enough for poor T. I asure you I know his taste and I know his embaresments I often picture him in the midst of a circle of 'blue stockings' offering this and that opinion for emprevement or omision I think to please all and offend all we should find out 215 pages of blank leaves and call it 'Clare in fashion'. . . . T. woud not be offended to find me vext and I think at the omisions he knows himself in so doing the gold is licked off the gingerbread—'Dolly's mistake' and 'my Mary' is by the multitude reckoned the two best in the book—I have lost my tail—by it.

(h) Hessey to Clare, 11 July 1820, Eg. 2245, foll. 172–3:

I am not at all surprised at your being vexed at the omission of any part of your Volume of Poems, and you may be assured that it was not resolved upon without the most mature deliberation & a firm conviction that your own Interest would be most essentially served by the Omission. The circumstance of their having been inserted at first, and again in the second Edition not withstanding the remonstrances of many of our friends & of yours, is sufficient evidence of Taylor's feeling as to their merit, and having given such a pledge of his opinion you may be sure he would not idly retract it. But he perceived that objections were continually made to them & that the sale of the Volume would eventually be materially injured & therefore he determined on leaving them out. Whether it be false or true delicacy which raises the objection to these pieces it is perhaps hardly worth while to inquire. If we are satisfied that in the Society which we frequent certain subjects must not be even alluded to, we must either conform to the rules of that Society or quit it. An author in like manner is expected to concede something to the tone of moral feeling of the Age in which he lives, and if he expects or wishes his works to be popular, to afford amusement, or convey instruction; he must avoid such subjects as are sure to excite a Prejudice against him & to prevent his works from being generally read. And, after all, there is no hardship in all this. There is plenty of room for a man of Genius, of Delicacy, of Taste, to exercise himself in, without touching upon such things as are of common consent now avoided in all good Society as repugnant to good Taste & real Delicacy. We make allowances for Shakespeares little touches of indelicacy & Double meaning, because such conversation was common in Society in his Day—but it would not be tolerated now, or if admitted at all, must be much more delicately wrapped up.

(i) Taylor to Clare, 27 September 1820, Eg. 2245, fol. 225. In this letter, continued on 29 September, Taylor reports Radstock's anger over the 'radical lines', and his intention to disown Clare. Because of this, Taylor is inclined to accede on this issue; but his bland assertion (fol. 225^v) that he is determined to avoid 'the Insertion of any Lines not absolutely yours. My province qualifies me to cut out but not to introduce anything' is less than totally convincing. Drury commented wryly in an undated letter to Clare, 'In the 4th Edit . . . the lines in Helpstone are cut out & mutilated to meet old Ld R's wish—thus it is with Taylor always, "firm in counsel but weak in purpose & doing"' (Eg. 2250, f. 146^v). Taylor wrote:

My opinion is fixed as to the Needlessness of these Omissions for the Reasons assigned, and there are no others that can weigh with me: but let them be expunged and welcome, since so decided. . . . Set is to be made against you if they are not. When the Follies of the Day are past with all the Fears they have engendered we can restore the Poems according to the earlier Editions.

(j) Clare to Taylor, 21 December 1820, LJC, pp. 81–2. This extract suggests Clare's equivocal attitude towards his patrons, in particular Lord Radstock and Mrs Emmerson.

. . . this moment I am interrupted with a parcel of News Papers from my old friend his Lordship but no letter—tis impossible to feel otherwise than gratful for the many trifling troubles he takes in my behalf weak as some actions may appear such trifles as these (whatever the simple design may be) warms & binds him closer in my esteem & affections & I really think I shall dye with his praises in my mouth do as he may do afterwards—I always told you to act as an Editor you may get above such insinuating bother I must knock under for my own advantage I find it far easier to have an hours work of flattery then I usd to do an hours threshing in a barn & tho I have not yet been swore at Highgate I have judgement enough to chuse the most easy method in such things—if E.L.E. & L.R. had found me out first & edited my poems what monsters woud they have made can it be possible to judge I think praises of self & selfs noble friend & selfs incomparable poems undoubtedly shovd into the bargain woud have left little room for me & mine to grow up in the esteem of the public but shoud end into a dark corner they woud have servd as a foundation for their own build-ings & dwindled away like the tree surrounded with Ivy while the names & praises of patron & poetess flourished in every page.

12. Eliza Emmerson on her admiration of 'Nature's Child'

1820

Eliza Emmerson to Clare, 21 February 1820, Eg. 2245, foll. 39–40ᵛ.

This was the first of hundreds of letters that poured into Help-stone from Stratford Place, London. For Mrs Emmerson, see No. 10a.

> To Mr. John Clare—Poet!
> Tho' lowly bred, and rude thy fare—
> I'll call thee friend! sweet poet Clare!
>
> ———

Chusing such a motto, be not alarmed at a stranger introducing herself to you:—I would indeed address you in the language of a real friend—

as one, more than anxious for your Fame—your welfare, and your happiness.

Your volume of Poems, fell into my hands a few days after they were published. I read them with attention, and delight; and felt most desirous to give them publicity and patronage! happily for you, and for your poems, I solicited to have the honour of presenting a volume of them to a Noble! and most benevolent friend—accompanying them with a short address, the effusion of my own heart! wherein, I entreated the patronage of *you*, and *your productions*! how far your exalted Patron has interested himself for you, and has succeeded—I need not explain: nor need I endeavour to impress on your mind the real benevolence of his Lordships character—the beautiful and devout volumes, which he has presented you with, will best convey his nature to you; and would *in itself*, be sufficient to *register him in your heart*, independant of his warm exertions to foster your superior genius, and be the means of removing you, in time, from that lowly situation of which you so often, and so feelingly, complain. . . .

Of your Poems, I am almost at a loss how to express my admiration of them. They are at once, simply beautiful—affecting—and occasionally sublime!—You prove yourself, in your scenes from nature—to be truly Nature's Child! In your domestic scenes, you bring the subject home to every feeling bosom—while in the Devout, and sublime! you create astonishment, and respect for your Moral and Religious reflections. May you *continue* to *indulge* your *Muse* in such truly sweet & fine productions; and that under the divine protection of a bountiful Providence! Fame! and ultimate independence and happiness may be yours—is my sincere wish.—

That your heart is susceptible of all the finer sensations, your poems sufficiently prove,—and, what may we not *further hope from you*, now, that your Genius can soar, freed from those depressions under which it has too long laboured.—How will *Gratitude* fill your soul—and inspire you, with song!— —

Your extraordinary patronage, will I hope remove from your mind those prejudices against the Great!—which your humble station had made you *too keenly* feel: you are now my friend—convinced that Greatness—goodness—kind heartedness and benevolence! dwell pre-eminent in the bosoms of the Rich and Great.—

I beg, you will not consider me, as wishing to dictate to you in the slightest degree—but believe that, I am anxious only, to light up *that beacon* which may lead you on to Fame! to fortune, and to happiness!

13. Charles Mossop on the source of Clare's success

1820

Charles Mossop to Clare, 25 February 1820, Eg. 2245, fol. 45.

The Rev. Charles Mossop was vicar of Helpstone, and involved with the Clare family over a long period. His warnings on the dangers of success and prosperity are typical of one kind of response to Clare's overnight fame.

Since I met you with the Printer of your Poems, I have read them with satisfaction I may say with pleasure. From the specimen you have given the Public I see a probability of your gaining applause from some men; but, I trust, you will ever recollect that whatever commendations you may receive from them, they are not to be considered as your own, further than as you acknowledge them to be the gift of *him*, from whom all good things do come, & with a grateful heart return them back to the right owner the Lord God of Xtians.

14. From an unsigned review, *New Monthly Magazine*

March 1820, xiii, 326–30

Without the knowledge of these [biographical] facts, indeed, any decision on the productions themselves would be premature; since, if they possess sufficient intrinsic merit to please, they will obtain some additional commendation from a consideration of the circumstances under which they were composed; whilst those circumstances may fairly be pleaded in extenuation of whatever defects they display, and may serve as an apology for the absence of that transcendent excellence which more favoured poets have attained. . . .

[Quotes from Introduction]

Of the subjects of these poems, and the style in which they are composed, two things are chiefly to be remarked: first, that they contain true and minute delineations of external nature, drawn from *actual observation*; and, secondly, that they abound with provincialisms, and are not unfrequently blemished by grammatical inaccuracies. Clare is strictly a descriptive poet; and his daily occupation in the fields has given him a manifest advantage over those minstrels whose pastoral strains are inspired by the contemplation of the furze and stinted herbage of Hampstead Heath, or the sooty verdure of a London square. In his descriptions we find no 'sweet buds' and 'wavy grass,' and 'leafy glories,' twice and thrice and thirty times repeated. He revels in an unbounded luxuriance of epithets; in his minuteness of detail he seems at a loss where to stop; he paints every mode of colour and of form, and when his attention is attracted by objects which he cannot define by ordinary language, he invents new forms of expression, as singular as they are vigorous and appropriate. 'Thus', it is observed in the introduction, 'he frequently makes verbs of substantives, as in the line

Dark and darker *glooms* the sky.

Or of adjectives, as in the following—

Spring's pencil *pinks* thee in thy flushy stain.

But in this he has done no more than the man who first employed *crimson* as a verb.' He looks on plants, insects, and animals with the eye of a naturalist, and his accuracy, in this respect, shews that he has been a watchful observer of their habits. Thus, in his 'Evening,'—

> The dew worms too in couples start,
> But leave their holes in fear;
> For in a moment they will part,
> If aught approaches near.

In his picture of 'Noon,' when, as he tells us—

> If we earnest look, it seems
> As if crooked bits of glass
> Seem'd repeatedly to pass.

Every thing is made to feel the effect of the scorching sun-beams; the bees 'cease to hum,' the birds are mute—

> ——No longer on the stream,
> Watching lies the silver bream.

The shepherds retire with their flocks to some friendly shade; of the cattle, some try to elude the rays of heat by motion; others again crouch under the hedgeside, or plunge into the wave.

> While to all the flowers that blow,
> If in open air they grow,
> Th' injurious deed alike is done
> By the hot relentless sun;
> E'en the dew is parched up
> From the teazle's jointed cup.

Again, when he describes 'Summer Evening,' he fails not to observe with Shakespeare the beetle's 'drowsy hum,' as well as the homeward flight of the crow, the rallying note of the partridge, the swallow resting on the chimney-top, the bat commencing its airy wheel, the leaps of the 'startled frog,' at which

> From the grass or flow'ret's cup,
> Quick the dew-drop bounces up.
> Now the blue fog creeps along;
> And the bird's forgot his song;
> Flowers now sleep within their hoods;
> Daisies button into buds;

> From soiling dew the butter-cup
> Shuts his golden jewels up;
> And the rose and woodbine, they
> Wait again the smiles of day.

If associations are only wanting to convey an image correctly to the mind, Theocritus or Virgil could bring forward none but what this untaught Northamptonshire hind enumerates. Their works are to him, as they were to the Ayrshire peasant, '*a fountain shut up, and a book sealed,*' but Clare is acquainted with a language less understood than Greek or Latin—the language of the human heart, and he reads in a book which requires no commentary—the book of nature. Of the figures of rhetoric he makes no display; but when he does employ them, he employs them with propriety. Thus, when he personifies the Storm, who, 'tyrant-like,'

> Takes delight in doing harm,
> Down before him crushing all,
> Till his weapons useless fall;
> And as in oppression proud,
> Peal his howlings long and loud,
> While the clouds, with horrid sweep,
> Give (as suits a tyrant's trade)
> *The sun a minute's leave to peep,*
> *To smile upon the ruins made.*

Can there be a personification more just, or an image more beautiful, than that with which it concludes? He imagines himself protected from the injuries of this tyrant by Plenty, and he has recourse to a simile, which might inspire the most polished poet with emulation.

> Oh, how blest 'mid these alarms,
> I should bask in Fortune's arms,
> Who defying every frown,
> Hugs me on her downy breast;
> Bids my head lie easy down,
> And on Winter's ruins rest.
> *Emblematic simile,*
> *Birds are known to sit secure,*
> *While the billows roar and rave,*
> *Slumbering in their safety sure,*
> *Rock'd to sleep upon the wave.*

The poems which please us best are, 'Noon;' lines 'To a Rosebud in humble Life;' the 'Harvest Morning;' lines 'On an Infant's Grave;' those addressed 'To an April Daisy,' 'Summer Evening,' 'Summer Morning,' the 'Dawnings of Genius,' and the Sonnets. The first are all too long to be extracted, but we will transcribe the sonnet to 'The Winds,' and that to 'The River Gwash;' the latter principally on account of the exceeding beauty of the epithets, and that happy sense of 'the light, shade, and mezzotint of a landscape,' which the introduction properly notices as the chief excellence of poetry of this species.

[Quotes 'To the Winds'; 'The River Gwash']

Clare, as his biographer admits, is addicted to imitation, and we think he imitates Burns too frequently. This is imprudent. The similarity of their conditions will so often induce a comparison, that it would be more judicious in Clare to attempt an original career, than to cramp the vigour of his muse by adopting a manner. He is, like his predecessor, 'Nature's never wean'd, though not her favour'd child;' and while he confines himself to the description of her charms, he needs not the aid of any mortal brother; but neither his songs and ballads, his 'Familiar Epistle to a Friend,' nor his 'Dolly's Mistake,' and 'My Mary,' which last are by far the worst pieces in the volume, will bear to be brought in competition with the deep pathos, the rich and genuine humour displayed in similar productions of the unequalled Scottish minstrel. Yet Clare has succeeded admirably in 'The Meeting,' which is imitated from Burns' 'O were I on Parnassus' Hill,' and which we feel a pleasure in transcribing, as we have no hesitation in saying we think these verses surpass their original. They were sent to the publishers after the volume was nearly printed, and are therefore inserted in the introduction, where, as they 'fitly close the chronicle of his (Clare's) poems,' they may also properly terminate our remarks.

[Quotes 'The Meeting']

To the poems is subjoined a glossary, that serves to explain the provincial expressions, 'many of which,' as the writer of the introduction acutely observes, were once general, and 'may be called part of the unwritten language of England.' We readily subscribe to his opinion, that some of them are 'as well sounding and significant as any that are sanctioned by the press.' But, surely, such expressions as 'bangs,' 'chaps,' (for 'young fellows,') 'eggs on,' 'fex,' (a petty oath,) 'flops,' 'snifting and snufting,' &c., are mere vulgarisms, and may as well be excluded from the poetical lexicon, as they have long since been banished from the dictionary of polite conversation: neither can we imagine, although we confess ourselves uninformed in this particular, that 'to pint it,' can be understood to signify, 'in the midland counties,' or elsewhere, 'to drink a pint of ale,' any more than to 'steak it,' or to 'chop it' would imply to eat a beaf steak or a mutton chop.

Our readers will, doubtless, now be anxious to learn what are the present prospects of this interesting young man, whose character and habits, we have reason to believe, both from what is stated in the introduction to his poems, and what we have ascertained from other sources, are as irreproachable as his talents are extraordinary. The success of his poems will, inevitably, render him dissatisfied with the situation of a daily labourer, earning 'nine shillings a week,' and 'working for any one who will employ him;' nor is it altogether to be wished that he should be suffered to remain in an occupation to which he must necessarily acquire an utter aversion, and for which his pursuits have obviously rendered him unfit. We would not be thought to undervalue the labours or the fruits of honest industry, but we consider it indispensably requisite, in order to insure content in this, as in any other station, that the disposition should correspond with the employment, and that the fancy should not be indulging in the contemplation of unattainable objects. As far as we can collect from his book, Clare's wishes are moderate. The political poet and courtly satirist of King William's reign, when he amused himself with wishing, desired to have—

——clear
For life six hundred pounds a year,
A handsome house to lodge a friend,
A river at my garden's end,
A terrace-walk, and half a rood
Of land set out to plant a wood.

Poor Clare's wants are more immediate. His anticipations have not yet learnt to take in superfluities. He asks for little more besides 'an easy chair,' 'a few books,' and, what we suspect to have been a deficiency, which he has hitherto had reason to complain of—

The barrel nigh at hand,
Always ready as I will'd,
When 'twas empty, to be fill'd!
And, to be possessed of all,
A corner cupboard in the wall
With store of victuals lin'd complete,
That when hungry I might eat. . . .

But we hope the readers of his poems will not confine their encouragement to barren praise; but will benevolently assist in supplying the wants and furthering the honest ambition of a man of talent; and we beg to add the recommendation of the editor of his poems; a recommendation at once judicious and humane, that 'those persons who intend to shew him kindness, will not do it suddenly or partially; but so as it will yield him permanent benefit.' It is proposed to establish a subscription for Clare, of which his respectable publishers and some gentlemen who interest themselves in his welfare, have undertaken to superintend the application.

15. From an unsigned review, *Monthly Review*

March 1820, xci, 296–300

Drury wrote of this review (21 July 1820), 'The Monthly Review contains a weak & washy critique upon you—but it is very harmless' (Eg. 2245, fol. 181ᵛ). See Introduction, p. 7.

A deep and intimate knowledge of the character and capabilities of the subject, and a profound sense of its effects on the heart, are the essential ingredients of poetic power; and, compared with these qualities, expression, and propriety of diction, though in themselves extremely important, are of secondary consideration. The mind of the true poet immediately acknowledges this truth, and seldom wanders without the bounds of its own capacity. To attempt the sublimer provinces of song, a mind richly stored with the philosophic treasures of the past and with the wisdom and beauty of antiquity is requisite, as well as a heart that is alive to the sublimity of the highest feelings of our nature; but to achieve a description of the external beauty of the creation requires no knowledge that gazing will not give. Hence the productions of men who have passed their days in the midst of rural scenery, and whose education has not been such as to pre-occupy the mind with other ideas, consist of a succession of rural images, mingled with representations of simple and natural feeling; and the compositions of such men are valuable, because they are artless and unsophisticated: not the effusions of a poet writing pastorals as he wanders through the fields to the north-east of London, or describing a battle after having seen a Review in Hyde Park. They are the delineations of *professors* in their own line; of men who have painfully and laboriously studied the face of nature in every changing shape, and in every varying season, when beaming with sunshine or when shadowed with tears.

In this point of view, the little volume before us is singularly curious, on account of the many most accurate and interesting pictures which it contains. At the same time, the unaffected and even rude style in which the poems are composed is a strong proof that the writer has been more wrapt up in his feelings than in his mode of expressing them; and we are convinced that the victory has been not of the poet over the muse, but of the muse over the poet.

Yet, however extraordinary these poems may be as the productions of a very uneducated man, and estimable as faithful representations of rural life and scenery, it would be injustice to their author to compare them with the writings of those whose superior stores of mind have enabled them to embellish the strong efforts of native genius with the ornaments of learning and refinement. So, likewise, it would be useless to plead in their favour the disadvantages and difficulties with which their author has been obliged to struggle; because, though it is very honourable to him that he has surmounted them, they can neither add to nor detract from their poetic excellence. If they were, indeed, totally devoid of this quality, Clare might be applauded, and rewarded for exertions so singular in his sphere of life, but the sooner his writings were forgotten the better. This, however, is not the case; since, though his pieces are very defective in expression, and frequently in grammar, they manifest the spirit and truth of poetry. As to the propriety of presenting such efforts to the public, when the writer's matured judgment might have clothed them in a more accurate form, we may perhaps feel a doubt; though the plea of the author's poverty and necessities should not be disregarded.

The pictures of rural life which Clare has drawn are true to nature; so true, that he frequently introduces images which, according to our preconceived notions, can scarcely be called poetical:—but notions like these are acquired by studying the works of poets who have *generalized* the beauties of nature, while Clare paints *in detail*, and with all the minuteness of one whose every-day occupation has led him to contemplate the objects which he represents. With him there is no *aristocracy of beauty*, but the stag and the hog, the weed and the flower, find an equal place in his verse. 'The Harvest Morning' is, perhaps, the best instance of this feature in his compositions:

[Quotes 'Cocks wake the early morn . . .' to '. . . dreads the sultry day!']

'The Summer Evening' also is remarkable for its very accurate and novel images, some of which are striking and beautiful:

[Quotes 'Round the pond the martins flirt' to '. . . their speckled sides']

When Clare attempts the delineation of more refined sentiments, he is by no means so successful: he is then not the master of his subject, and is compelled to become a mere imitator, without possessing a matured and extended taste to assist him in his selection of models. When his topic admits an allusion to natural objects, his compositions of this higher class possess considerable merit; of which the ensuing sonnet is a fair instance:

Anxiety.

One o'er heaths wandering in a pitch dark night,
   Making to sounds that hope some village near;
Hermit, retreating to a chinky light,
   Long lost in winding cavern dark and drear;
   A slave, long banish'd from his country dear,
By freedom left to seek his native plains;
   A soldier, absent many a long, long year,
In sight of home ere he that comfort gains;
A thirsty labouring wight, that wistful strains
   O'er the steep hanging bank to reach the stream;
A hope, delay so lingeringly detains,
   We still on point of its disclosure seem:
These pictures weakly 'semble to the eye
A *faint* existence of Anxiety.

In the structure of these sentences, we strongly perceive the want of education under which the author labours. . . .

[Biographical details]

In mentioning a peasant-poet, we immediately remember Burns: but Clare must not be ranked with him whose talents would bear a comparison with the noblest intellects of modern times, and whose compositions, though perpetually enriched with illustrations from the beauties of nature, were filled with the deepest and truest sentiment, or lightened up with the most brillant wit. Clare, moreover, possesses but a small share of the acquirements of Burns, whose mind was well stored with much useful knowlege.—To extend judicious encouragement, however, to a man who has so laudably displayed the wish for advancement, and the powers and energies which distinguish the writer of these poems, is only an act of justice.

16. Unsigned notice, *Monthly Magazine*

March 1820, xlix, 164

Poems descriptive of Rural Life and Scenery, by John Clare, a Northamptonshire peasant, have lately been edited and published by a gentleman well known in the literary world, for the benefit of the author. To judge from the sketch given of the humble and laborious life of this obscure genius, we are surprised to discover such a display of poetical talent and force of mind in circumstances so little favourable to the development of the human faculties. Considered as the productions of a common labourer, they are certainly remarkable, and deserving of encouragement and commendation: but, to maintain that they have the smallest pretensions to comparative excellence with the writings of others out of his own sphere, would be ridiculous and unjust, and would be trying them by a poetical law from which they ought to be exempt. We do not therefore require that they should possess the correctness and elegance of more classic bards. We must decide upon them by their own merits, and the positive degree of excellence they may possess. We shall not even insist upon Horace's rule, that neither gods nor men will listen to mediocrity in poetry, as we are aware such a radical latitudinarian principle would prove highly detrimental to the claims of the majority of our countrymen from the throne to the cottage. As it is an art of entertainment, however, rather than of use and necessity, we have a right to expect some sort of good in it. The value of poetry must depend upon its positive powers of pleasing and instructing. Without these requisites, it is vain and foolish to offer the excuse of untoward circumstances and luckless fates 'dooming the morn of genius to the shade.' Without intending directly to apply these remarks to the present publication, we are of opinion, that there is often much mistaken kindness in the idea of patronizing neglected worth, as there is seldom one out of ten humble aspirants after fame, who have finally justified the hopes entertained of them. The patrons and the protegées are often both equally mistaken. The opinion, that much is to be conceded to them, from a consideration of the difficulties under which they wrote, is apt to mislead them. These will be forgotten, and they will then be tried by their own native merit. The reputation of Burns and Bloomfield was not granted to them in consideration of their humble station in society, but to their superior excellence as poets. Though Mr. C.'s poems are not devoid of merit, they will not stand the test of a trial by themselves. That he is not without the elements that constitute a poet, the following quotation will sufficiently evince:

[Quotes 'Evening': 'Now glaring daylight . . .']

We must, in justice to Mr. C. mention that there are many pieces of equal merit to this, and that one favourable feature of his poetry is, that it evidently improves. He has still, however, much to overcome.

17. John Scott, from an unsigned review, *London Magazine*

March 1820, i, 323–8

John Scott (1783–1821), who was the first editor of the *London Magazine*, died in a duel with Jonathan Christie, a friend of the influential J. G. Lockhart (see No. 27). There had been a fierce running quarrel with Lockhart over the criticism contained in *Blackwood's Edinburgh Magazine*. In London literary circles, Scott was thought of very highly, especially after the flying start that he gave to the *London Magazine*.

An esteemed correspondent introduced the interesting author of this little volume to public notice, in our first number, and we have now before us the offering itself of the humble and rustic poet, which will, we hope, make good what has been already done for him. John Clare cannot be put forth as the rival of Burns, for the latter, as has been remarked of him by others, is misrepresented when described as an un-lettered peasant. The intellectual powers of Burns were aided by edu-cation almost as far as education can aid, for it is more than doubtful whether the higher branches of academical tuition have any effect in quickening the fancy, or even strengthening the judgment. There is even reason to believe that their effect, on the former faculty at least, is prejudicial rather than advantageous. Burns was placed amongst intelli-gent and thoughtful persons: the powers of his mind were excited by grave and sublime themes, which occupied much of the conversation that passed in his hearing; and he possessed, from his youth, a general knowledge of the events of the day, and of the contents of history, as well as of literary incidents and characters.

John Clare's situation has been, and is, in every respect, far more untoward. A feelingly and neatly-written introduction is prefixed to this volume, which details the case of his family and himself, and, in so doing, proves that no one has ever worshipped the Muse with zeal, in despight of a greater number of painful circumstances, caused by poverty and distress, weighing on, and depressing, his spirits:

[Quotes extensively from the Introduction]

An intense feeling for the scenery of the country, a heart susceptible to the quietest and least glaring beauties of nature, a fine discrimination and close observation of the distinguishing features of particular rural seasons and situations, and, a melancholy sense of the poet's own heavy, —and as he has had too much reason to consider it,—hopeless lot;— such are the qualities of character most prominent in these poems, and which shed over them a sweet and touching charm, in spite of some inaccuracies and incoherencies in their language and arrangement. The sentiment is every where true, and often deep: there is no affectation visible: no bad taste, at least not in the serious pieces: the discontent expressed is not querulous: the despondency is not weak:—the author feels acutely the calamity of his fortune, but he preserves, in the midst of his distress, a quick eye and an open heart for the works of Providence, and an unchangeable faith in its goodness.

Nothing in these pieces has touched us more than the indications they afford of the author's ardent attachment to places, that can have witnessed little but his labour, his hardships, and his necessities. It would seem, that, in the dearth of congenial society, and the absence of benefits from the hands of his fellow men, his love and gratitude had turned towards the inanimate scenes of nature, and fastened with more than usual force on the recollection of favourite spots. The first poem of the collection, 'on Helpstone,' his native place, illustrates this amiable tendency in a very remarkable manner: the conclusion runs in a strain of correct and harmonious poetry, which is really calculated to excite astonishment, when the situation of the writer is taken into account.

> Thou dear, beloved spot! may it be thine
> To add a comfort to my life's decline,
> When this vain world and I have nearly done,
> And Time's drain'd glass has little left to run.
> When all the hopes, that charm'd me once, are o'er,
> And warm my soul in extacy no more,
> By disappointments prov'd a foolish cheat,
> Each ending bitter, and beginning sweet;
> When weary age the grave, as rescue, seeks,
> And prints its image on my wrinkled cheeks,—
> Those charms of youth, that I again may see,

May it be mine to meet my end in thee:
And, as reward for all my troubles past,
Find one hope true—to die at home at last!

The feeling of the descriptive parts of these poems causes them to steal upon the reader with all the moral and poetical influence that belongs to the objects themselves. We do not think that the following verses, taken from a poem to 'Evening,' need fear a comparison with those of Collins.

[Quotes selectively]

Some touching and harmonious verses on a lost greyhound follow these: but the 'Address to Plenty' seems to us fuller of poetical fancy than almost any other piece in the collection.

[Quotes 'Hills and dales no more are seen' to 'In no prospect to be paid'; 'Troubles then no more my own' to 'Then proceed as heretofore']

The 'Summer Evening' is another very fine picture, pleasantly harmonized, all through, to the pensive colour of the poet's disposition.

[Quotes 'The sinking sun . . .' to '. . . her absent love'; 'From the haycock's moisten'd heaps' to '. . . his corn begin'; 'The night-wind now . . .' to the end]

We wish rather to be profuse of our extracts than of our observations in this case. The latter might be regarded with jealousy; but the former put the case of John Clare fairly before those to whom an appeal in his behalf is made by one who has counselled and superintended this interesting publication. If any person can read the compositions it contains, and afterwards reflect without emotion on the fate of the author, should he be still doomed to pursue the weary way in which his life hath hitherto proceeded, either such person is very differently constituted from what we would wish to be, or our estimate of the poetical merit of the book is more grossly wrong than we are willing to believe it will be found. It has been said of this poor young man, that, amongst poets, 'he is, perhaps, the least favoured by circumstances, and the most destitute of friends, of any that ever existed.' He certainly does not merit to be left so circumstanced; and if he should be so left, he may find consolation in the consciousness that his distress is at least unmingled with disgrace to himself, while it attaches much odium elsewhere.

18. John Clare and the *Morning Post*

1820

The *Morning Post* (like the *New Times*), thanks largely to Mrs Emmerson and Lord Radstock, contained a number of 'puffs' on Clare, who soon tired of these attentions. Writing to Taylor on 3 April 1821, Clare referred to 'those silly beggarly flattery in the Morning Post &c &c &c—I think Ive gaind as much harm as good by it— & am nothing in debt on that quarter' (*LJC*, p. 111); his sentiments were pre-echoed by Taylor in a letter of 31 May 1820 to his brother James, after the third edition of *Poems Descriptive* had appeared: 'I am much annoyed by Lord R's puffing in the *Post* & *New Times* & am determined to put an end to it, for I cannot but think it is disgraceful to me & injurious to Clare's Fame as well as Feelings.' Later in the same letter, Taylor gloomily prophesied, 'Poor Fellow! I question if his advancement will make him much happier.' (Quoted in Olive Taylor, 'John Taylor, Author and Publisher', *London Mercury*, July 1925, xii, 262.)

(a) From a letter from 'A Well-Wisher to Merit', *Morning Post*, 11 February 1820. The writer, referring to 'this surely *heaven-born Poet*', asks, 'what is best to be done for this wonderful child of Nature?' The solution offered is to make him a '*nominal under* gardener.' The writer then turns to the question of a second edition:

Another advantage would likewise accrue from a second edition, that is, some two or three poems in the present edition might be expunged, in order to make room for others of riper and purer growth. It is probable that the compiler of the present volume might have chosen his selection with a view of making more fully known the versatility of the youth's genius; or perhaps the stock was so scanty as not to admit of choice. At any rate much allowance must be made for a seeming want of refinement, which it must be confessed appears in one or two instances, in this otherwise most admirable little work. . . .

(b) From a brief account headed 'John Clare, The Peasant Poet', *Morning Post*, 3 March 1820. For William Gifford, editor of the *Quarterly Review*, see No. 25.

Nothing can more fully evince the innate love of poetry which reigns so triumphantly in the mind of our Heaven-born Poet, and the indomitable ardour with which he so nobly pursues it; than the following spirited and energetic lines [Quotes 'An Effusion to Poesy'].

Strong, however, as is our predilection in favour of this wonderful Child of Nature, and sanguine as we are to behold these hopes realized, perhaps we should not have ventured to speak so decidely to this point, had we not been borne out in our opinion by that *judgment* already pronounced, and from which there is *no appeal*, that of our Prince of Critics, William Gifford, Esq; for we have been assured, from indisputable authority, that this Gentleman has declared that he already perceives in his 'Dawnings of Genius', more innate poetic fire, and traits of true genius, than were ever discoverable in Bloomfield, even when he was at the very zenith of his glory.

(c) A letter, signed 'Q', *Morning Post*, 15 May 1820. Edward Drury, in a letter of 17 May 1820, guessed this to be from Captain M. E. Sherwill, and commented, 'Said letter is worded judiciously, and not so offensive as some that have appeared in the Journals' (Eg. 2245, fol. 129). Markham Sherwill wrote several letters to Clare (see Introduction, pp. 4–5), and was a writer himself: his *Poems* appeared in 1832. Drury's guess could be correct: Clare hoped (in vain) that Sherwill would get for him a signed copy of 'The Lady of the Lake'. 'Q's letter ran:

If I were not thoroughly convinced of your earnest desire to lend at all times a fostering hand to genius, when employed in purity of thought and moral rectitude, I ought certainly to apologize for this intrusion on your valuable columns; but I am well assured you will do John Clare, the Northamptonshire Peasant Poet the favour to give publicity to the following pleasing and gratifying truths.

Early in the present year his little volume of poems was ushered into the world, and coming from an unknown pen, their fate was as doubtful as the success is certain when a similar production is given by a valuable and good writer. Merit was the only foundation they possessed, for in the short space of six weeks the whole of the first Edition, consisting of one thousand copies, was sold and dispensed. The very kind and liberal publishers, Messrs. Taylor and Hessey of Fleet-street, immediately printed a second edition of the same extent, which experienced a similar rapid sale, and it is now with difficulty a copy can be procured. This unprecedented demand for a volume of Poems from an obscure individual like Clare, will and must lead a discerning reader to coincide in the general opinion that great originality of idea in his '*Dawnings of Genius*', purity of thought, as may be seen in his poem of '*What is Life?*' added to a natural beauty of language, exist in this poor fellow's compositions; and I am heartily rejoiced to learn a third edition will speedily be offered to the patronage of a generous Public.

The great encouragement Clare has received, not only from Noblemen of the highest rank, but also from the soundest critics, as well as our most eminent Poets, will, I am sure, induce many more of your enlightened readers to seek his little volume.

Clare has been accused of plagiarism, which, in a very few words, I will endeavour to shew is a very unjust and false opinion. In a letter I received from him *after* the publication of his first edition, he writes, 'When your letter arrived, I was reading Scott's "Lady of the Lake", the first of that great Poet's works I ever saw'. In several other letters, he repeatedly writes, I have *heard* of such and such works, but they are far beyond my capacity. In short, Sir, I know what his library consisted of at that time (if that name may be applied to his books), and he certainly had not more than eight or ten volumes, and those decidedly were not of a character from which a natural genius like Clare would ever attempt to transcribe one idea. He owes no debt to any dead or living author, not even the general obligation which men of education owe to the classics of antiquity. An important scrutiny therefore into Clare's Poems will at once convince the reader of my observations, and I hope, by your insertion of these remarks, a still further spirit to support the native genius of Britain, and of an unlettered Peasant, will be engendered, while at the same time, Charity may lend her healing wing; for poor Clare's health is very much lessened of late; he is unable to endure hard labour, and can alone look for support to the further sale of his excellent little volume, added to the benevolent assistance of his noble and liberal patrons. . . .

19. Eliza Emmerson on the certainty of ultimate success

1820

Eliza Emmerson to Clare, 15 March 1820, Eg. 2245, foll. 60–1.

Mrs Emmerson reveals the current preoccupations of these months: the willing and noble patronage, the need to have heart and confidence, the irrelevance of adverse criticism. Mrs Emmerson presumably had in mind the reservations expressed by the *Monthly Magazine* and the *Monthly Review* (see Nos 15 and 16); the doubts of the *Guardian* (No. 26) and *Blackwood's* (No. 27) were not yet public. The letter begins with talk of a rent-free cottage to be provided by Lord Milton (see No. 11c).

. . . I indeed think, that with *peace* of *mind*, a very little would suffice to make you contented! And why my good friend, should you not enjoy peace of mind, now, that *your Genuis*—is *encouraged*—your *character esteem'd*, & your prospects so smiling, that they cannot but be followed with *complete success?* You have *noble* and *sincere friends*, who have *hearts* and *understandings* to *appreciate your real worth*, and who will *never* neglect your welfare, while you have the want and *wish* of their protection! Be *not* then, my dear Clare *discouraged*—but continue to indulge, and *exercise* those *powers*, with which a kind Providence has so eminently blessed you; and never let the voice of the *cold-hearted Critic intimidate* or *depress you*: What is the opinion of a *Cynical Few*, to compare with a liberal and *discerning multitude?* Be *assured*, of your *ultimate success*; and believe the truth, of our immortal Bard 'Shakespeare' who says 'The only way, to *conquer difficulties*, is *daring* to *surmount* them'— In the course of which meritorious exertion, you may rely on my friendship to serve you, in *thought, word* & *deed*, my advice, or opinion you shall have to the *best* of my *abilities*—and *my sympathy* shall *always attend you*! But *do not* let any thing from me, create in your bosom the

84

sense of *obligation*, for you would do *injustice* to *me*, and to *yourself.* Your *confidence* and *esteem* I shall ever be proud and happy to enjoy—it will be a grateful return, to friendship, such as I feel for you: but my soul disclaims, the wish to make *others* feel the weight of obligation, who are *themselves* too noble! *too pure of heart* to 'flatter 'or seek *favour thro'* *dissimulation*—no, my friend! *your nature*, is above such artifice, and it will be valued by me for its *intrinsic worth*!

20. An enquirer after Clare's welfare

1820

(a) M. Hoare to Clare, 17 March 1820, Eg. 2245, fol. 64:

I have met with your Poems and admire them exceedingly and wish to know if you receive all the advantage from the sale of them, or whether you have disposed of the copyright as my buying some copies would not then benefit you—Who is yr Bookseller in Town? and are you in tolerable circumstances now?

(b) Gilchrist writes to Clare, 28 March 1820, that Hoare is 'a man of the first eminence as a Banker in London, and has the reputation of adding the most aimiable manners and liberal disposition to very great wealth. Such a person interesting himself in your behalf, it would be desirable on every account to conciliate' (Eg. 2245, fol. 70). Clare had mistaken Hoare, irritably, for another huffing bookseller (*LJC*, p. 40).

21. Eliza Emmerson on critical reactions

1820

Eliza Emmerson to Clare, 3 April 1820, Eg. 2245, foll. 79ᵛ–80ᵛ.

The opening pages (foll. 78–9) regret Clare's lack of gratitude; Mrs Emmerson then expands on this theme.

More than half of the Second Editions are already sold, and your *fame* as a Poet widely circulated in the way most likely to be beneficial to you:— I know also that *considerable* additions have been made by my Noble friend, to the *funds* in Mr Taylors hands for your benefit—and which ere long you will feel the sweets of—Let nothing then, in the shape of reproach against the higher orders enter your heart, or flow from your pen—recollect that *others* are as sensative [sic] as yourself—and surely my d<ear> Clare since you have been made known, you have no cause for complaint. To suffer your mind to be *sour'd* by improper feelings, in consequence of the *critical* opinions that have been given upon your poems, would be unworthy of your understanding and your heart: your productions only share the same fate that others (of great Poets) have done before: and so it will ever be while Critics exist! It is not their *business* to point out the *beauties* of a work; they are to be *seen without their aid*—the *faults* are their object—and, perhaps 'tis right to guard against a recurrence of the same error—*if any really exists*; and who of us my friend can continue to say, I am without a fault—I cannot improve—I am perfect!—You are charged with imitating 'Burns'—but I think unjustly, as your *ideas* are *original*, then where can the imitation be? Why only in the *measure*—which cannot be considered as an imitation—but I perfectly agree with you, 'let the *comparison decide*'. . . .

86

22. Octavius Gilchrist on having to write another article on Clare

1820

Gilchrist to Clare, 10 April 1820, Eg. 2245, fol. 84. For the finished article, see No. 25.

What's to be done now Measter? Here's a letter from William Gifford, saying I promised him an article on one John Clare for the Quarterly Review. Did I do any such thing? Moreover, he says he has promised Lord Radstock, and if I know him, as he thinks I do, I know that the Lord will persecute him to the end. This does not move me much. But he adds, 'do not fail me, dear Gil: for I count upon you:—tell your simple tale, and it may do the young bard good.' Think you so; then it must be set about! But how to weave this old web anew, how to twist the same rope again and again, how to continue the interest to a twice-told tale. Have you committed any rapes or murders, that you have not yet revealed to me? if you have, out with 'em straight, that I may turn 'em to account before you are hanged; and as you will not come here to confess, I must hunt you up at Helpstone, so look to it, John Clare, for ere it be long, and before you expect me, I shall be about your eggs and bacon. I have had my critical cap on these two days, and the cat-o-nine-tails in my hands, and soundly I'll flog you for your sundry sins, John Clare, John Clare!

23. From an unsigned review, *Eclectic Review*

April 1820, n.s. xiii, 327–40

It is possible that this review, and also that of *The Village Minstrel* in the *Eclectic Review* (No. 60), was by the poet Josiah Conder (see No. 81). See Introduction, p. 7.

If it be the characteristic privilege of genius, as distinguishable from mere talent, 'to carry on the feelings of childhood into the powers of the man,'—to combine the child's sense of wonder and novelty with the every day appearances of nature,

> With sun and moon and stars throughout the year,
> With man and woman,—

and if there be any truth in the assertion, that, 'so to represent familiar objects as to awaken the minds of others to a like healthy freshness of sensation concerning them, is its most unequivocal mode of manifestation,'[1]—there can be no hesitation in classing the Author of these poems, to whatsoever rank in society he should prove to belong, among the most genuine possessors of this dangerous gift. That a peasant should write verses, would, in the present day, afford no matter of astonishment; and did the individual challenge attention in the character of a prodigy, the wonder would soon be over. There is nothing prodigious in real genius, under whatsoever circumstances it has been developed. But a genuine and powerful interest, that does more honour to its object, cannot fail to be excited by the perusal of these exquisitely vivid descriptions of rural scenery, in every lover of nature, who will feel a sort of affinity to the Author; and the recollection that the sensibility, the keenness of observation, and the imaginative enthusiasm which they display, have discovered themselves in an individual of the very humblest station in society, in a day-labourer, whose independence of spirit alone has sustained him above actual pauperism, will be attended by sensations similar to those with which he would recognise some member

[1] Coleridge, *Biographia Literaria*, ch. iv.

88

of his own family in a state of degradation. Talent is, we admit, cheap enough in the present day: the average stature of mind has been raised pretty extensively throughout society. But genius such as characterises these productions of John Clare, is not common in any rank; and that state of things cannot be favourable to the general welfare, which offers to such an individual no means of rising above the condition of extreme indigence in which, almost literally with his spade in the one hand, and his pencil in the other, Clare has hitherto been earning the scanty pittance of hard labour among the most vulgar of mankind. We feel confident, however, that the present appeal to the public on his behalf, will not disappoint the expectations of his friendly and intelligent Editor, nor crush the modest hopes of 'better life' which he has been the means of awakening. Let our readers say whether the Author of the following lines, is a man that should be thrown back into obscurity.

[Quotes 'Helpstone': 'Hail, scenes obscure! . . .' to the end]

For minute fidelity and tastefulness of description, we know scarcely any thing superior to the sketches of Noon, Summer Morning, and Summer Evening. It is evident from a line introduced between inverted commas in the first of these, that the Author had seen Cunningham's 'Day.' This, however, is the extent of his obligations. Clare's descriptions are as far superior in spirit, and picturesque beauty, and tasteful expression, to the namby pamby style of Cunningham's pastorals, as the scenes from which he derives his inspiration, are to Vauxhall gardens. It is, indeed, remarkable, that Clare's style should be so free from the vices of that school of poetry, to which his scanty reading appears to have been confined. Colloquialisms and provincialisms abound in his poems, and attest its substantial originality; but of the grosser vulgarity of affected expression, of all attempt at fine writing, he has steered most commendably clear. We must make room for the whole of

SUMMER EVENING.

[Quotes]

The Village Funeral is a very touching little poem: the following stanzas in particular, are exquisitely beautiful.

> There the lank nettles sicken ere they seed,
>   Where from old trees eve's cordial vainly falls
> To raise or comfort each dejected weed,
>   While pattering drops decay the crumbling walls.

Here stand, far distant from the pomp of pride,
  Mean little stones, thin scatter'd here and there;
By the scant means of Poverty applied,
  The fond memorial of her friends to bear.

O Memory! thou sweet, enliv'ning power,
  Thou shadow of that fame all hope to find;
The meanest soul exerts her utmost power,
  To leave some fragment of a name behind.

Now crowd the sad spectators round to see
  The deep sunk grave, whose heap of swelling mold,
Full of the fragments of mortality,
  Makes the heart shudder while the eyes behold.

After describing the grief of the helpless orphans on leaving behind them in the dust, their only friend and provider, the Poet feelingly exclaims:

Yon workhouse stands as their asylum now,
  The place where poverty demands to live;
Where parish bounty scowls his scornful brow,
  And grudges the scant fare he's forced to give.

Oh, may I die before I'm doom'd to seek
  That last resource of hope but ill supplied;
To claim the humble pittance once a week,
  Which justice forces from disdainful pride!

There are some very fine poetical thoughts in the Address to Plenty, but we have quoted enough for our purpose. We must, however, make room for two noble sonnets; the first for its picturesque beauty, the second for its sentimental excellence.

[Quotes 'To the Winds'; 'To Religion']

We hope we have by this time amply substantiated the opinion we gave at the outset, as to the extraordinary merit of these productions: if so,—if, instead of thinking them *very clever considering they are by a day labourer*, our readers agree with us in conceding to them a high degree of poetical merit quite independent of the circumstances of their Author, they will be prepared to enter with the requisite sympathy, into the simple details of his history. . . .

[Biographical details]

We deem it a very happy circumstance, that Clare has apparently fallen into so good hands; and we earnestly hope that no ostentatious act of injudicious kindness on the part of any who may feel disposed to serve poor Clare, will frustrate the object which his friends have in view. A situation of honourable industry, in which, while elevated above the fear of want, he should not be discharged from the necessity of daily exertion, in which poetry should still continue to be, not his occupation, much less his trade, but his solace and his pride,—would be the most conducive to his happiness. Let him not be cursed with an Exciseman's place, nor fettered with a scanty pension from a titled patron, nor imprisoned in a town till his mind becomes morbid, or his morals tainted by its atmosphere, nor tempted to play the idler. Let him still be suffered to live, and to labour too, in the presence of Nature, but to live free, and to labour for an object that shall sustain and compensate his exertions.

One word to the Editor of the present volume. We are not disposed under present circumstances, to find fault with any of the specimens which he has presented to us, of Clare's genius; and it was quite proper that they should appear with all their inaccuracies and provincialisms, just as they proceeded from his pen. But as the permanent interest of the volume will depend on the intrinsic merits of the composition, we cannot imagine that a few corrections from the hand of Clare himself, at the suggestion of his Editor, would render a new edition less valuable. We by no means intend this remark to apply to the greater number of the words thrown into the glossary,—some of them needlessly enough; as, for instance, 'folds,' 'standard trees,' 'tools,' 'won't,' &c. Many of the provincial terms are forcibly expressive, and can scarcely fail to be understood. What we chiefly refer to, is, an occasional grammatical blemish, although both the diction and the construction of the periods, are, upon the whole, singularly chaste and correct. A more important improvement, however, would consist in a careful revision of the selection of pieces offered to the Public. Several in the present volume, we should be extremely glad to see displaced by subsequent productions; in particular, 'My Mary,' 'Dolly's Mistake,' and 'The Country Girl.' Clare does not succeed in humour: his poems display a playful fancy, but it is a playfulness quite distinct from the unbridled joyousness of dramatic humour, or the epigrammatic smartness of wit. Humour belongs to other scenes than the quiet landscape of human life: it draws its materials from the fantastic modifications of character which are given birth to by the action of men upon one another in an artificial state of society. What may be the effect of further cultivation and a more extended experience, on the mind of Clare, we will not venture to predict. It belongs to the nature of real genius, to convert all knowledge to its own nutriment, and to enrich itself with the spoils of time. There have, however, been instances in which the imagination has been confused, and its vigour impaired, by the attempt to improve upon the finer instincts of nature by means of subsequent cultivation. Clare is hardly likely to produce anything much more beautiful than some of the descriptive passages in the present volume. However this may be, he will not in future be able to yield with the same zest and simplicity of feeling, and in the same unsolicitous mood as formerly, to the tide of his own emotions; and though he may write better, he will scarcely enjoy in an equal degree the luxury of his solitary thoughts. But he may, and we trust he will, be put in possession of the more substantial means of permanent enjoyment. Society owes it to itself, to prevent the Author of these poems from adding another name to the annals of unbefriended genius.

24. James Plumptre on rural poetry according to particular principles

1820

James Plumptre to Clare, 26 April 1820, Eg. 2245, fol. 99.

James Plumptre (1770–1832), a fellow of Clare College, Cambridge, became Vicar of Great Gransden, Huntingdonshire, in 1812. His self-appointed task was to clean up the English stage, and to this end, published, in three volumes, in 1812, *The English Drama purified; being a specimen of select plays, in which all the passages . . . objectionable in point of morality, are omitted or altered.* In this letter, he seems to be referring to two works in particular: *A Collection of Songs, Selected and Revised*, 1806–8, and *Four Discourses on subjects relating to the amusement of the Stage*, 1809. But in Clare's library, it is Plumptre's *Original Dramas*, 1818, that survives. Taylor was right to tell Clare to have nothing to do with him or his advice; he wrote on 17 May 1820, 'I know Mr Plumptre and am not surprised at what he recommended, but it would have been wonderful indeed had he convinced you of the Truth of his Opinions, or the Propriety of your adopting them. Keep as you are: your Education has better fitted you for a Poet than all School Learning in the World would be able to do' (Eg. 2245, fol. 126).

I have myself, for some years, been a writer and a publisher of Rural Poetry, but upon particular principles; and I wish to interest all, especially those who can write better poetry than myself, to consider and adopt these principles. . . . You will probably write and publish much more, and I hope you will turn your thoughts towards some instructive popular Songs for the lower classes. Your knowledge of rural life and your sweet 'Oaten Reed' would charm them. On reading my Introductory Letter you will conclude that there are many things in your Poems which do not accord with my ideas, as your use of *Fate* and *Fortune* a<nd> some *curses*. I am pleased, however, to see occasional marks of a 'love' for religion. . . .

25. From an unsigned review, *Quarterly Review*

May 1820, xxiii, 166–74

This was mainly the work of Octavius Gilchrist (see Nos 22; 18b); but William Gifford (1756–1826), editor of the *Quarterly Review*, seems to have helped. The *Gentleman's Magazine*, June 1844, xxi, 578, was quite wrong to suggest that Southey was the author. Gilchrist told Clare on 22 April that he had 'got very impatient, and fear I have slubbered it. I have not, certainly, instituted the enquiry I proposed to myself, but that may be, perhaps, as well for both of us' (Eg. 2245, fol. 92). Taylor had little to say about the 'critique': 'I am very indifferent myself to what is said of the "Booksellers metropolitan or provincial", but I think Henson is placed higher than he deserves' (6 June, Eg. 2245, fol. 139); to which Clare replied on 10 June, 'I have seen the critique in the Quarterly & a deal softer it is then I expected as for what he says of booksellers care not I dont' (*LJC*, p. 51). The *Monthly Magazine*, June 1820, xlix, 495, discussing this particular number of the *Quarterly*, comments: 'The *eighth* article respects a volume of pretty descriptive poems, by John Clare, a Northamptonshire peasant; and for once the disadvantages of education are treated with indulgence by the high bred Mr. Gifford. We had supposed that the extraordinary academical pampering which his own genius received in his youth, had rendered him incapable of appreciating the merits of talent struggling with indigence.—We had never presumed to think that *he* could have any sympathy for such a thing, but we have been mistaken.' Gifford survived an odd and difficult childhood, before going up to Oxford with help from a subscription; there were, then, reasons for his sympathy towards Clare. E.P., in *Gentleman's Magazine*, January, April 1821 (see No. 34) discusses in an article on native genius, Chatterton, Burns, Gifford, Clare, and Kirke White. See Introduction, p. 7.

We had nearly overlooked, amidst the bulkier works which incessantly solicit our attention, this interesting little volume; which bears indubitable evidence of being composed altogether from the impulses of the writer's mind, as excited by external objects and internal sensations. Here are no tawdry and feeble paraphrases of former poets, no attempts at describing what the author *might* have become acquainted with in his limited reading: the woods, the vales, the brooks—

> the crimson spots
> I' the bottom of a cowslip,—

or the loftier phenomena of the heavens, contemplated through the alternations of hope and despondency, are the principal sources whence the youth, whose adverse circumstances and resignation under them extort our sympathy, drew the faithful and vivid pictures before us.

Examples of minds, highly gifted by nature, struggling with and breaking through the bondage of adversity, are not rare in this country; but privation is not destitution; and the instance before us is, perhaps, one of the most striking, of patient and persevering talent existing and enduring in the most forlorn and seemingly hopeless condition, that literature has at any time exhibited. . . .

[Biographical details]

'The fate of Amy' is one of those stories with which every village, more especially every secluded village, abounds; and the pool, from her catastrophe named the haunted pool, is still shewn, while the mound at the head of it attests the place of her interment. We do not propose to institute a very rigid criticism on these poems, but we must not omit to notice the delicacy with which the circumstances of this inartificial tale are suggested, rather than disclosed; indeed it may be remarked generally that, though associating necessarily with the meanest and most uneducated of society, the poet's homeliest stories have nothing of coarseness and vulgarity in their construction. Some of his ballad stanzas rival the native simplicity of Tickel or Mallett.

> The flowers the sultry summer kills,
> Spring's milder suns restore;
> But innocence, that fickle charm,
> Blooms once, and blooms no more.
>
> The swains who loved no more admire,
> Their hearts no beauty warms;
> And maidens triumph in her fall,
> That envied once her charms.

95

Lost was that sweet simplicity,
  Her eye's bright lustre fled;
And o'er her cheeks, where roses bloom'd,
  A sickly paleness spread.

So fades the flower before its time,
  Where canker-worms assail,
So droops the bud upon the stem,
  Beneath the sickly gale.

For the boisterous sports and amusements which form the usual delight of village youth, Clare had neither strength nor relish; his mother found it necessary to drive him from the chimney corner to exercise and to play, whence he quickly returned, contemplative and silent. His parents—we speak from knowledge—were apprehensive for his mind as well as his health; not knowing how to interpret, or to what cause to refer these habits so opposite to those of other boys of his condition; and when, a few years later, they found him hourly employed in writing,—and writing verses too,—'the gear was not mended' in their estimation. 'When he was fourteen or fifteen,' says Dame Clare, 'he would shew me a piece of paper, printed sometimes on one side, and scrawled all over on the other, and he would say, Mother, this is worth *so* much; and I used to say to him, Aye, boy, it looks as if it warr! —but I thought he was wasting his time.' Clare's history, for a few succeeding years, is composed in two words, spare diet and hard labour, cheered by visions of fancy which promised him happier days: there is an amusing mixture of earnestness and coquetry in his invocation 'to Hope,' the deceitful sustainer, time immemorial, of poets and lovers.

Come, flattering Hope! now woes distress me,
  Thy flattery I desire again;
Again rely on thee to bless me,
  To find thy vainness doubly vain.

Though disappointments vex and fetter,
  And jeering whisper, thou art vain,
Still must I rest on thee for better,
  Still hope—and be deceived again.

The eccentricities of genius, as we gently phrase its most reprehensible excesses, contribute no interest to the biography of Clare. We cannot, however, regret this. Once, it seems, 'visions of glory' crowded on his sight, and, he enlisted at Peterboro' in the local militia. He still speaks of the short period passed in his new character, with evident satisfaction.

After a while, he took the bounty for extended service, and marched to Oundle; where, at the conclusion of a bloodless campaign, his corps was disbanded and he was constrained to return to Helpstone, to the dreary abode of poverty and sickness. His novel occupation does not appear to have excited any martial poetry; we need not therefore 'unsphere the spirit of Plato,' adequately to celebrate the warlike strains of the modern Tyrtæus.

The clouds which had hung so heavily over the youth of Clare, far from dispersing, grew denser and darker as he advanced towards manhood. His father, who had been the constant associate of his labours, became more and more infirm, and he was constrained to toil alone, and far beyond his strength, to obtain a mere subsistence. It was at this cheerless moment, he composed 'What is Life?' in which he has treated a common subject with an earnestness, a solemnity, and an originality deserving of all praise: some of the lines have a terseness of expression and a nervous freedom of versification not unworthy of Drummond, or of Cowley.

[Quotes]

That the author of such verses (and there are abundance of them) should have continued till the age of twenty-five unfriended and unknown, is less calculated perhaps to excite astonishment, than that devotedness to his art, which could sustain him under the pressure of such evils, and that modesty which shrunk from obtruding his writings on the world. Once, indeed, and once only, he appears to have made an effort to emerge from this cheerless obscurity, by submitting his verses to a neighbour, who, it seems, enjoyed a reputation for knowledge 'in such matters.' Even here his ill-fortune awaited him; and his muse met not only with discouragement but rebuke. The circumstance is however valuable, since it serves to illustrate the natural gentleness of the poet's disposition. Instead of venting his spleen against this rustic Aristarch, he only cleaves to his favourite with greater fondness.

> Still must my rudeness pluck the flower
> That's pluck'd, alas! in evil hour;
> And poor, and vain, and sunk beneath
>   Oppression's scorn although I be,
> Still will I bind my simple wreath,
>   Still will I love thee, Poesy. . . .

Looking back upon what we have written, we find we have not accomplished our intention of interspersing with our narrative such extracts as might convey a general character of Clare's poetry,—we have used only such as assorted with the accidents of the poet's life, and the tone of them has necessarily been somewhat gloomy. The volume, however, offers abundant proofs of the author's possessing a cheerful disposition, a mind delighting in the charms of natural scenery, and a heart not to be subdued by the frowns of fortune; though the advantages which he might have derived from these endowments have been checked by the sad realities which hourly reminded him of his unpromising condition. Misery herself cannot, however, keep incessant watch over her victims; and it must have been in a happy interval of abstraction from troublesome feelings that Clare composed 'the Summer Morning,' the result, we believe, of a sabbath-day walk; the lively pictures of rural occupation being introduced from the recollections of yesterday, and the anticipations of the morrow. We have only room for a few stanzas of this little poem, which is gay, and graceful, possessing the true features of descriptive poetry, in which every object is distinct and appropriate.

[Quotes 'The cocks have now the morn foretold' to 'A hailing minstrel in the sky']

It will have appeared, in some measure, from our specimens, that Clare is rather the creature of feeling than of fancy. He looks abroad with the eye of a poet, and with the minuteness of a naturalist, but the intelligence which he gains is always referred to the heart; it is thus that the falling leaves become admonishers and friends, the idlest weed has its resemblance in his own lowly lot, and the opening primrose of spring suggests the promise that his own long winter of neglect and obscurity will yet be succeeded by a summer's sun of happier fortune. The volume, we believe, scarcely contains a poem in which this process is not adopted; nor one in which imagination is excited without some corresponding tone of tenderness, or morality. When the discouraging circumstances under which the bulk of it was composed are considered, it is really astonishing that so few examples should be found of querulousness and impatience, none of envy or despair.

The humble origin of Clare may suggest a comparison with Burns and Bloomfield, which a closer examination will scarcely warrant. Burns was, indeed, as he expresses it, 'born to the plough,' but when in his riper years he held the plough it was rather as a master than as a menial. He was neither destitute nor uneducated. Secure from poverty, supported by his kindred, and surrounded by grand and exciting scenery, his lot was lofty and his advantages numerous compared with those of the youth before us. There is almost as little resemblance in their minds. To the pointed wit, the bitter sarcasm, the acute discrimination of character, and the powerful pathos of Burns, Clare cannot make pretension; but he has much of his tender feeling in his serious poetry, and an animation, a vivacity, and a delicacy in describing rural scenery, which the mountain bard has not often surpassed. In all the circumstances of his life, the author of the 'Farmer's Boy' was far more fortunate than Clare. Though his father was dead, Bloomfield had brothers who were always at his side to cheer and sustain him, while an early residence in the metropolis contributed largely to the extension of his knowledge. To want and poverty he was ever a stranger. Clare never knew a brother; it was his fortune to continue till his twenty-fifth year without education, without hearing the voice of a friend, constrained to follow the most laborious and revolting occupations to obtain the bare necessaries of life. The poetical compositions of the two have few points of contact. The 'Farmer's Boy' is the result of careful observations made on the occupations and habits, with few references to the passions of rural life. Clare writes frequently from the same suggestions; but his subject is always enlivened by picturesque and minute description of the landscape around him, and deepened, as we have said, with a powerful reference to emotions within. The one is descriptive, the other contemplative.

A friend of Clare has expressed a doubt of his capacity for the composition of a long poem:—we have no wish that he should make the experiment; but we have an earnest desire that he should be respectable and happy; that he should support a fair name in poetry, and that his condition in life should be ameliorated. It is with this feeling that we counsel—that we entreat him to continue something of his present occupations;—to attach himself to a few in the sincerity of whose friendship he can confide, and to suffer no temptations of the idle and the dissolute to seduce him from the quiet scenes of his youth—scenes so congenial to his taste,—to the hollow and heartless society of cities; to the haunts of men who would court and flatter him while his name was new, and who, when they had contributed to distract his attention and impair his health, would cast him off unceremoniously to seek some other novelty. Of his again encountering the difficulties and privations he lately experienced, there is no danger. Report speaks of honourable and noble friends already secured: with the aid of these, the cultivation of his own excellent talents, and a meek but firm reliance on that GOOD

POWER by whom these were bestowed, he may, without presumption, anticipate a rich reward in the future for the evils endured in the morning of his life.

26. Unsigned article, *Guardian*

28 May 1820, i

This article, headed 'Clare, the Northamptonshire Poet', is referred to by J. G. Lockhart in his brief discussion of Clare in *Blackwood's Edinburgh Magazine* (No. 27). The view expressed here may seem unduly harsh, but it was the inevitable result of the publicity Clare had received.

The public efforts which have been made to place this man above the common struggles of his place in life, are honourable to English liberality. Scotland has been reproached, and deservedly reproached, with the fate of Burns, to whom a hundredth part of the money that its opulent ostentation is now lavishing on stones and mortar to his memory, would have been affluence. A more feeling plan seems to be adopted, to secure Clare from penury; and the sums set down in the names of his distinguished patrons, are proofs at once of good sense and timely generosity. But in this, as in all matters where publicity is to be won, there are foolish and noisy intruders, who throw the wisest plans into hazard, and, not unfrequently, conclude by making that absurd or impossible, which was in the commencement, liberal, rational, and humane. Some of those dangerous and active persons have already gone the first downward step, by 'out-heroding Herod' in their panegyrics of this poor man as a genius. The natural and most unfortunate result of this folly is, to turn the object of their praise into a fool. The lower orders are singularly apt to place an idle estimate upon their own powers, to be of course easily inflated, and in their inflation to desert the easy path of wisdom. It requires an educated mind to make the true estimate of itself, and feel the deference due to the talents and to the common sense of society. Burns, a true poet, was made insolent, reckless, and worthless by this disastrous extravagance of praise. But Clare, and we say it without any wish, but for his better interests, has not the same claims as the Scotchman, whose career yet shut in, in drunkenness, beggary, and half idiotism. The Northamptonshire peasant is simply a tolerable versifier. He has hitherto exhibited nothing of the spirit, feeling, or original views of genius. We pass over the vulgarisms of his verses; they are incidental to his condition. But all that he has done, is daily done in every school in England by boys of 12 years old. The panegyrics of his bustling friends are ridiculous, and, if he has not a higher understanding than theirs, he will abandon his natural calling, bind himself to a desk and disease, write middling verses year by year, and after having exhausted the liberality of his noble benefactors, and wearied the ear of the public by compliment and complaint, will go as the victims of unfounded applause have always gone, and perish in desertion and decay. We are extremely glad that his poems have had an unusually large sale, and there can be no offence in his writing while to write can be productive. But his true wisdom will be in adhering to the advice of those honourable and intelligent patrons who have desired him to continue his old avocations; and, while they hold out a security against the actual distress of a peasant's life, have warned him against abandoning, in bodily industry, the best preservative of his health, humility and happiness. The following sonnet by Mr. Hare Townsend, of Cambridge, is rather at variance with some of our opinions, but it is lively and ingenious—

[Quotes 'Sonnet', No. 10c]

27. J. G. Lockhart on Clare, *Blackwood's Edinburgh Magazine*

June 1820, vii, 322

From 'Extracts from Mr. Wastle's Diary', no. ii.

This is by J. C. Lockhart; Mrs Emmerson hinted at the possibility of his authorship in a letter to Clare (10 July 1820), in which she referred to the '*slight, but not liberal* mention' of him, and scornfully remarked, 'If this is all he could say for you . . . why better he had said nothing about you! Your *Patrons* are treated most ungraciously, for their "fuss", & "great zeal" for you:—so much for the author of the "Lady of the Lake" and your friend "Peter"!!!' (Eg. 2245, fol. 167ᵛ). Lockhart (1794–1854) was Scott's son-in-law, and a frequent contributor to *Blackwood's*. He edited the *Quarterly Review* from 1826 to 1853. For the article in the *Guardian*, see No. 26. James Hogg (1770–1835), 'The Ettrick Shepherd', was another instance of talent overcoming adversity. He formed a close friendship with the Scots poet Allan Cunningham (1784–1842), author of the drama *Sir Marmaduke Maxwell*, 1820, which appealed to Clare.

When one thinks of Hogg, and of the silent but sure progress of his fame—or of Allan Cunningham, and of the hold he has taken of the heart of Scotland almost without being aware of it himself—one cannot help feeling some qualms concerning the late enormous puffing of the Northamptonshire peasant, John Clare. I have never seen Clare's book, but from all the extracts I have seen, and from all the private accounts I have heard, there can be no doubt Clare is a man of talents and a man of virtue; but as to poetical genius, in the higher and the only proper sense of that word, I fear it would be very difficult to shew that he deserves half the fuss that has been made. Smoothness of versification and simplicity of thought seem to be his chief merits; but alas! in these days these are not enough to command or to justify such a sounding of the trumpet. The Guardian takes by far the best view of this subject—Clare has exhibited powers that not only justify but demand attention and kindness—but his generous and enlightened patrons ought to pause ere they advise him to become anything else than a peasant—for a respectable peasant is a much more comfortable man, and always will be so, than a mediocre poet. Let them pause and think of the fate of the far more highly-gifted Burns, and beware alike of the foolish zeal and the sinful neglect of *his* countrymen.

28. From an unsigned review, *British Critic*

June 1820, n.s. xiii, 662–7

The *British Critic* took a rather cool view of Clare (see No. 35b). There is considerable scorn in the italics inserted into the quotation from Taylor's Introduction.

[Begins with biographical details]

It is not likely, after this account, that our strictures should be very formidable. We most cordially and sincerely hope that Clare will reap a substantial advantage by the publication of this collection, and that he will be placed at once beyond the reach of poverty. The extracts which we shall select from his volume will themselves speak sufficiently as to the poetical rank to which he may be entitled; and his peculiar situation effectually disarms our criticism. The tendency of his book throughout is moral, and if a single piece, the *grossièreté*[1] of which cannot fail to offend every reader, has been suffered to creep in, it must be set down to a cause which is connected with that which in reality forms the principal merit of the poems before us—the circumstances of the writer.

1 'coarseness'.

[Extracts from 'Helpstone', 'What is Life?', 'The Village Funeral']

The following was written before Clare was seventeen; it has more condensation and point than he generally manifests, and might not disgrace a pen of established reputation.

[Quotes 'The Universal Epitaph']

The lines below partake of the same manner, and it is that in which we think him most fortunate.

[Quotes 'On an Infant's Grave']

One more extract must suffice, and we give it with pleasure, for its unaffected piety.

[Quotes 'To Religion']

The humorous, perhaps, is the rock upon which Clare most frequently splits; it is too delicate for his touch, and when he attempts it, he becomes downright boisterous. If he wishes to write more, we would whisper to him one other word of advice, and upon his observance or disregard of it, we are convinced that all his rhyming hopes are suspended. Let him avoid any emulation of Burns, as he would a bottomless pit-fall: Burns is of quite another metal, and it is not wise to remind us of him. Such defects as are the necessary result of situation, we willingly forgive, even without the adumbration of his benevolent Editor; who states in excuse of false grammar, that 'another peculiarity in Clare's writing, which may occasion some misunderstanding to those who are *critically nice in the construction of a sentence*, is the *indifference with which he regards words as governing each other.*'

29. From an unsigned review, *Antijacobin Review*

June 1820, lviii, 348–53

This little volume is the production of a second Burns; a poet in humble life, whose genius has burst through the fetters with which his situation had surrounded it; and astonished the neighbouring villages with the brilliancy of his song. Amidst all the privations attendant on the life of the labouring peasant, this genuine child of poesy has written a volume, many articles in which would reflect no disgrace upon a far nobler name, and we are glad, that a public-spirited individual has snatched them from obscurity; we rejoice, that they are not doomed

> To blow unseen,
> And waste their sweetness on the desert air. . . .

[Biographical details]

The volume thus compiled, consists of a number of miscellaneous poems, descriptive and pathetic; tales, songs, ballads, and sonnets. They display considerable poetic talent and a genius peculiarly his own; delighting to celebrate nature in her homeliest dress, and painting, with the force of truth, the wants and miseries of poverty's hapless children. Yet no envious spirit, no carping discontent, is to be traced in Clare's Poems. Resignation to his lot appears to be a prominent feature in his character, combined with that love of his native village, which frequently bears such potent sway in the mind of the unlettered rustic. The conclusion of the first Poem in the collection, called 'Helpstone,' displays, in no unfavourable point of view, both the poetical talent, and the disposition of the writer. For, it may be fairly presumed that, writing with no view to fame, either present or posthumous, he did not 'affect a virtue, if he had it not;' but portrayed the genuine effusions of his heart.

[Quotes 'Helpstone': 'Oh happy Eden . . .' to the end]

We did not commence this article with a view to write an elaborate critique upon poems written under the circumstances in which Clare wrote his. Though, were we inclined to do so, we are of opinion, we could shew, that the beauties far outnumber the defects. The latter are chiefly those resulting from a want of education; which has led him to violate, in a few instances, the rules of construction; and to use words, perhaps, not the very best that could have been selected, in order to render his meaning intelligible. The former are, however, peculiarly his own; and the perusal of his work cannot fail to afford much pleasure to every admirer of honest simplicity, and natural genius. If they do not possess the polish of Bloomfield, or the wild energy of Burns, they are free from those impurities (and even impieties) which disgrace the latter; and equal the former in unaffected piety; and in giving a true picture of rustic life, and those scenes with which the author was best acquainted. We will give, as further specimens of his talent, the two sonnets we have before alluded to.

[Quotes 'The Setting Sun'; 'The River Gwash']

Our limits will not allow us to give any further extracts; but we hope we have said enough to excite the curiosity, at least, of our readers; and to induce them to purchase the book, in order to fully gratify that feeling. We assure them they will not deem their money thrown away.

30. Robert Bloomfield on the pleasure afforded him by Clare's poems

1820

Robert Bloomfield to Clare, 25 July 1820, Eg. 2245, fol. 186.

Robert Bloomfield (1766–1823) was the Suffolk poet, author of *The Farmer's Boy*, 1800, whom Clare greatly admired, to the extent of planning a biography of him.

I am however very glad to have lived to see your poems: they have given me and my family an uncommon pleasure, and, they will have the same effect on all kindred minds and that's enough; for, as for writing rhimes for Clods and sticks and expecting them to read them, I never found any fun in that in all my life, and I have past your age 26 years. I am delighted with your 'Address to the Lark', 'Summer Morning', and 'Evening' &c &c. In fact I had better not turn critic in my first letter, but say the truth, that nothing upon the great theatre of what is called the world (our English world) can give me half the pleasure I feel at seeing a man start up from the humble walks of life and show himself to be what I think you are,—What that is, ask a higher power,—for though learning is not to be contemn'd it did not give you this.

31. An admirer comments on Clare's poetry

1820

R. V. Hankinson to Clare, 29 July 1820, Eg. 2245, foll. 192ᵛ–3.

Hankinson, of whom nothing is known, writes from a 'Revd. Mr. Handyman's', North Luffenham; his home address is near Lynn, Norfolk.

The perusal of your poetry has afforded me great pleasure: it is stampt with the true seal of Genius. Imagination delights to embody these scenes which you have so faithfully described. Yours is not that Panoramic view of Nature, which (imposing while viewed at a distance) only gives an idea of the general effect of the landscape: but you have touched your miniature with the finest pencil; every leaf and every flower is there accurately delineated; & the minutiae of natures treasures revealed. I much admire your sonnet on 'The Setting Sun', both for the elegance of the poetry, and the moral that is deduced for [sic] it, it shews that while gazing on the inexhaustible & varied beauties of Nature, the mind is rapt aloft to Nature's God—Poetry, I believe, is generally found to be the child of misfortune, since it is then that fancy is most vivid and feeling most acute. . . .

32. Eliza Emmerson on reactions in Bristol

1820

Eliza Emmerson to Clare, 25 November 1820, Eg. 2245, fol. 241.

The Bristol people, are very difficult to please in matters of Literature, particularly poetry.—They are lovers of the earlier poets in the time of 'Elizabeth'—some few I met with who could only admire 'Burns'— and it was only with warm argument, and by daring *comparison*, that, they would believe, that you had not imitated 'Burns' too closely to be called an original poet yourself—I however, aided by the more powerful arguments of Mr. Emmerson, who was equally warm in *my poets* cause—brought our friends to allow you many claims as a poet, both for originality and beauty—and above all for simplicity, and tenderness of feeling.—They *all lamented* that yᵣ publishers, introduced in your Volume—'Mary', 'Dollys Mistake' 'Lubin' and 'the Country Girl'— considering as *spots*, to what could otherwise *be pure*.

33. Edward Drury on the poems people like

[1820]

Drury to Clare, no date, Eg. 2250, fol. 135.

Your later pieces I do not like so well as the first, and in my opinion, those trifles recommended by Mr. Mossop are not so natural to you, or worthy your attempts, as moral and rural subjects.

As a proof of what I say, the Primrose, Setting Sun, Autumn, Gipsey's Evening Blaze—are the only pieces that many friends I have shewn them too [sic] (for the sake of Counsel) think above the common regiment of poets.

34. Clare and 'Native Genius'

1821

From two articles, signed 'E.P.', of Melksham (unidentified), entitled, 'Remarks on the spontaneous display of Native Genius', *Gentleman's Magazine*, January, April 1821, xci, 32–5; 308–12. See Introduction, p. 6.

I

It was finely said by Akenside,—

> from Heaven descends
> The flame of *Genius* to the human breast;

and it has been generally acknowledged that the aspirations of true Genius, if they have been regulated by, have not been dependant upon the advantages of Education, or the light of Learning.

It has, on the contrary, been thought, that although Education, including all the means of intellectual culture, has afforded facilities in calling forth and directing the fine suggestions of Genius,—yet her native and indigenous creations of fancy, the teeming images of a mind finely oppressed by a generous enthusiasm, will burst forth in spite of the rustic garb and the inauspicious circumstances which, perchance, environ and obscure it; although capricious fortune has thrown her numerous obstacles,—of poverty, want of education, and want of patronage around it.

The exquisite paintings of a mind, tuned by nature to the mental enjoyment of vivid impressions of imagery, or of fine and illimitable prospects of imaginary existence;—the bursts of feeling and of sentiment which gains utterance,—not perhaps in the chastised and measured flow of eloquence, which distinguishes the man of extensive intellectual cultivation, and refined habits of thought,—which attends the periods of the student long inured to polished numbers and academical honours, —but rather in the simple, but plaintive language and thoughts which is understood in every age and every nation, which commands respect

III

and admiration among every class of society whose 'mind's eye' is capable of opening to pleasure beyond those of sense,—of feeling a sympathy with passion and sentiment abstracted from mercenary views and sordid joys,—these artless but fervid emanations of a mind alive to 'gentlest beauty' must be ever read with peculiar interest and avidity, by all descriptions of mankind, who can appreciate the generous flow of a heart cast in a fine mould, and fired by emotions far above those of his own level and occupation.

Whether it is that the child of Nature, in her rude unlettered character, has peculiar appeals of his own, and that his beauties, from their intrinsic pleadings, find their way at once to the hearts of all;—or from the benevolent wish to foster and animate to still greater things the humble but aspiring swain, in whom dawns the fire of Genius,—it is certain, that all ranks feel a sudden impulse within them (although that impulse may possibly never realize any active or permanent display of patronage), to eulogize, and render honours and assistance to him whose productions gild, with a new radiance, the intellectual horizon.

The appearance of these literary phenomena or anomalies in the moral and mental world may likewise give birth to speculations to their existence and formation.

The philosophic investigator on the subject of mind,—its laws, its component principles and its stimulative mediums, might, perhaps, find scope for theories variously connected with the openings of the human faculties.

Whether from his birth, the peasant who rises to literary honours and immunities, possessed a secret power and propensity, which led him to poetry and to song; or whether certain associations in early childhood or infancy opened, at once, his perceptions and his taste to a range of thinking vastly superior to the standard of his ordinary compeers, has been a question, which, in the opinions of many, is still undecided.

Whatever be assumed as the operative cause, or whether there be any cause which may be termed operative or secondary, (thus referring this disparity to the immediate decree of the Deity,) the fact has repeatedly of late been sufficiently evident to the world,—of Genius, in the more refined studies of the human mind, rising, as it were, from the clods and the dunghill, and attaining, from its own native stores of imagery and force of sentiment, eminence, and justly-merited fame among the productions of those higher lucrubators, who, from the appointment of nature, or certain favourable circumstances connected with their moral being, retain, in general, an exclusive dominion in the empire of mind.

It is certain that the powers of mind or of understanding are as un-equal among subordinate and labouring classes, as among those where mind is cultivated, and endowments carefully expanded.

Observe two peasants of equal birth and fortune, perhaps the one appears stupid and dull as the clods which his industry attempts to fertilize and animate, and his sordid soul revolves in a narrow circle of gross enjoyments, whilst the other enjoys his faculties in far brighter vigour,—thinks with greater precision and correctness, and looks upon men and things with more acute and aspiring views.—But he may be equally far from seeing nature, and nature's scenery, through the delightful medium of Poetry; or of measuring the fitness of things, material and immaterial, through the subtle and profound theory of metaphysics.—His faculties, so far as the finer operations, necessary to render him a proficient in these pursuits, were concerned, remained equally barren and deaf to every outward solicitation.

Many instances have occurred in which peasants have evinced an acuteness and sagacity in mechanical invention,—have made discoveries far beyond any thing which their rank and level would warrant an expectation of, but still the association of mind here argued, are of a subordinate description to the mental standard of thought which shall view nature and mankind as the common materials by which its Genius should rise to the attainment of new truths, or by which it should create fresh systems of intellectual delight.

This vast disparity, however, in the thinking conceptions of indivi-duals of the same rank and occupation, must be assumed to militate very powerfully against the hypothesis of Helvetius, and others, who have taught that it is education alone, combined with certain favourable circumstances and moral temperaments, which constitutes the sole difference between the understandings and capacities of men.

The passions, which the French philosopher speaks of, as the con-stant excitements to Genius, can hardly be reconciled with a sober examination of facts, as clowns may be often observed, whose animal passions and temperaments are ardent, and easily excited, whose mind and imagination seem, yet, wholly dead to the finer intellectual passions, incapable of exercising abstractions, and of creating, in idea, an associ-ated thought, or a poetical image,—while, on the other hand, those who have drawn the eyes of their contemporaries from their extraordinary conceptions and endowments of mind, have often been of a retiring disposition, and have been by no means distinguished by the warmth or impetuosity of their animal passions.

The capabilities, in this last case, seem to depend, not upon the passions or the moral temperament, although these are often useful in aiding the flow of mind, and although certain circumstances, often, considerably facilitate their expansion,—but, rather upon a decided, and peculiar pre-disposition implanted originally by the Author of Nature, for these pursuits, and these associations. Indeed it may be thought that sufficient grounds exist for concluding that, although the intellectual perceptions are often elicited and determined by extrinsic means, a settled bias for this or that pursuit is always originally latent in the human mind previous to its actual development.

The Literature of our Island may be said to have, of late years, exemplified the truth of reflection of this nature, as it may also be said to have been fruitful in generating Poetical talents, of no inferior order, emerging from plebeian rank and station, and the actual progress which they achieved in polite literature and sciences, when this genial principle of mental emancipation has struggled into birth, surrounded by poverty, and by every other deteriorating circumstance in the shape of coarse and sordid minds in those to whom they would naturally look for example, for patronage, and support.

Generous and emulative spirits,—emulative of that high and heaven-born genius which disdains to be fettered by the dull range of thoughts, which circumscribes the souls of those among whom they were bred, —they have, at length, risen to a standard of excellence which has extorted the suffrage of honourable eulogium, even from the fastidiousness of criticism.

This may, perhaps, be said with justice of Chatterton, of Burns, of Bloomfield, of Drew, of Gifford, of Clare, and of Kirke White. . . .

Of the genius of Clare and Kirke White we may, without incurring the charge of tediousness, go a little into detail.

The Poems of Clare, a Northamptonshire peasant of the lowest order, which have recently been given to the world, may be thought well calculated to generate the reflections in which we just now indulged. It is not too much to say that the genius of their author, for poetic imagery of a genuine class and character, stands high among his contemporaries, while his means of intellectual culture were unprecedentedly low;—such indeed as, without very extraordinary energy of mind and imagination, aided by every parsimony of time and attention, he could not have succeeded in giving his embryo conceptions intelligible utterance to the world.

II

It has been observed of Thomson, that in his admirable descriptions—where he appears equally original and obvious,—that, whilst he selected those appearances alone most characteristic in the things which he describes, he imparts the air of novelty to objects, which, when pointed out by the exquisite colouring of his pencil, appear sufficiently known and familiar.

It may be said of CLARE, and without the imputation of bestowing unmerited praise, that, while from the constant opportunities, which his manner of life afforded him, in common with all other peasants, of observing Nature under all her forms, and with all her accompaniments, he was capacitated to delineate her minutest beauties,—these opportunities were not neglected, and he has happily illustrated her more trivial phenomena.

We are tempted to rank among the number of Poetical images, things which, until touched by his creative and fertilizing pencil, had appeared devoid of any thing which could impart dignity or grace to a literary description.—His invocations and descriptive tales usually bear the genuine stamp of a heart kindled to action and sentiment by the pure emotions of her own dictates, unschooled by the polish of art, but giving utterance to those ideas which Nature, with all her sublime and interesting garniture, is capable of inspiring.

Warm with the grateful acknowledgments of the swain looking around on all about him with generous enthusiasm, responsive to the call of piety,—and minutely descriptive, from the habitual views which his occupation enabled him to take at once of all the phenomena which characterize the revolution of the seasons, and the incidents which diversify the life and employments of a rustic,—these compositions must always obtain that dominion over the heart and sensibilities, which Poetry of far higher classical pretensions often fails in exciting. They may be said to call forth that feeling of mental delight, generated we know not why, but that they seem to have a secret affinity with certain sympathies and affections which dwell within us.

Clare, as his Editor has observed, had numerous difficulties to struggle with, unknown to almost all others, whose minds have opened to the power and perceptions of Genius.

Nursed in the lap of poverty of the most chilling description, he was long unable to acquire even the commonest rudiments of education,—until, by excessive parsimony, coupled with unwearied assiduity, he attained some knowledge of reading and writing, and, hence, was proportionately facilitated in giving utterance to the pictures which 'imagination bodied forth.'—Hence arises his occasional unpleasing collocations of words,—which indeed he, doubtless, it may be presumed, found most intelligibly expressive of his ideas, but, from the scanty limits of his vocabulary, he was unable, in his phraseology, to make those selections of copiousness which would have imparted a more modulated flow of harmony to his periods.

The minor deficiencies of this kind, however, do not materially deteriorate the Poetry of Clare,—they even add to its general effect, as the heart, while it feels the power of vigour, and artless beauties stealing over its susceptibilities, so far from regretting the absence of a more elaborate diction, is tempted to rank that writer in a higher class who can accomplish the ends of Poetry without using all those weapons which skilful practitioners often employ with success.

Among the many specimens of beauty, of imagery, and pathos, and tenderness of sentiment, which Clare has given us in the small volume which has called forth the present animadversions, several may be quoted as pre-eminently indicative of ardour of feeling and elevation of thinking, certainly vastly above the general standard of his own rank and occupation.

In description and vigour of imagination, 'Summer Evening,' 'Summer Morning,' an 'Address to Plenty in Winter,' 'Harvest Morning,' 'Evening,' 'Noon,' may be adduced as Poems which, for the felicity and propriety of the images employed, possess claims upon the reader of taste and sensibility which will not be neglected, while it may be said with equal justice, that 'Helpstone,' an 'Address to a Lark singing in Winter,' 'Elegy to the Ruins of Pickworth, Rutlandshire,' and 'The Dawnings of Genius,' may, for the fine tone of their sentiment, the dignity, and, withal, the warmth, tenderness, and simplicity of their style, vie with the admired productions of many, who have long ranked deservedly high in the annals of Poetical fame.

In the 'Ruins of Pickworth,' the measured and solemn flow of numbers happily illustrate the melancholy tinge of sentiment and of feeling which seems to animate the author, and swells his soul to something like sublimity. Although to the reader, impressed with classic veneration for names hallowed by the high suffrage of criticism, it may appear bold to mention him in connection with Gray, justice will not refuse to acknowledge that there is, in the general flow of sentiment and style which pervades this Elegy, much that forcibly reminds us of the sublime and impassioned moral painting which characterizes the 'Church-yard.' . . .

Many pictures of genuine beauty strike the reader in the 'Sonnets,' of which it must be said generally, that they proclaim a high degree of delicacy of thinking in their author, and exhibit much warmth of colouring, expressed with simplicity and purity of language. It may not be thought exaggerated commendation, to say, that they sometimes unite dignity with force of feeling and of passion, and discriminative thought with quick sensibility.—Of these, 'The Setting Sun,' 'The Moon,' 'The Gipsey's Evening Blaze,' 'To Hope,' 'Evening,' 'To the Glow Worm,' 'To Religion,' and 'Expectation,' may be esteemed the best. Indeed those on the subjects of 'Hope' and to 'Expectation,' when read under a full impression of the circumstances of the author's life and occupations, must certainly be pronounced extraordinary effusions, and, argue powers of thought and combination of a standard with those who have been long admired for their genius, exhibited under far more auspicious circumstances, rather than the artless and plaintive strains of a peasant. . . .

35. Some brief comments on Clare

1821

(a) From a review of *Amarynthus, the Nympholept: A Pastoral Drama* (an anonymous poem, modelled on Fletcher, by Horace Smith (1779–1849), the co-author, with his brother James, of the celebrated *Rejected Addresses*, 1812), *Monthly Review*, April 1821, xciv, 386:

Pastoral poetry has long been on the decline in England. We have indeed in our own times had Bloomfield, and more lately Clare, both of whom are exclusively pastoral poets, but the classical pastoral had almost become extinct among us.

(b) From a review of Robert Millhouse, *Vicissitude: a Poem, in four Books*, *British Critic*, June 1821, n.s. xv, 660–1:

If a volume of poems be not good in themselves, we certainly do not see in what respect their merit, to the public, is enhanced, by having been produced under unfavourable circumstances; and, as a general principle, we feel disposed rather to set our faces against all claims to the patronage of the public, that are founded merely upon this plea. If prizes are to be held out to the labouring classes for the production of such poetry as is here before us, or even for such as Clare's, about which so much nonsense was talked, we will venture to predict that we shall soon have competitors in abundance: but whether either the interests of poetry, or of the lower orders themselves are likely to be benefited by this misplaced sort of indulgence, is a question about which some variety of opinion will, we should hope, be found to exist. Nothing is more easy than for any person, of moderate talents, be his situation in life what it may, who can read and write, and is in possession of Thomson's Seasons and Beattie's Minstrel, and one or two other poems of that class, to cultivate a talent for making verses;—to learn to cut out watch-papers with his toes would be far more difficult;—but it is surely highly inexpedient, more especially in the present times, when the whole of our population are, in some degree, educated, that literature should be made a walk into which the working classes should be invited to enter, by means of bounties. Let it be a walk from which none are excluded, if we please; and if another Burns should arise, let him stand, as that unfortunate person stood, upon the privilege of his genius; but it should be well understood that no man is to be allowed to plead *in formâ pauperis*,[1] for reward. Such a plea can only gain a hearing so long as it is rare; but every new precedent will render it less rare; and in the meanwhile the number of disappointed candidates will increase; and without perhaps one single good line of poetry being produced, we shall have geniuses starting up in every village, to the great detriment, we will venture to say, both of the happiness and morality, not only of these unhappy persons themselves, but of the little communities over which they will probably preside.

(c) From a review of C. H. Townsend, *Poems* (see No. 10c), *Eclectic Review*, July 1821, n.s. xvi, 50:

Of the luxuriant accumulation of poetry to which the present age has given birth, it is but a small proportion that can have room made for it. . . . [Most will have to be discarded, but in these discarded

[1] 'as a poor man'.

volumes] there will remain the materials of a most elegant anthology. The works of Anacreon Moore, R. W. Spenser, Smyth, Leigh Hunt, Lloyd, Neale, Jane Taylor, Barton, Keats, Barry Cornwall, Wilson, Clare, and some other minor writers, whose entire works have no claim to preservation, would furnish a selection equal to almost anything in the language.

THE PERIOD PRIOR TO PUBLICATION OF *THE VILLAGE MINSTREL*: INCIDENTAL COMMENTS

March 1820—August 1821

36. Some opinions on 'Solitude'

1820

(a) Taylor to Clare, 16 March 1820, Eg. 2245, fol. 62:

I received the Poem safe, and like it very much, but from an apprehension that it contains rather too much minute Description I feel desirous of cutting out a Couplet here & there.—The Difficulty is the greater in parting with them, as they are generally excellent in their way. . . . [Talks of Keats] When I read Solitude to him he observed that the Description too much prevailed over the Sentiment.—But never mind that—it is a good fault. . . .

(b) Clare to Taylor, 19 March 1820, *LJC*, p. 37:

You Talk of cutting me about in 'Solitude' I can only say have mercy I have provd your judgement & patiently submit—my lodge house I think will be above your thumbs & Keats' too it as undergone the Critiscism of my father & mother & several rustic Neighbours of the Town and all aprove it you will agree they beat your polite Critics in that low nature which you never prove but by reading & which them & I have daily witnessed in its most subtle branches. . . .

(c) Eliza Emmerson to Taylor, 25 April 1820, NMS. 44. 'The Lodge House' was one of Clare's many narrative poems that were not published.

I admire the 'Solitude' excessively—but the 'Lodge House' is not to my taste: I could almost wish it may never be published: it is laboured and incoherent: has very little to interest, and much less to delight. These are not the subjects wherein Clare excels.

Of the 'Solitude', I would presume to say very much in its praise— all the early part of the Poem is beautifully descriptive of rural scenery: the *personification* of Solitude is very original, and pathetically lovely— as, are all her favourite haunts,—Indeed, there is throughout this Poem, a sweetness, simplicity and pathos, which subdue the heart, and bid me say—that, I find a charm in the uncultivated language of Clare, which I look in vain for among our more learned Poets. There is a loveliness, and tenderness of feeling, joind with a comprehensiveness of thought, and originality of expression, with which I am delighted: he leads me on thro' every scene of nature with him; I am the companion of his wanderings, and identify every object of his contemplation! This, I own, is the poetry in which I can delight, it springs genuine from the Soul! Unfetter'd by the studied rules of rigid correctness, it requires no depth of learning to discover its beauties; for having pure unsophisti- cated Nature for its model—it enchains the hearts of those who are admirers of its sweet original!

(d) Eliza Emmerson to Clare, 8 May 1820, Eg. 2245, fol. 112ᵛ:

['Solitude' is] full of poetic loveliness of description. . . . I would have you soar to the loftier regions of poesy—for you have abundant means of imaginative power, observation, and reflection: facility of language only is wanting, to enable you, to do all, that our sweetest, & most moral poets, have, or can do—and this will imperceptibly be gained by reading those esteem'd Authors, which you are in possession of—and the benefit of your corresponding with a few sensible persons, will be of the greatest advantage to you.

(e) Taylor to Clare, 14 August 1820, Eg. 2245, fol. 202ᵛ:

It is a pity that 'Solitude' shoᵈ so much resemble in its plan & structure the 'Contemplation' of H. K. White——As you seem to like those Subjects best which have been treated by others I would recommend in future that you should take them from some prose writer, where these Resemblances would be thought no Disadvantage to your Poem.

(f) Taylor to Clare, 27 September 1820, Eg. 2245, foll. 225–6:

I think he [Keats] wishes to say to you that your Images from Nature are too much introduced without being called for by a particular sentiment. . . . his Remark is only applicable now & then when he feels as if the Description overlaid & stifled that which ought to be the prevailing Idea.

37. John Taylor on narrative poetry

1820

Taylor to Clare, 18 April 1820, Eg. 2245, foll. 90^v–1.

You must not mind my Criticisms, Clare, but *write away*—only if you tell a Story again, like the Lodge House, don't let the Circumstances occupy so much of your Attention to the Exclusion of that which is more truly poetical.—I have not Time today to tell you exactly what I mean—But I can conceive that as a Story this of Lodge House may appear to all your Hearers capitally told, and yet that it has not the Superiority about it which makes Good Poetry—Poets do not tell Stories like other people; they draw together beautiful & uncommon but very happy Illustrations, and adorn their subject, making as much Difference as there is between a common Etching and a full painted Picture.

38. Edward Drury with some good advice

1820

Drury to Clare, 9 May 1820, Eg. 2245, foll. 115–16.

I assure you that I consider that they [Clare's poems] possess undeniable merit of no common stamp; yet some there are not fitted for our purpose because of absolute indelicacy in the images, and further because there is a roughness of measure in some unsuitable to the tender feeling the words express: this destroys the effect of all your fine thoughts, and must greatly cramp your mind.

If you would prepare yourself by reading a few of Burns' & Allan Ramsey's best pieces, & wait for the moment of inspiration, I dare pledge myself for your success. One great thing is the identifying yourself with the subject. . . . [Mentions 'The Meeting'] It is as fine and as complete as can be written. The words are astonishingly simple and suitable, and the rhythm is accordant. You always excel when you write as you would have spoken and acted in the reality. . . .

Do not force your mind to produce anything it is disinclined to; and disregard all kinds of recommendation to any particular subject. Let your mind ever keep virtue, & honour in esteem, as the only truly inestimable things, and you will never want for subjects. I would not urge this so strongly were I not conscious that you have a talent within you of which you are scarcely aware as yet, & which may be turned to profitable account.

Sonnets are beautiful, but everybody can write a Sonnet, if they bestow labour and time, and have any idea of poetry—they may even produce sonnets of tolerable merit, but none but a real poet can produce a song like the Meeting.

39. John Taylor on the next volume

1820

Taylor to Clare, 16 May 1820, Eg. 2245, fol. 124.

. . . my surprise, Clare, with all my Experience of your Abilities, is very considerable at some of the Pieces in the Collection which E.D. has sent me. I have merely dipt into them, & read one here and there, but judging from what I have seen I think it pretty certain that the next Volume will contain much better things than the one now printed.

40. Edward Drury on the songs

1820

Drury to Clare, 17 May 1820, Eg. 2245, fol. 128ᵛ.

Drury had been copying out a batch of Clare's recent songs.

As to my opinion of them, I can say, that some will stand the test of the nicest ear & the nicest eye—and those which from their individuality of feeling will not do for 'Songs' will rank as no mean station as rural Love Songs.

41. John Clare and C. H. Townsend on plagiarism

1820

(a) Clare to Townsend, May 1820, *LJC*, p. 48. Townsend (see No. 10c) had sent Clare a copy of Beattie's *Minstrel*.

'The Minstrel' is a sweet poem & far as I have read a many thoughts occur which are in my 'Peasant Boy' I doubt the world will think them plagarisms, therefore I must alter or cut them out altogether, but nature is the same here at Helpstone as it is elsewhere.

(b) Townsend to Clare, 5 September 1820, Eg. 2245, fol. 212ᵛ:

It does not surprise me, that there should be coincidences between your own poetry, & Beattie's, since you both copied from Nature, but sure I am, that there exists sufficient diversity in your pictures to prevent the alarm you feel of being charged with plagiarism. Do not alter one line from this fear. There will always be a freshness in your nature-painting strains, which will distinguish them from copies. Every original mind (and such is yours) will ever treat even a hacknied subject in an original manner.

42. John Clare on the judgments of others

1820, 1821

(a) Clare to Taylor, May 1820, *LJC*, p. 46:

I have been trying songs & want your judgment only either to stop me or to set me off at full gallop which your disaproval or applause has as much power to effect as if spoken by a magician the rod of criticism in your hand has as much power over your poor sinful ryhmer as the rod of Aaron in the Land of Egypt.

(b) Clare to Taylor, 10 June 1820, *LJC*, p. 51:

I think your taste & mine had I education would be as like 'as pin to pin' your selection of my poems gave me plenty of consciet of your abilities I asure ye— & if I have any fault it bears to the flattering side more for that.

(c) Clare to Hessey, 4 July 1820, *LJC*, p. 56. Clare had been reading Keats, in particular *Lamia, Isabella, and other Poems*.

. . . he is a child of nature warm and wild Campbell & Rogers must be fine very fine Because they are the critics own children nursd in the critics garden & prund by the fine polishing knives of the critics— they must be good no soul dare say otherwise—it woud be out of the fashion—don't ye think a critic like a gardener uses his pruning knife very often to keep it in action & find as he calls it a job—an old proverb is among us 'a gardener woud cut his fathers head off were he a tree' so woud the other if his father was a book—to keep his hand in. . . .

(d) Clare to Taylor, 2 January 1821, *LJC*, p. 84. 'Ways in a Village' was the work that became *The Village Minstrel*.

I have somthing I think that will struggle and hobble out of me better than I have yet done only tell me my faults in long poems of the Ways in a village you last got & I shall know how to escape shipwreck for the future with your Compass I cannot feel satisfied without leading strings yet tho I think I want them less then before.

(e) Clare to Taylor, 6 or 7 March 1821, *LJC*, p. 103. There had been discussion over what should be included in *The Village Minstrel*.

. . . your taste is preferable to any I have witnessd & on that I rely—mines not worth twopence— & a critics is too severe for me—a man of feeling that looks on faults with indulgence & never willfuly passes by a blossom he may chance to find on his journey is a man to my mind & such a one (no flattery mind from me) I reckon John Taylor.

(f) Clare to Taylor, 10 July 1821, *LJC*, pp. 120–1. Clare had seen the proofs of *The Village Minstrel*.

You rogue you, the pruning hook has been over me agen I see in the Vols but vain as I am of my abilities I must own your lopping off have bravely amended them the 'Rural Evening' & 'Cress Gatherer' in particular are now as compleat as anything in the Vols. but the 'Pastoral' & 'death of Dobbin' are left out to save the public 6d expense—but why do I rant & rattle on at this rate—friend I believe you are a caterer of profound wisdom in these matters you know what sort of a dish will suit the publics appetite better then I at all events you'll say 'I ought to do'.

43. More advice from Eliza Emmerson

1820

(a) Eliza Emmerson to Clare, 10 July 1820, Eg. 2245, fol. 168. Similar advice was given by Taylor on 12 February 1820, 'I think you will find old Poetry more powerful than the new in stimulating you to fresh Performances—there was so much more truth in the old Poets—they looked and thought for themselves;—but I would not give you any advice on what you should do—you will feel your own way best' (Eg. 2245, fol. 38). Clare was soon writing pastiches of the older poets, which he sent to newspapers as rediscovered poems by Marvell, Sir

John Wotton, and so on. There was even talk of a collection being made of such pieces, for publication. In this extract, Mrs Emmerson refers him to Percy's *Reliques*:

. . . all ancient poetry must have a charm for you; but particularly that of the Elizabethan time, as having much of your own feeling and simplicity, in it.

(b) Eliza Emmerson to Clare, 7 August 1820, Eg. 2245, fol. 197:

I have not yet expressed my admiration of your 'address to the rural muse'—I think it equal in *poetic beauty* to anything you have *ever written*, with a tenderness of feeling throughout, which no other Poet of the present day could express!

(c) Eliza Emmerson to Clare, 23 August 1820, Eg. 2245, fol. 205. Clare had been disclosing his plans for 'Ways in a Village' (see No. 42d).

Your Subjects will afford you good scope for simple, and sweet description, also matter, and opportunity for much reflection—'tis in *these* you *excel*; therefore I entreat you, not to bestow your attention on any thing that can partake of the harmonious, or familiar, in the *vulgar sense*, for they would only serve as *spots* to darken your sun!

(d) Eliza Emmerson to Clare, 4 September 1820, Eg. 2245, fol. 211. For the 'Peasant Boy', see No. 48; for 'Solitude', see No. 36.

Your 'Peasant Boy' is *uniformly* sweet and simple:—your 'Solitude' is very lovely and poetical: your 'Thunder Storm' truly natural, and sublime! but your *Sonnets*—ah, there my dear friend—*you stand alone*, you are yourself—all simplicity—all feeling all soul—I could almost add —you are *perfection* for when—a *lonely feeling* is to be expressed, arising from a simple object in Nature—I have never before met the poet, who spoke so truly, and so tenderly as yourself: *this* is no 'flattery' 'tis *my honest sentiments* believe me however incapable I may be of giving a correct opinion, in the judgment of others.

44. John Clare on one of his poems

1820

Clare to Hessey, 1 December 1820, *LJC*, p. 72.
'The Wild-Flower Nosegay' was not published in Clare's lifetime.

I am glad you like the wild flowers the last verse is such a favourite of mine that it is the only one I can repeat of any of my poems & my selfish consiet is constantly repeating it twas first pointed out by a stranger on reading the M.S. who begd to transcribe it.

45. John Taylor on Clare's good taste

1820

Taylor to Clare, 12 December 1820, Eg. 2245, fol. 255.

I did not tell you before, but I hope you have had no Doubt that I was much pleased with the last Poems you sent me:—I don't like to particularize for I wish your own Mind & good Taste to lead you; it has prompted you to your best things, and will again; but I cannot help remarking the Sonnet to the Ivy in which you say 'Where thou in *weak Defiance* strives with Time, & holds his weapons in a dread suspense': this Figure is I think of the highest order of Poetry; and I would also observe the happy Epithet of 'thy *Green Darkness* over-shadowing me.'

46. John Taylor on true poetry

1821

Taylor to Clare, 1 January 1821, Eg. 2245, fol. 267ᵛ.

It is not clear what poem Taylor means; it could be 'To Lord Radstock', sent in a letter of 30 December 1820. Taylor has been talking about Lord Radstock in the previous paragraph of this letter, and the asterisks are a joke between Taylor and Clare, representing the false delicacy required to satisfy Radstock's sensibilities.

Thank you for the Sonnet.—It is * * * * * * * without doubt; but perhaps the Author does not further to his own Feelings out of Respect to established usage—If he has a soul of native Fancies, let him study to express what it dictates in that Language it will bring with it; then he will write like himself & no one else: if he has not that innate Poesy he may write clever Poems like many others who are called Poets, but he will have no just claim to the Title.

47. Edward Drury on 'The Last of Autumn'

1821

Drury to Clare, 3 January 1821, Eg. 2245, fol. 269.

This poem was included in *The Shepherd's Calendar*, 1827.

I am now nearly through the last of Autumn & scarcely 18 pages remain uncopied; the subject, as I proceed excites the warmest feelings—in one couplet the setting-sun described as peeping beneath the meadow bridges quite struck me mute with admiration. There is a sweet strain of reflexion, pensiveness, and regret throughout the whole of this which will render the Last of Autumn a very great favourite of mine.

48. Some opinions on 'The Peasant Boy'

1821

This poem was the first version of what later became 'The Village Minstrel'. It was in the first place a longer, more diffuse work; Taylor had not taken much notice of it at first, partly because Drury had scribbled at the top 'let it pass in obscurity'.

(a) Clare to Taylor, ?6 January 1821, *LJC*, pp. 74–5:

I have been looking over that hasty scribbled thing the 'Peasant Boy' & find some of the best rural descriptions I have yet written such as the Feast & the Statute & some touches on Love & Scenery I feel little pleasure after a second reading of one's ryhmes in general but the thing is quite decievd me & I think it will take when your Pencil has just gone over it here & there as its printing.

(b) Clare to Taylor, 9 January 1821, *LJC*, p. 88. Lord Radstock had written in the manuscript that the poem was 'radical slang'.

I am glad you like the 'Peasant Boy' for I have read the rough sketch a second time & think some of the things the best I have written. . . . Never mind Lord R.'s pencilings in the 'Peasant Boy' what he dont like he must lump as the dog did his dumpling I woud not have 'there once were lanes, etc' left out for all the Lord R.'s in Europe d-n it do as you like I tell you if you like to print 'cursed' too print it—' & a fig for the sultan & sophy'.

(c) Taylor to Clare, 23 January 1821, Eg. 2245, fol. 277:

There are too many of those 'feeble expletives' as Pope calls them *did* and *does*, but I fear they cannot be expell'd without doing harm. I have left out the Song of Lubin and the Pauper's Story, & Woodcroft Castle —They were less poetical than the other parts, and only broke in upon the leading Interests to no good End. . . . Woodcroft Castle is almost too common-place in its Language you tell the tale too much in the Words in which a prose Narrator would tell it—and you can do something much more than that when you are *poetical*.

49. John Taylor on the prospects of success

1821

Taylor to Clare, 17 February 1821, Eg. 2245, fol. 296ᵛ.

We shall greatly surpass our former Volume, & take a higher Rank among the Poets when this is published: in consequence of which I am the more solicitous about certain matters of refinement, which '*you know, you do*' my own Opinion jumps with yours in Otherwise. But we shall be attacked I foresee by his Lordship & *such*, therefore let us be as free from Indelicacy as he would call it as possible, that he may find no Handle against us on that Side.

50. Comments on 'prettiness' in poetry

1821

(a) Clare to Taylor, 24 April 1821, *LJC*, pp. 113–4. Dr Noehden, from the British Museum, had visited Clare.

. . . he odd enough said 'he had seen my *pretty poems* & that curiosity had urged him to seize the first opportunity of seeing the author'. . . . I didnt much like pretty but will alter these things when out a second time twas natural enough—children say so about playthings— & this first book is our plaything I consider it nothing more now—the muse is there in the bud in the next she will be in the blossom If I mistake not— & these will alter the note a little—a smile shoud dimple to say them pretty—but admiration shall redden the cheek with pronouncing they are good— & if not in the next—if we are left as I hope we shall to wind up the story: in the last admiration shall let fall her muscles into reverence. . . .

(b) Taylor to Clare, 1 May 1821, Eg. 2245, fol. 313ᵛ:

I know Dr. Noehden only by Name—Never Mind what Epithet people use—the *Feeling* you anticipate will have its full Effect in their hearts at some Time or other—if they have any Taste or Feeling. Go on & prosper.

(c) Drury to Clare, no date, Eg. 2250, fol. 121:

That word 'pretty' is an odious appellation to a vol. of Poems—and if you call them 'pretty' you have said the severest & most provoking thing that can be said. Therefore I hope you will back my endeavours to avoid the idea of 'prettiness' being attached to the book.

51. Comments in anticipation of the new volume

1821

(a) Eliza Emmerson to Clare, 25 April 1821, Eg. 2245, foll. 96ᵛ–7:

Your 'Pathetic Narratives' will also afford you ample room to indulge in that, wherein you excel—In animated descriptions of Nature! heightened by the finer sensibilities of the Soul! But why say 'we are not to expect any more publication of yours, after these in the press, for 3 years'—surely, if the forth coming Vols. are successful there should not be such delay in offering to the World, further poems? I am happy to find a 4th Edition of your 1 Volume is announced, and knowing, as *I do*, the *merits* of *these* in the *press*, what may we not expect from them? . . . Indulge my dear Clare! to the fullest degree your *imagination*, write that, which suggests itself to your mind, without repressing the ardour of your feelings with *doubts*, or fears—let your *Genius lead you*; and in following her dictates you cannot err!

(b) Hessey to Clare, 12 May 1821, Eg. 2245, fol. 320:

I must say I am the more pleased the more I see of these Volumes. You have made a great advance on your former productions & I think the Public will admit it—this was necessary and I am happy you have (or will have) fulfilled the natural expectations of the Public.

(c) Clare to Hessey, 17 May 1821, *LJC*, p. 105:

'Criticism may do her worst'— & be d-d when shes done it—to escape the hell of party-political criticism is impossible—so I am prepared— I am glad your opinion of my advancement is so favourable—I think much of it and feel its value.

THE VILLAGE MINSTREL

September 1821

52. John Taylor, from the Introduction to *The Village Minstrel*

1821

The former volume of JOHN CLARE's Poems was published on the 16th of January, 1820. It immediately received the most flattering notice from several periodical publications, and the interest which was directly taken in the Poet's fate by all ranks, is a circumstance most clearly indicative of the good taste and generous feelings of the nation. A pleasant and judicious account of the author, which was published in the first number of the London Magazine, greatly contributed to this rapid acknowledgment of the merits of the work, and of the justice of the author's pretensions to the distinction of public patronage. It was written by Mr. Gilchrist, of Stamford, whose kindness to CLARE did not cease with that effort in his favour. To him, and all those who, by sympathising with CLARE in the days of his distress, have a peculiar title to be named among his benefactors, the pleasure of befriending a man of true genius is of itself a sufficient reward:—

> ———The praise is better than the price,
> The glory eke much greater than the gain—

In the summer of 1817 CLARE left Helpstone and went into the employment of Mr. Wilders, of Bridge Casterton, Rutlandshire. Here he first met with Patty, who was destined to be his future companion through life—but as he observes in one of his letters at this period, 'a poor man's meeting with a wife is reckoned but little improvement to his condition, particularly with the embarrassments I laboured under at that time.' With the view of relieving himself from some of these troubles, and thinking it but fair that his love of poesy should contribute to his support as well as his amusement, the latter only being too great a luxury for a poor man to indulge in, he began to consider seriously about publishing a small volume of Poems by subscription, and having some time before ascertained, from a Printer at Market Deeping, that the expense of three hundred copies of a Prospectus would not be more than one pound, he set himself resolutely to work to obtain that sum. . . .

In the Spring of 1820, CLARE married 'Patty of the Vale,'—'the Rosebud in humble Life,'—or, to speak in prose, Martha Turner, the daughter of a cottage farmer residing at Walkherd Lodge in the neighbourhood of Bridge Casterton, whose portion consisted of nothing beyond the virtues of industry, frugality, neatness, good-temper, and a sincere love for her husband; qualities, indeed, which contribute more than wealth to the happiness of the marriage state; but money is still a desirable accompaniment, and for want of it our Poet's finances are somewhat too much straitened to support his family with comfort. His household consists at the present time of his father and mother, who are aged and infirm, his wife, and a little girl who bids fair to be the eldest of a family, which at this rate may be expected to be pretty numerous. They all live together in the cottage in which CLARE was born.

Since sending his former Poems to the press, CLARE has written the whole of the following collection, with the exception of the Excursion to Burghley Park, Helpstone Green, To the Violet, The Wood-Cutter's Night Song, To the Butterfly, To Health, May-Day, William and Robin, and the first five Sonnets.—The third Sonnet and May-Day were written on the illness and death of a youth who was CLARE's earliest friend and favourite play-fellow, and the brother of John Turnill, the excise-man who taught CLARE to write. Some of these Poems are ten or twelve years old. The pastoral, William and Robin, one of his earliest efforts, exhibits a degree of refinement, and elegant sensibility, which many persons can hardly believe a poor uneducated clown could have possessed: the delicacy of one of the lovers towards the object of his attachment is as perfectly inborn and unaffected as if he were a Philip Sidney.—It also shews that a style of writing, caught from the accredited pastoral poets, which so many admire, was not above CLARE's reach, had not his good sense taught him to abandon it for the more difficult but less appreciated language of nature.

The Village Minstrel was begun in the autumn of 1819: the writer of these lines saw in November about one hundred stanzas of it, and it was finished soon after the former volume made its appearance. To the fate of that volume the author alludes with much natural anxiety at the end of this poem,

> And wishes time her secrets would explain,
> If he may live for joys, or sink in 'whelming pain.

And the state of dreary misery in which he then lived must be his excuse for some apparently discontented stanzas about the middle of the poem, if any excuse be necessary for some of the most vigorous and beautiful ebullitions of true poesy that can be met with in our language.

The regret of a poet for the loss of some object in nature, to which many of the dearest recollections of his earliest and happiest days had attached themselves, is always vehement; but who can wonder at or condemn it? If an old post had such attractions for Pope, surrounded as he was with comfort and luxury, what allowance ought not to be made for the passionate regard of poor CLARE for things which were the landmarks of his life, the depositaries of almost all his joys? But the poet can be as much a philosopher as another man when the fit is off: in a letter to the writer of these lines he laments the purposed destruction of two elm trees which overhang his little cottage, in language which would surprise a man whose blood is never above temperate; but the reflection of a wiser head instantly follows:—

My two favourite elm trees at the back of the hut are condemned to die—it shocks me to relate it, but 'tis true. The savage who owns them thinks they have done their best, and now he wants to make use of the benefits he can get from selling them. O was this country Egypt, and was I but a caliph, the owner should lose his ears for his arrogant presumption; and the first wretch that buried his axe in their roots should hang on their branches as a terror to the rest. I have been several mornings to bid them farewel. Had I one hundred pounds to spare I would buy them reprieves—but they must die. Yet this mourning over trees is all foolishness—they feel no pains—they are but wood, cut up or not. A second thought tells me I am a fool: were people all to feel as I do, the world could not be carried on,—a green would not be ploughed—a tree or bush would not be cut for firing or furniture, and every thing they found when boys would remain in that state till they died. This is my indisposition, and you will laugh at it. . . .

It is not our province to comment on the following Poems,—we must leave it to the professed critics to exercise their usual discrimination, in bringing forward the faults and beauties of the author. Of the former the detection is not difficult,—but it requires something of

generosity and high-mindedness to perceive and appreciate beauties,—
some consanguinity with the poet to feel what we would express,—
and some wisdom to admit, in doubtful places, where the judgment of
the poet and the critic differ, that he may be right, and that an appeal
ought not to be made from the higher to the lower tribunal:—for the
critic is not the poet's superior, though he often affects to be so, on the
strength of having had, probably, a better education; as if the Latin and
Greek which can be driven into a boy's head at school, for a certain sum
of money, were a more valuable possession than the rarely found, un-
bought, unpurchasable endowment of genius from the hand of the
Creator.

> What more felicity can fall to creature
> Than to enjoy delight with liberty,
> And to be lord of all the works of nature,
> To reign in th' air from th' earth to highest sky,
> To feed on flowers and weeds of glorious feature,
> To take whatever thing doth please the eye?—

The poet enjoys all this right royally, but he does not reserve it for his
own gratification: he makes all the rest of his fellow-creatures happy,
in the same degree, by placing before them 'whatever thing doth please
the eye.' Thus CLARE bids his inspired flowers and trees grow up in our
sight, and assume characters which we did not discover in them before.
He saw them, having his vision cleared by the euphrasy of a poetical
imagination: he brings them out into the clear light of day, and sets
them as pictures and statues in a gallery, to be the charm and glory of
many a future age; 'such tricks hath strong imagination,' even in the
mind of an illiterate peasant.

> Thus Nature works as if to mock at Art,
> And in defiance of her rival powers;
> By these fortuitous and random strokes
> Performing such inimitable feats
> As she with all her rules can never reach.

CLARE has created more of these never-dying forms, in the personification of things inanimate and abstract,—he has scattered them
more profusely about our paths, than perhaps any poet of the age
except one;—and having contributed so much to our gratification,
what ought we to render in return to him?—He deserves our favour, as
one who tries to please us—our thanks, for having so richly increased

the stores of our most innocent enjoyments—our sympathy, and something more substantial than mere pity, because he is placed in circumstances, grievous enough to vulgar minds, but to a man of his sensibility more than commonly distressing;—and our regard and admiration, that, sustaining so many checks and obstructions, his constant mind should have at length shone out with the splendour which animates it in these productions:

> For who would ever care to do brave deed,
> Or strive in virtue others to excel,
> If none should yield him his deserved meed,
> Due praise, that is the spur of doing well?

Poets of all ages have been cherished and rewarded, and this, not as of mere favour, but from a feeling that they have a claim to be so considered. If of late years a less generous treatment has been experienced by any, it is not chargeable on the nature of man in general, but on an illiberal spirit of criticism, which, catching its character from the bad temper of the age, has 'let slip the dogs of war' in the flowery fields of poesy. We may hope that kinder feelings are returning, that 'olives of endless age' will grace the future Belles Lettres of our country, and that especially the old and natural relation of poet and patron may be again acknowledged, as it has been in the present instance:—

> The kindly dew drops from the higher tree,
> And wets the little plants that lowly dwell.

53. John Clare on popularity

1821

Clare to Taylor, 6 September 1821, *LJC*, p. 126.

I am sought after very much agen now 3 days scarcly pass but sombody calls—some rather entertaining people & some d-d knowing fools— surely the vanity woud have kill'd me 4 years ago if I had known then how I shoud have been hunted up— & extolld by personal flattery—but let me wait another year or two & the peep show will be over— & my vanity if I have any will end in its proper mortification to know that obscurity is happiness & that John Clare the thresher in the onset & neglected ryhmer in the end are the only two comfortable periods of his life.

54. From an unsigned review, *Literary Gazette*

6 October 1821, No. 246, 625–8

See Introduction, p. 9, and No. 58.

The publishers of these volumes have done themselves everlasting honour, by the liberality and friendship which they have exercised towards John Clare. Through their means, his first essay saw the light in 1820; and their continued exertions have mainly contributed to the knowledge, and with the knowledge to the popularity of an individual, as meritorious as remarkable in the annals of song. . . .

[Biographical details]

It is impossible to contemplate in detail, even the imperfect detail which happier stars put it in the power of the more fortunate to imagine, the difficulties opposed to the child of want, to the mean, the friendless, the beggared hind, who feels impregn with the ecstasies of inspiration, without wonder at their ever being surmounted. The simplest aids, within the reach of loftier bards, are to him inaccessible; what they attain with ease, are to him obstacles of hopeless anxiety. But true talent loves to cope even with impossibilities. The Peasant, whose exertions have been rewarded and longings gratified by procuring the bare materials with which to give his fancies their first rude form, is, if truly a poet, far above the exalted Would-be, who is courted to compose by all the luxuries of literature and 'all appliances to boot.' Their different fates are in poesy as in the slumbers so finely described by our immortal Swan of Avon,—the coy visitant flies from the couch of vainly-wooing monarchs, to dwell in contentment with the happy lowly clown.

Several of the poems in this collection will raise the reputation of the rustic bard above his former fame; though, perhaps, it might have been better for him, in this respect, to have limited the publication to one volume, and expunged the less striking compositions. At the same time we can readily suppose, that the kind idea of securing him a larger reward, led to the present arrangement, which is only to be regretted on account of its mixing up, with pieces of great interest, others which are less worthy of the poet, his patrons, or the public. Of these, however, we shall take no further notice: the extraordinary instance which the writer exhibits of pure inspiration, in the midst of every thing which could depress man, and plunge genius into despair, is a theme more pleasing to us to dwell upon, and if we mitigate our admiration with any alloy, we trust it will be received, not as censure, but as advice—not as stinting applause of the past, but as suggesting hints for future improvement.

Clare, in these volumes, takes a station in many points above Bloomfield, though in other particulars he is inferior to the author of the 'Farmer's Boy.' The peculiarities which render him so, consist chiefly in the frequent use of words radically low and insignificant, which mar the effect of his best passages; in the employment of others too decidedly provincial, or coined without taste to suit his own occasions; in the admission of expletives to eke out the verse; in harsh ellisions unsanctioned by any good authority; in deficiency of humour where humour is attempted; and in the want of interest in things which he laments as if they were of essential value. Most of his deficiencies may, we think, be traced to these sources; to which, perhaps, we may add, that his lyrical are, with one or two exceptions, manifestly so much weaker than his descriptive powers, as to cause a regret that he should have tuned his pipe to that chord. . . . The lack of humour we refrain from exemplifying; but the want of interest in the objects of his theme is of so much greater consequence to his after-labours, that we beg to call his regards especially to that defect. It is obvious that this has arisen in great measure, if not entirely, from the nature of the country, in which the author's life has been spent. The rushes, the sedges, the 'willow groves,' and the sluggish rivulets of a marshy part of North-amptonshire, are to him what the forest, the mountain, the lake, and the ocean, are to other poets. Now, though these are genuine sources of feeling, to him who has wandered from childhood to maturity among flat, unpicturesque and swampy fields, it is hardly possible to excite a like feeling in the general bosom, for such scenes——

> Swamps of wild rush-beds, and sloughs' squashy traces,
>   Grounds of rough fallows with thistle and weed,
> Flats and low valleys of kingcups and daisies,
>   Sweetest of subjects are ye for my reed:

is a fitting invocation for the vicinity of Helpstone; but as Clare's vision becomes extended to landscapes of a more sublime and beautiful order, it is to be hoped he will turn his vivid descriptive talent to paint them. As yet, his subjects seem to limit him to the single praise of being admir-ably natural;—a Morland in poetry, but without so much glow of colour or skill in art.

Having premised thus much, we shall now apply to the agreeable task of displaying a few of the examples which stamp the author to be a true and original poet. The leading piece is called 'The Village Minstrel,' and has evidently had Beattie's Minstrel for its model. It was begun, we are told, in Autumn, 1819, and was finished in the ensuing Spring. In the person of Lubin, Clare draws his own portrait, and largely insists on his love of Nature—the grand fountain of all his emotions and of all his writings. Of this the following stanzas are proof:—

[Quotes 'But who can tell the anguish . . .' to '. . . the birds have took to wing'; 'Ye fields, ye scenes . . .' to '. . . old "Lea-close Oak" adieu!'; 'O who can speak his joys . . .' to '. . . the aid of art supplied']

Nor is his address to poverty, real poverty, less forcible:—

> O Poverty! thy frowns were early dealt
> O'er him who mourn'd thee, not by fancy led
> To whine and wail o'er woes he never felt,
> Staining his rhymes with tears he never shed,
> And heaving sighs a mock song only bred:
> Alas! he knew too much of every pain
> That shower'd full thick on his unshelter'd head;
> And as his tears and sighs did erst complain,
> His numbers took it up, and wept it o'er again.

In more cheerful strains he pourtrays bumkin sports, (some of them not worth the pains,) and from his account of the revels of harvest home, we shall select such stanzas, as best evince his manner, and give a lively picture of Northamptonshire customs:—

[Quotes 'The muse might sing too . . .' to '. . . and morts of things were done']

This characteristic and clever passage, leaves us little room for longer illustration, and therefore, from the Village Minstrel we shall only quote two very brief similes more of poetical grace:—

> Nor could the day's decline escape his gaze;
> He lov'd the closing as the rising day,
> And oft would stand to catch the setting rays,
> Whose last beams stole not unperceiv'd away;
> When, hesitating like a stag at bay,
> The bright unwearied sun seem'd loth to drop,
> Till chaos' night-hounds hurried him away,
> And drove him headlong from the mountain-top,
> And shut the lovely scene, and bade all Nature stop.
>
> *   *   *   *   *   *   *   *
>
> No insect 'scap'd him, from the gaudy plume
> Of dazzling butterflies so fine to view,
> To the small midges that at evening come,
> Like dust spots, dancing o'er the water's blue;

In his picture of a Cotter's evening, Clare comes into too direct comparison with Burns, to be read with advantage: indeed it is in compositions liable to this dangerous contrast, (witness 'Disappointment, in vol. 1.') that he is seen in the faintest light. The greater genius of Cæsar predominates over his lesser fire till it is nearly extinguished, and we are glad to escape from the darkness to view him in his own brighter beaming. To this belong two pieces intitled, 'Rural Morning' and 'Rural Evening', which we esteem to be altogether his most perfect productions, and which we are sorry we cannot transplant into this Number of our Gazette. But we purpose at an early period to do him that justice, and in the mean time commend the annexed from among his minor pieces to our readers as satisfactory evidence, if any more were needed, that John Clare is a genuine poet, and richly entitled to the fostering smiles of the liberal and enlightened:—

[Quotes 'To the Clouds'; 'Song: Of all the days in memory's list'; 'Song: There was a time . . .']

The variety of verse which Clare has tried, shows that he has read a good deal, and studied both our ancient and modern bards. A poem on 'Sunday,' is full of simplicity, and at once eminently descriptive and meditatively soothing; but we have been seduced, past all bounds, by this interesting peasant, and must bid him farewell.

55. Two views of Clare, *Literary Chronicle*

1821

(a) From an unsigned review, 6 October 1821, no. 125, 623–5.

When we saw two new volumes of poems, by Clare, announced, within so short a period since his first collection was published, we acknowledge we were afraid that his friends were drawing too freely on his genius, and forcing him before the public somewhat too hastily; we must, however, confess, that this is not the case, and numerous as are the pieces in these volumes, there are scarcely any that we would have wished to be withheld. The whole of these poems, with the exception of about a dozen pieces (some of which are his earliest productions), have been written since his former volume went to press. The principal poem, the 'Village Minstrel,' was begun in the autumn of 1819, and finished soon after the former volume made its appearance. Clare is himself the hero of his poem, and paints, with glowing vigour, the misery in which he then was, and his anxiety for his future fate. It is a fine picture of rural life, and the author luxuriates in his love of natural objects and his description of rustic sports and village scenes, notwithstanding the melancholy reflections and forbodings with which they are accompanied. A few stanzas will justify our remark. The author is describing his own feelings and character:—

[Quotes 'And dear to him the rural sports of May' to '. . . and bade all nature stop'; 'It might be curious . . .' to '. . . Crusoe's lonely isle'; 'There once were springs . . .' to '. . . as parish kings allow']

This is the last extract which we shall make from the 'Village Minstrel,' a poem which of itself would justify all the praise that has been bestowed on John Clare, who, in vivid descriptions of rural scenery, in originality of observation and strength of feeling, richness of style and delicacy of sentiment, may rank with the best of poets of the day, though a humble and untutored peasant.

Among the minor poems in these volumes, we have been much pleased with 'Autumn,' 'Cowper Green,' 'Song of Praise,' and some of the pastorals, a style in which Clare would have been successful, had he not abandoned it early in his poetic career. The songs and sonnets are many of them very pretty, and some of them possess considerable merit. We shall enrich our present article with a few of these pieces. The first is a sweet ballad:—

[Quotes 'I love thee, sweet Mary . . .'; 'There was a time . . .']

Though there is no species of poetry more common than the sonnet, yet there are few who succeed in it. Clare has indulged in it largely, and given us no less than sixty specimens of his talents in this species of composition, in which we think him very successful. We quote three of them:—

[Quotes 'A Wish'; 'To Time'; 'To Autumn']

With all our predilections for the first fruits of natural genius, we must admit that Clare has improved by cultivation; and though some of his earlier productions are striking from their neatness and simplicity, yet his more matured efforts, though not deficient in this respect, have a refinement of language and a correctness of style, which give them an increased value. Should these new volumes extend the public patronage sufficiently to relieve him from that oppressive anxiety which still bears him down, we may fairly expect the poet to take a loftier and more extensive range of subject, and to add new claims to those he already possesses as a man of genius; though stronger claims to public sympathy and public support no one can present, than the poor Northamptonshire peasant; and with all the warmth of admiration for his talents, and sympathy for his miseries, we recommend him and his works to the public.

(b) A letter, signed Mus., 21 October 1821, no. 127, 665–6.

SIR,—With much respect for your impartial review of Mr. John Clare, the Northamptonshire Peasant's poems, I venture to call his attention, through your pages, to the observations which I am about to make, that he may be further encouraged to pursue the celestial art of poetry, with the easiest and best success. It is well understood that many original geniuses have become ruined imitators by yielding their judgment to the voice of *party* criticism, and have sunk into oblivion under the pressure of envy and malice, as though originality should be clipped and toned into a particular school, intimating the unworthiness of genius being schooled by nature and operated on by inspiration. Whoever is versed in periodical literature knows how poor Keats was buffeted from one page to another, how much ill-nature was shed in lines of ink, and what rancorous spleen appeared in print,—because he was fostered by a *political* writer.

Fortunately, however, for classical and self-taught writers too, history presents a long roll of geniuses who have treated unjust criticism with that neglect which it has merited. Keats is an exception, but his constitution, like his taste, was delicate; like a rose-leaf, he was easily blown upward in his fancy, or driven downward by the sadness of his lonely spirit. Mr. Clare is otherwise. His genius is of the masculine order, from whose manly nature the sensibilities of feeling issue, but never more successfully than when he describes the crinkle of a primrose-leaf or the fluttering of love's confusion. His element is under a hedge, among the various grasses and herbs and mosses; whatever little object draws his eye in the sun-beam wins his admiration and love. His first conception is natural and striking; therefore, the crown of his hat aids his memory to paper; the lines are written, and require but little more embellishment or correction. The advantages of a thousand hallowed volumes of English poets, I conceive, would be of injury rather than service to him, for his poetic reading is already manifest, and imitation, however humble or elegant, will be the result; that

> Young Edwin was no vulgar boy;

and—

> Deep thought oft seemed to fix his infant eye.

One reason, why so many strike 'their lyre in praise of poesy' is, that they partly acquire a good ear for rhyme, a correct method for the delivery of it, and attempt, but seldom produce, more than excellent verses. Mr. Clare is aware that poems, like timber, can be measured by feet, and finished off like picture frames, yet, if the timber be unsound at heart, or the frames without good pictures, neither the one nor the other are of much value. Poems should be skilfully put together, contain solid sentiments, and the most touching pathos of nature,—

> Divinely felt, to make another feel.

Shakespeare, with a few original authors, should be the only ones worthy of great application. I believe Bloomfield's amiable muse was never much benefited by listening to the sound of 'read the poets!'— 'study the A's down to the Z's,'

> Range them by day and meditate by night.

This is an affectation for perfection, at which *soi-disant* critics have themselves failed. Who questions that Lord Byron is not, in some respects, the worse for his poetical reading? How many 'Deserted Villages' have been attempted since Goldsmith's career, yet unsuccessfully. The habitual reading of poetry alone is sufficient to make a poetaster feel his way through a monthly periodical. But, allowing one exception, I verily believe, now and then, a fine poem *is* scattered in periodical pages, far exceeding half, nay, four-fifths of puffed off published poetry; and I have often wished that a work were patronised by the literati to select the best pieces for 'after ages' from those which are destined for 'the soap and candles.' I would not keep Mr. Clare in ignorance of the silliness of some poets, the eccentricity of some, and the disproportionate nonsense of others; but I would not advise him to trust to the strength of their weakness, which is irretrievable, from vain notions and obstinate party considerations. If he march the fields with his eye directed to *nature* he will be *original*; if he closet himself and *imagine* nature, he will be an *imitator*. London has given birth to poets, but the country has made them. Edinburgh will produce a 'Pirate,' but his attributes have been drawn from the scenes of action. Ramsay and Burns danced with the shepherdesses and sung with hobbinols. Cunningham used to sit on the furrows, like Prior's 'Cupid's ploughboy,' and listen to the calm wanderings of the stream. Morland loved to lean over bridges and broken trees, in *sober* abstraction, before he soiled his brush. Falconer had never written his 'Shipwreck' but for a tempest; Somerville the 'Chace' but for his actual experience in field sports; and Olney's harp might have been unstrung but for its attractive ruralties. Hence, if Mr. Clare will be great, and form a constellation for the heaven of eternity, let him read good *prose* with assiduous and ardent attention: let his mind be stored with a clear knowledge of things in and out of their nature; let him reason with truth and virtue: his beauties will touch the heart while they strike the eye, and do much towards refining the understanding, which is the spiritual essence of true poetry. Well then, after all, it will appear, that I would have him unacquainted with metrical authors, ancient and modern,—not so; I would warn him against the *danger* of the *shallows*, the rocks, and the storms: he may dip, but not meditate; skim, but not dive. He may consult, but only with a view of correcting his errors. He will have to occupy his niche in 'Fame's proud temple.' He should watch the ellipsis and the eclipses. The apostrophe is a very useful little fellow, but should not be abused. *That is* is preferable to *that's*; *against* to *'gainst*. A *hobbling* line is, like a lame ploughman, out of its place. *Inferior* is not full enough for three syllables at the close of a 'Sonnet.' Mr. Clare will comprehend me by re-perusing his works.* It is true, many provincialisms, with other eccentricities, might be brought forward, but his experience will tutor him to expunge them as he advances towards beatified love and eternal triumph.

* The trifles which I have mentioned are only intended as *examples* of *carelessness* and not as *injurious* to the tenor of the volumes.

56. From an unsigned review, *Monthly Magazine*

November 1821, lii, 321–5

Naturâ fieret laudabile carmen an arte
Quæsitum est: ego nec studium sine divite venâ,
Nec rude quid prosit video ingenium: alterius sic
Altera poscit opem res, et conjurat amicè.[1]

Under the sanction of this high authority, we trust it may be permitted us to express, without reserve, the reflexions that have been suggested by the perusal of these interesting, but very unequal, volumes; without being suspected of a wish to crush the attempts of any meritorious, though humble, aspirant to public fame, or incurring the imputation (to use the language of the eulogium prefixed as an introduction to the work) of cherishing 'an illiberal spirit of criticism, which, catching its character from the bad temper of the age, has let slip the dogs of war in the flowery fields of poesy.' The present production contains much that is good, and even beautiful; and we are disposed not only to point out its merits with readiness, but to acknowledge them with pleasure, as sincere, perhaps, as that of eulogists, whose undiscriminating praises have a tendency rather to alienate, than to conciliate, more discerning judges. But considering these poems with reference only to their literary excellence, the meed of commendation to which some parts of them may be justly entitled, is altogether a distinct question from the necessity, or even the propriety of bringing them before the tribunal of the public. The latter is what Partridge would have termed a *non sequitur.* We are willing to give full credit to the motives of those, whose benevolence has prompted them to introduce the effusions of the Northamptonshire peasant to general notice, but we may reasonably doubt how far they have been the means of enriching, in any great degree, our stores of national poetry, or are likely to bind a wreath

---

[1] 'It is asked whether a praiseworthy poem comes into being through nature or through art. I myself do not see the use either of study without nature's rich vein, or of raw talent; each in fact asks help of the other, in friendly co-operation', Horace, *Ars Poetica,* 408–12.

more permanent than that woven by the caprice of fashion, or the pre-vailing appetite for novelty, round the brows of the object of their patronage.

From the time that the poetical labours of Burns and Bloomfield gained for their authors that deserved popularity, to which genuine talent, wherever found, is justly entitled, various candidates for like success, prompted either by their own self-love, or by the favourable opinion of partial friends and patrons, have made their appearance; resembling the gifted writers of the 'Farmer's Boy,' or the 'Cotter's Saturday Night,' in nothing but their want of early education, and their obscure situation in life. Ploughmen, milkmaids, and other similar prodigies have thus acquired an ephemeral celebrity; and the error of these writers appears to us far more excusable than that of their pro-fessed admirers, in mistaking the very common disease of a love for rhyming, for that rare poetic genius which, in all ages, has been accorded only to a favoured few. Most of these have flourished their brief day, indebted for their temporary success principally to that feeling of the mind, which has been happily defined 'the effect of novelty upon ignorance.' We are far from being disposed to regret that such attempts should have contributed to the comforts or enjoyments of those who have made them; but every principle of sound judgment and impartial criticism lead us to deplore the influence which even the short-lived favour with which they have been received has had, in vitiating the taste of no small portion of the public. In opposition to the judicious assertion of an elegant writer of our own, that

> True ease in writing comes from art, not chance,

an opinion has been engendered among many unreflecting persons, that the most natural and pleasing poetry is the offspring of mental powers intuitive and uncultivated; and instead of requiring that marked superiority of knowledge, which the sage in Rasselas regarded as in-dispensable to the formation of the poetic character, they appear to hail the existence of consummate ignorance as a happy omen of success in the votary of the muses. While such sentiments prevail, the evil of in-competent intruders into the walks of literature will obviously be an increasing one; and the *scribimus indocti doctique*,[1] a complaint better founded than ever.

Though the author of the poems before us is undeniably superior in correct observation, vigour of intellect, and native talent, to many

[1] 'we [all] write [poetry], learned and unlearned [alike]', Horace, *Epistles*, II, i, 117.

others who have come before us with pretensions of a similar description, we do not consider him as forming an exception to the general
tenor of the observations with which we have introduced our notice of
his volumes. We do not conceive that occasional sweetness of expression, or accurate delineations of mere exterior objects, can atone for a
general deficiency of poetical language, or the indulging in a style
devoid of uniformity and consistency. The Village Minstrel is the
principal poem in the collection, and is evidently intended to afford a
picture of the peculiar circumstances and early scenes of the author's
life. To himself this topic is no doubt peculiarly interesting; and his
descriptions may very probably be productive of amusement to those
who are familiar with the originals. To us, however, the writer's
mention of himself appears, in general, too egotistical and querulous,
and the local subjects and rural amusements, whatever opinion may be
entertained of the colours in which he has pourtrayed them, have not,
we think, been very judiciously selected for the purpose of inspiring
general interest. There is, besides, something more than homeliness,
approximating to vulgarity, in many of his themes, and it must be
admitted that these are described in most suitable language. What shall
we say, for instance, of lines like the following?

> But soldiers, *they're the boys to make a rout.*

> The *bumptious* serjeant struts before his men.

> His friends so poor and clothes *excessive dear.*

> And *don't* despise your betters *'cause* they're old.

> Up he'd *chuck sacks* as one would hurl a stone.

> And in disgrace at last each jockey *bumps* adown. . . .

If it be urged that such language is appropriate to the subjects treated
of, we reply, that subjects to which such language is best adapted, are
not those which a poet should have chosen; or, if selected for the
exercise of his muse, he should have spoken of them in the dialect that
'the muses love.' When a writer who had submitted his production to
the inspection of Voltaire, contended, in defence of some passage which
the latter censured as low, that it was natural, the wit replied, *Avec
permission, Monsieur, mon —— est bien naturel, et cependant je porte des
culottes.*[1]

Another disadvantage attending the Village Minstrel, is, the in-

[1] 'May I point out, Sir, that my —— is quite natural, but I none the less wear trousers.'

voluntary comparison which it forces on the mind with the exquisite poem of Beattie; a comparison that can hardly prove favourable to the Northamptonshire bard. We do not allude to the plan of the poem, for Mr. Clare's Minstrel appears to be without any, and is composed principally of detached descriptions, most of which might change places with one another, without the reader's being conscious of the alteration. But not only in the structure of the verse, but in many imitative passages, we seem to perceive an attempt to present us in Lubin, with a species of travestie of our old acquaintance Edwin, and we cannot approve of the experiment. Indeed the author of the present collection seems, on more than one occasion, to have lost sight of his ground, being previously occupied by those whom he could hardly expect to displace. We could have dispensed with his verses on Solitude, after Grainger's Ode on the same subject; his 'Sorrows for the Death of a favourite Tabby Cat,' will hardly be sympathised in, by those who bear Gray's Selima in remembrance, and it is very unfortunate for his 'Song to a City Girl,' that it cannot be read without recalling to our minds the inimitable old ballad, 'Oh, come with me, and be my love.'

An allusion has already been made to the productions of Burns and Bloomfield. In both these writers, the defect of early education appears to have been in great measure supplied, in the former by such natural abilities, as perhaps, with the exception of Shakspeare, scarcely any other man ever possessed; and in the latter, there is strong reason to suspect, by the refining touches of the fostering hand, by which they were first presented to the public. But in the volumes before us, the consequences of this defect are perpetually visible. The author seems always incapable of sustaining an equal flight; and hence, if we meet with a passage we are disposed to approve, it is frequently but an introduction to specimens of the bathos, which could not be exceeded by the citations of the learned Scriblerus himself. . . .

The following verses we have no hesitation in pronouncing beautiful; indeed it appears to us, that there are no others equal to them in the whole collection:

> I cannot pass the very bramble, weeping
>   'Neath dewy tear-drops that its spears surround,
> Like harlot's mock'ry, on the wan cheek creeping,
>   Gilding the poison that is meant to wound.

But would any one imagine, that they are almost immediately preceded, in the same piece, by such a line as,

Winding the zig-zag lane, turning and turning?

Again, speaking of the lark, Clare says,

> With day-break's beauties *I have much been taken*,
> As thy first anthem breath'd its melody.

Can there be a greater contrast, than that between the richness and force of the latter of these two lines, and the feeble vulgarity of that which precedes it?

We must likewise mark our strong disapprobation of the innovating style introduced in many parts of these volumes, by the employment of unauthorised contractions, and the use of words that have hitherto been strangers alike to our prose and poetry. Take, out of many, the subjoined specimens.

> And then, for sake *of's* boys and wenches dear.
>
> *And's* merry sport when harvest came again.
>
> And *well's* he knows, with ceremony kind.
>
> While I, as unconcern'd, went *soodling* on.
>
> He heard the *tootling* robin sound her knell.
>
> If *yah* set any store by one *yah* will.
>
> How he to scape *shool'd* many a pace beyond.

We leave it to the sober judgment of our readers, to decide, whether these, though indisputable, are desirable additions to our language. We may perhaps be told, that a Glossary is annexed to the book; but this does not alter our view of the subject. If the example of Burns, Ramsay, Ferguson, or other Scottish poets be pleaded, we answer, that they employed a dialect in general use through an entire country, and not the mere *patois* of a small district. If the peculiar phraseology of the Northamptonshire rustics is to be licensed in poetry, we see no reason why that of Lancashire, Somersetshire, and other counties should not be allowed an equal currency; and thus our language would be surprisingly enriched, by the legitimization of all the varieties of speech in use among the *canaille*[1] throughout the kingdom.

Our surprise is not unfrequently excited, by meeting with lines whose weakness can scarcely be exceeded.

> As grinning north winds horribly did blow,
> And pepper'd o'er my head their hail and snow.

[1] 'riff-raff'.

Last spring he was living, but now he's no more!

The following effusions of filial affection may perhaps do honour to the heart of the writer, but certainly reflect little credit on his muse.

> Bless thee, my father! thou'st been kind to me,
> And God, who saw it, will be kind to thee.

> My mother too, thy kindness shall be met,
> And e'er I'm able, will I pay the debt;
> For what thou'st done, and what gone through for me,
> My last earn'd sixpence will I break with thee.

The annexed instances, as well as numerous others, of 'vile alliteration,' are likewise to us, who are no admirers of that figure of speech, a strong impeachment of the author's good taste.

> While maidens fair, with *bosoms bare*,
> Go *coolly* to their *cows*.

> Now wenches *listen*, and *let lovers lie*.

> *Hay-makers hustling* from the rain to *hide*.

> Keep off the bothering bustle of the wind.

We trust our readers will readily perceive that the above strictures have not been dictated by a spirit of fastidious or splenetic criticism; they have been prompted solely by a wish to rescue our literature from the inroads attempted to be made upon it by false taste or mistaken benevolence. It is with real pleasure that we turn from this unwelcome part of our task, to point out some favourable specimens of the native talent which we have already said the author possesses, and which would, we doubt not, in other circumstances than those in which he has been placed, have developed themselves to much greater advantage. . . .

In our opinion, however, the writer of the present collection has excelled in his sonnets more than in any other species of composition that he has attempted. The second volume contains upwards of fifty of these short poems, many of which need not shrink from a comparison with the productions of loftier bards in the same department. Our limits will not admit of extracting more than two or three among those that have struck us most: but justice to the poet requires us to observe, that several others are to be found, not at all inferior in merit to those that we have inserted.

[Quotes 'Hereafter'; 'Peace'; 'Autumn']

Several passages in the above extracts are very pleasing, and in no small degree poetical; indeed, they must be confessed to be very superior to any thing that could have been anticipated from the limited resources and defective education of a man like Clare. So far, therefore, he is certainly entitled to praise. But we fear, when every allowance is made, that sober judges will hardly be disposed to assign these poems at the utmost, a place above mediocrity; and the elegant critic of antiquity expressly tell us,

> ———Mediocribus esse poetis,
> Non dî, non homines, non concessere columnæ.[1]

We cannot but regret, that those who were disposed to serve the author, have not hit upon a better expedient than that of endeavouring to force public patronage in his favour, on the ground of claims which we cannot consider as established, notwithstanding the imposing assertions of an anonymous writer, in an introduction prefixed to the poems, that 'Clare has created more never-dying forms in the personification of things inanimate and abstract, and has scattered them more profusely about our paths, than perhaps any poet of the age, but one'. Such extravagant commendation could hardly be admitted on the mere *ipse dixit*, even of a judge of recognised and unquestionable ability; much less can it be acceded to on the ground of unknown authority.

[1] 'Neither gods, nor men, nor booksellers would allow mediocrities to be poets', Horace, *Ars Poetica*, 372–3.

57. John Taylor on Clare, *London Magazine*

1821

From 'A Visit to John Clare', *London Magazine*, November 1821, iv, 540–8.

This (unsigned) account by Taylor was, as it turned out, instead of a review of *The Village Minstrel*. Allan Cunningham, the poet, had sent in a review which dissatisfied Taylor (see *Life*, pp. 169–70). Mrs Emmerson thought the article a 'great credit to its author' (Eg. 2245, fol. 376). Taylor was by now in control of the *London Magazine*.

I have just returned from visiting your friend Clare at Helpstone, and one of the pleasantest days I ever spent, was passed in wandering with him among the scenes which are the subject of his poems. A flatter country than the immediate neighbourhood can scarcely be imagined, but the grounds rise in the distance clothed with woods, and their gently swelling summits are crowned with village churches; nor can it be called an uninteresting country, even without the poetic spirit which now breathes about the names of many of its most prominent objects, for the ground bears all the traces of having been the residence of some famous people in early days. 'The deep sunk moat, the stony mound,' are visible in places where modern taste would shrink at erecting a temporary cottage, much less a castellated mansion; fragments of Roman brick are readily found on ridges which still hint the unrecorded history of a far distant period, and the Saxon rampart and the Roman camp are in some places seen mingled together in one common ruin. On the line of a Roman road, which passes within a few hundred yards of the village of Helpstone, I met Clare, about a mile from home. He was going to receive his quarter's salary from the Steward of the Marquis of Exeter. His wife Patty, and her sister were with him, and it was the intention of the party, I learned, to proceed to their father's house at Casterton, there to meet such of the family as were out in service, on their annual re-assembling together at Michaelmas. I was very unwilling to disturb this arrangement, but Clare insisted on remaining with me, and the two chearful girls left their companion with a 'good bye, John!' which made the plains echo again, and woke in my old-bachelor heart the reflection 'John Clare, thou art a very happy fellow.'

As we were within a hundred yards of Lolham Brigs, we first turned our steps there. 'Tradition gives these brigs renown,' but their antiquity is visible only to the poet's eye—the date of the present structure is 1641; still, the Roman road crossed over on the same foundation, and that is enough; or if more certain evidence of Roman origin were wanted, a fragment of a most ancient wall runs into the road diagonally at this place, leaving the mind in that degree of obscurity, with respect to its age or use, which Burke esteems to be essentially connected with the sublime. Of the Poem, Clare gave me the following account. He was walking in this direction on the last day of March, 1821, when he saw an old acquaintance fishing on the lee side of the bridge. He went to the nearest place for a bottle of ale, and they then sat beneath the screen which the parapet afforded, while a hasty storm passed over, refreshing themselves with the liquor, and moralizing somewhat in the strain of the poem. I question whether Wordsworth's pedlar could have spoken more to the purpose. But all these excitations would, I confess, have spent their artillery in vain against the woolpack of my imagination; and after well considering the scene, I could not help looking at my companion with surprise: to me, the triumph of true genius seemed never more conspicuous, than in the construction of so interesting a poem out of such common-place materials. With your own eyes you see nothing but a dull line of ponds, or rather one continued marsh, over which a succession of arches carries the narrow highway: look again, with the poem in your mind, and the wand of a necromancer seems to have been employed in conjuring up a host of beautiful accompaniments, making the whole waste populous with life, and shedding all around the rich lustre of a grand and appropriate sentiment. Imagination has, in my opinion, done wonders here, and especially in the concluding verse, which contains as lovely a groupe as ever was called into life by the best 'makers' of any age or country.

[Quotes 'The Last of March']

From Lolham Brigs we turned towards the village of Helpstone, and at a distance I saw 'Langley Bush,' which Clare regretted was fast hastening to utter decay; and could he have the ear of the noble proprietor, he said, he would beg that it might be fenced round to preserve it from unintentional as well as wanton injury. There is a melancholy cadence, in the construction of the little poem which he addressed to this Bush, that chimes on my ear whenever its name is mentioned, and seems to attach me to it as to a rational object, though I know nothing further of its history than is contained in the following lines.

> What truth the story of the swain allows,
>   That tells of honours which thy young days knew,
> Of 'Langley Court' being kept beneath thy boughs
>   I cannot tell—thus much I know is true,
> *That thou art reverenc'd:* even the rude clan
>   Of lawless gipsies, driven from stage to stage,
> Pilfering the hedges of the husbandman,
>   Spare thee, as sacred, in thy withering age.
> Both swains and gipsies seem to love thy name,
>   Thy spot's a favourite with the sooty crew,
> And soon thou must depend on gipsy-fame,
>   Thy mouldering trunk is nearly rotten through.
> My last doubts murmur on the zephyr's swell.
>   My last look lingers on thy boughs with pain;
> To thy declining age I bid farewel,
>   Like old companions, ne'er to meet again.

The discretion which makes Clare hesitate to receive as canonical all the accounts he has heard of the former honours of Langley Bush, is in singular contrast with the enthusiasm of his poetical faith. As a man, he cannot bear to be imposed upon,—his good sense revolts at the least attempt to abuse it;—but as a poet, he surrenders his imagination with most happy ease to the illusions which crowd upon it from stories of fairies and ghosts. The effect of this distinction is soon felt in a conversation with him. From not considering it, many persons express their surprise that Clare should be so weak on some topics and so wise on others. But a willing indulgence of what they deem weakness is the evidence of a strong mind. He feels safe there, and luxuriates in the abandonment of his sober sense for a time, to be the sport of all the tricks and fantasies that have been attributed to preter-natural agency. Let them address him on other subjects, and unless they entrench themselves in forms of language to which he is unaccustomed, or take no pains to understand him according to the sense rather than the letter of his speech, they will confess, that to keep fairly on a level with him in the depth and tenour of their remarks, is an exercise requiring more than common effort. He may not have read the books which they are familiar with, but let them try him on such as he has read, (and the number is not few, especially of the modern poets,) and they will find no reason to undervalue his judgment. His language, it is true, is provincial, and his choice of words in ordinary conversation is indifferent, because Clare is an unpretending man, and he speaks in the idiom of his neighbours, who would ridicule and despise him for using more or better terms than they are familiar with. But the philosophic mind will strive to read his thoughts, rather than catch at the manner of their utterance; and will delight to trace the native nobleness, strength, and beauty of his conceptions, under the tattered garb of what may, perhaps, be deemed uncouth and scanty expressions. But why do I plead for his language? We have nothing in our poetry more energetic or appropriate than the affecting little poem of

CHILDISH RECOLLECTIONS.

[Quotes]

If elegance and tenderness of expression are required, from what author in our language can we adduce more delightful instances than are found in the following

BALLAD.

[Quotes 'Winter's gone; the summer breezes . . .']

In the following little poem the art of the composition, admirable as it is, and yielding to no other in this respect, is yet exceeded and kept properly under by the easy grace and delicate fancy with which the lover urges his passion.

[Quotes 'I love thee, sweet Mary, but love thee in fear . . .']

One more quotation, and I return to my companion. Is it possible, that any mode of education, or any rank in life, could have taught Clare to express, in better language than he has chosen, the lovely images under which he commemorates

PLEASURES PAST.

Spring's sweets they are not fled, though Summer's blossom
  Has met its blight of sadness, drooping low;
Still flowers gone by find beds in memory's bosom,
  Life's nursling buds among the weeds of woe.

Each pleasing token of Spring's early morning
   Warms with the pleasures which we once did know;
Each little stem the leafy bank adorning,
   Reminds of joys from infancy that flow.
Spring's early heralds on the winter smiling,
   That often on their errands meet their doom,
Primrose and daisy, dreary hours beguiling,
   Smile o'er my pleasures past whene'er they come;
And the speckt throstle never wakes his song,
But Life's past Spring seems melting from his tongue.

I have dwelt more at length than may be necessary in a letter to you, on the subject of Clare's power of language, but some of his friends object, in my opinion most unreasonably, to his choice of words: one wishes that he would *thresh* and not *thump* the corn, another does not like his eliding the first syllable of some of his words, as "'proaching, &c.' Every one seems to think that the words or phrases which are in common use in his native place, or where he happened to pass the greater part of his life, ought to be reckoned the true and entire 'world of words' for all Englishmen; and so each disallows by turns almost every expression which has not received the sanction of the court. At this rate, Spenser and Shakspeare ought to be proscribed, and Clare may be well content to endure their fate. But in reality, Clare is highly commendable for not *affecting* a language, and it is a proof of the originality of his genius. Style at second-hand is unfelt, unnatural, and commonplace, a parrot-like repetition of words, whose individual weight is never esteemed,—a cluster-language framed and cast into set forms, in the most approved models, and adapted for all occasions,—an expedient, in fact, to give an appearance of thinking, without 'the insupportable fatigue of thought.' It suits the age, for we abound with machinery, invented to supersede man's labour; and it is in repute, for it 'is adapted to the meanest capacities;' but there never was a great poet, or grand original thinker in prose, who did not compose his phraseology for himself; words must be placed in order with great care, and put into combinations which have been unknown before, if the *things* which he is solicitous to express, have not been discovered and expressed before. In poetry, especially, you may estimate the originality of the thoughts by that of the language; but this is a canon to which our approved critics will not subscribe: they allow of no phrase which has not received the sanction of authority, no expression for which, in the sense used, you cannot plead a precedent. They would fetter the

English poet as much as they circumscribe the maker of Latin verses, and yet they complain that our modern poets want originality!

Helpstone consists of two streets, intersecting each other at right angles. In the middle stand the church and a cross, both rather pictures-que objects, but neither of them very ancient. Clare lives in the right hand street. I knew the cottage by the elm trees, which overhang it:

> ——The witchen branches nigh,
> O'er my snug box towering high—

and was glad to hear that they are not now likely to be cut down.

On a projecting wall in the inside of the cottage, which is white-washed, are hung some well engraved portraits, in gilt frames, with a neat drawing of Helpstone Church, and a sketch of Clare's Head which Hilton copied in water colours, from the large painting, and sent as a present to Clare's father. I think that no act of kindness ever touched him more than this; and I have remarked, on several occasions, that the thought, of what would be his father's feelings on any fortunate circum-stance occurring, has given him more visible satisfaction, than all the commendations which have been bestowed on his genius. I believe we must go into low life to know how very much parents can be beloved by their children. Perhaps it may be that they do more for them, or that the affection of the child is concentrated on them the more, from having no other friend on whom it can fall. I saw Clare's father in the garden: it was a fine day, and his rheumatism allowed him just to move about, but with the aid of two sticks, he could scarcely drag his feet along: he can neither kneel nor stoop. I thought of Clare's lines:

> I'll be thy crutch, my father, lean on me;
> *Weakness knits stubborn while it's bearing thee:*
> And hard shall fall the shock of fortune's frown,
> To eke thy sorrows, ere it breaks me down.

The father, though so infirm, is only fifty-six years of age; the mother is about seven years older. While I was talking to the old man, Clare had prepared some refreshment within, and with the appetite of a thresher we went to our luncheon of bread and cheese, and capital beer from the Bell. In the midst of our operations, his little girl awoke, a fine lively pretty creature, with a forehead like her father's, of ample pro-mise. She tottered along the floor, and as her father looked after her with the fondest affection, and with a careful twitch of his eyebrow when she seemed in danger, the last verse of his Address to her came into my mind:

Lord knows my heart, it loves thee much;
And may my feelings, aches, and such,
The pains I meet in folly's clutch
    Be never thine:
Child, it's a tender string to touch,
    That sounds 'thou'rt mine.' . . .

Our meal ended, Clare opened an old oak bookcase, and showed me
his library. It contains a very good collection of modern poems, chiefly
presents made him since the publication of his first volume. Among the
works of Burns, Cowper, Wordsworth, Coleridge, Keats, Crabbe, and
about twenty volumes of Cooke's Poets, I was pleased to see the Niths-
dale and Galloway Sang of our friend Allan Cunningham, to whom
Clare expresses a great desire to be introduced; he thought, as I did,
that only 'Auld Lang Syne' could have produced such poems as The
Lord's Marie, Bonnie Lady Anne, and the Mermaid of Gallowa'. The
Lady of the Bishop of Peterborough had just made him a present of
Miss Aikin's Court of Queen Elizabeth. From Sir W. Scott he received
(I think) the Lady of the Lake, and Chatterton's Poems of Rowley, in
lieu of two guineas which were offered him; he had requested to have
the value of the gift enhanced by the autograph of Sir Walter, in one or
both the volumes, but his wish was refused. Crabbe's Works were sent
him, by Lord Milton, on the day I called at Helpstone. To see so many
books handsomely bound, and 'flash'd about with golden letters,' as he
describes it, in so poor a place as Clare's cottage, gave it almost a romantic air, for, except in cleanliness, it is no whit superior to the habitations
of the poorest of the peasantry. The hearth has no fire-place on it,
which to one accustomed to coal fires looked comfortless, but Clare
found it otherwise; and I could readily picture him enjoying, as he
describes himself in one of his early Sonnets,

    ——The happy winter-night,
When the storm pelted down with all his might,
    And roar'd and bellow'd in the chimney-top,
And patter'd vehement 'gainst the window-light,
    And on the threshold fell the quick eaves-drop.
How blest I've listen'd on my corner stool,
    Heard the storm rage, and hugg'd my happy spot,
While the fond parent wound her whirring spool,
    And spar'd a sigh for the poor wanderer's lot.
In thee, sweet hut, this happiness was prov'd,
    And these endear and make thee doubly lov'd.

163

Having directed my man to set off in an hour's time, and wait for me at the top of Barnack Hill, I walked with Clare to the lower end of the street, to see the place where 'Jenny' drowned herself. It is a large pond, partly overhung with trees; a deep wood backs the field; and in front is an ancient building, which looks like an old manor-house, but it is now in ruins: the scene is, perhaps, the most picturesque of any in the neighbourhood. Here let me refer you at once to the poem of Cross Roads, or the Haymaker's Story. It is so true to nature, so full of minute incidents, all telling the story in the most dramatic way, that any attempt to glance at it otherwise than in the words of the original, would be to destroy some portion of its interest; and altogether it is a most affecting narrative. The following lines are beautifully characteristic of those numberless recollections, which rush upon the memory after an irreparable deed is done, and seem to have been so strikingly prophetic of the fact, that our indifference to them assumes even a culpable taint, and we almost feel as if we might have prevented the mischief. An old woman, who was Jenny's companion, thus narrates the story:

[Quotes 'Poor thoughtless wretch! . . .' to '. . . her passing bell'; 'That very morning . . .' to '. . . hop'd to be forgiven']

The tale is a true one, and in a little village it would doubtless make a deep impression at the time; but Clare received it from tradition, for the circumstance happened long ago: he would learn therefore the mere fact, that such a girl was drowned in such a pond, and all those particulars which constitute the poetry of the story, would remain to be created by the activity of his own imagination. The true poet alone could so faithfully realize to himself, and few of that class would dare to dwell so intensely upon, the agonizing considerations which pass in the mind of a person intent on self-destruction: the subsequent reflections of the narrator on her own indifference in passing the pond where Jenny lay drowned, and on the unconcern of the cattle and the insects, may be, perhaps, more easily conceived, but are no less faithfully and eloquently uttered.

In our way to Barnack, we skirted the 'Milking pasture,' which, as it brought to my mind one of the most delicious descriptions I ever saw of the progress of love, shall be my apology, if any is necessary, for the following quotation.

[Quotes 'Rural Evening': 'Now from the pasture . . .' to '. . . and seals it on her lips']

But you are tired, or at least I am, with this long letter. Briefly then, suppose that I parted with my interesting companion, on the top of Barnack Hill, a place which he has celebrated in his poems; that he pursued his way to Casterton; and that after dinner I tried to put these my imperfect recollections of the day on paper for your amusement.

58. From an unsigned review, *European Magazine*

November 1821, lxxx, 453–8

As some apology for our too long neglect of these interesting and un-assuming little volumes, we beg to assure our friends, that it arose from accidental circumstances, over which we had no controul; and that our feelings towards them are distinctly the reverse of those, which with-held us from noticing the inflated quartos of Lady Morgan. In the present instance we are gratified with simple nature, seen with a Poet's eye, and depicted in a Poet's language; while in the nondescript volumes of her radical Ladyship, we have every thing but nature. Her pages of history are, for the most part, filled with a senseless tirade against all established authorities and all national institutions; and her style consists of a series of unmeaning rhapsodies, far nearer approaching to her Ladyship's old vocation of novel writing, than befitting a recorder of historical facts; while her political self importance, her religious quackery, and her unbounded egotism, are positively more repelling than downright ignorance. We may reasonably hope to be forgiven this almost unintentional digression, even upon such a disagreeable subject, as we have had no previous opportunity of noticing her Ladyship in *propria persona*; and we can faithfully assure our readers, that this will be our only transgression. Leaving Lady Morgan, therefore, to amend her Irish Tour in Italy as she feels best inclined, we now turn with additional pleasure to young Clare's Poetry, as the first fruits of that partial respite from severe labour, which literary benevolence has purchased for their amiable and deserving author. And however we may be usually compelled to coincide in that worldly wisdom, which invariably insists, that to encourage the 'idle trade' of verse-making is to spoil useful mechanics; yet deeply indeed should we condemn that avarice of humanity, which could for a moment hesitate in assisting and encouraging such an individual as John Clare. Real talent, however, loves to contend not merely with difficulties, but with impossibilities, and we can participate the almost rapture, that, with such vivid feelings as our author is gifted with, he must have hailed his benefactors' kindness. We can, in our 'mind's eye,' contrast the poor friendless beggared rustic, often perhaps without even the bare materials with which to give his poetic breathings their first rude form;—with the same individual raised to hope, happiness, connubial bliss, and domestic comfort, through the offerings of liberality at the shrine of genius, and the tributes of warm-hearted benevolence to industrious virtue. Clare may indeed exclaim,—

> Once on the cold and winter shaded side
> Of a bleak hill, mischance had rooted me;
> Transplanted now to the gay sunny vale,
> Like the greenthorn of May, my fortune flowers!

—But we must dispense with any further observations of our own, to have the pleasure of attending to the gratifying duty more immediately before us. Clare's earlier history, detailed in the introduction to his *Poems on Rural Life and Scenery*, is too extensively known to demand repetition, and we resume it therefore where it is again taken up in the present volumes, from which we quote the following additional particulars. . . .

59. Unsigned review, *New Monthly Magazine*

November 1821, iii, 579

The manner in which the first productions of this 'Northamptonshire peasant',—the 'Poems on Rural Life and Scenery', were received by the public, evinced a degree of feeling and benevolence which we were glad to find could rise above the cold and petty system of carping criticism and chilling ridicule, that act like a mildew upon the present age, wherein they are unhappily encouraged with an ungenerous avidity that threatens destruction to every nobler sentiment and more refined pursuit. We hope the 'Village Minstrel' will not be received with less favour than has already been shown to its author; for its poetical merits are quite sufficient to enable it to give pleasure to the reader, and it is calculated to excite in him feelings of sympathy and compassion, which will at any rate make him rise from the perusal of it with his heart amended, whether his taste be gratified or not. And this is Clare's peculiar excellence. He does not bring before us individual pictures, in all their provincial peculiarities, as Bloomfield does; nor can he awaken in us that deep train of reflections on life which the vigorous mind of the better educated Burns perpetually lays open to us; but he can teach us to feel for his poverty, and for the privations of that large class of society to which he belongs; he can teach us to rejoice in the pleasures and enjoyments, scanty as they may be, that fall to their lot; he can teach us to value their labours, and to extend our charities beyond the cold and calculating limits of parish dues. As a proof of his powers in this way, we would refer our readers to the poems in this collection entitled 'An Effusion'—'Address to My Father'—'Sunday'—'The Woodman'—'Sunday Walks', and 'The Cress Gatherer'. Those who have read Beattie's Minstrel with the delight which it will ever inspire in the enthusiastic, the ingenuous, and the young, will be pleased also to trace, in the artless description of the 'Village Minstrel's' feelings, the same causes producing the same effects, differing only in the modes of expression, which convey in each poem so faithful a picture of the situation and peculiar habits of the writer. It would be easy for us to interest our readers by extracts from these poems, illustrative of the various merits we feel inclined to assign to them; but, as this would carry us beyond the brief boundary to which we limit ourselves, we can only refer them to the work itself, which will be found well deserving the attention of all who take pleasure in rural imagery, in faithful delineations of nature, in the artless expression of pure and virtuous feelings,—and, above all, in the delightful contemplation of the heavenly gift of genius, yielding good and happiness to its possessor, even amid the pressure of poverty, hunger, anxiety, and almost every ill 'that flesh is heir to'. It is gratifying to reflect that most of these evils have been removed from the subject of this article by the benevolence of those to whom his merits and his privations became known by his first publication; and we trust his present performance will add alike to the modest fame and to the decent comforts which his earlier attempts were fortunate enough to procure for him.

60. From an unsigned review, *Eclectic Review*

January 1822, n.s. xvii, 31–45

This is conceivably by Josiah Conder, the poet (see Nos 23 and 81).

It still holds as true as ever, that a poet must be born a poet, he cannot grow into one; but then this must be understood not of the poetical talent so much as of the poetical character. An ear for verse and a command of language are accomplishments not less within the reach of moderate faculties and ordinary characters, than a taste in the arts, or musical skill; but not so an eye and a heart for nature, not so the calm intellectual enthusiasm, the passion for beauty, and the self-drawn happiness of the genuine poet. This is the age of mechanism. Mechanism of all kinds has been carried to its utmost perfection; and poetry, that exquisite species of mechanism, has, like every thing else, been wrought up to a steam-engine nicety. The same increased facility of production, too, which has overstocked with cottons our foreign markets, has produced a glut of literary commodities, especially in the article of verse, at home. Nor is there much fault to be found with the average quality of the article produced: if not of so durable a texture as the coarser fabric which it once cost ten times the labour to produce, it is far more smooth, brilliant, and ornamental. In other words, there is no want of good poetry; that is, lively, sparkling, elegant, classical, clever composition,—composition as superior to these poems of our Northamptonshire Peasant, as a Dutch tulip is to a hedge-row violet. But then Clare's poems have just this peculiarity, that, how inferior soever, in some points of comparison, to the works of literary artists born under a happier star, they are spontaneous, and, in the true sense, original. Though of modest pretensions, they are perfect in their kind, like every thing which Nature gives birth to. Such a poet as John Clare, education could not have made, not could adversity destroy. We may apply to him the beautiful lines of Wordsworth:

> Then Nature said.............
> This lad I to myself will take,
> He shall be mine, and I will make
> A *Poet* of my own.

These poems breathe of Nature in every line. They are, like Morland's inimitable drawings, not studies from nature, but transcripts of her works: his cattle, his birds, his trees and bushes are all portraits. There is a literal fidelity in the sketches, which only true genius could keep from sinking into vulgarity; while the rural feeling which pervades and characterizes them, gives meaning and animation to the tameness of the rural scene. The best substitute for a walk in the country —we do not mean Hampstead—to those who are immured in the metropolis, would be, so far as the mind is concerned, the perusal of some of the poems of John Clare. . . .

[Biographical details]

But we must now turn from the man to the Author. The Village Minstrel, the principal poem in the present volumes, was begun in the autumn of 1819; and was finished soon after the appearance of his former publication. To the fate of that volume, the Author alludes with natural anxiety at the end of the poem; 'and the state of dreary misery in which he then lived,' is suggested by the Editor as an 'excuse for some apparently discontented stanzas about the middle of the poem,—if any excuse be necessary for some of the most vigorous and beautiful ebullitions of true poesy, than can be met with in our language.' Lubin, like Giles in the Farmer's Boy, is at once the hero and the minstrel; but there is more of 'Edwin' than of Giles about Clare, and had Beattie been living, he might have been surprised to find the half-allegorical idea which he has imbodied in his elegant villager, realized in a living wight, who comes forward to tell his own tale. In place of the lazy young enthusiast who had nothing else to do but pipe to the rustics, or stroll for whole days among rocks and woods, and listen to a philosophical hermit, we have here a substantial English labourer, a consumer of bread and cheese and porter, who has been compelled to work hard for a bare livelihood; and if, like Edwin, he is 'no vulgar boy,' it is because his mind has been borne up by the elasticity of genius, above the vulgarizing influence of his circumstances and employment.

[Quotes 'Young Lubin was a peasant . . .' to '. . . humm'd o'er his simple song']

We have neither comments nor criticism to bestow on this simple and authentic description of Lubin's childhood, but must confess that, in interest and character, it far exceeds any imaginary picture. It is not Westall, but Wilkie, that could alone transfer the portrait to canvass. We transcribe the following stanzas, for the minute accuracy of observation which they display.

[Quotes 'And he would mark in July's rosy prime' to '. . . and still the place is seen']

'Autumn time—the cornfield—harvest-home—harvest supper—the statute—the poor sailor—the recruiting serjeant—the village feast—rural love—village sports'—these form a series of rural sketches equally graphical. But we pass them over to insert the Poet's indignant deprecation of that mistaken policy which has pushed the system of enclosure to so vexatious and ruinous an extent. Poets are not always sound political economists, in proof of which, Goldsmith's Deserted Village has often been adverted to; but it is our firm persuasion, that the changes deplored by Lubin, have, in a large proportion of instances, been decidedly prejudicial.

[Quotes 'There once were springs . . .' to '. . . old "Lea-close Oak" adieu!']

But we must not multiply our extracts; nor will it be necessary in order to interest our readers in these volumes. We shall merely, therefore, select from the minor poems, two or three specimens, which will amply shew that neither is our Poet's vein exhausted, nor has his mind stood still. There is no diminution of vigour in his later productions, although there is a visible improvement of taste. He has evidently not relaxed in his efforts, nor grown indolent from success, but has presented us with two volumes which entitle him at once to the thanks and the admiration of every lover of rural Nature.

[Quotes 'The Last of March']

There is in the first volume a very pleasing poem entitled Sunday, which we are tempted to transcribe; but as it is in the same stanza as the longer poem from which we have made so copious extracts, and has less pretensions to originality than most of the poems, we pass it over for the sake of presenting a few specimens of the sonnets. It is not a little remarkable, that Clare should have so perfectly succeeded in catching the genuine spirit, as well as mastering the rhythmical difficulties of this most artificial and delicate species of poem. He is quite as much at home in the sonnet as in the ballad. Nothing can be more unaffected, free, and natural than the flow of his versification. If he had invented the sonnet, or it had been invented on purpose for him, it could not better suit the genius of his poetry. Take for instance, the exquisite little amber gem in which he has enclosed

THE ANTS.

[Quotes]

Here are a pair of drawings fit for framing.

[Quotes 'Noon': 'The mid-day hour of twelve . . .'; 'Twilight']

We transcribe another pair; the first for its vivid and masterly colouring, the second for its beauty of sentiment; and with these we reluctantly close our extracts. The sonnets entitled, The Last of April, Summer, A Copse in Winter, Summer Morning, To an Early Butterfly, and to Autumn, are particularly beautiful; scarcely inferior, if, indeed, at all, to those which we have selected.

[Quotes 'Summer Tints'; 'Early Spring']

61. C. H. Townsend on *The Village Minstrel*

1822

C. H. Townsend to Clare, 17 January 1822, Eg. 2246, fol. 5ᵛ.

For Townsend, see No. 10c.

They [the 2 volumes] are indeed replete with the true spirit of poetry. As I predicted, the Village Minstrel does not at all interfere with Beattie's on a similar subject. It is my sincere opinion, that, in Nature, you have far exceeded his celebrated compositions. His Edwin is an impossible being, with too much sentiment, and refinement both for his age, and his situation in life—whereas your hero is, in *keeping*, throughout the poem. He feels with delicacy, and yet with truth—he is alive to the influences of nature, and yet is never seduced into unmeaning declamation.

With what delightful sonnets you have enrich'd your volumes! The sonnet was always a favourite mode of composition with me, and you excel particularly in that forcible conciseness, which presents the eye with a vivid picture, and the heart with a poetical feeling, in the short space of fourteen lines. . . . Your reputation cannot fail to be highly raised by the publication of these volumes.

62. John Clare on the disappointing response

1822

Clare to Taylor, 8 February 1822, *LJC*, pp. 131–2.
For 'The Dream' see No. 68.

I rather feel hipt[1] at the Village Minstrels success the Old Vol had gone thro 2 editions ere this & I think a notice in the London agen of a New Vol of Poems preparing is nessesary as a stimulant to revive the flatness of these for I am jealous of their ill success at least I feel something that tells me they don't go off like the others & I prevent that feeling as much as ever I can from damping my further exertions but I cannot help it doing so at some times—still I'm determined in the teeth of vexation to surmount dissapointment by unwearied struggles—under these feelings the dream was written & that is the reason of their explanation.

[1] 'vexed'.

63. An admirer on *The Village Minstrel*

1822

Henry Hawkes to Clare, writing from Lincoln, 19 April 1822, Eg. 2246, fol. 50^v.

I have just spent an hour very pleasantly in reading your 'Village Minstrell' [sic]. I love the Spenserian metre, & think you have done it justice in your easy flowing numbers. I am much delighted with the descriptions of Rural Sports, &c interspersed through the Poem, but I hope you will excuse me when I honestly tell you that I think 'Lubin' (which I suppose is a poetical appellation for the narrator himself!) was scarcely made of sufficient importance!

64. Charles Lamb on the 'true rustic style'

1822

Charles Lamb to Clare, 31 August 1822, Eg. 2246, fol. 99 (*Letters of Charles and Mary Lamb*, ed. E. V. Lucas, 1935, ii, 327–8).

Clare met Lamb (1775–1834) at Taylor's *London Magazine* dinners. Thomas Hood, in 'Literary Reminiscences No. IV', *Hood's Own*, 1839, 555–6, told how Lamb addressed Clare as 'Clarissimus' and 'Princely Clare'.

The quantity of your observation has astonished me. What have most pleased me have been Recollections after a Ramble, and those Grongar Hill kind of pieces in eight syllable lines, my favorite measure, such as Cowper Hill and Solitude. In some of your story telling Ballads the provincial phrases sometimes startle me. I think you are too profuse with them. In poetry *slang* of every kind is to be avoided. There is a rustick Cockneyism as little pleasing as ours of London. Transplant Arcadia to Helpstone. The true rustic style, the Arcadian English, I think is to be found in Shenstone. Would his Schoolmistress, the prettiest of poems, have been better, if he had used quite the Goody's own language? Now and then a home rusticism is fresh and startling, but where nothing is gained in expression, it is out of tenor. It may make folks smile and stare, but the ungenial coalition of barbarous with *refined* phrases will prevent you in the end from being so generally tasted, as you deserve to be.

65. The Rev. W. Allen on Clare

1823

From *Four letters from the Rev. W. Allen, to the Right Hon. Admiral Lord Radstock, on the Poems of John Clare, the Northamptonshire Peasant*, 1823.

This was the first, lengthy, independent assessment of Clare's poetry. Mrs Emmerson (14 March 1823) was ecstatic about it: the promise she had suspected 'has been *fulfill'd*, but, in so masterly, so sensible and so liberal & feeling a way—that any thing which I can say in favor of the Critique wd be *worthless*—so *perfect is it*, as to poetical taste & refined judgment, in my opinion' (Eg. 2246, fol. 161ᵛ). Taylor was refusing to publish it in the *London Magazine*, on the grounds that his readers were already aware of Clare. Clare seems to have thought this sensible enough. Mrs Emmerson then announced (6 May 1823) that she and Lord Radstock were going to publish Allen's work at their own expense; Murray was to print 500 copies (Eg. 2246, fol. 189). She was convinced that the critique would help Clare 'without the use of flattery', and a month later it was out (13 June), published by Hatchard and Booth. Not everyone was pleased with it. Mrs Emmerson complained that *John Bull*'s review was too partial, and Charles Elton, author of *The Idler's Epistle* (No. 67) told Clare on 8 September 1824, that 'the allusions [in the *Epistle*] to coxcomb patrons was meant for Mr. Allen, who wrote the letters on your poetry: and Rip and I both thought him a blockhead for his pains' (Eg. 2246, fol. 379ᵛ). Rip was the artist E. V. Rippingille (1798?–1859) with whom Clare struck up a lasting friendship. Allen, the incumbent of Peel, Lancashire, had his sermons published in two volumes in 1835.

LETTER I

My dear Lord,

A friend of mine, who, though he has some good points, is certainly not overcharged with brains, considers genius and great talents as public evils; and would have the possessors of them punished, in proportion to their eminence,—the little offenders with imprisonment for life, and the more daring ones with burning at the stake. Now, according to this scheme, I am afraid that your favourite Clare would meet with a hotter death than we wish. His three volumes, which you were kind enough to send me, have afforded me an unexpected pleasure; as I was not prepared to find in them any thing beyond the ordinary productions, that are courteously styled Poems. . . .   (p. 1)

In 'Summer Evening', Clare displays his talent for description, leaving, however, nothing to the imagination of his reader. He places before us an entire scene, from which we may cut out as many little pictures as we choose. For this reason, he appears to greater advantage in *extract* than most writers do. What can be finer than this delineation,— making allowance for the roughness of the fifth line, where the sound is an echo to the sense:

> The sinking sun is taking leave,
> And sweetly gilds the edge of eve,
> While huddling clouds of purple dye,
> Gloomy hang the western sky.
>
> Crows crowd croaking over-head,
> Hastening to the woods to bed.
> Cooing sits the lonely dove,
> Calling home her absent love.

Among your collection of paintings, have you a Claude that represents this?—Or this, from 'Summer Morning', to form a pair?—

> The cocks have now the morn foretold,
>   The sun again begins to peep;
> The shepherd, whistling to his fold,
>   Unpens and frees the captive sheep.
>
> Now every leaf that forms a shade,
>   And every flow'ret's silken top,
> And every shivering bent and blade
>   Stoops, bowing with a diamond drop.

> But soon shall fly those pearly drops,
>> The red, round sun advances higher;
> And stretching o'er the mountain tops,
>> Is gilding sweet the village spire.

The representation here of every leaf, flower, and blade of grass, bending with a dew-drop, reminds me of an anecdote that I must tell your Lordship:—A country painter, who was upon very good terms with himself, was employed by an ale-house keeper, to paint the sign of the Magpie, which he finished in his best style, placing the bird on the twig of a bush. When he brought it home to the purchaser, he said, 'There's a sign for you! I'll give any man a guinea that can find a single fault in it.' 'Why,' said a little boy that stood by, 'I can find a fault in it; the twig that the magpie stands upon, ought to *bend* a little.'—Now this is what Clare thoroughly understands; he makes his twigs bend when they ought. He discovers, in almost every page, an exact attention to the minutiæ of landscape circumstances. As he justly says of himself, in his *Village Minstrel,*

> ——Many a way of nature he could tell,
> That secrets are to undiscerning eyes,
> As how the bee most careful closed her cell,
> The mouse with far-fetched ear his hole supplies,
> And moles root deeper down, from winter's frowning skies.

Look, if you please, at the description of the squirrel, in the next stanza of the Minstrel,—of the rabbits coming out at evening, in the twenty-second stanza,—and of the stubble crackling with the heat of autumn, at page 89 of the same volume;—and before you lay down the book, which I advert to here by anticipation, read the lines beginnning

> And full sweet it was to look,

in 'Recollections after a Ramble'; and this part of the poem of Holywell:

> And just to say that spring was come,
> The violet left its woodland home,
> And, hermit-like, from storms and wind
> Sought the best shelter it could find,
> *'Neath long grass banks, with feeble powers*
> *Peeping faintly purple flowers;*
> And bobbing rabbits, wild, and shy,
> *Their white tails glancing on the eye,*
> Just prick'd their long ears list'ning round,
> And sought their coverts under ground.

This I consider to be the peculiar excellence of Clare. We do not find much of it in Pope,—perhaps not in Virgil,—but we do in Thomson. . . .

(pp. 13–17)

The 'Songs and Ballads' are of various merit, and I shall despatch them briefly.—They shew, that if he studied it, Clare would excel in song-writing; an art which, unfortunately, is now almost lost.—The English are grown too refined to celebrate the simplicity of Arcadian love;—and Colin, with his sweet Chloe, is driven from the plains. We have not had a new hunting song, except one from Helpstone, for many a long year; and now that Charles Dibdin is dead, the dangers and exploits upon *your* element, the ocean, will be left unsung:

————carent quia vate sacro.[1]

In exchange for all this, we have the squallification of Catalani, and the bravura of Braham; tunes without words, and words without sense; the *science* of music, and the Logierian System; and the piano-forte, through all ranks of executioners, from my Lady Duchess, down to Miss Elizabeth at the Red Lion. Clare, in this department, may be a public benefactor, if his charming and natural songs are well set to music.

I come now to the Sonnets.—This species of composition, if considered strictly, and according to the laws of such critics as Boileau and others, is the nicest, the most mechanical and therefore the least successful, in the whole range of poetry. Our modern sonneteers have contented themselves with writing fourteen lines of equal length, and have disregarded the technical division of quatrains and tercets. Clare, as might be expected, is one of these. Yet his Sonnets are his best productions. He uses them as the vehicles of his choicest thoughts, when he indulges in that loneliness of feeling, which seems to have formed his natural character. They have more strength, more finish, and, if I may use the expression, more enamel, than his longer pieces. 'The Setting Sun' I consider to be one of his happiest efforts, combining poetry with religion:—

(pp. 20–2)

[Quotes]

LETTER II

My dear Lord,

In the two volumes, containing *The Village Minstrel, and other Poems,* I expected to find some improvement in Clare, and have not been

[1] 'because they do not have a sacred bard', Horace, *Odes*, IV, ix, 28

disappointed. He retains the simplicity and originality that appeared in his former publication; but he takes now a wider scope; is generally more correct, and has more of brilliancy and polish.

His 'Minstrel' is so far upon the plan of Beattie's, that the measure of the stanza, in both, is the same; and so is the turn of expression, in some very few places. Beattie, indeed, is the philosophizing poet. He views Nature through a pair of spectacles, to which Virgil has furnished one glass, and Aristotle the other. He has the art of giving a lesson, in the most stately manner imaginable. Aiming at magnificence and romantic grandeur, he is kept in check by the dread of 'rising to faults.' He takes you to the mountains, to see the landscape, and to hear a declamation on the sciences and arts. You would suppose that he owed his poetry altogether to his education, if he did not, now and then, make free with himself, and accost you in the most delicious strains that the Muses can inspire:—

> O how canst thou renounce the boundless store
> Of charms which Nature to her votary yields;
> The warbling woodland, the resounding shore,
> The pomp of groves, the garniture of fields,
> All that the genial ray of morning gilds,
> And all that echoes to the song of even,
> All that the mountain's sheltering bosom shields,
> And all the dread magnificence of heaven;—
> O how canst thou renounce, and hope to be forgiven!

Clare is, in most points, the opposite to this. He is the unshackled poet, who looks minutely into objects, without the aid of the optician. He has no philosophy, but what is forced upon him. He is the child and pupil of Nature alone—cherishing, with filial affection, her sensibilities, doating upon her simple discipline, and living in her smiles. You can, therefore, depend upon him as her interpreter. He is the only man that can 'shew the Lions.' He takes you to the fields and woods, and points out all their beauties, in a way that enables you to see them with the same eyes that he does. In doing this, he is the poet, the painter, and the gentleman. He introduces you to the neighbouring rustics, whom you attend in their every-day pursuits, and in the celebration of their galas, till you almost become one of them. You learn, from him, their language, and their habits of thought; you see how they behave at home, abroad, and at church; you penetrate into their social and private feelings;—and return wiser and better than you went.

There is a difference, also, betweeen the purposes of the two poets,

as there is between the materials they had to work upon. Beattie's purpose was, to teach; Clare's simply to describe. Beattie endeavours to
bring natural genius under the control of education; Clare determines
to let genius wander as it will. The former was placed amidst that
mountainous scenery which is confessed to be of itself poetical;—the
latter is confined to a country naturally flat and uninteresting, and not
otherwise suitable to poetry, than his own skill can represent it.

The Village Minstrel is, as the comparison implies, the history of
Clare himself; but more circumstantial and interesting than that which
his biographer has given in the Preface. He is here, as he generally is
elsewhere, busied in his own feelings and his own descriptions,—in
descriptions that are lively and exact; and in feelings that are delicate,
tender, and melancholy. Here too, as elsewhere, he distinguishes himself
from most other poets, in being entirely free from affectation. . . .

(pp. 25–8)

The Village Minstrel is a valuable addition to our stock of English
poetry. It is full of *bijoux*. It will be a treat to the admirers of nature and
of genius. The philosopher may trace in it the effects of sensibility
and self-cultivation on the human mind. It records habits, customs, and
sentiments, which might not otherwise have been recorded but by
tradition. As a faithful and distinct portraiture of rural life in England,
it is unequalled: and it will, in proportion to its extent, supply to the
critic, if our language should become obsolete, as much scope for
inquiry and acumen, as Aristophanes himself.   (pp. 41–2)

LETTER IV

Now, my dear Lord, you will be glad that we have done. If I have
invaded your time longer than I ought, you will impute it to the difficulty of expressing myself, by letter, so briefly and intelligibly as in
conversation. I have endeavoured to shew you what *I think* of Clare;
and you will have the goodness to receive it, not as a critique, but as an
opinion. Others, whose business it is to examine such matters strictly,
may not agree with me. They may require, in a poet, more extent of
thought, more warmth of fancy, more condensation, flexibility, and
triteness of language;—in short, more of art, and less of nature, than
Clare can lay claim to. As far as the poet's province is to please and
to instruct, he has acquitted himself creditably; for his wild notes,
like those of the birds he celebrates, are highly pleasing,—and, in the
display of his subjects, there is something from which the wisest may

condescend to learn. He has done well, what would be thought difficult for *him* to have done at all. His poems are curious, as shewing the force and delicacy of native genius; and they will be acceptable, to every one to whom the language of the heart is not a dead language. (pp. 76–7)

66. John Clare on the neglect of true genius

1824

Clare to Thomas Inskip, 10 August 1824, *LJC*, p. 158.

Inskip, a watchmaker, was a friend of the Suffolk poet Bloomfield and a constant help to Clare in the early asylum years (see Introduction, p. 14). Inskip had several of Clare's poems published in local newspapers. In this letter, Clare is mourning Bloomfield's death in 1823.

I am grievd to hear of his family misfortunes were are the icy hearted pretenders that came forward once as his friends—but it is no use talking this is always the case—neglect is the only touchstone by which true genius is proved look at the every day scribblers I mean those nonsense ginglings calld poems 'as plenteous as blackberrys' published every now and then by subscription and you shall find the list belarded as thickly with my Lord this & my Lady tother as if they were the choicest geniuses nature ever gave birth too while the true poet is left to struggle with adversity and buffet along the stream of life with the old notorious companions of genius Dissapointment and poverty tho they leave a name behind them that posterity falls heir too and Works that shall give delight to miriads on this side eternity well the world is as it is and we cannot help it.

67. Charles Abraham Elton, 'The Idler's Epistle to John Clare'

1824

From the poem which appeared, anonymously, in *London Magazine*, August 1824, x, 143–5, with some omissions that were restored when the poem was printed in *Boyhood and other Poems*, 1835.

Elton (1778–1853), scholar, poet and politician, contributed several articles to the *London Magazine*. The poem, with its references to other members of Taylor's circle, pleased Clare.

So loth, friend John, to quit the town?
Twas in the dales thou won'st renown:
I would not John! for half-a-crown
  Have left thee there;
Taking my lonely journey down
  To rural air.

The paven flat of endless street
Is all unsuited to thy feet;
The fog-wet smoke is all unmeet
  For such as thou;
Who thought'st the meadow verdure sweet,
  But think'st not now.

'Time's hoarse unfeather'd nightingales'*
Inspire not like the birds of vales;
I know their haunt in river dales
  On many a tree,

* Namely, Watchmen: authority, Samuel Taylor Coleridge.

And they reserve their sweetest tales
John Clare! for thee.

I would not have thee come to sing
Long odes to that eternal spring,
On which young bards their changes ring
With birds and flowers;
I look for many a better thing
Than brooks and bowers.

Tis true thou paintest to the eye
The straw-thatch'd roof with elm-trees nigh;
But thou hast wisdom to descry
What lurks below:
The springing tear, the melting sigh,
The cheek's heart-glow.

The poets all, alive or dead,
Up Clare! and drive them from thy head;
Forget whatever thou has read
Of phrase or rhyme;
For he must lead and not be led
Who lives through time.

What thou hast been the world may see,
But guess not what thou still may'st be;
Some in thy lines a Goldsmith see,
Or Dyer's tone:
They praise thy worst; the best of thee
Is still unknown.

Some grievously suspect thee, Clare!
They want to know thy form of prayer;
Thou dost not cant, and so they stare
And smell free-thinking;
They bid thee of the devil beware,
And vote thee sinking.

With smile sedate and patient eye
Thou mark'st the creedmen pass thee by,

To rave and raise a hue and cry
      Against each other:
Thou see'st a father up on high,
      In man a brother.

I would not have a mind like thine
Thy artless childhood tastes resign,
Jostle in mobs, or sup and dine
      Its powers away;
And after noisy pleasures pine
      Some distant day.

And, John! though you may mildly scoff,
That curst confounded church-yard cough
Gives pretty plain advice, be off!
      While yet you can;
It is not time yet, John! to doff
      Your outward man.

Drugs?—Can the balm of Gilead yield
Health like the cowslip-yellowed field?
Come sail down Avon and be healed,
      Thou cockney Clare!
My recipe is soon revealed;
      Sun, sea, and air.

What glue has fasten'd thus thy brains
To kennel odours and brick lanes?
Or is it intellect detains?
      For 'faith I'll own
The provinces must take some pains
      To match the town.

       ★   ★   ★   ★   ★   ★

But, Clare! the birds will soon be flown;
Our Cambridge wit resumes his gown;
Our English Petrarch[1] trundles down
      To Devon's valley;

[1] Charles Strong, a popular translator and writer of sonnets.

Why, when the *Mag* is out of town,
      Stand shilly-shally?

The table-talk of London still
Shall serve for chat by rock and rill;
And you again may have your fill
      Of season'd mirth;
But not if spade thy chamber drill
      Six feet in earth.

Come then; thou never sawest an oak
Much bigger than a waggon-spoke:
Thou only couldst the Muse invoke
      On treeless fen;
Then come and aim a higher stroke,
      My man of men!

The wheel and oar by gurgling steam
Shall waft thee down the wood-brow'd stream;
And the red channel's broadening gleam
      Dilate thy gaze;
And thou shalt conjure up a theme
      For future lays.

And Rip Van Winkel[1] shall awake
From his loved idlesse for thy sake;
In earnest stretch himself, and take
      Pallet on thumb;
Nor now his brains for subjects rake;
      John Clare is come.

His touch will hue by hue combine
The thoughtful eyes that steady shine,
The temples of Shakspearian line,
      The quiet smile,
The sense and shrewdness which are thine,
      Withouten guile. . . .

[1] E. V. Rippingille, the artist; see No. 65.

January 1822–December 1826

68. Eliza Emmerson comments on 'Superstition's Dream'

1822

Eliza Emmerson to Clare, 1 January 1822, Eg. 2246, foll. 1–4.

This is a good example of Mrs Emmerson's desire to tinker with Clare's text (none of her suggestions was incorporated into the final version), and also of her love of the sublime. The poem, printed in the *London Magazine*, February 1822, was later included in *The Shepherd's Calendar*. Taylor told Clare on 7 August 1826 that it was 'perhaps the best poem you have written' (Eg. 2247, fol. 202). Clare sensed the originality of the piece when he saw it in print; as he told Taylor on 8 February 1822, 'I can see in a moment the Dream will do 'tis the best I've done yet' (*LJC*, p. 131). Mrs Emmerson did not want the poem to be published in the *London Magazine*; Taylor insisted, and Mrs Emmerson commented, when she saw it on 5 February, 'since it must be introduced to public notice through the medium of a half-crown publication, I am truly rejoic'd now that your name is not affixed to it' (Eg. 2246, fol. 17ᵛ). Taylor reported on 18 February, 'I don't hear so much Inquiry after the author of the Dream as you suspect would be made, but it is thought very clever' (Eg. 2246, fol. 44).

What a *Treasure* have you this day placed before me, in your 'Superstition's Dream'—speak no more to me of the 'dreadful sublimities of Byron'—for what have I to fear from them, after *your* magnificent flights of the terrible and sublime! would, my dear Clare! that I were capable of giving a *just judgment* of the *merits* of this extraordinary production of your mind—but I *dare* not *touch* upon its *beauties*! and, its faults are indeed so few, so trivial, that it were like pointing out 'spots in the sun' to name them. . . . [There is] a little occasional *obscurity*, which even seems to add a beauty to the vision—(for dreams are ever obscure), with, now & then, a *repetition* of nearly the same idea—such as 'howling prayers' 'wild confusion'—'Hope stood watching like a *Bird to fly*' instead of which might be said 'and Hope stood looking *to a Power on High*! the figure would be more powerful— & would leave your after beautiful idea of nearly the same—free to its object—'And the pale *Morn*' &c &c—'Like startled Bird whose wings are stretch'd for flight' this is a lovely figure *thus applied*! . . .

You have taken up your Subject with a high feeling of Superstitious dread—and you have supported it throughout with general perspicacity, force and beauty—not unattended with Magnificence! I should suppose my dear Clare! there is little room to enlarge upon it, from the *nature* of the *last two* lines! unless, it might be deem'd advisable *after* all y^r *trials* to add—

And still I dream'd—by Earth's destruction hurl'd
My Spirit wander'd to another World—
Where all was Heavenly, solemn, sweet, serene:
Where sat my Maker! with benignant mien—
Who stretch'd his arm, and bade my troubles cease,
There dwell, with Him, in realms of lasting Peace!!—

. . . As a *Whole* I should pronounce it the finest thing you have written, and certainly, for originality, depth and sublimity—you have not produced its equal . . . you have used the painters pencil, with the poets pen, in your delineation of the destruction of natures simple beauties. . . . And now let me *pray* of you not to allow, this *splendid effort* of yr Genius, to appear in a Magazine—it would be a *Sin*, a *shame* to do so; let it be kept sacred for your next volume.

69. Octavius Gilchrist on a magazine poem by Clare

1822

Gilchrist to Clare, 1 February 1822, Eg. 2246, fol. 13.

The poem that 'shocks' Gilchrist is 'To ★★★★' ('O lovely maid, though thou art all/That love could wish to find thee . . .'), *London Magazine*, February 1822, v, 128.

I have just opened the London, and find a poem to some wanton hussey or other by John Clare, which has so shocked me that I can write no more—fie upon it,—fie upon it!

70. John Clare on inspiration and isolation

1822

Clare to Taylor, 8 February 1822, *LJC*, p. 132.

. . . the Muse is a fickle Hussey with me she sometimes stilts me up to madness & then leaves me as a beggar by the wayside with no more life then whats mortal & that nearly extinguishd by mellancholy forbodings—I wish I livd nearer you at least I wish London woud creep within 20 miles of Helpstone I don't wish Helpstone to shift its station

I live here among the ignorant like a lost man in fact like one whom the rest seems careless of having anything to do with—they hardly dare talk in my company for fear I shoud mention them in my writings & I find more pleasure in wandering the fields then in mixing among my silent neighbours who are insensible of everything but toiling & talking of it & that to no purpose.

71. John Taylor on the need to avoid vulgarity

1822

Taylor to Clare, 18 February 1822, Eg. 2246, fol. 43.

What you ought to do is to elevate your Views, and write with the Power that belongs to you under the Influence of true Poetic Excitement—never in a low or familiar Manner, unless at the Time some strong Sensibility is awakened by the Situation of the Writer or those he writes about. For this Reason I cannot quite admire your Imitation of Wordsworth, though it is very clever—to him it is out of the Way to write on the familiar Topics of humble Life—His education has made a retired, a proud philosophic Poet of him, and when he chuses a Simple Theme, it is interesting to see how such a Man will treat it. But it has a Poetry also then, from various Singular Associations which are unexpectedly conjoined with it, which it cannot have when actually written in Simple Life—it seems then too *real* to be very poetical—You should write as you would suppose he would think, to be even with him when he writes as he imagines you would think—Try by way of Experiment some little piece of the Kind I allude to—Don't make it artificial but avoid what you know & feel to be vulgar.—Between affectation on the one hand, & the common plain homely language of every Day Life on the other, there is a vast Field for your Genius to roll over in, & frolic, & kick about like a young Colt in a Pasture.

72. Some comments on 'The Parish'

1823

Clare's lengthy attempt at satire forms a companion piece to *The Shepherd's Calendar*. It was not published in Clare's lifetime, although at one stage plans were afoot (Eg. 2247, fol. 102). Clare told Taylor on 12 May 1826 that it was 'the best thing in my own mind that I have ever written' (*LJC*, p. 192). The fullest version available of the poem is in *Selected Poems*, ed. Elaine Feinstein, 1968.

(a) Eliza Emmerson to Clare, 3 February 1823, Eg. 2246, fol. 152^v. (Lord Radstock was clearly thinking along similar lines when he sent Clare some quotations from Hugh Blair on the dangers of Satire: Eg. 2246, fol. 56).

How goes on your 'Satire' 'The Parish'—is it in verse or prose?—though, in any form, I almost hate the name of Satire—however ably indulged, it is an *unamiable* use of abilities, and often serves to destroy our better faculties & feelings.

(b) Eliza Emmerson to Clare, 23 March 1823, Eg. 2246, foll. 167^v–8:

I like your 'Parish'—very much, it is powerfully written— & you have contrived to admirably blend *feeling* with severity—your 'Overseer' is represented in biting language—and the higher authority of Justice is little less keenly treated by you—however, you temper all this, by tender & pathetic appeals to their human & private characteristics as

Men! I *admire* this part of the poem exceedingly: and in short, if the *whole of it* partakes of the same feelings as the portion you have sent me, it will be a valuable addition to your stock—but *not* for *present* publication.

(c) T. Henderson to Clare, 21 May 1823, Eg. 2246, foll. 198ᵛ–9. Henderson, the head gardener at Milton, was a close friend of Clare's, and a regular correspondent.

. . . no one possesses in a greater degree the natural simplicity of language fitted for such a subject & few are better acquainted with the general details of the subject. Your general plan, and the characters you have marked out, are in my opinion just what should be. . . . I will now tell you what in my humble opinion is objectionable in it. . . . It is rather too severe—too pointed, & perhaps too personal,—not that I think you have overdrawn any character or thrown his delinquencies into broader light than they deserve,—but that I think the poem would be equally effectual, gain more readers, & more admirers, if it were less pointed & less severe.—In passing from one character to another in some instances it is rather too abrupt. . . .

73. Two brief comments on a sonnet by 'Percy Green'

1823

'Percy Green' was one of the pseudonyms adopted by Clare; there was a feeling that there had been too many sonnets in the magazines, especially the *London*, under Clare's name. The poem referred to here appeared in *London Magazine*, July 1823, viii, 46 ('Sweet brook, I've met thee many a summer's day').

(a) Taylor to Clare, 2 July 1823, Eg. 2246, fol. 219^v (for H. F. Cary, see No. 75):

You saw the Sonnet by Percy Green in the last mag, it has been much admired by our Friend Cary, who had no Suspicion that you were the Author.

(b) Eliza Emmerson to Clare, 15 July 1823, Eg. 2246, fol. 222^v:

I read the 'Sonnet' in the 'London' and instantly said to Mr. E. 'Surely this must be Clare!'

74. James Hessey on *The Shepherd's Calendar*

1823, 1824

(a) Hessey to Clare, 13 October 1823, Eg. 2246, foll. 245–6. This is an extremely important letter, for from it springs the final form of the poem. The long delay over *The Shepherd's Calendar* suggests, amongst other things, a radical rethinking of Clare's particular qualities as a poet. Hessey (see No. 11g) is referring to a batch of manuscript poems, intended for the projected new volume; he picks out some which he likes, such as 'Daydream in Summer' and continues:

I do not mean to say that several of the others are not good, but they are all so very like what you have written before that they would not do to publish. I can read them myself with great pleasure—my knowledge of the author, & my former familiarity with such scenes & objects give a charm to the descriptions which is not felt by all (by the way I should relish them much more if you would bestow a little more pains on the writing, the mechanical operation of writing I mean). The descriptions however are too personal to excite much Interest—their wants a human interest—a Story or a more particular delineation of character, and this might easily be given from the experience *you* must have had of life as well as from your own power of Invention & Combination. The Shepherds Calendar should consist of delineations of the face of nature, the operations of the husbandman, the amusements, festivals, superstitions, customs &c of the Country, and little stories introduced to illustrate these more accurately and to fix an Interest on them.

(b) Hessey to Clare, 3 November 1824, Eg. 2246, foll. 405ᵛ–6ᵛ:

I am sorry to say they [the MS. poems] are by no means fit for the public eye at present, and they will require much more alteration than we or any one but yourself can give to make them so. In each of the Poems now sent there are many beauties, but they have evidently been written in too much haste and without the fear of the Public before your eyes. The great fault of the whole of them is that they abound too much in mere description & are deficient in Sentiment and Feeling and human

Interest. You have already described in admirable colours the Morning & the Noon & the Evening, & the Summer & the Winter, & the Sheep & Cattle & Poultry & Pigs & Milking Maids & Foddering Boys—but the world will now expect something more than these— let them come in incidentally—let them occupy their places in the picture, but they must be subordinate to higher objects. A man who has travelled & mixed in Society, and read, and reflected, as you have, should give us some of the fruits of his experience & the result <of> his refl<ection>s. You may still be a descriptive poet if <you> please, but, when you describe Nature to those who see but little of her or to those who daily live with her, shew her as she appears to the Poet & the Man of Mind. Your colouring and your sketching are excellent but your Landscapes want Life and human Feelings. . . . We are anxious that you should do something to raise your Name still higher, and as you know our motive, I am sure you will pardon the freedom of our remarks.

75. H. F. Cary on *The Shepherd's Calendar*

1824

H. F. Cary to Clare, 3 January 1824, Eg. 2246, fol. 138ᵛ.

The Rev. H. F. Cary (1772–1844), the translator of Dante, wrote for the *London Magazine*, and was a sympathetic friend to Clare. In 1826 he was appointed assistant keeper of printed books in the British Museum.

I am glad to see a New Shepherds Calendar advertised with your name. You will no doubt bring before us many objects in nature that we have often seen in her but never before in books, & that in verse of a very musical construction. These are the two things, I mean description of natural objects taken from the life, & a sweet melodious versification, that particularly please me in poetry; & these two you can command if you chuse.

76. John Taylor on *The Shepherd's Calendar*

1825, 1826

(a) Taylor to Clare, 18 March 1825, Eg. 2246, fol. 469. The delay in the editing and publication of the volume was causing great annoyance to Clare; Mrs Emmerson kept prodding Taylor, who grew increasingly irritated. He explains his delay in part here: he is convinced 'that I could not make up Such a Volume from the whole Collection, answering to the Title of The Shepherd's Calendar, as would surpass the others or equal them in the Estimation of the public'.

(b) Taylor to Clare, 28 January 1826, Eg. 2247, fol. 133. Taylor comes out into the open about the delays; the MSS. are illegible, and

. . . the Poems are not only slovenly written, but as slovenly *composed*, & to make Good Poems out of some of them is a greater Difficulty than I ever had to engage with in your former Works,—while in others it is a complete Impossibility. . . . Instead of cutting out of the Poem on July what is bad, I am obliged to look earnestly to find anything that is good—Pray look it over yourself, & tell me whether there are in this long Piece any Lines worth preserving but these which I am happy to say are very beautiful [16 lines, beginning 'Noon gathers, with its blistering breath']. This is in my opinion the only *Poetry* in this long Poem. The rest is a descriptive Catalogue in Rhyming Prose of all the occupations of the Village People, scarcely one Feature of which has not been better pictured before by you.
On 17 February, Taylor wrote, 'I received the Poem of July yesterday, & was highly delighted with it.—I have not altered one word at present. . . . I feel greatly relieved by seeing that you retain all your original Powers' (Eg. 2247, fol. 146).

(c) Taylor to Clare, 4 March 1826, Eg. 2247, fol. 152:

I have often remarked that your Poetry is much the best when you are not describing common Things, and if you would raise your views generally & Speak of the Appearances of Nature each Month more philosophically (if I may so say) or with more Excitement, you would greatly improve these little poems; some parts of the November are extremely good—others are too prosaic—they have too much of the language of common every Day Description;—faithful I grant they are, but that is not all. . . . You wish to make it a complete Record of Country affairs. I would have you only make a Selection of the Circumstances that will best tell in Poetry.

77. A 'chorus of praise' for Clare

1826

Frank Simpson to Clare, 7 December 1826, Eg. 2247, fol. 236.

Simpson was a nephew of Mrs Elizabeth Gilchrist (widow of Octavius), an artist and something of a literary man. 'The Memory of Love' was one of the tales finally included in *The Shepherd's Calendar*.

I have been just reading to our Coterie one of the most beautiful poems ['The Memory of Love'] . . . & before I go to bed must attempt to describe the affect it had on us all. From the beginning to the End all was breathless Silence, a Circumstance not usual in our Readings for the wanderings to our various & incongrous occupations generally interrupt the Story, . . . but for the movement of my Father who used the Snifters by Stealth, all around me were wondering Statues. When finishd each made their Remark one admired the moral & connexion of the Story another rejoiced at the punishment of the once reckless Hero of the Tale while he whom his Friend Clare is pleased to call his Freind [sic] also & who is accustomed to peep for Beauties in Detail & Minutiae (in the Cowslips Eye) pickd out the exquisite painting of ye troubled fountain, or the twittering movements of the hopping Gold-finch &c All joined in the Chorus of Praise & rejoiced that our poet was himself again nay more than himself. . . .

9 Dec: I have been reading more of your poems & with every succeeding one am more & more delighted. I can not think it possible that he who could write such admirable things as are contained in this Vol: could have any apprehension, about the reception, they will meet with in the World of Letters, but if doubts do come across you, disregard them for when Men having one Flash of Taste, one Spark of Feeling or one Grain of Sense do not admire the unaffected Narrative of the 'Progress of Love', the Simplicity & Nature that runs thro' the 'Pastorals' or the Sublimity of the 'Dream' then is Chaos come again. The Publication of these Efforts will choke the vain railings of your envious contemporaries & smother all they have said or dare say. If this Prophecy is not fulfilled then henceforth I shall set myself Down an arrant Fool & in Matters of this Sort will forever hold my Tongue.

78. Eliza Emmerson on Clare

1826

Eliza Emmerson to Clare, 8 December 1826, Eg. 2247, fol. 238ᵛ.

Mrs Emmerson tells Clare what she has said to Taylor.

Clare's Mind, and heart, are alive to every object in Nature—*he* is the *Crucible* to receive all the scents, and hues, & forms, of simple, & material things—to analyze, and purify them, and give them forth in sweetest Song!—But in this Vol.—he proves himself capable of higher subjects than—talking of birds & flowers.

THE SHEPHERD'S CALENDAR

April 1827

---

79. John Clare, the Preface to *The Shepherd's Calendar*

1827

Hessey told Clare on 5 September 1826 that both he and Taylor thought Clare should write the Preface himself (Eg. 2247, fol. 211ᵛ). Clare drafted his Preface almost immediately on the back of a letter (Eg. 2247, fol. 212), wisely deleting suggestions of excessive gratitude and hints of his 'inability to write what my feelings are anxious to dictate'.

Prefaces are such customary things, and so often repeated, that I think good ones cannot always be expected; and I am glad that they are so, for it gives me an opportunity of saying something which I am anxious to say, and at the same time leaves me the hope that I shall be pardoned for saying it so ill. I feel desirous to return thanks to my friends, who, I am happy to say, are too numerous to speak of here in any other than a general manner. To the Public, also, I return my hearty acknowledgments; and, however awkwardly I may write them here, I feel them at heart as sincerely as any one can do; in fact, I ought, for I have met with a success that I never dare have hoped to realize, before I met it.

I leave the following Poems to speak for themselves,—my hopes of success are as warm as ever, and I feel that confidence in my readers' former kindness, to rest satisfied, that if the work is worthy the reward it is seeking, it will meet it; if not, it must share the fate of other broken ambitions, and fade away. I hope my low station in life will not be set off as a foil against my verses, and I am sure I do not wish to bring it forward as an excuse for any imperfections that may be found in them. I cannot conclude without making an apology for the long delay in publishing these Poems, which, I am sure will be readily forgiven when it is known that severe illness was the cause.

80. Unsigned notice, *Literary Gazette*

31 March 1827, no. 532, 195

Mrs Emmerson wrote on 16 June 1827, 'I am very well content with this review—it is fairly said without acrimony or jealousy— I only wish the "New Monthly" had been civil enough to have taken notice of your Book—but neither it or the "Magnet" have done so' (Eg. 2247, fol. 297). The *Literary Magnet*, however, did mention the book (see Introduction, p. 12).

There is a great deal of sweet poetry in this little volume,—snatches of song springing like wild flowers on the heath, or in the green lanes. It makes us votaries to the fine creed which in olden time esteemed the minstrel's gift 'a light from heaven,'—when the young peasant, filled with his own warm feelings, with heart attuned and awakened to the natural loveliness around, pours them out in careless, untutored, but still musical song. With much at which the critic might carp—much to which the general reader will be indifferent,—there is yet in these pages what will interest and please lovers of the gentle art. For the truth of this we appeal to the following selections.

[Quotes from 'Wanderings in June'; 'To the Cowslip']

We like the narrative parts the least: there is but little romance in vulgar life,—too much regular routine comfort in our English peasantry, to be very picturesque; and pastoral poetry partakes much, we doubt, of the general flatness of the landscape, but without its rich harvest to make the amends.

81. Josiah Conder, unsigned review, *Eclectic Review*

June 1827, n.s. xxvii, 509–21

Of the reviews, Clare preferred this: he thanked Taylor, 10 December 1827, for the reviews,'which are as usual talking of what I know not and as usual liking that least which I think best but I like the Eclectic much the best in fact I always liked it there is a heartiness in the praise and that coming from a Poet pleases me much better' (*LJC*, p. 207). Josiah Conder (1789–1855) was proprietor and editor of the *Eclectic Review* from 1814 to 1837, and a poet himself: *The Star in the East, with other Poems*, 1824, was carefully read by Clare. It is possible that Conder wrote earlier notices of Clare in the *Eclectic* (see Nos 23 and 60).

John Clare, we confess, is a favourite with us; we hope he is with our readers, and for a similar reason; he is so true to nature, that his verse may be said to reflect the very images and colouring of the scenes he describes, rather than to be the tapestry-work of the fancy. His poetry seems to have no other business than simply, as it murmurs on, to image to the mind's eye the natural objects which the season and the place may present. There they are, softened by the reflection, but just as they breathe or bloom; and any poor wight, in cities pent, by means of this *camera lucida*, may see them as he sits with his book in his hand, by the side of his hanging garden of flower-pots, uttering his melancholy *O rus, quando te aspiciam*?[1] We dare not vouch, however, that every one

[1] 'O country home, when shall I see you?' Horace, *Satires*, II, vi, 60.

of his readers will have true pastoral taste enough fully to relish his poetry, or be able to appreciate the nice observation which it discovers. To those who would think the country dull, John Clare's poetry must needs be insipid. He is professedly but a landscape-painter, and not of Turner's school; he might rather be compared to Morland, only that, in sentiment and feeling, he rises so far above him. But we are not sure whether we may not have said all this, or something like it before; and as it is only five years since we had the last occasion to speak of the merits of our Village Minstrel, our readers will doubtless have in recollection the critique which we then offered. We shall, therefore, without further prologue, advert to the contents of the present volume.

We know not whether our Poet is aware that he has been forestalled in his title by Spenser, who has also a Shepherd's Calendar, written in the fantastic style which was then so fashionable. But his amorous shepherds and goatherds, Cuddy and Colin, Hobbinol and Diggon, are mere awkward maskers, while the scenery is all pasteboard. Nothing is more astonishing than the total absence of descriptive beauty, and rural feeling, and observation of nature, from these eclogues, and from almost all the pastorals of the old school The scene is laid in a cockney Arcadia, and the lady and gentlemen shepherds are evidently pining for want of fresh air. As Dan Spenser singeth,—

> All as the sheep, such was the shepherd's look,
> For pale and wan he was, alas! the while:
> 'May seem he lov'd, or else some care he took;
> Well couth he tune his pipe and frame his stile,
> Tho' to a hill his fainting flock he led,
> And thus he plain'd the while his sheep there fed.

Cowley, though by no means a natural poet, except in his prose, revels in his garden; and Milton, when he gets a holiday, plays L'Allegro to admiration,—although he soon grows tired of Buckinghamshire, and

> Towered cities please us then,
> And the busy hum of men.

Milton nevertheless loved nature, and could paint a paradise. But after him comes a dreary interval. From Dryden to Thomson, it has been remarked, that scarcely a rural image drawn from life is to be found in any of the English Poets, except Gay. Thomson deserves great credit for the choice of his subject, and though his theme and his genius were not very well suited to each other, it was a fortunate match for the fame of

the Poet: the Author of Liberty and Britannia would have been forgotten. Thomson undoubtedly takes us into the country, but we feel, in
his philosophic company, too much like school-boys taking a walk with
their master in rank and file, who long to run away from his sage
lectures, to gather cowslips or go birds' nesting. Cowper was the first
poet who taught his readers how to look at the country, and to love it
for its own sake, and to turn to nature as a living fountain of consolation.
Since Cowper, a wonderful revolution has taken place in English
poetry. Our lakes and mountains have been vocal with poets, and the
consequence has certainly been, the infusion of a most healthful vigour
into our poetical literature. For nice observation, and fidelity, and native
feeling, Clare however, will stand a comparison with any of our descriptive poets. If we meet with few elevated sentiments or philosophic
remarks, which in him could only be affectation, it is high praise, but
well deserved, that he is always natural and in character, and never aims
at a style above his compass.

The Shepherd's Calendar consists of twelve poems on the several
months of the year, written in different measures, and with a happy
variety of style. We take the fourth of the series, as being of convenient
length; and it recommends itself also by a touching sort of beauty, like
that of the spring leaf which seems to have lent its vivid colour to the
verse.

[Quotes 'April']

The opening lines of 'May' would form a good subject for Wilkie,
were it not that painting cannot be so picturesque as language, which
can express, as Dugald Stewart remarks, picturesque sounds as well as
sights, and picturesque sentiments also. The 'swarthy bee teazing the
weeds that wear a flower',—the school-boy 'viewing with jealous eyes
the clock,'—the driving boy 'cracking his whip in starts of joy,'—
these are images full of life and beauty, which cannot be expressed on
the canvas. Having thus long dwelt upon the Spring, we must take one
specimen from Summer.

[Quotes 'July']

Nothing, we think, can be more perfect than this summer picture of
still life, with its entomological embellishments. While we dwell upon
the scene, we seem to become boys again, and long to have a pelt at that
same squirrel. And though our heart has never 'danced with daffodils,'
as Mr. Wordsworth has it, many a time have we watched the insect

sports which Clare has so happily described. But, perhaps, we should have done better to select extracts more intelligible to the uninitiated in these minute mysteries of nature. The volume appears without any table of contents. and we must therefore supply one. The Shepherd's Calendar is followed by three beautiful narrative poems, entitled, The Sorrows of Love, The Progress of Love, and The Memory of Love; and a 'Pastoral,' or what some would have called an eclogue, entitled, The Rivals. The remainder consists of miscellaneous poems. Among these, it is with sincere satisfaction that we perceive an occasional thoughtful reference to such topics as death and eternity; the total avoidance of which in most of the poems, excites the fear, that the Poet has not yet learned to look upon the beauties of Nature as faint types at best of a far more exceeding and eternal glory,—has not yet drunk into that spirit which should enable him, amid the scenes of his rural wanderings, to

> lift to Heaven an unpresumptuous eye,
> And smiling say, My Father made them all.

We do not now speak as critics, for it were not fair to find fault with his poems for what they do not contain; nor would we wish the Poet to affect sentiments he does not feel, and to *hitch in* an awkward sentence or two of a religious complexion. There are 'tongues in trees' and 'sermons in stones,' and in this species of divinity, Clare's poetry is not deficient. It is for his own sake, as much as for that of his readers, that we could wish him oftener to

> reach the Bible down from off the shelf,
> To read the text, and look the psalms among:—

till, haply, he might imbibe from the sacred page a higher inspiration, and perceive, not only how 'the heavens declare the glory of God,' but that 'the statutes of the Lord are right, rejoicing the heart, and his testimonies sure, making wise the simple.' Then, should he live, as we hope he will, to produce a fourth volume, we should expect to find him reaching a higher strain.

The present volume, as compared with Clare's first efforts, exhibits very unequivocal signs of intellectual growth, an improved taste, and an enriched mind. This progressive improvement is one of the surest indications of a mind endowed with the vigorous stamina of genius. When he first appeared before the public, it was as a Northamptonshire peasant, in fact a day labourer; and the public were led to wonder how an individual so circumstanced should have been capable of writing genuine poetry,—how such a flower should have sprung up under the very harrow of poverty. It is seven years since that volume appeared, and we reflect with satisfaction, that, from our Journal, Clare met with (we believe) the earliest notice and the most cordial praise. We could not, however, refrain from expressing our doubt as to the possible effect of further cultivation upon the native originality of his mind. We hardly ventured to hope that he would so far excel his early efforts as he has since done. In the preface to the present volume, he expresses a just and manly confidence of success. 'I hope,' he says, 'my low station in life will not be set off as a foil against my verses; and I am sure I do not wish to bring it forward as an excuse for any imperfections that may be found in them.' We like this spirit. There is a sort of praise which, in its tone, differs little from contempt, and with which no poet would be satisfied. His compositions may now challenge admiration on the ground of their intrinsic merit and interest. Although we have already extracted somewhat largely, it would hardly be doing justice to the volume, to withhold a specimen of his success in narrative poetry; but we can make room for only a short specimen, with which we shall conclude this article.

[Quotes from 'The Sorrows of Love']

82. Unsigned notice, *London Weekly Review*

9 June 1827, i, 7

We happened to open this little book in so pleasant a mood, that we almost felt our judgment might be somewhat improperly biassed in the estimate of its intrinsic merits. We had not, however, perused many pages before we discovered that our self-suspicions were wholly ground-less. Wretched taste, poverty of thought, and unintelligible phraseology, for some time appeared its only characteristics. There was nothing, per-haps, which more provoked our spleen than the want of a glossary; for, without such an assistance, how could we perceive the fitness and beauty of such words as—*crizzling*—*sliveth*—*whinneys*—*greening*—*tootles*—*croodling*—*hings*—*progged*—*spindling*—*siling*—*struttles*, &c. &c.

We observed also in the author a servile imitation of some of the most objectionable peculiarities of other poets. He abounds with such lines as the following, which are marked by the vices of Crabbe's singular style, without one redeeming trait of that forcible and graphic poet.

> But *turned* a look on Jockey as she *turned*.

> To *miss* whose tasting seems a heaven to *miss*.

> And *sighed* and urged, and Jenny could but *sigh*.

> And *please* a maiden whom he wished to *please*.

But it is by no means our intention to pass an unqualified condemnation on the whole of this little work, towards the close of which there are many passages of great beauty. We must except, however, from all praise, an absurd piece of doggrel and bombast, styled 'A DREAM.' It appears to have been suggested by Lord Byron's extravagant but powerful poem, entitled 'DARKNESS.' As a sufficient proof of the justice of our censure, we extract the following specimen taken almost at random:—

> Amid the dread of Horror's dark extreme,
> I lost all notion of its being a dream!!
> Sinking, I fell through depths that seemed to be
> As far from fathom as eternity.
> Where dismal faces from the darkness came,
> With wings of dragons, and with fangs of flame;
> Writhing in agonies of wild *despairs*,
> And giving tidings of a doom like theirs.

As we shall not have space for complete poems, we shall extract a few detached verses, which will, we hope, sufficiently testify that the author has feelings and powers not unworthy the notice of the lovers of genuine poetry; and that, when he chooses to observe nature with his own eyes, and write from his own impulses, he is often eminently happy in his images and descriptions. . . .

[Quotes selectively]

83. Unsigned review, *Literary Chronicle*

27 October 1827, no. 441, 674–5

Clare told Harry Stoe Van Dyk, a friend of whom had written this review, 'tho I feel highly pleased with it I cannot dare to take all the praise to myself which you & some friend of yours has kindly given me' (*LJC*, pp. 206–7). Van Dyk, a minor versifier, had helped to edit *The Shepherd's Calendar*; he had told Clare on 19 October that 'your new poems please me exceedingly—some of the thoughts are beautiful & their beauty is heightened by the simplicity & nature with which you have expressed them. I like thoughts as I like pretty women—the less dress upon them the better' (PMS. F1, p. 82).

We have been always admirers of John Clare, and were among the first to acknowledge his claims to that station in the poetical literature of our country, to which his native and undefiled genius entitled him; and which he has now for several years occupied with great and increasing reputation. We saw in him more than in any of the rustic bards who have arisen in a period so prolific in versifying talent—that delicate sense of the beautiful in nature, and that varied and comprehensive facility in describing the rural objects with which he was most familiar, —that strength of imagination and intensity of feeling, without which there can be no real poetry, nor any lasting fame. In these respects, and, we trust, with no unjustifiable enthusiasm, we have not scrupled to consider him the English rival of the bard of Ayr. Of each, it may be said with equal justice:—

> The linnet in simplicity;
> In tenderness, the dove;
> But more, oh, more than all, is he
> The nightingale in love;

and the parellel holds good, not less in the genius than in the checquered fortunes of both these delightful poets.

The Shepherd's Calendar, as will be readily conceived, is indeed a *shepherd's* description of the varying phenomena of the months, and only in its general features resembling the Seasons of Thomson, and the Months of Leigh Hunt. Less imaginatively poetical than the former, and not quite so fanciful or full of sentiment as the latter; yet are these pictures sketched with a master-hand, and possess the vivid colouring and peculiar freshness with which it is the province of genius to invest every the most exhausted subject. From this part of the volume we select November, and when we say that the other portions of the Calendar are rarely inferior to that most powerful poem, we have said enough to recommend the whole:—

[Quotes 'November']

The Village Stories consist of the Sorrows of Love, the Progress of Love, the Memory of Love, and the Rivals. The last is an ingenious pastoral, and all are exquisitely written. We can afford but one example of the blended power, pathos, and simplicity which characterize these stories. Our quotation is from the Sorrows of Love, and describes the final sufferings of a maiden whose heart has been won and trifled with by

> A clown, as wild as young colts free from plough,
> Who saw a prison in a marriage vow.

[Quotes 'Her friends, no longer with false hopes beguiled' to 'Who sang the psalm bareheaded by the grave']

We need not call the attention of our readers to the Shakspearian splendour of the line which we have marked.[1] A distinguished friend of Clare has quoted it in his Gondola, and we remember being struck with its powerful originality long before we were aware of its being the property of the latter.—There are several minor poems, of which the Wanderings in June, the Approach of Spring, and the Last of Autumn, bear the genuine impress of the Village Minstrel; whilst the Dream and Antiquity aim at higher praise, are conceived in a loftier spirit, and possess, in our opinion, an almost Byronic strength and originality. We give one passage of the first:

[Quotes 'Fierce raged Destruction . . .' to '. . . lick'd their master's feet']

---

1 'While anguish rush'd for freedom to her eyes'. *The Gondola* was a novel, published in 1827, by Van Dyk.

This volume is an additional confirmation of our opinion, long ago expressed, that its author in accurate pictures of rural scenery, in depth of feeling, and originality of observation, is inferior to no poet of the day. We had almost forgotten to notice a very sweet frontispiece, after Dewint, most beautifully etched by Finden. It is illustrative of August; a group of harvesters are enjoying themselves at 'bevering time;' the maidens seated on the sheaves, and the swains beside them on the ground. We know of no artist whose style is so peculiarly adapted to the illustration of our poet as that of Dewint; for the same graceful touch, the same truth to nature, and the same sunny beauty equally distinguish the artist and the bard.

THE PERIOD PRIOR TO PUBLICATION OF *THE RURAL MUSE*: INCIDENTAL COMMENTS

January 1828–January 1833

---

84. Some comments on 'Autumn' and 'Summer Images'

1828, 1829, 1830, 1831

These two poems showed the clear influence of Collins on Clare; both poems were very carefully worked over in rough drafts.

(a) Eliza Emmerson to Clare, 18 January 1828, Eg. 2247, foll. 393ᵛ–4. She thanks Clare for his 'charming "Ode to Autumn"'; it is 'by far the best, & choicest thing you have produced—it is well constructed—your *Images*, & *Epithets*, are admirably chosen, & beautifully supported thro'out the poem!' Of the last 3 stanzas she exclaims, 'If this is not poesy & pathos & simplicity and originality, I have no *discrimination*, or *feeling*, or taste in the composition of the pastoral Ode!'

(b) Allan Cunningham to Clare, 20 March 1828, Eg. 2247, fol. 422. Cunningham (1784–1842) published the slightly altered poem in his *Anniversary*, 1829, 75–9, as an 'Ode to Autumn'. He told Clare that it was 'one of the very happiest Poems you have written—full of nature and truth.'

(c) Eliza Emmerson to Clare, 26 February 1829, Eg. 2248, fol. 121ᵛ:

Why not . . . write, an *Ode* to Spring, as following up your successful

Autumn, write in the same *lovely* & *familiar style* of language, & I am sure you will have it much admired.

(d) Eliza Emmerson to Clare, 10 November 1830, Eg. 2248, fol. 294:

What a train of lovely visions she [your Muse] hath brought unto me— 'Summer Images' yea, in all their glowing beauty, in all their native freshness, and simplicity of attire:—truly, this muse of thine, is a most *bewitching* sort of *modeller*—she makes dame Nature and her progeny (tho' always the same) ever varying, *ever new*—she robes them with such peculiar grace. Such resistless modesty—that, we can only stand and gaze and gaze, and wonder at the artist's skill!

(e) Taylor to Clare, 6 July 1831, Eg. 2248, fol. 371:

I cannot altogether approve the Poem of 'Summer Images', in many Parts it is as good as anything you ever wrote, but it is too long, too little select—you have gathered into it many Images which you have given before in Language sometimes more happy,— & it rambles too much.

85. Thomas Pringle on Clare and fashion

1828

Thomas Pringle to Clare, 16 August 1828, Eg. 2248, fol. 29.

Thomas Pringle (1789–1834), the Scots poet, edited, amongst other things, *Friendship's Offering*, to which Clare contributed several poems.

I see you as a manly straight forward honest man—such another as our mutual friend Allan Cunningham— & your native taste has not been spoiled by the puling fastidiousness of literary fashions.

86. John Clare and George Darley on action in poetry

1829

Clare told Taylor at the end of December 1828 that he was at work on a new poem, 'The Pleasures of Spring'. Taylor had his reservations; Clare replied on 3 January 1829. The poem was not published in Clare's lifetime, but it is included in W. K. Richmond, *Poetry and the People*, 1947, pp. 230–42 (see No. 139). George Darley (1795–1846), poet and mathematician, seems to have agreed with Taylor over the shortcomings of the poem.

(a) Clare to Taylor, 3 January 1829, *LJC*, p. 222:

Your opinion of my intended Poem is in some instances correct for the same images must certainly occur of which I have written before yet if I could succeed others would be added that would do away the impression of repetition but action is what I want I am told & how action is to get into the pleasures of Spring I cannot tell

I think many of the productions of the day that introduce action do it at the expense of nature for they are often like puppets pulled into motion by strings & there are so many plots semiplots and demiplots to make up a bookable matter for modern taste that its often a wonder how they can find readers to please at all.

(b) Darley to Clare, 14 March 1829, Eg. 2248, fol. 130 (C. Colleer Abbott, *Life and Letters of George Darley*, 1928, pp. 77–8):

There have been so many 'Pleasures of So-and-So', that I should almost counsel you against baptizing your Poem on Spring—the 'Pleasures' of anything. Besides, when a poem is so designated, it is almost assuredly prejudged as deficient in *action* (about which you appear Solicitous). 'The Pleasures of Spring', from you, identified as you are with *Descriptive* Poesy, would, almost without doubt, sound in the public ear as the

213

announcement of a series of literary scene-paintings. Beautiful as these may be, and certainly would be from your pencil, there is a deadness about them which tends to chill the reader. . . . But I cannot see why you might not infuse a dramatic Spirit into your poem on Spring, which is itself only the development of the living principle in Nature. See how full of life those descriptive scenes in the Midsummers' Night's Dream, and the Winter's Tale are! . . . The hooks with which you have hitherto fished for praise in the ocean of literature, have not been garnished with *live-bait*; and none of us can get a bite without it. How few read 'Comus', who have 'The Corsair' by heart! Why? because the former, which is almost 'dark with the excessive bright' of its own glory, is deficient in human passions and emotion; while the latter possesses these, altho little else.

87. Derwent Coleridge on Clare

1831

Eliza Emmerson to Clare, 22 January 1831, Eg. 2248, fol. 307.

Mrs Emmerson is reporting a conversation with Rev. Derwent Coleridge (1800–83), the younger brother of Hartley; she was elated when she 'discovered' him in 1822, before he became a schoolmaster in Cornwall. He produced an edition of William Praed's *Poems*, with a memoir, in 1864, as well as a biography of his brother (1849).

. . . *you* were a favourite theme with us—he talked most kindly about you, said many things, to me, in the form of *advice* in your poetic character, as *to subjects* & the mode of expressing your *feelings* & *ideas* —he admires your *tender* compositions very much.

88. Some practical advice

1831

Frank Simpson to Clare, 5 February 1831, Eg. 2248, fol. 325ᵛ.

Clare was by now becoming increasingly depressed and ill. For Simpson, see No. 77.

I will conclude with advising you to keep *your Bowels open & the Fear of God before your eyes* not jocosely but seriously & sincerely.

89. John Clare on Southey's view of uneducated poets

1831

Clare to Taylor, 7 March 1831, *LJC*, p. 254.

Clare was angry at Southey's account which appeared in *Attempts in Verse, by John Jones, an old Servant, with some account of the writer by himself, and an Introductory Essay on the Lives and Works of our Uneducated Poets*, 1830. Two reviews in particular of this work are instructive: that by J. G. Lockhart in *Quarterly Review*, January 1831, xliv, 52–82, and that by Thomas H. Lister (1800–42) in *Edinburgh Review*, September 1831, liv, 69–84. Lister commented ominously: 'Experience does not authorize us to regard it as probable, that the world will be favoured with any poetry of very exalted merit from persons in humble life and of defective education.'

Mr Southey seems to hold uneducated poets in very little estimation & talks about the march of mind in a sneering way—as to education it aids very little in bringing forth that which is poetry— & if it means [a] humble situation in life is to be the toleration for people to praise him I should say much admiration is worth but little.

90. Thomas Crossley, a sonnet to Clare

1831

Dated 19 December 1831, Eg. 2248, fol. 408.

Thomas Crossley, who lived at Halifax, published *Poems, Lyric, Moral and Humorous*, 1828, and *Flowers of Ebor*, 1837 (which included this poem and also a sonnet 'To Helpstone Cottage, The Birth Place of John Clare').

Bard of the Pastoral reed! if aught of song,
   Or poesy, a stranger should inspire,
(Whose ear, old Ebor's heathery hills among,
   Has heard the magic of thy soothing lyre;)
To thee should swell the chords of harmony,
   And to the world those feelings should impart,
Which in his bosom struggle to be free,
   And thro' his soul their quick vibrations dart.—
Oft has he conn'd, with ever-glowing heart,
Thy rural themes beneath the woodland tree, ·
   Till fast the sympathetic tears would start
From Rapture's fountain. Hence, sweet bard, would he
For thee, (O poor return for gifts like thine!)
Amid thy bays this simple flower entwine.

91. John Clare on ambition and independence

1832

Clare to Eliza Emmerson, 13 November 1832, *LJC*, p. 275.

Clare had been upset by a heated controversy over his move to a cottage at Northborough, three miles from Helpstone,—and by the desire of some to paint his benefactors in a bad light (see *Life*, pp. 357–61).

. . . all I wish now is to stand on my own bottom as a poet without any apology as to want of education or anything else & I say it not in the feeling of either ambition or vanity but in the spirit of common sense.

92. Two reactions to 'The Nightingale's Nest'

1832, 1833

(a) Eliza Emmerson, 'On reading the Nightingales Nest by John Clare', 31 December 1832, Eg. 2249, fol. 118:

> 'Up the green woodland'—did he say,
> He heard her chanting forth her lay?
> Oh! no—'tis in the *Poet's brest*
> The nightingale hath made her 'nest'—
> And given her soul of melody
> Unto the bard! Hark—cannot we

Hear in his love-inspired note,
The very warblings of her throat—
The jug-jug-jug! the plaintive moan—
The self-same spirit in each tone?
'Clare' and the 'Nightingale' are one!

(b) Frank Simpson to Clare, 20 January 1833, Eg. 2249, fol. 126ᵛ:
'. . . it is the most exquisite *bit* I ever read.'

93. John Clare, the Preface to *The Rural Muse*

9 May 1835

It is necessary that I should say something respecting the following Poems. They are selected from a great many, written at different times and under very different feelings; and if I do not crave the reader's indulgence for them, I shall be heartily satisfied of his good opinion, if he gives me the same encouragement as he has done with the others I have published; for if I wished to have it thought that I was careless of censure, or heedless of praise, I should contradict my feelings. They were written to please my own mind; but it will be a most gratifying addition to find that my old friends are as warm as usual, and waiting to cheer me with the welcome praises that encouraged me in the beginning, though ill health has almost rendered me incapable of doing anything. If I write a short Preface, it is from no vanity of being thought concise, but on the contrary, from a feeling of inability to say anything more to the purpose, and with much confidence I leave my little book to the kindness of the reader and the public.

94. Unsigned notice, *Athenaeum*

25 July 1835, no. 404, 566–7

Of all those whose genius has struggled to light through the dis-advantages of humble fortune, there have been few who, however they may have begun, can, in the end, justly be called peasant-poets—few, in whose verses, as they advance in life, traces of cultivation and book-learning do not increasingly appear either in the enlargement of the circle of their subjects, or their improved use of language and allusion. This change is natural and delightful to witness, when it does not involve the loss of that simple freshness of spirit, which is the peculiar and compensating gift of those born under such circumstances; it gladdens us to watch one fertilizing influence after another enriching a mind of high natural endowments—to observe experience and know-ledge adding to, without alloying, the rich native ore: but there is also to us something unspeakably pleasant, in these days of pretence, to light upon some lowly but not mean-minded singer, who, in his own retired corner of the world, continues to pour out the thoughts which rural life awakens, in a strain full, it may be, of delicate observation, but as artless and unworldly as that which he first spontaneously uttered on hedge-row stile, or in the loneliness of green meadows. Such a one was Bloomfield—such a one is John Clare: in fact, the verses he addresses to his predecessor might be not unaptly applied to himself.

[Quotes 'To the Memory of Bloomfield': 'Sweet unassuming Min-strel! . . .']

Hear, too, with what happy and homely simplicity he describes the sources of his inspiration; every line contains a picture.

[Quotes 'Pleasant Places': 'Old stone-pits . . .']

It will be easily gathered, then, that the songs of 'The Rural Muse' are in favour with us. Some of them are old acquaintances, but the greater number we have never seen before: we shall give a specimen or two of these.

[Quotes 'The Evening Star': 'How blest I've felt . . .']

221

We find the poet improved since we met him last; though he writes of his own progress in such a strain of pleasant and self-deceiving melancholy as the following:—

[Quotes five stanzas from 'Decay']

But, since the world began, have authors been unjust judges of their own capabilities and performances: and we can by no means agree in the last lament. In taking leave of John Clare's volume, we give it our hearty recommendation; which it deserves, were it only for these four lines, which might fitly have served it for motto.

> Joys come like the grass in the fields springing there,
> Without the mere toil of attention or care;
> They come of themselves, like a star in the sky,
> And the brighter they shine when the cloud passes by.

95. Unsigned notice, *Literary Gazette*

25 July 1835, no. 966, 465–6

O rus, quando te adspiciam![1] has been echoed by every being in city close ypent since the Roman poet uttered that nature-loving sentiment. With us it is a passion. We could babble o' green fields for ever. Even these poor geraniums, and myrtles, and roses, which cheat our window into a horticultural sort of aspect, are dear to us, independently of their price in Covent Garden market. Peter Pastoral could not love the spring more, nor ride his hobby with greater avidity at the risk of spring guns. What pleasure, therefore, it is to pore over such a number of rural images as are here presented to us. The thermometer 114 in the shade—the lightest character of dress which propriety demands—every casement staring open—punkah refrigeration throughout, *à la* Nisbett —position horizontal—the legs of the sofa iced—and this small tome in hand, it is really delightful to 'unfatigue' oneself in these dog-days, wherein, if we may judge by the heat, according to the ancient proverb, every dog has his day.

A modest preface, we are sorry to say, mentioning ill health as a companion of the bard, ushers in the sweet rustic compositions contained in this volume: and Mr. Clare thus naturally addresses his theme:—

[Quotes 'To the Rural Muse', first two stanzas]

The poet loves the country, and observes it with a lover's fondness; finding out and dwelling upon every beauty; now expatiating in their minute detail, and now clustering them together in their own wild profusion. 'Summer Images' offer many examples:—

[Quotes 'Rich Music breathes in Summer's every sound' to 'To greet me in the field']

'Thoughts in a Churchyard,' hackneyed as is the subject, breathe a tender melancholy:—

1 'O country home, when shall I see you?' Horace, *Satires*, II, vi, 60.

[Quotes]

A Sonnet to Napoleon follows this, and seems to us to be sadly misplaced amid the pathos and peace of the *Rural Muse*. What has she to do with warriors and conquerors? the true lovers of nature ought not to sing those by whom nature and the fairest things in creation are ruthlessly defaced. Mr. Clare should have kept his admiration of Napoleon for another place.

> As looking at the sun,
> So gazing on thy greatness, made men blind
> To merits, that had adoration won
> In olden times. The world was on thy page
> Of victories but a comma. Fame could find
> No parallel, thy greatness to presage.

How much better than this discordant note, is 'The Nightingale's Nest!'

[Quotes 'These harebells all . . .' to the end]

How pretty, also, is the following thought on 'Insects:'—

> One almost fancies that such happy things,
> With coloured hoods and richly burnished wings,
> Are fairy folk, in splendid masquerade
> Disguised, as if of mortal folk afraid,
> Keeping their joyous pranks a mystery still,
> Lest glaring day should do their secrets ill.

The adventures of a grasshopper are worthy of Æsop, and we regret that the poem is too long for quotation. Our limits restrict us to two examples more brief, though not less illustrative of the author: (we mean no offence)—

[Quotes 'The Ass']

Our last specimen will save us the trouble of recommending the poet and this work to the public. Certainly do we rely upon it to cause his lowly estate and poor health to be remembered where they ought to be.

[Quotes 'On Leaving the Cottage of my Birth': 'I've left my own old home of homes . . .']

96. John Wilson, unsigned review, *Blackwood's Edinburgh Magazine*

July 1835, xxxviii, 231–47

John Wilson—or 'Christopher North'—(1785–1854) was a way-ward, temperamental critic, and Professor of Moral Philosophy at Edinburgh. His review, important for its basic seriousness, did not please Taylor who told Clare on 3 August 1835 (Eg. 2249, fol. 295):

The Review is a very poor one, very Scotch & very much inferior to what it should have been. Its author has no conception of the Imaginative Faculty in Poetry, in which your Genius excels, & which is the highest Faculty of the Poet. He therefore fails to estimate properly your character as a Poet, and advises you to imitate Bloomfield! This is sad Foolery, but we must be content. I hope the Review will help the Sale of the Work—Everybody says it is the best Volume you have yet published & I am sure it is.—Had you heard what James Montgomery said of yourself & your Poems one day lately to me, you would have been very much pleased. The praise of such a man is worth having.

On the other hand Mrs Emmerson exclaimed on 10 August, 'I am rejoiced to find "The Rural Muse" meets with such *gracious* notice—all the Journals I have seen speak of your "Poems" in terms of high commendation—"Blackwood" has a very ample notice . . . the article is written with great *good feeling* in judgement.' The review reappeared, substantially the same, in *Recreations of Christopher North*, 1864, i, 313–21, with one significant alteration: 'His mind is an original one, and this volume proves it' becomes 'His mind is an original one, and his most indifferent verses prove it.' See Introduction, pp. 12–13.

It is with heartfelt pleasure that we take up a new volume of Poems by John Clare, the Northamptonshire Peasant. Some fifteen years or thereabouts, we believe, have elapsed since he earned that title which, to our ears, has almost as pleasant a sound as that of the Ettrick Shepherd. We rejoice to find that the Rural Muse has been with him during his long retirement—that his fine sensibilities have suffered no abatement under the influence of time—and that, though he says 'ill health has almost rendered me incapable of doing any thing,' it has not in any degree weakened his mental powers or dulled his genius. Let us hope that ill health may soon take its departure from 'the Poet's Cottage, Northborough,' of which, facing the titlepage, we have here so pretty an impression—and that as he is yet in the prime of life, he may live to sing many such sweet songs as these—and in domestic peace and comfort long enjoy his fame. Yes—his fame. For England has singled out John Clare from among her humble sons (Ebenezer Elliot belongs altogether to another order)—as the most conspicuous for poetical genius, next to Robert Bloomfield. That is a proud distinction—whatever critics may choose to say; and we cordially sympathize with the beautiful expression of his gratitude to the Rural Muse, when he says—

> Like as the little lark from off its nest,
> Beside the mossy hill, awakes in glee,
> To seek the morning's throne, a merry guest—
> So do I seek thy shrine, if that may be,
> To win by new attempts another smile from thee.

The poems now before us are, we think, at least equal to the best of his former productions, and characterised by the same beauties—among which we may mention as the most delightful—rich and various imagery of nature. England is out of all sight the most beautiful country in the whole world—Scotland alone excepted—and, thank heaven, they two are one kingdom—divided by no line either real or imaginary—united by the Tweed. We forget at this moment—if ever we knew it—the precise number of her counties—but we remember that one and all of them—'alike, but oh! how different'—are fit birth places and abodes for poets. Some of them, we know well, are flat—and we in Scotland, with hills or mountains for ever before our eyes, are sometimes disposed to find fault with them on that ground—as if nature were not at liberty to find her own level. Flat indeed! So is the sea. Wait till you have walked a few miles in among the Fens—and you will be wafted along like a little sail-boat, up and down undulations green and gladsome as waves. Think ye there is no scenery there? Why, you are in the heart of a vast metropolis!—yet have not the sense to see the silent city of mole-hills sleeping in the sun. Call that pond a lake—and by a word how is it transfigured? Now you discern flowers unfolding on its low banks and braes—and the rustle of the rushes is like that of a tiny forest —how appropriate to the wild! Gaze—and to your gaze what colouring grows! Not in green only—or in russet brown doth nature choose to be apparelled in this her solitude—nor ever again will you call her dreary here—for see how every one of those fifty flying showers lightens up its own line of beauty along the waste—instantaneous as dreams—or stationary as waking thought—till, ere you are aware that all was changing, the variety has all melted away into one harmonious glow attempered by that rainbow.

Let these few words suffice to show that we understand and feel the flattest—dullest—tamest places, as they are most ignorantly called— that have yet been discovered in England. Not in such doth John Clare abide—but many such he hath traversed; and his studies have been from childhood upwards among scenes which to ordinary eyes might seem to afford small scope and few materials for contemplation. But his are not ordinary eyes—but gifted; and in every nook and corner of his own country the Northamptonshire Peasant has, during some two score years and more every spring found without seeking either some lovelier aspect of 'the old familiar faces,' or some new faces smiling upon him, as if mutual recognition kindled joy and amity in their hearts.

It is usual to speak of the hidden beauties of nature. But what is there to hide the most secret from our eyes? Nothing. Nature wears no veil —at least it is transparent—and often laid aside; but most men are at the best sand-blind. Their eyes are not to blame—but their minds—their hearts—and their souls. Poets alone see. Poetry shows this earth to those who have been looking at it all their days and yet have seldom seen the sights that make it so beautiful. They have indeed seen many of its things—but not felt their spirit—and what are mere phenomena to the senses? Pleasant indeed—for the senses have their own delight almost unaffected by thought—some sentiment too will belong to them by inevitable associations—but imagination's eye is spiritual, and matter seems to become so too wherever falls its transforming and creative light. All descriptive poetry is good—if it be indeed poetry; for a mere enumeration of the phenomena of nature, however accurate or exten-sive, is not poetry, nor has it ever been so esteemed; yet he must be a dunce indeed who, with any feeling accompanying his perceptions, can deal for long and at large with what nature yields, and yet never partake of her spirit, nor yet ever infuse into hers his own—so as occasionally to be inspired with song. Even in the poorest and meanest versifiers are now and then to be met with movements that show the breath of poetry was there—while the poetical reader is often so affected by the very words, however ill-assorted and uninspired, that denote things most dear, that in his delusion he attributes to the genius of him who has no genius, the delight which he in truth owes to his own instructed and easily awakened heart. But such delusion soon dies—and the power of true poetry alone is perpetual and crescent for ever.

True descriptive poetry, however, does not at any time consist in the attributing to nature whatever qualities it may please a self-conceited coxcomb, in the superabundance of his egoism, to bestow upon our gracious mother—nor in the pouring out into her lap all the diseased feelings that may happen to have been generated in his—however *intense*. The inferior followers of Shelley, Keates, Hunt, and Tennysson, are all addicted to this disgusting practice—and show it chiefly in sonnets. The men we have named are all poets—the creatures we have hinted are not even poetasters—and have brought a reproach on mere versifiers to which in their silliness they used not to be liable; while such of them as must needs be critics too, the most rickety of the set, are beginning to pollute our periodical literature. They bespatter with their praise all that is bad in their masters—and with their abuse all that is best in those who do not belong to that school. But write what they will—creeping prose or fugitive verse—they still look like creatures in a cholic. We hope they will not meddle with Clare.

The Northamptonshire Peasant always writes with sincerity and simplicity—like one to whom 'dear is the shed to which his soul conforms.' Indeed the great charm of his poetry is that it deals with what is nearest and dearest to him—and that much as he loves nature, that sweet and humble nature in midst of whose delights he lives—he never flies into any affected raptures—never seeks to intensify beyond the truth any emotion he owes to her—but confides in her inspiration with a grateful and a filial heart. And verily he has had his reward. For thus has he been privileged to converse with nature, who is well-pleased with her pious son—and makes revelations to him, at her own sweet will—as he sits beneath the old pollard, a few steps from his own cottage door, or walks

> By overshadowed ponds, or woody nooks,
> With crowning willows lined, and ramping sedge,
> That with the winds do play,
> And with them dance for joy;
> And meadow pools, torn wide by lawless floods,

Where water-lilies spread their oily leaves
On which, as wont, the fly
Oft battens in the sun;

Where leans the mossy willow half way o'er,
On which the shepherd crawls astride to throw
His angle, clear of weeds
That crowd the water's brim;

Or crispy hills, and hollows scant of wood
Where step by step the patient lonely boy,
Hath cut rude flights of stairs
To climb their steepy sides;

Then track along their feet, grown hoarse with noise,
The crawling brook, that ekes its weary speed,
And struggles through the weeds
With faint and sullen brawl—
These haunts I long have favoured.

These lines are truly descriptive—and the volume abounds with as
good and better—as our quotations, selected with little care, will show;
but Clare is profuse of images—and though very often one or two,
taken singly or by themselves, *tell* so as to give us the character of the
whole landscape to which they belong—yet full justice can be done to
his power of painting, only by presenting a whole composition—or if
not a composition, an entire series of images all naturally arising, as it
were, out of each other—as in the strain—too long, however, for
quotation—entitled 'Summer Images;'—nor less so in 'Autumn,' from
which we have taken the above stanzas. What can be more picturesque
than this—

The green lane now I traverse, where it goes
Nought guessing, till some sudden turn espies
Rude battered finger-post, that stooping shows
Where the snug mystery lies;
And then a mossy spire, with ivy crown,
Cheers up the short surprise,
And shows a peeping town.

We do not believe that any bard before Clare ever mentioned the
frog and the lark in the same stanza; yet nothing can be better than

I love at early morn, from new mown swath,
    To see the startled frog his route pursue,
To mark while, leaping o'er the dripping path,

His bright sides scatter dew,
The early lark that from its bustle flies,
To hail the matin new;
And watch him to the skies.

And having lost him there, the poet is pleased to note, with eyes withdrawn from heaven,

The jetty snail creep from the mossy thorn,
With earnest heed and tremulous intent,
Frail brother of the morn.

As the frog and the lark had been sleeping in the same new mown swath—and the poet equally rejoiced to see the one leaping over the dripping path and so pursuing his route, and the other soaring to hail his matin new—so he equally rejoices to see the snail and the swallow—the one 'from the tiny bent's dewy leaves withdrawing his timid horn,' the other (how poetically painted!)

On smoke-tanned chimney top,
Wont to be first unsealing morning's eye,
Ere yet the bee hath gleaned one wayward drop
Of honey on his thigh;
To see him seek morn's airy couch, to sing
Until the golden sky
Bepaint his russet wing.

Or sauntering boy by tanning corn to spy,
With clapping noise to startle birds away,
And hear him bawl to every passer by
To know the hour of day;
While the uncradled breezes, fresh and strong,
With cooling blossoms play,
And breathe Æolian song.

We ought to have quoted all the stanzas—but you will read them for yourselves in the little book—and will be still more tempted to do so, we are sure, by the following most natural, and, with the exception of the second one, which, however, could not well be avoided—original lines.

See how the wind-enamoured aspen leaves
Turn up their silver linings to the sun!
And hark! the rustling noise, that oft deceives,
And makes the sheep-boy run:
The sound so mimics fast-approaching showers,

> He thinks the rain's begun,
> And hastes to sheltering bowers.

But we cannot glance our eye over almost any one single page without seeing some such true beauty as these, or others of pensive, moral sentiment, let fall from an overflowing heart; as, for example, when he says that play—pastime—all that time had seemed to conceal,

> Comes like a new-born joy,
> To greet me in the field;

or when more touchingly still he calls

> The primrose, too, a doubtful dream
> Of what precarious spring may be;

or when he exclaims,

> O put away thy pride,
>   Or be ashamed of power,
> That cannot turn aside
>   The breeze that waves a flower;

or when he somewhat sadly breathes,

> The sweetest flower in pleasure's path
> Will bloom on sorrow's grave;

or, moralizing beneath the evening star, sings thus:—

> O'er the wood-corner's sombre brown
>   The lamp of dewy eve,
> No sooner up than sloping down,
>   Seemed always taking leave.

John Clare often reminds us of James Grahame. They are two of our most artless poets. Their versification is mostly very sweet, though rather flowing forth according to a certain fine natural sense of melody, than constructed on any principles of music. So, too, with their imagery, which seems seldom selected with much care; so that, while it is always true to nature, and often possesses a charm from its appearing to rise up of itself, and with little or no effort on the poet's part to form a picture, it is not unfrequently chargeable with repetition—sometimes, perhaps, with a sameness which, but for the inherent interest in the objects themselves, might be felt a little wearisome—there is so much still life. They are both most affectionately disposed towards all manner of birds. Grahame's 'Birds of Scotland' is by far his best poem;

yet its best passages are not superior to some of Clare's about the same delightful creatures—and they are both ornithologists after Audubon's and our own heart. We cannot show the genius of the Northampton-shire Peasant in a pleasanter light than by giving entire—after our use and wont—and ours alone—some of his most charming strains, sung to and of his brother choristers of the fields and woods.

[Quotes 'The Pettichaps's Nest'; 'The Skylark'; 'The Nightingale's Nest'; 'The Autumn Robin']

Were all that has been well written in English verse about birds to be gathered together, what a set of delightful volumes it would make! And how many, think ye—three, six, twelve? That would be indeed an aviary—the only one we can think of with pleasure—out of the hedge-rows and the woods. Tories as we are, we never see a wild bird on the wing without drinking in silence 'the cause of liberty all over the world!' We feel then that it is indeed 'like the air we breathe—without it we die.' So do they. We have been reading lately, for a leisure hour or two of an evening—a volume by a worthy German doctor whose name escapes us—on Singing Birds. The slave-dealer never for a moment suspects the wickedness of kidnapping young and old—caging them for life—teaching them to draw water—and, *oh nefas!* to sing! He seems to think that only in confinement do they fulfil the ends of their existence—even the nightingale. Yet he sees them, one and all, subject to the most miserable diseases—and rotting away within the wires. Why could not the Doctor have taken a stroll into the country once or twice a-week, and in one morning or evening hour laid in sufficient music to serve him during the intervening time, without causing a single bosom to be ruffled for his sake? Shoot them—spit them—pie them—pickle them—eat them—but imprison them not; we speak as Conservatives—murder rather than immure them—for more forgiveable far it is to cut short their songs at the height of glee, than to protract them in a rueful simulation of music, in which you hear the same sweet notes, but if your heart thinks at all, 'a voice of weeping and of loud lament' all unlike, alas! to the congratulation that from the free choirs is ringing so exultingly in their native woods.

Clare gives us some very feeling, fanciful, and elegant lines on 'Insects.'

[Quotes]

Time has been—nor yet very long ago—when such unpretending

poetry as this—humble indeed in every sense, but nevertheless the product of genius which speaks for itself audibly and clearly in lowliest strains—would not have past by unheeded or unbeloved; now-a-days it may to many who hold their heads high seem of no more worth than an old song. But, as Wordsworth says,

> Pleasures newly found are sweet,
> Though they lie about our feet;

and if stately people would but stoop and look about their paths, which do not always run along the heights, they would often make discoveries of what concerned them more than speculations among the stars.

It is not to be thought, however, that the Northamptonshire Peasant does not often treat more directly of the common pleasures and pains, the cares and occupations of that condition of life in which he was born and has passed all his days. He knows them well, and has illustrated them well, though seldomer in this volume than in his earlier poems; and we cannot help thinking that he may greatly extend his popularity, which in England is considerable, by devoting his Rural Muse to subjects lying within his ken and of everlasting interest. Bloomfield's reputation rests on his 'Farmer's Boy'—on some exquisite passages on 'News from the Farm'—and on some of the tales and pictures in his 'May-day.' His smaller poems are very inferior to those of Clare—but the Northamptonshire Peasant has written nothing in which all honest English hearts must delight, at all comparable with those truly rural compositions of the Suffolk shoemaker. It is in his power to do so—would he but earnestly set himself to the work. He must be more familiar with all the ongoings of rural life than his compeer could have been; nor need he fear to tread again the same ground, for it is as new as if it had never been touched, and will continue to be so till the end of time. The soil in which the native virtues of the English character grow, is unexhausted and inexhaustible; let him break it up on any spot he chooses, and poetry will spring to light like clover through lime. Nor need he fear being an imitator. His mind is an original one, and this volume proves it; for though he must have read much poetry since his earlier day—doubtless all our best modern poetry—he retains his own style, which, though it be not marked by any very strong characteristics, is yet sufficiently peculiar to show that it belongs to himself, and is a natural gift. Pastorals—eclogues—and idyls—in a hundred forms— remain to be written by such poets as he and his brethren; and there can be no doubt at all, that if he will scheme something of the kind, and begin upon it, without waiting to know fully or clearly what he may be intending, that before three winters, with their long nights, are gone, he will find himself in possession of more than mere materials for a volume of poems, that will meet with general acceptation, and give him a permanent place by the side of him he loves so well—Robert Bloomfield. Of that blameless bard how affectionately does he speak in these beautiful lines! and let them be followed by a sonnet equally so to that delightful painter of the 'level pastures'—Dewint.

[Quotes 'To the Memory of Bloomfield'; 'To Dewint']

These sonnets are in all respects honourable to John Clare. The first shows that his heart is not only free from the slightest taint of jealousy, but full of all affectionate feelings of the best kind towards his brother bard. Were Bloomfield and he personal friends? We hope so, and can hardly doubt it—though in this strange world people, whom nature made that they might love one another, pass to and fro for years almost within hand-reach, and never once meet.

Ebenezer Elliot claims with pride to be the poet of the poor—and the poor might well be proud, did they know it, that they have such a poet. Some—not a few of them, know it now—and many will know it in future; for a muse of fire like his will yet send its illumination 'into dark deep holds.' May it consume all the noxious vapours that infest such regions—and purify the atmosphere—till the air breathed there be the breath of life. But the poor have other poets besides him—'two will I mention dearer than the rest'—Crabbe and Burns. We mention their names—and no more. Kindly spirits were they both—but Burns had experienced all his poetry—and therefore his poetry is an embodiment of national character. We say it not in disparagement or reproof of Ebenezer, for let all men speak as they think and feel; but how gentle in all his noblest inspirations was Robin! He did not shun sins or sorrows, but he told the truth of the poor man's life, when he showed that it was, on the whole, virtuous and happy—bear witness those immortal strains—'The Twa Dogs,' 'The Vision,' 'The Cottar's Saturday Night,' the sangs voiced all braid Scotland thorough by her boys and virgins, say rather her lads and lasses—while the lark sings aloft and the linnet below, the mavis in the golden broom accompanying the music in the golden cloud. We desire—not in wilful delusion—but in earnest hope—in devout trust—that poetry shall show that the paths of the peasant poor are paths of pleasantness and peace. If they should seem in that light even pleasanter and more peaceful than they ever now can be below the sun, think not that any evil can arise 'to mortal man who liveth here by toil,' from such representations—for imagination and reality are not two different things—they blend in life—but there the darker shadows do often, alas! prevail—and sometimes may be felt even by the hand—in poetry the lights are triumphant—and gazing on the glory men's hearts burn within them—and they carry the joy in among their own griefs, till despondency gives way to exultation, and the day's darg of this worky world is lightened by a dawn of dreams.

This is the effect of all good poetry—according to its power—of the poetry of Robert Bloomfield as of the poetry of Robert Burns. John Clare, too, is well entitled to a portion of such praise; and by following our advice his name may become a household word in the dwellings of the rural poor. Living in leisure among the scenes in which he once toiled, he can contemplate them all without disturbance—having lost none of his sympathies, he has learnt to refine them all and see into their source—and wiser in his simplicity than they who were formerly his yoke-fellows are in theirs, he knows many things well which they know imperfectly or not at all, and is privileged to be their teacher. Surely in an age when the smallest contribution to science is duly estimated, and knowledge not only held in honour but diffused, poetry ought not to be despised, more especially when emanating from them who belong to the very condition which they seek to illustrate, and whose ambition it is to do justice to its natural enjoyments and appropriate virtues. In spite of all they have suffered, and still suffer, the peasantry of England are a race that may be regarded with better feelings than pride. We look forward confidently to the time when education—already in much good—and if the plans of the wisest counsellors prevail, about to become altogether good—will raise at once their condition and their character. The Government has its duties to discharge—clear as day. And what is not in the power of the gentlemen of England? Let them exert that power to the utmost—and then indeed they will deserve the noble name of 'Aristocracy.' We speak not thus in reproach—for they better deserve that name than the same order in any other country; but in no other country are such interests given to that order in trust—and as they attend to that trust is the glory or the shame—the blessing or the curse—of their high estate.

It is right that every Poet, high or humble, should be an egotist. Clare speaks much—but not too much—of himself—for always in connection with his lot, which was a lot of labour from which his own genius—and we believe the kindness of friends—(are we mistaken in naming Lord Fitzwilliam and John Taylor?)—have set him free. The grateful lines with which the volume concludes, seem to us to be addressed to Mr Taylor—and we remember that he was an active friend of Clare's on his first appearance before the public. Here is a pleasant picture of the Northamptonshire Peasant's domestic life.

[Quotes 'Home Happiness']

Our eye has this moment fallen on a few lines in a different strain—which seem to us very beautiful—and therefore we quote them, though in this part of our critique they may not be quite in place.

[Quotes 'On an Infant Killed by Lightning']

But perhaps the pleasantest portion of the volume is that which consists of sonnets—no fewer than eighty-six—and almost all expressive of 'moods of my own mind,' when meditating either on his own lot or on that of his rural neighbours. Why does our able friend, the literary critic in the *Spectator*, when speaking of the Reverend Charles Strong's sonnets—which are excellent—say—'But we have already stated our *indifference* to this mode of composition; and Mr Strong cannot overcome the *antipathy* which Milton and Wordsworth fail in conquering?' Indifference and antipathy seem to us scarcely to be synonymous—but the feeling must be as strong as it is strange—and, pardon us for saying so—irrational—which the united power and majesty of Milton and Wordsworth fails to conquer. Let us hope that it is merely monomania —and that our friend is otherwise sane. In the humble hands even of John Clare, the sonnet discourses most excellent music. Here are Twelve. Let our good Spec avert his eyes from them with indifference and antipathy, while, well-pleased, run over and then rest upon them all eyes besides—and smile thanks to Maga for the rural feast.

[Quotes 'Sedge-bird's Nest'; 'The Thrush's Nest'; 'The Happy Bird'; 'The Mole'; 'The Shepherd's Tree'; 'The Shepherd Boy'; 'A Pleasant Place'; 'The Milking Shed'; 'Sudden Shower'; 'The Old Willow'; 'First Sight of Spring'; 'Pleasant Places']

We have now done what we could to bring before the public the new merits of an old favourite—and we hope that he will meet with something more substantial than praise. All that they who wish to befriend him have to do is to buy each a copy of the Rural Muse. A few editions will thus soon slip off—and the poet's family be provided with additional comforts. The pigeons are sitting on the roof, cooing their sweet undersong, and get peas and barley in abundance at home or afield—but there are other creatures below that roof not so easily fed—though they have never yet been heard to murmur but in happiness—and the poor, far beyond the reaches of the souls of the rich, feel that Scripture—'the day cometh in which no man can work.' The creeping plants look pretty in front of the poet's cottage, but they bear no fruit. There is, however, a little garden attached—and in it may he dig without anxiety—nor need to grudge among the esculents the gadding flowers. Does he keep bees? He does. Then we know how to enable him to increase the number of his hives. A cow? Probably. Let us take care she has both grass and fodder, and become a miracle of a milcher. Call we this charity? Not at all. Clare is contented, and his Patty has her handful for the beggar at the door, her heart-full for a sick neighbour. His volume is worth ten times over what you will have to give for it—and on your side, in good troth, should be the gratitude. Purchase then pleasant thoughts, and it will be your own fault if you cannot enjoy them—should that be the case you are but a trifle out of pocket, and can have recourse to turtle, venison, and pine apple—and again be blest.

Our well-beloved brethren—the English—who, genteel as they are —have a vulgar habit of calling us *the Scotch*—never lose an opportunity of declaiming on the national disgrace incurred by our treatment of Burns. We confess that the PEOPLE of that day were not blameless—nor was the Bard whom now all the nations honour. There was some reason for sorrow—perhaps for shame—and there was avowed repentance. Scotland stands where it did in the world's esteem. The widow out-lived her husband nearly forty years—she wanted nothing—and was happy; the sons are prosperous—or with a competence—all along with that family all has been right. England never had a Burns. We cannot know how she would have treated him—had he 'walked in glory and in joy upon *her* mountain-sides.' But we do know how she treated her Bloomfield. She let him starve. Humanly speaking we may say that but for his imprisonment—his exclusion from light and air—he would now have been alive;—as it was—the patronage he received served but to protract a feeble, a desponding, a melancholy existence,—cheered at times but by short visits from the Muse, who was scared from that dim abode—and fain would have wafted him with her to the fresh fields and the breezy downs—but his lot forbad—and generous England. There was some talk of a subscription—and Southey, with hand 'open as day to melting charity,' was foremost among the Poets. But somehow or other it fell through—and was never more heard of—

and mean while Bloomfield died. Hush then about Burns. Pretend to admire what you cannot read—leave *the Scotch* to their own reflections on the fate of their Ploughman—and explain to us at your leisure in what lay the grace of English gratitude to your Farmer's Boy.

97. Two readers on *The Rural Muse*

1835

Eliza Emmerson to Clare, 26 July 1835, Eg. 2249, foll. 292ᵛ–3.

Mrs Emmerson had presented a copy to Derwent Coleridge (see No. 87), and Alaric Watts discussed the merits of the new volume with her. Watts (1797–1864) was a poet of sorts, a contributor to the *Literary Gazette*, and from 1824 editor of the *Literary Souvenir*, one of the most popular of the annuals.

Mr Coleridge considers *this volume* to be a very great advancement to your literary fame, he particularly noticed your *improved style* and *increased power* of *language*—with many other kind & flattering remarks, he concluded by saying 'If this little volume of Clare's had come out *twenty* years *ago*, it would have made a great sensation in the poetic world—and it is certain to greatly increase his reputation as a Poet *now* & *hereafter*!'

[Alaric Watts told her] it was one of the sweetest and best little books of poetry he had seen for many years.

98. Unsigned notice, *New Monthly Magazine*

August 1835, xliv, 510

Mr. Clare's muse, at all times chaste and elegant, and frequently reaching a pathos and feeling uncommon enough in these days of superficial writing, has contributed some of his happiest productions to grace the present volume. The reader will also be pleased to observe a far superior finish, and a much greater command over the resources of language and metre in the later compositions of this truly pastoral writer, who, presented at first to the public notice by the genuine spirit of poetry displayed in his less experienced days, has gone on constantly improving, and enlarging his claim to popular approbation. The poem which opens his last work, an 'Address to the Rural Muse,' will be found a very favourable illustration of what we have observed. It is a fine specimen of manly feeling, and of that quiet inspiration which, without any ostentatious attempt at display, speaks directly and powerfully to the heart. 'Summer Images' is another beautiful poem, and affords a pleasing example to show from what common materials a superior composition may be produced under the touch of a skilful hand. The pieces which follow are of various degrees of merit, but almost all of a character likely to add to Mr. Clare's fame. We would particularly specify 'The Eternity of Nature,' Stanzas 'On seeing a Skull on Cowper Green,' 'The Autumn Robin,' and 'The Skylark.' Of the sonnets we are not inclined to think so highly. It is given but to few names in literature to overcome the difficulties attending the most common, and at the same time most wayward and perplexing kind of composition. The simply pathetic and pleasing,—all the more gentle emotions, whether joyful or melancholy,—which the contemplation of Nature in her most familiar garb is qualified to inspire, fall legitimately within the province of Mr. Clare's singularly felicitous power of song. As long as he keeps to these, there is no fear of his being accounted otherwise than as a poet who must be a general favourite with all in whom a love of his art is inherent; to his name, we may add, the volume he has just published will add no trifling increase of reputation.

99. Unsigned review, *Druids' Monthly Magazine*

1835, n.s. ii, 131-4

> Then Nature said
> This lad I to myself will take
> He shall be mine, and I will make
> A poet of my own.

The readers of 'The Druids' Magazine' will remember that it contained some short time since, one or two original poems by John Clare; such as are admirers of the loveliness and truth of poetry, will be glad that the 'Northamptonshire Peasant' has just published a new volume, under the most appropriate title of *The Rural Muse*.

The poetry of Clare is entirely distinguishable from all others, by the richness and profusion of its imagery: an observer the most acute—an admirer the most passionate—a painter the most graphic of the beauties of nature,—his poetry is a beautiful scene laid before us of woodland, copse, field, meadow, and roadside, with the voices of birds and the humming of insects coming on the gentle breezes, and the delicate perfume of field-flowers, making the air faint with its luxuriance: there is not perhaps a single verse in all Clare's descriptive poetry which is not as distinct and perfect a picture as the most finished delineator of nature might give; it is true he has not 'dipped his pencil in the rainbow' to give a more alluring or artificial effect—he has described things as they exist, with the fidelity to the original, that we cannot separate the reality from the description. Every one who has visited the country—and who has not?—must see at once the most perfect beauty of the following lines:—

PLEASANT PLACES.

> Old stone-pits, with veined ivy overhung;
> Wild crooked brooks, o'er which is rudely flung
> A rail, and plank that bends beneath the tread;
> Old narrow lanes, where trees meet over-head:
> Path-stiles, on which a steeple we espy,
> Peeping and stretching in the distant sky;

Heaths overspread with furze-bloom's sunny shine,
Where Wonder pauses to exclaim, 'Divine!'
Old ponds, dim shadowed with a broken tree;—
These are the picturesque of Taste to me;
While painting Winds, to make complete the scene,
In rich confusion mingle every green,
Waving the sketchy pencils in their hands
Shading the living scenes to fairy lands.

Why every line is in itself the spot that it describes,—a picture worthy of the pencil of Gainsborough! Was there ever a better expressed line than

Old ponds, dim shadowed with a broken tree?

It is not only in the outline of nature that Clare excels; in the very minutiæ of insect and vegetable life he is equally correct: in all the shades and changes of rural scenery, and every object connected with it, they are all depicted with the same skilfulness and truth.

Look at his description of 'THE YELLOWHAMMER'S NEST'.

[Quotes]

In pathos Clare has proved himself a master. We shall say nothing of some of his earlier productions, in which he has spoken of his own struggle with 'chill penury,' and his sufferings under 'the heartsickness of hope deferred,' but we shall mention those which have spoken of the tears and the griefs of others. Some 'Stanzas on a Child' of his sister's, who died suddenly, we remember somewhere to have seen; they are some of the most touching and eloquent in the language. Why are they not included in the present volume? We may ask the same question of other poems we have seen in a newspaper, published at Stamford, under the title of 'The Bee.'—Where are the most exquisite verses 'On Childhood' which appeared in that journal? Verily, we are sorry John's book is not larger,—much, very much more has he written than has appeared in his books: this should not be; he should have published a larger volume—particularly when poetry like his is so scarce; when immense volumes are issuing from the press,—some epics of thousands of lines; some with titles as absurd as they are affected, and which show the character of their authors in their title-pages. It is refreshing after being annoyed and fatigued with such productions, which Clare has defined in one of his sonnets, as

Automatons of wonder-working powers,
Shadows of life and artificial flowers,

to open a book like *The Rural Muse*, to look upon the beauties of Nature in her unadorned simplicity, well may we echo his own line respecting Old Poesy, when we think of his own writing—

Sweet are these wild flowers in their disarray!

While speaking of some of Clare's poems which have appeared in print, and are not included in this volume, we may mention one under the title of 'The Cottager.' In the admirable review of the 'Rural Muse,' which appeared in *Blackwood*, the writer has suggested to Clare, that he would make himself even more generally read than he now is among the lower orders, did he devote himself to some poem descriptive of the manners and feelings of that class, and it prognosticates him equal to it. Cristopher North is right: the specimen Clare has given of his talent in that department, in 'The Cottager,' leaves no doubt of his success in a continued series. His 'Village Doctress,' too, has only appeared in the newspaper we have before mentioned; both that and 'The Cottager' are worthy of a place beside 'The Cotter's Saturday Night' of Burns, and the sketches of 'The Schoolmaster' and 'Clergyman' of Goldsmith. It is to be hoped, that we shall not be long before we have another volume from Clare's pen; how delighted many would be to see one under some such a title as 'Village Portraits.'

In some touches of sublimity, Clare has been most happy: there are some admirable ones in his 'Antiquity.' A sonnet from *The Rural Muse* may also be quoted:—

[Quotes 'Earth's Eternity']

By the kindness of a near and dear relative, who has since sunk into the repose of death, I was favoured with an introduction to Clare, at Northborough. My friend had been long acquainted with the peasant poet; he had edited the newspaper at Stamford which Clare had written for; and one morning in the autumn of three years agone, we started in a chaise and one from Stamford to Northborough, a distance of nine miles: the roadside, and the scenery about us, was that which the earlier poems of Clare have described. We visited the cottage of his birth, at Helpstone; his mother still lived there; she was out gleaning! Clare's cottage at Northborough is large and commodious; is situated in a nice flower-garden with an orchard attached to it; the view given in the frontispiece to *The Rural Muse* is correct. We found Clare and his 'Patty' surrounded by their family of six children. The first glance at Clare would convince you that he was no common man: he has a forehead of a highly intellectual character; the reflective faculties being exceedingly well developed; but the most striking feature is his eye, light-blue, and flashing with the fire of genius: the peculiar character of his eyes are always remarked by persons when first they see him: his height is rather below the common. His conversation is animated, striking, and full of imagination, yet his dialect is purely provincial; his ideas being expressed in the most simple manner, you can compare his conversation to nothing but the line of Goldsmith—

> Like a fair female, unadorned and plain.

He walked with us round his garden and orchard,

> Rubbing the perfume from the black-currant leaves.

He pointed out to us a spot in the hedge of his orchard where a nightingale had built her nest, which some rude hand had removed, and he expressed his sorrow at the spoliation, and his indignation at the offender, in no measured terms. There is in Clare a simplicity of heart and manner which endears him to you with the first knowledge of him: he is subject to melancholy moments; but when he has a friend with him, he can share the 'flow of soul,'—his manner and his conversation are most enchanting and delightful. We look upon the few hours we spent at his cottage at Northborough as among the happiest of our life.

Clare has suffered for some time from ill-health, the heir-loom of many a genius; it is the effect of that intensity of thought that preys upon the physical frame of the gifted. He may rest assured, however, of one thing, that his old friends are as warm as usual, and will cheer him with the praises that encouraged him in the beginning.

And now a word at parting with our old friend—and that is, respecting his *Rural Muse*. The readers of the Magazine, united by the tie of 'Brotherhood,' must respect and admire a man like Clare, who has raised himself from the humble 'Shepherd Boy,' to be placed among the immortal on the scroll of fame, by the side of Burns, and of Bloomfield. Do they love Nature? They do: her glories—her beauties—her ever-varying, yet ever-lovely face; then must they love the works of Him who hath painted her with a most cunning hand:—

> Whose breathing lines are Nature's counterpart.

Amid the struggle, and the toil, and the turmoil of life, a few moments occasionally snatched from its activity to the perusal of *The Rural Muse* will be as sweet as the calmness of repose to the weary and overladen.

Though Clare is not in distress, 'the night cometh in which no man can work,' his family are growing up around, and clinging to him for support, as the ivy clingeth to the oak. Druids! friends! *The Rural Muse* is worthy of many editions. Oblige yourselves by taking copies of it; shew that you have the true respect and admiration of Genius, which will support it not with words only, but more substantially.

100. Thomas De Quincey on Clare

1840

From 'Sketches of Life and Manners', *Tait's Edinburgh Magazine*, December 1840, vii, 765–76 (the section on Clare is on pp. 771–2). *Collected Writings*, ed. David Masson, 1897, iii, 144–5.

Our Scottish brethren are rather too apt, in the excess of that nationality which, dying away in some classes, is still burning fervently in others, and which, though giving a just right of complaint to those who suffer by it, and though direfully disfiguring the liberality of the national manners, yet stimulates the national rivalship usefully,—our Scottish brethren, I say, are rather too apt to talk as if in Scotland only there were any precedents to be found of intellectual merit struggling upwards in the class of rustic poverty: whereas there has in England been a larger succession of such persons than in Scotland. Inquire, for instance, as to the proportion of those who have risen to distinction by mere weight of unassisted merit, in this present generation, at the English bar; and then inquire as to the corresponding proportion at the Scotch bar. Oftentimes it happens that in the poetry of this class little more is found than the gift of a tolerably good ear for managing the common metres of the language. But in Clare it was otherwise. His poems were not the mere reflexes of his reading. He had studied for himself in the fields, and in the woods, and by the side of brooks. I very much doubt if there could be found in his poems a single commonplace image, or a description made up of hackneyed elements. In that respect, his poems are original, and have even a separate value, as a sort of calendar (in extent, of course, a very limited one) of many rural appearances, of incidents in the fields not elsewhere noticed, and of the loveliest flowers most felicitously described. The description is often true even to a botanical eye; and in that, perhaps, lies the chief defect; not properly in the scientific accuracy, but that, in searching after this too earnestly, the feeling is sometimes too much neglected. However, taken as a whole, his poems have a very novel quality of merit, though a quality too little, I fear, in the way of public notice. Messrs. Taylor & Hessey had been very kind to him; and, through them, the late Lord Fitzwilliam had settled an annuity upon him. In reality, the annuity had been so far increased, I believe, by the publishers as to release him from the necessities of daily toil. He had thus his time at his own command; and, in 1824, perhaps upon some literary scheme, he came up to London, where, by a few noble families and by his liberal publishers, he was welcomed in a way that, I fear, from all I heard, would but too much embitter the contrast with his own humble opportunities of enjoyment in the country. The contrast of Lord Radstock's brilliant parties, and the glittering theatres of London, would have but a poor effect in training him to bear that want of excitement which even already, I had heard, made his rural life but too insupportable to his mind. It is singular that what most fascinated his rustic English eye was not the gorgeous display of English beauty, but the French style of beauty, as he saw it amongst the French actresses in Tottenham Court Road. He seemed, however, oppressed by the glare and tumultuous existence of London; and, being ill at the time, from an affection of the liver, which did not, of course, tend to improve his spirits, he threw a weight of languor upon any attempt to draw him out into conversation. One thing, meantime, was very honourable to him,—that even in this season of dejection he would uniformly become animated when anybody spoke to him of Wordsworth—animated with the most hearty and almost rapturous spirit of admiration. As regarded his own poems, this admiration seemed to have an unhappy effect of depressing his confidence in himself. It is unfortunate, indeed, to gaze too closely upon models of colossal excellence. Compared with those of his own class, I feel satisfied that Clare will always maintain an honourable place.

101. Cyrus Redding visits John Clare

1841

From *English Journal*, 15 May 1841, 20, 305–9; 29 May 1841, 22, 340–3.

This was the first extended account to be published of Clare as he was in the asylum. It is therefore important in the development of the Clare myth, as well as for its critical comments. Shortly after this visit Clare escaped from Matthew Allen's asylum in Epping Forest. Redding relied on this account in two subsequent works, *Fifty Years' Recollections*, 1858, and *Past Celebrities whom I have known*, 1866. Cyrus Redding (1785–1870), who had been the effective editor, with Thomas Campbell, of the *New Monthly Magazine* (1821–30) started the *English Journal* in 1841, but it did not last long; the same was true of his *London Journal*. Redding was an expert on wines, and known for his *History and Description of Modern Wines*, 1833. There is nothing to indicate that he was the author of the notices of Clare's poems that appeared in the *New Monthly* (see Nos 14 and 59): there is an account of his connection with the *New Monthly* in *Fifty Years' Recollections*, second, revised edition, 1858, ii, 353–60. In the same work, discussing Clare's circumstances since his visit to Epping Forest, Redding refers to the poem, 'I am': 'We have never read any [lines] in which even an unerring intellect was more nobly distinguished. Could the writer be really a bewildered spirit? If so, then are sense and madness much nearer allied than the world generally thinks' (ii, 146).

I

A few days ago we visited JOHN CLARE, the 'Peasant Poet,' as he styles himself, at present in the establishment for the insane of Dr. ALLEN, at High Beach, in Essex. We were accompanied by a friend, who had formerly known CLARE. The situation is lofty; and the patients inhabit several houses at some distance from each other. These houses stand in the midst of gardens, where the invalids may be seen walking about, or cultivating the flowers, just as they feel inclined. The utmost politeness was exhibited upon making our object known; and we were informed that CLARE was in an adjacent field, working with four or five of the other patients.

We accordingly proceeded thither, and saw the 'Peasant Poet,' apart from his companions, busily engaged with a hoe, and smoking. On being called, he came down at once, and very readily entered into conversation. Our friend was surprised to see how much the poet was changed in personal appearance, having gained flesh, and being no longer, as he was formerly, attenuated and pale of complexion. We found a little man, of muscular frame and firmly set, his complexion fresh and forehead high, a nose somewhat aquiline, and long full chin. The expression of his countenance was more pleasing but somewhat less intellectual than that in the engraved portrait prefixed to his works in the edition of 'The Village Minstrel,' published in 1821. He was communicative, and answered every question put to him in a manner perfectly unembarrassed. He spoke of the quality of the ground which he was amusing himself by hoeing, and the probability of its giving an increased crop the present year, a continued smile playing upon his lips. He made some remarks illustrative of the difference between the aspect of the country at High Beach and that in the fens from whence he had come—alluded to Northborough and Peterborough—and spoke of his loneliness away from his wife, expressing a great desire to go home, and to have the society of women. He said his solace was his pipe—he had no other: he wanted books. On being asked what books, he said BYRON; and we promised to send that poet's works to him.

The principal token of his mental eccentricity was the introduction of prize-fighting, in which he seemed to imagine he was to engage; but the allusion to it was made in the way of interpolation in the middle of the subject on which he was discoursing, brought in abruptly, and abandoned with equal suddenness, and an utter want of connection with any association of ideas which it could be thought might lead to the subject at the time; as if the machinery of thought were dislocated, so that one part of it got off its pivot, and protruded into the regular workings; or as if a note had got into a piece of music which had no business there. This was the only symptom of aberration of mind we observed about CLARE; though, being strangers to him, there might be something else in his manner which those who knew him well could have pointed out. To our seeming, his affection was slight; and it is not at all improbable that a relief from mental anxiety might completely restore him. The finer organisation of such a humanity, if more easily put out of order than that of a more obtuse character, is in all probability more likely to re-tune itself, the evil cause being removed.

It is proposed, and advertisements have already appeared in pursuance of the object, that a subscription shall be opened for raising a sufficient sum of money to increase the little income of poor CLARE, which amounts only to £13. 10s. per annum, exclusive of £10. from Earl SPENCER and £15. from the Marquis of EXETER, who, when affected admirers and patrons fell off and forgot him, have, with truly honourable feeling, continued him their subscriptions to this day. The increase proposed, is £21. 10s. per annum; so as to raise his present £38. 10s. to £60., in the whole; and thus to place him beyond the reach of that care for his subsistence which is the main cause of his present mental hallucination. The object is a worthy one, and we do trust will be carried into effect. When we reflect upon the sums expended by every individual amongst the least wealthy in the middle classes of society, and how very small a portion from each, among a number comparatively inconsiderable, would effect the desired end, we are sanguine in the hope that the object may yet be achieved. True it is that a taste for the simple and beautiful, for the imaginative and elegant, is fast fading away before the vulgar realities of modern existence. We do not expect the many to be moved by the claims of genius, for the many are little susceptible of its influence; but we trust the comparatively few, and they are enough, who still cast the 'longing, lingering look,' towards those better things which the cold world's collision no longer permits them leisure to enjoy—all such whose snatches of thought renew the pleasures that exist but in recollection—will consider the subject not in vain. The young, with the spirit fresh from Creation's bosom, with uncorrupted hearts and pure impulses—they, kindred to genius itself, which is an eternal juvenescence—may still feel for the 'Peasant Poet,' as poor CLARE styles himself, like the 'Je suis Vilain' of BERANGER. Thus, their mite for the muse of simple, eloquent Nature, will return back warm in benefit to the givers. Formerly, when the love of poetry was universal, and pent-up cities did not cut off all communing with Nature—when the elegant and natural were not overlayed by the vulgar and demoralising in literature, and the gratification of the intellect harmonised with a refined and moral end, there would have been no hazarding a doubt about the result of such an application as the present.

In 1835, Professor WILSON made an appeal to the public in CLARE's behalf, which did high honour to his feelings. In that appeal, in *Blackwood's Magazine*, WILSON very appropriately twitted the English people for their censure of the Scotch neglect of BURNS, and cited their own conduct towards BLOOMFIELD, and how they let that amiable man starve. 'Leave the Scotch,' says WILSON, 'to their own reflections on the fate of their ploughman; and explain to us, at your leisure, in what lay the grace of English gratitude to your "Farmer's Boy?"' Well and truly is this said. Among sixteen millions of people laying claim to every virtue under heaven beyond all others, two individuals, in BLOOMFIELD and CLARE, have exhibited surprising examples of genius—of that rare but undying gift which confers its most enduring glory upon empires—two have appeared among the ranks of poverty; and one was left to starve, as Professor WILSON observes; and as to the other, except Lords SPENCER and EXETER already mentioned, his rich patrons of wealthy professions have forgotten him. His position has preyed upon his mind, and consigned him to a lunatic asylum.

Two men of genius in half a century—certainly not a very burthensome number—have been thus treated by sixteen millions, among whom their appearance is an honour. Quacks, impostors, the obscene, who mock Nature in posture-making, and

> Twirl the light leg that scorns the needless veil,

—the parasites of luxury, the panders to bad morals, to the gambling-table, the race-course, and the dog-kennel, with all their brutal adjuncts —consume hundreds of thousands annually among some people, who too often ask, when solicited for the very smallest aid on an occasion like the present, 'What! this for a song?'

Then again, the mass of the people in middling circumstances have little community with the productions of imagination of a simple and natural character, particularly the inhabitants of large cities, who, with those in the ranks above them, seek their reading in writers of more congenial feeling with their own—panting for intellectual excitement from the pages of the emasculating novel, or the vulgar and demoralising romance. It is true that they who draw their earliest breath in the carboniferous atmosphere of cities, amid large congregations of men, must take for granted the emotions and descriptions of a rural poet.

Their sympathies lie another way than with mountains, vales, and brooks. The Poet of Nature can hardly expect that those reared in the hotbed of artificial life can feel much sympathy for him or his productions; yet while no appeal of charity, except such a one as the present, wants its supporters in large communities of individuals in this country, it does seem singular that, 'few and far between' as such calls are upon the public of any class, it is responded to as it was in BLOOMFIELD's case.

No one who is born and bred out of a city atmosphere, who has loved the country, and knows more of it than he who merely passes over a turnpike road, or sees it from the vehicle which transports him rapidly along—no one of such a character can read CLARE's poetry, and not be struck with its beautiful simplicity, its adherence to nature, and the amiable and pure character which in these times of artificial life can set its heart upon them, and make them the themes of its verse under privation and sorrow, melancholy proof as it affords of the fast hold that genius takes of the soul, loosing its bonds but with life itself.

In the paper in *Blackwood* to which we have alluded, WILSON made copious extracts from CLARE's second publication. The first publication of CLARE's was entitled *Poems Descriptive of Rural Life and Scenery*. It came out in 1820, and went through four editions—for good poetry was read by many, and enjoyed too, twenty years ago. To this volume, succeeded, in the same year, *The Village Minstrel, and Other Poems* which, in 1827, was followed by *The Shepherd's Calendar*, a very beautiful volume of poetry; the success of which we do not know, but its success was well merited, for it was the best volume CLARE ever published.

In 1835, however, when the public dreamed so erroneously that the puling, wordy, pseudo-sentimental effusions of boarding-school misses, and verses that said much and meant nothing—when the public were wearied and nauseated by a poetical salivation—just then CLARE published *The Rural Muse*, of which WILSON wrote so excellent an account. That volume, notwithstanding, did not sell at all. The very word 'rural' was enough; but the namby-pamby in annuals and in all sorts of ephemera, that had overlain the market to the exclusion of better things, began about that time to sink poetry. Hence that the volume of poor CLARE did not meet with the success it merited is not extraordinary. We must refer the reader to *Blackwood*, for August, 1835. In that is a far better analysis of the volume than we can pretend to give. We think with WILSON, that BLOOMFIELD's poems generally, except 'The Farmer's Boy,' are inferior to those of CLARE, and we only except *that* in deference to such an authority. Some are eminently beautiful. CLARE is indeed—with BURNS, CRABBE, ELLIOT, and BLOOMFIELD—the 'Poet of the Poor.' His sympathies, his enjoyments, his habits, and aspirations, are all those of the poor man. Despised as the poor are in England, they who despise them cannot rob them of their intellectual pleasures—of their purer sensations—of fair Nature's light. The poor then must look to their own poets. A mite from each—a penny a head in one of our populous manufacturing districts—might place CLARE where he ought to be, and enable him to continue to delight them, and the wise and feeling of every rank, with his simple and touching verse—might relieve him from his mental disease, which on good authority is believed to depend more upon the pressure of his wordly circumstances than any other cause.

If the rich will not contribute, let the poor shame them; that England may not incur the reproach, under her burthen of wealthy affluence, of suffering her men of genius, who so rarely appear, to languish in privation, and die of want, like CAMOENS, to whom Portugal owes almost all her poetical renown.

We will here drop this part of the subject, leaving what we have said to the reader's own breast, and turn to a remarkable circumstance connected with CLARE's position. Many of our readers may not know that SMART, an author of note, when in the cell of a madhouse, in 1763, wrote a poem, entitled 'A Song to David,' with charcoal on the wall, some say indented it with a key on the wainscot; and that it betrays nothing of mental aberration, but is a most powerful and admirable production. In the same way the later compositions of CLARE show nothing of his mental complaint, as if the strength of the poetic feeling were beyond the reach of a common cause to disarrange. We were gratified with several pieces of CLARE's, written at High Beach; and we shall insert a few of them, not less confirmatory of our observation, than as presenting a proof of the extraordinary phenomena of mind, and of the limited knowledge we possess of them. The following, 'To the Nightingale,' is one of these:—

[Quotes]

The following, which the author styles 'A Sonnet,' is very beautiful. Whence springs the delicate inspiration in the breast of the peasant, to which such lines owe their origin, but in a great mystery of the mental constitution, which spurns the ordinary limits of human action, mocks conventional ideas, and gathers its vigour from an immortal principle.

> Maid of Walkherd, meet again,
> By the wilding in the glen;
> By the oak against the door,
> Where we often met before.
> By thy bosom's heaving snow,
> By thy fondness none shall know;
> Maid of Walkherd, meet again,
> By the wilding in the glen.
>
> By thy hand of slender make,
> By thy love I'll ne'er forsake,
> By thy heart I'll ne'er betray,
> Let me kiss thy fears away!
> I will live and love thee ever,
> Leave thee and forsake thee never!
> Though far in other lands to be,
> Yet never far from love and thee.

[Quotes 'Sighing for Retirement'; 'The Forest Maid'; 'On the Neglect of True Merit'; 'The Sequel to John Barleycorn']

We must close with the following sonnets, and resume this subject in a second article, only making enquiry of the reader, if he does not marvel at the nature of that genius, which, under the yoke of a mind in delusion, still retains its skill in composition undiminished, and pours forth in this way the playings of its fancy. We know no parallel instance but that of SMART already alluded to.

[Quotes 'A Walk in the Forest'; 'To Wordsworth'; 'The Water Lilies'; 'The Frightened Ploughman']

II

That the taste which reigns paramount in what is styled the 'Literature of the hour' will soon have run its cycle, and die of its own excitement, is scarcely to be doubted. There will some day be a return to the simply beautiful, when the love of Truth and Nature will again cause the dust to be blown off the volumes of such poets as CLARE, and the merit of similar verse be again acknowledged; as certainly will this be as that Nature must ever triumph over puling sentimentality, false pathos, puerile complexity of verbiage, and ignorance of sound principles.

Where is the school of poetry so greatly the rage about the time of

POPE, which that exquisite satirist so well ridiculed in the stanzas beginning—

> Fluttering spread thy purple pinions?

Where is the tinsel of DARWIN, and the fashionable mannerism of HAYLEY, belonging to a later period? buried 'in the tomb of all the *Capulets*.' COWPER, and BURNS, and CRABBE, contemporaries of these 'lost Pleiads,' have endured and brightened their fame by time; but they were poets who belonged to the great school of Nature and of Truth, though taking a higher flight than CLARE or BLOOMFIELD.

The malady of CLARE introduced him to scenery of a different character from that to which he had been accustomed. It was scarcely possible that one of his temperament should be insensible to the change, and we find, accordingly, that the wildness of Epping Forest has called forth his verse in its celebration. . . .

[Quotes several poems with brief comments: 'A Walk on High Beech, Loughton'; 'London *versus* Epping Forest'; 'Greatness of Mind'; 'The Gipsey Camp'; 'Love and Beauty'; 'The Courtship'; 'The Cowslips'; 'The Mock Bird'; 'The Botanist's Walk']

The artless description of Nature's works in CLARE is, in reality, the result of very close observation, and the recapitulation of that which is not only familiar, but to which the Poet is ardently attached, whether under delusion or in perfect possession of his mental faculties. Wherever he goes, Nature, in the general form obvious to all, is his theme, but he is versed in her minuter aspects. Those who do not observe minutely cannot describe with fidelity; close observation only coming from preference, that which is preferred being naturally loved even from familiarity, were there no auxiliary aid to quicken the impression it produces. Common minds get attached to things because they are in continued intercourse with them, but genius attaches itself besides to what is excellent in the view of superior intellect, however insignificant, and raises and adorns it, dresses it in 'orient pearl and gold,' casts round it a witchery of its own, and places it before the 'wondering upturned eyes' of mortals as something well nigh divine.

The simple subjects upon which CLARE delights to dwell most persons pass by, or have deemed beneath their notice, as inferior in the order of Nature, and wonder how such charming things can be said of what appears to them insignificant. They are ready to admit the merit of the Poet, but they cannot imagine how a flower, an insect, or a combination of similar objects, can be invested with such interest, and they undervalue that which gives them pleasure in the imaginary depreciation which it causes of their own consequence by concerning themselves with such common subjects. Yet, in reality, all Nature's works are beautiful to the Poet as they are intrinsically, the daisy as well as the rose. Were poetry to bind itself by conventional notions, it would at best be but a tawdry harlot.

True, there are repetitions in the verses of CLARE, and much similarity of metaphor and subject. It would be wonderful if this were not the case with one who has been educated at the plough, and toiled in fields through the first years of existence, in place of passing his time in academic bowers. A few grammatical lapses and indefensible elisions may well be excused. Let those who can only see these things, albeit well grounded in grammar, write with equal excellence destitute of the genius which breaks through trammels genius alone could overcome. It is that mysterious power which leads to the productions of such writers as CLARE, so seldom seen—productions, simple as they are, that hundreds and thousands who could write a volume without one repetition or one breach of PRISCIAN, could no more rival than they could ride to the moon upon LINDLEY MURRAY's pedantic and lumbering 'Grammar.'

But they are not alone the trivial things of Nature that occupy the verse of CLARE. The expansive landscape so varied and beautiful, the hill and stream, the humanities of life, are all equally subjects of his poetry. In CLARE, too, there is a peculiar locality always prevalent, his themes belonging to that part of England frequented by the nightingale, which goes no further north than York, and enters not the mild climate of Devonshire and Cornwall. His subjects come out of the very heart of England, and many of the words he uses are unknown beyond the central part of the island. Another quality remarkable in CLARE is his admiration of woman; a fond, respectful, 'true love' attachment to the sex distinguishes his writings.

CLARE may be styled the illustrator of the rural scenery of his native land to a degree of fidelity, as well as minuteness, that has not been before approached; almost every flower, tree, and shrub that springs freely from the free soil of England has been noticed in his verses in its proper site, as it bourgeons and blows. BLOOMFIELD generalises more; indeed, it may be questioned if he knew a tithe of what CLARE knows of the minutiæ of Nature, the result of position and his love of beautiful things.

It is to be lamented, perhaps, that he has not taken his rural muse sometimes a higher flight; but his leisure for a work of any considerable length must have been scanty, and his excellencies may, perhaps, be best exhibited as they are now written down before us.

In the poems we have published in the present and foregoing papers we do not say that CLARE has surpassed his preceding productions; moreover, they are printed rough and uncorrected, as they were first committed to paper. They have been composed under the shadow of insanity, in circumstances to which the Poet is well awake, and the irksomeness of which he feels. We ask, however, whether the inhabitant of an asylum for lunatics ever wrote, in assimilation to preceding works, so well before; and whether it be not a discredit to the age that such a man should be permitted to wear out his days under the depression of a cankering care for his future support, which outrages reason painfully, though not heavily? Thanks to the excellent Dr. ALLEN and his mode of treatment at High Beach, no pleasures that the exciting neighbourhood of the Forest can afford to this Poet of Nature have been wanting under poor CLARE's slight delusion. He may enjoy Nature in her simple or grander aspect, he may cultivate a garden or a field, he may write or read as he pleases: but, as he observed to us, 'I want to be with my wife and family; there is none of woman here.'

Here we must leave this subject, hoping that shortly some effort will be made to place CLARE with his family; for which end, twenty-one pounds a-year, in addition to what he possesses, is all that is required. Until his mind is made easy, he can be better nowhere than where he is. In the asylum of Dr. ALLEN, as already observed, no restraint is exercised. The patients are attached by kindness and a course of treatment calculated to soothe and please, in place of engendering irritation and disgust. This system is carried out further by Dr. ALLEN, we believe, than by any other medical gentleman who has made the management of the insane a profession, upon principles of the beneficial effect of which a very long course of habitual exercise has only served to show, more and more, the great efficacy.

102. Edwin Paxton Hood on Clare

1851

From 'John Clare, the Peasant Poet' in Hood's *Literature of Labour*, 1851, pp. 128–64.

Edwin Paxton Hood (1820–85), a Congregational minister, contributor to (and for some time editor of) the *Eclectic Review*, was the first to write so expansively about Clare (see Introduction, pp. 14-15). It was he who wrote the unsigned account of Clare in the *Eclectic*, August 1865, n.s. ix, 101–38. A chapter on Clare appeared in his *Peerage of Poverty*, 5th edition, revised, 1870. Both these later accounts leaned heavily on the chapter in *Literature of Labour*, without adding much. (See Introduction, note 60.)

But never have Literature and Labour been more beautifully combined than in the instance of John Clare, the Northamptonshire peasant. Perhaps none of those who have attained any degree of eminence in literature from the lowly walks of life, ever had to contend with difficulties so stern and severe as this noble soul.

[Biographical details]

At present he is confined in an asylum in the neighbourhood of Northampton. It is not to be supposed that the mind has really tottered from its throne: the fact appears to be that the body is too weak for the mind. Some of the most pleasant and touching verses have been written since his affliction, and in the course of a few pages we shall lay before our readers some of these curiosities of literature. The memory of the Poet has not during his long estrangement passed away from his native village. From its excellent rector, the Rev. Mr. Mossop, we derived much of the information we have detailed above. In a recent pilgrimage to the Poet's birthplace, he most courteously received and furnished to the writer the mournful details of the swan of Helpstone. And from thence we passed to the cottage of Northborough, and spent a few moments with Mrs. Clare—'Patty,' and we thought the tears with which she told us some of the incidents of the old time, so long ago, the best testimony to the soundness and healthiness of Clare's home affections. The old violin hung on the wall with which the cottage used to echo to the song in the old days; when the verses were read by the fireside as soon as made. 'We were all so happy in those days,' said the poor woman, in a tone that sounded like the wail of a heart sadly learned in the lesson of endurance and suffering. Intemperance has been the sad cause of much of the misery of those, who, from the fields of labour have elevated themselves to be the bards and the singers to their fellows. It is very delightful to record that from this frailty Clare was exempt: not that he did not enjoy a can of beer. He, however, never went to the Public House. His wont seems to have been to purchase occasionally his mug of beer, and going frequently among the very poorest of his neighbourhood to sit with them talking, and probably observing while contributing something to their enjoyment. Many illustrations might be given of his extreme sensitiveness; the delicacy and refinement with which he invariably speaks of Woman, is one proof of this. His words never burn with passion—they glow with modesty and sensibility. Woman, however, is the secret spring of his inspiration: indeed, he says

> I wrote my better poems there—
>   To Beauty's smile I owe it;
> The Muses they get all the praise,
>   But Woman makes the poet.
> The Muses they are living things,
>   But Beauty still is dear;
> But though I worshipped stocks and stones,
>   'Twas Woman everywhere.

And is there not an extreme sensibility indicated in the following strange extract from one of his letters. How affectingly does the vehemence of the former portion contrast with the wisdom of the latter:—

My two favourite elm trees at the back of the hut are condemned to die—it shocks me to relate it, but 'tis true. The savage who owns them thinks they have done their best, and now he wants to make use of the benefits he can get from selling them. O, was this country Egypt, and was I but a caliph, the owner should lose his ears for his arrogant presumption, and the first wretch who buried his axe in the roots should hang on their branches as a terror to the rest. I have been several mornings to bid them farewell. Had I one hundred pounds to spare, I would buy them reprieves—but they must die. Yet this mourning over trees is all foolishness—they feel no pains—they are but wood, cut up or not. A second thought tells me that I am a fool: were all people to feel as I do, the world could not be carried on; a green would not be ploughed; a tree or bush would not be cut for firing or furniture; and everything they found when boys would remain in that state till they died. This is my indisposition, and you will laugh at it.

But, notwithstanding the distinguished patronage which at one time Clare received, he was never lifted beyond the avenues of Poverty, although, we believe, he has never since the period we have referred to, known absolute want, nor have his poems ever been extensively popular; and now, even in literary circles, they are unreferred to, if not entirely unknown. Their purity, their excessive modesty, their intense devotion to Nature in the woods and the fields, in an age when the woods and fields have been comparatively forsaken, these may be assigned as some of the reasons for the obscurity which has gathered round the name of one of the sweetest singers of the children of Labour. Clare is Bloomfield's successor, and he is very far his superior, dwelling among the ever-varying scenes of Nature, and abounding, as he un-questionably does, with homely images, he is yet not merely a rustic Poet, or a rural Bard. Such poets receive, but do not give; they take passing sensible impressions of the Georgic world, but they do not reflect themselves. From such writers we scarcely expect reflection; their Bucolics abound in prettinesses and generalities, without the bold-ness of generalization; but Clare has more fully individualized his scenery than any poet of his class, always excepting Burns: it is the poetry of Rural Life and Taste—but it is Rural Life with the dignity of the man, not with the rudeness or mannerism of the clown. It is worth some inquiry what makes the evident distinction between the methods of Cowper, and Wordsworth, and Keats, and Tennyson; and between all these again and our humbler friend, of whom we are now speaking, all love the country, but few love it as Clare loves it. Yet, it seems in-dispensable to the proper appreciation of rural scenery, that we should not only take our walks there, but find our work there. Clare writes, as Gilbert White would have written, had he been a poet. He threads his way through all Nature's scenery with a quiet meditation and reflection, and frequently those reflections, if not the result of profound thought, yet bear the stamp of profound beauty. Clare's life is in the country. There are those who study the country, and read the volume of the town by its side; there are those who bring to the study of the country extensive readings and learning; there are those who make each scene of country life only the key to their own imaginations, and move, indeed, very far from the scenery of their original thought: but Clare takes the country literally as it is; he brings to it no learning, no historical suggestion; he seeks in the country none of the monuments of haughty human grandeur; he unfolds no political philosophy; he seeks no high idealization; he takes the lesson lying on the surface, and frequently it is so simple and natural that it affects us to tears. The fields of Nature are not so much a study to which he retires, or an observatory which he mounts; they are rather a book which he reads, and, as he reads, turns down the page. We should be prepared to expect after this, what we do actually find—an extreme homeliness of style and thought —we mean homeliness in its highest and best sense—not lowness, not vulgarity—the very reverse of all these. Clare walks through the whole world around him with the impression, that he cannot go where 'universal love smiles not around.' His whole soul is a fountain of love and sensibility, and it wells forth in loving verse for all, and to all creatures. The lessons of his verses may be described as coming, rather than being sought; for they grow up before him; he does not dig for them, and, therefore, his poems are rather fancies and feelings than imaginations. He throws his whole mind, with all its sensitiveness, into the country; yet, not so much does he hang over its human life as the life of Nature, the love and the loveliness of this beautiful world. Traditional tales he does not narrate. A bird's nest has far more attraction to his eyes than the old manor-house, or the castle. The life of the cottage, too, is a holy life for him; his home is there, and every season brings, day by day, its treasures of enjoyment and of peace to him. In a new and noble sense all his poems are pastorals; he sings of rural loves and trystings, and hopes, and joys. He never, indeed, loses himself, as many of us do, in vague generalities, for he has seen all he mentions in his song; he has been a keen observer of the ways of Nature, he knows her face in all its moods, and to him the face is always cheerful. Other poets go out into the walks of Nature to spend a holiday, they love her, but to see her is an occasional pleasure, but to Clare it is an every-day existence. He has no holiday with Nature, he walks with her as friend with friend. Other poets select a river, or a mountain, and individualise it, but to Clare all are but parts of the same lovely Home, and as every part of the home is endeared—the chair, the shelf, the lattice, the wreathing flower, the fire-place, the table—so is every object in Nature a beloved object, because the whole is beloved. Other poets entertain, as they enter the avenues of Nature, a most solemn awe and dread: we have said that Clare never forgets himself in low coarseness, so neither does he ever shrink or shiver beneath the dread of an overaweing presence; he walks with Nature as an angel walks with goodness— naturally, cheerfully, fraternally.

Fancy, Feeling, and Philosophy or Reflection, these are the character-istics of the verses before us. Most rural poets have indulged merely in the Feeling, but the Feeling has not been sufficiently sensitive or pro-found for Reflection, and the mind has not been active enough for Fancy—that is rich and ariel humour of our poet, in which he enters into the life of an insect. Insects, which to many are, have been, and will be, simply an annoyance, are to him fairies with coloured hood and burnished wings, disguised in a sort of splendid masquerade, rocked to sleep in the smooth velvet of the pale hedge rose, or slumbering like princes in the heath bell's purple hood, secure from rain, from dropping dews, in silken beds and painted hall; a jolly and a royal life this seems, this band of playfellows mocking the sunshine on their glittering wings, or drinking golden wine and metheglin from the cup of the honied flower. It is in a deeper mood that the ploughman reflects upon the eternity of Nature; to the simplest things in Nature, to his eye, there is entwined a spirit sublime and lasting: the daisy, trampled under foot strikes its root into the earth, and in the distant centuries of time, the child will clap its tiny hands with pleasure and cry 'A Daisy!' its little golden bosom frilled with snow, will be the same, as bright as when Eve stooped to pluck it in Eden. Cowslips of golden bloom, will come and go as fresh two thousand years hence as now; brooks, bees, birds, from age to age, these will sing on when all the more ambitious things of earth shall have passed away; and not only the fact continues, but the fact in the same form; for Clare, like Audubon, is not content to be merely sentimental, he fixes his eye on the proprieties and ever recur-ring mysteries of Nature, all Nature's ways are mysteries, hence 'the red thighs of the humble bee' travel wide and far, when he

> Breakfasts, dines, and most divinely sups
> With every flower, save golden buttercups,
> On whose proud bosoms he will never go,
> But passes by with scarcely 'How do 'e do?'
> Since in their snowy, shining, gaudy cells,
> Haply the Summer's honey never dwells.

Eternal youth and eternal mystery, the unfading beauty and the unfading sublimity of Nature—these are everywhere seen; seen as remarkably in the most insignificant as in the most majestic. The fancies and the freaks of Nature are a sort of pledge of unfailing truthfulness.

[Quotes 'Eternity of Nature': 'With the odd number, *five* . . .' to the end]

The Laureat of the Birds' nests—nests often seen, but never disturbed. The nest of the Pettichap, close to the rut-gulled waggon-road, so snugly contrived, although with not a clump of grass to keep it warm, or shielding thistle spreading its spears abroad—built like an oven, through a little hole—

> Scarcely admitting e'en two fingers in,
> Hard to discern, the birds' snug entrance win;
> 'Tis lined with feathers, warm as silken stole,
> Softer than seats of down for painless ease,
> And full of eggs, scarce bigger e'en than peas;
> Here's one that's delicate, with spots, as small
> As dust, and of a faint and pinky red:
> Well, let them be, and Safety guard them well—
> A green grasshopper's jump might break the shell.

In the same strict individuality of description we have the nest of the nightingale, whose

> Melody seems hid in every flower
> That blossoms near her home. These harebells all
> Seem bowing with the beautiful in song;
> And gaping cuckoo flower, with spotted leaves,
> Seems blushing at the singing it has heard.

Stepping from the nightingale, we come to another nest, with

> Five eggs, pen scribbled o'er with ink their shells,
> Resembling writing scrawls, which Fancy reads,
> As Nature's poesy, and pastoral spells.
> They are the yellowhammer's; and she dwells
> Most poet-like, where brooks and flowery weeds,
> As sweet as Castaly her fancy deems;
> And that old mole-hill is Parnassus' hill,
> On which her partner haply sits and dreams
> O'er all his joys of song.

These citations are very far from being in our Bard's highest voice of song, but they show, in his walk, an English Audubon; they reveal an intimacy and acquaintance with Nature; an eye perpetually on the watch to notice the colouring and the scenery of things, as well as the thing itself. We remember no Poet of any walk, who has lived so much with Nature; who has pressed so far within her visible portals; who has so reverently gathered the mosses and the wild flowers growing in the neighbourhood of her temple. Ambition to reach the glory of the Shekinah has frequently interfered with the perception of the beauties in the outer court; it is not from inability to penetrate so far, but from modesty and sensitiveness, that Clare has taken his chief delight in lingering over common things, and folding in fondness to his heart the least and most fragile of Nature's forms, and finding the things of beauty and the joy for ever where none but those who love Nature with a lover's passion ever look. But the individuality of colouring is preserved when any other objects of Nature are referred to, the two developements aways attendant upon a love of Nature, namely, exceeding tenderness, and delicate and truthful painting are found in ample abundance in these verses. How feelingly is the universal love of the Robin sketched:—

[Quotes from 'The Autumn Robin']

Listen to the following descriptive touches of a Summer Morning.

[Quotes from 'Summer Morning': 'The cocks have now the morn foretold . . .']

All these illustrations prove how literal is Clare's rendering of the Truth of Nature; he indulges in no extravaganzas; all his images are simple, natural, and affecting; he never selects images he has not seen: perhaps, the words *mountain* and *forest* do not occur throughout his poems. They are moulded from the long level wastes and fens, the vast moors of his own and the adjacent counties. Some have scouted the idea of poetry, and boldness of thought and variety of conception in the fen country; they have not been there, nor have they learned the philosophy of our poet when he says:—

> Be thy journey e'er so mean,
>   Passing by a cot or tree,
> In the rout there's something seen,
>   Which the curious love to see.
> In each ramble, Taste's warm souls,
>   More of Wisdom's self can view,
> Than blind Ignorance beholds
>   All life's seven stages through.

Of course, scenery materially influences character, and gives tone and colouring to the poet's mind; yet the richness, the strength, the melody are not in the scenery, but in the Poet's soul, and that soul finds its beauties and its interests everywhere: and the Fens, and the scenes about them have their own peculiar impressions, and those frequently of a highly interesting and pictorial character. From scenes like those in which Clare was born and reared, Alfred Tennyson derives his inspiration, where

> The long dun wolds were ribb'd with snow,

where

> A sluice of blackened waters slept;
> And o'er it, many, round, and small,
> The clustered marish mosses crept.

Of course, if the proposition is to be put, the vote we give is our voice for the mountains, but the lowland levels must not be despised. Is there monotony in the landscape, or in the mind that surveys it? mountains and cataracts are monotonous to the idealess mind. Look out upon those long lines of road, and field, or in winter, all this wide landscape turned into a kind of inland ocean, over which the boats drift to and fro in pursuit of the long caravans of wild fowl. Is there nothing inspiring to the reflective mind, too, in the fact that human industry and enterprise have turned the swamp into a fruitful field? that those long lines of dyke and ditch are the evidences of man's conquest over Nature in her most unpropitious moods? In thoughts like these may not even the Fen land wear a sublimity and a majesty beyond even the mountain and the waterfall? To some minds Northamptonshire and Lincolnshire may seem the very Nazareth of Poetry; but they have there, and have ever had, grange, and park, and meadow; skylarks from of old have sung there behind the broken cloud; winds have panted over the moor. The fountains of admiration and of mystery well up, even in those lands for those who like to drink of those waters; and to such, the country becomes as suggestive as a prairie or a savannah. Men and women, we may further say, too, were born in those regions, and they have become learned in the art and mystery of loving and of mourning; there, they have their church-yards and their ingle nooks; and where all these are, can man help occasionally uttering himself in poetry? Passion, is it not within him, and is it not this that wakens the inspiration around him. And injustice, and wrong, and poverty, are not they there? and where they are, will they not occasionally flood the heart with a current of song? It is thus then we vindicate from contempt the *study* of our Poet.

At the risk of exciting a misunderstanding and a sneer, we may call Clare the Wordsworth of Labour. In saying this, the great distance both of attainment and position is borne in mind, and perhaps the immeasureable distance of original genius. Of this, however, it is well nigh impossible to speak. Clare's genius is one of that order depending greatly upon cultivation and communion with exalted minds; Wordsworth is a teacher, appearing once in the course of many ages, and combining in himself some exquisite sympathies never found, in the same degree, in any poet of any previous age. All that learning, travel, education in the most sublime scenery of Nature, leisure, solitude, association with the most gifted spirits, long life—all that these combined could do was lavished upon him. The reverse of all these forms the history of Clare; yet in him we notice the same intense affection for the simplest things in Nature—the same disposition to self-communion—the same power to reflect back a lesson, and to treat Nature in all her visible manifestations as an intimation and a prophecy; the same exuberant overflowing of tenderness and love—the same disposition to preserve the soul in 'a wise quietness'—the same love of the sonnet and ease of utterance through that formal barrier of expression. Is there not a vein of our old Patriarch's feeling in this, called 'Pleasant Places'.

[Quotes]

When it is remembered how Clare received his education, how little opportunity he has had of cultivating acquaintance with books, and how few associations he can have had of a refining character, the affluence of his language, and its exquisite music and freedom from every jarring coarseness become truly astonishing. The patronising tone in which some critics have spoken is most unjust, and, therefore, mean and tasteless. In the higher flights of song no comparison must be drawn between Bloomfield and Clare; the shoemaker must unbonnet his brow to the ploughman; the former never exercises or seems to possess a reflective power. We have here linked together a series of poems, several unpublished in any edition of our poet's works, and the four first written in lucid intervals in the lunatic asylum, and with these remarkable beauties of composition, we shall close the notice of this beautiful and exemplary genius.

[Quotes 'Loves and Beauty'; 'The Modesty of Great Men']

The following lines are very touching, when it is remembered that they are the pensive utterances of a soul ill at ease from the very frailty of the tabernacle in which it is confined—a house too fragile for the strong spirit within it—the cause at once of every poet's madness. His organic sensibility, his nervous nature responding to every varying tone and intimation, and his strong soul desiring to overleap the material pales and boundaries, and live entirely in the land, visiting it in his poetic dreamings,—'Sighing for Retirement'.

[Quotes; also quotes 'To the Nightingale'; 'Home Happiness'; 'On an Infant Killed by Lightning']

103. A biographical sketch of Clare

1856

From *Men of the Times, Biographical Sketches of Eminent Living Characters*, new edition, 1856, pp. 155–6.

This new edition of a popular work was edited by Alaric Watts (see No. 97). Earlier editions (the first appeared in 1852) had no mention of Clare.

For some years past Clare has been living in a state of mild lunacy, his chief delusion being that all the best poetry of Byron, Wordsworth, Campbell, and others, was written by him! He is allowed to wander about at will, although perfectly unconscious. For many years he has been wholly lost to the world, without any hope of his restoration. The last volume published by him, in 1836 [sic], previous to his illness, *The Rural Muse*, presents a vast improvement on its predecessors, and contains many poems of great simplicity and beauty. Without being chargeable with want of originality, moreover, they display an acquaintance with the great poets of his country, which is exceedingly remarkable.

104. Clare in passing

1857

Thomas James, from an unsigned review-article, 'The History and Antiquities of Northamptonshire', *Quarterly Review*, January 1857, ci, 1–56.

Thomas James (1809–63) was honoured by a separate reprinting of this article, under his own name, in 1864.

. . . his true and loving descriptions of natural objects, his picturesque and nervous language, and the pure vein of poetry and feeling that runs through all he wrote, might claim for him a kindly remembrance even in days which would look upon his themes as antiquated and insipid. There are lines called 'First Love's Recollections' in his last volume, which, coming from a man of his class, strike us as one of the most remarkable expressions of refined feeling we know; and there is a singularly wild and strange beauty in some verses, still unpublished, written by him while an inmate of the asylum; but we regret that these and further details of his story are beyond our present limits. . . .

(p. 45)

105. John Plummer on a forgotten poet

1861

From a signed article, *Once a Week*, 11 May 1861, iv, 539–41.

John R. Plummer, a local poet from Kettering (his *Songs of Labour, Northamptonshire Ballads, and Other Poems* were published in 1861), sent a rather similar communication to the *Northampton Mercury* on 24 June 1861, which ended:

Whether Clare will ever recover from his malady is a problem difficult to solve: but whether such be the case or not, he has left the world a legacy which will ever entitle him to be ranked amongst the most natural and truehearted of poets; and though the gay world of fashion may have forgotten even the name of its former idol, it will be many, very many years before it is effaced from the glorious roll of English poets.

Forty years ago the literary world was thrown into a ferment by the appearance of an article in the *Quarterly Review*, in which the poetical productions of a young and humble farm-labourer were noticed with a degree of favour somewhat unusual in the pages of the Giant of Criticism; and well did the poor poet sustain the reputation thus unexpectedly thrust on him, for seldom has an individual been more blameless in his private character, or more deserving in his public capacity, than John Clare, whose mild disposition furnishes such a genial and pleasing commentary on his vivid and ofttimes exquisitely beautiful delineation of rustic life and manners. . . . So intent had Clare been on rectifying his educational deficiencies, that his *Rural Muse* displayed an amount of grace and polish totally unexpected by his admirers, but, alas! in proportion to the development of his powers, the poet's popularity waned, and the unsold copies of his works which crowded the publishers' shelves but too truly testified to the neglect and indifference of the fickle public. Poor Clare felt the blow, and became more moody and sad in his demeanour, till at last the springs of his

268

overwrought mind gave way, and he became hopelessly insane.★ He was, after awhile, removed to the Northampton County Lunatic Asylum, where he still remains; and where we recently visited him by the courteous permission of the medical superintendent, who generally refuses the same favour to others, because he deems, and rightly too, that his patients should not be made an 'exhibition' of. Passing through several of the wards, we were ushered into what we at first deemed to be a gentleman's private sitting-room, but which was the ordinary sitting chamber of the better class of patients; and which appeared very cosy and comfortable with its mahogany chairs, table, and couch, warm soft carpets, and cheerful fire. Several patients were lounging about, and in a recess formed by one of the windows, which commanded a beautiful view of the large and spacious gardens belonging to the establishment, sat John Clare. Time had dealt gently with the poet, who —making allowance for his increased years—bore a very striking resemblance to the portrait of him prefixed to *The Village Minstrel*. He was rather short in stature, with a very large forehead, and mild benevolent-looking features. On our approaching him, we found him to be extremely taciturn, but the attendant informed us that in general Clare was good humoured, obedient, and cheerful.

He was reading a somewhat bulky volume, which he had obtained from the extensive library belonging to the institution, and appeared deeply interested in its contents. He still amuses himself by writing short pieces, of which the following is a fair specimen:

The Daisy

The daisy is a happy flower
    That comes with early spring;
And brings with it the sunny hour,
    When bees are on the wing.

It brings with it the butterfly,
    And humble early-bee;
The polyanthus goldeneye,
    And blooming apple-tree.

Hedge sparrows form their mossy nests
    By the old garden hedge,
Where schoolboys, in their idle glee,
    Seek 'pooties' as their pledge.

★ I do not think this was the cause of his madness.—J. P.

The cow stands browsing all the day
   Over the orchard gate;
And eats her bits of sweet old hay,
   While Goody stands to wait;

Lest what's not eaten the rude wind
   May rise and snatch away,
Over the neighbour's hedge behind,
   Where hungry cattle lay.

March 20, 1860   John Clare.

The last two verses contain some faint traces of the humour which formed such a conspicuous feature in his earlier works, while the poem itself is remarkable for its extreme simplicity, and its evidence of poor Clare's deeply-rooted fondness for old associations. Miss Mitford, in her *Notes of a Literary Life,* has given some account of the delusions of the poet; and in the *Quarterly Review* for January, 1857, there is a powerful and graphic paper on Northamptonshire, in which some account is given of the olden home of Clare at Northborough, where his wife resides; and which we are informed 'shows in the neatness of its arrangement and furniture marks of a higher cultivation than the ordinary labourer's home: in its books, many of them the gift of friends, —in the framed engravings, portraits of his benefactors—in flowers more abundant and more choice than in common cottage gardens—just such a holding as one would wish the Village Minstrel to enjoy.'

Whether Clare will ever recover from the malady with which he is afflicted, is a matter of doubt; but so many of his old friends and benefactors have been removed by the hands of death, that it is perhaps better for him to be as he is, than to awaken to reason and find himself amongst a new generation who know, and yet know him not, so little is he in fashion with the present generation.

106. John Askham on Clare

1863, 1864

A sonnet and a letter, both in *Northampton Mercury*, 28 May 1864, cxliii, 7.

John Askham (1825–94) was another 'uneducated poet', a shoe-maker, who became Librarian of the Literary Institute at Welling-borough, Northants, and had five volumes of verse to his credit. The same issue of the *Northampton Mercury* concluded an obituary:

He continued the habit of poetical composition to the last, and among those which have been preserved are some which are said to possess the beauty and coherency of the writings of his healthier days; but assuredly many of them have all the inconsecutiveness of a mind ungoverned— 'Like sweet bells jangled, out of tune and harsh'.—If it should be pro-posed to publish any of them, they will require very careful editing at thoroughly competent and congenial hands.

(a) 'Sonnet to John Clare': this first appeared in Askham's *Sonnets on the Months, and other Poems* (1863).

> Son of the Muses, Nature's favourite child,
>   Hushed are thy numbers, silent is thy song;
> The sun of Poesy that on thee smiled
>   Is set in gloomy night: thy harp, unstrung,
> Neglected hangs—its wonted music flown;
>   Reason, dethroned, hath fled her fair domain;

Thine eye hath lost its light, thy voice its tone;
   Thy fire is quenched, thy mantle rent in twain;
Nature shall woo thee to her haunts no more—
   The whispering woods, the softly-singing winds,
The brooklet's song, and all thou loved'st of yore,
   In thy lorn breast no voice responsive finds.
Alas! we mourn thy fate, poor hapless Clare,
That such a night should follow morn so fair.

(b) From a letter to the editor, *Northampton Mercury*, 28 May 1864:

It was with mingled feelings of sorrow and pleasure that I read in last week's *Mercury* the announcement of the death of John Clare, the peasant poet of our county. Sorrow to think that for so many years his bright intellect should have been overclouded with the awful shadow of insanity, and a melancholy pleasure to think that at last his long night of sorrow and disease was ended in death. I have always been an admirer of Clare's poetry; there is a truthfulness and sincerity in it that wins upon the reader as he peruses his verse. He was perhaps the most natural poet that ever wrote, and certainly one of the most original. . . . He uses none of the hackneyed phrases of mere rhymesters: there is no spasmodic raving, no straining for effect, in all his verse. . . . He is almost purely a descriptive poet; a true painter of nature in all her varied moods. . . . What he might have done had his reason been spared of course is mere conjecture, but what he *has* done is a rich addition to our poetic literature. . . .

107. John Dalby, a poem on Clare

1864

John Watson Dalby (1799–1883?) was a prolific sonneteer. *His Tales, Songs and Sonnets*, 1866, included this poem, entitled 'John Clare', which first appeared in *Northampton Mercury*, 4 June 1864, cxliii, 3. G. J. de Wilde was the author of *Rambles Round About*, ed. E. Dicey, Northampton 1872, in which Clare was mentioned. For Thomas Inskip, see No. 66.

John Clare

A life of dreams! the first, and the most real,
    Began in boyhood, when his spirit went,
    Mate of birds, trees, and flowers, glad and content;
'Mong sylvan haunts, embracing the ideal,
Which is the poet's workshop, who would see all
    God gives of true and good and lovely, blent
    In nature and man's heart; then fame was sent,
The dream of dreams! the towering hope to be all
    Man can be of supreme in worlds of thought;
        Then came the last dream, in our sight how sad!
And yet, perchance, unfettered fancy caught
    From that more joy than when cool reason had
Its reign, and ranged o'er realms too darkly fraught
    With cloud and change to keep such spirit glad.

Let me recal him when kind Inskip led
    The unconscious poet to your home, De Wilde,
    And we sat listening as to some fond child,
The wayward unconnected words he said—
Prattle, by confused recollections fed.
    Of famous times gone by—how Byron piled
    Praise on him in the *Quarterly*, and styled

Him of all poets as the very head!
Still dreaming! Happy dreamer! all is o'er!
All earthly visions, sober or insane;
Discord shall mar the harmony no more
That poured upon us, and, like summer rain
To the parched earth, oft filled the bosom frore
With sunshine as it drank the flowing strain.

108. John Plummer, again, on Clare

1864

From 'John Clare', *St James's Magazine*, July 1864, x, 438–47.
For Plummer, see No. 105.

(a)

It is impossible to imagine a greater contrast than that presented by the productions of Dryden and Clare, a contrast so marked and vivid as to leave few points of resemblance between the two poets. Dryden was vigorous, authoritative, yet formal withal; Clare was timid, delicate, and natural, even to a fault. . . . But who was John Clare? The ignorance of the present generation respecting the once popular poet is perfectly natural and excusable, considering how long he had been as one dead to the world, taking no pains or unable to inform his admirers that he still lingered amongst them—living yet dead, dead yet living!

(p. 438)

(b)

To those who admire an earnest love of nature, expressed in simple yet appropriate language, breathing a pure and reverent spirit, touching from its utter simplicity, the poems of John Clare will always be welcome; and should they be published in a collected shape, there will be few bookshelves on which their presence will be unknown. (p. 447)

109. Spencer T. Hall on Clare and Bloomfield

1866

From chapter 12, 'Bloomfield and Clare', *Biographical Sketches of Remarkable People*, Burnley 1873, 155–70. The essay is dated March 1866.

S. T. Hall (1812–85) co-edited the *Sheffield Iris* with James Montgomery, and was popularly known as the 'Sherwood Forester'. He was a man of many parts, defending phrenology, lecturing on mesmerism, practising as a homoeopathic doctor.

The Rural Muse and his long insanity were, in my opinion, about the two best friends under a merciful Heaven by which John Clare was ever visited. If you doubt it, read his painfully interesting biography by Frederick Martin. Read Clare's poetry too; and, while you feel thankful for your own sake that such a poet ever lived, if you happen to have a child gifted with a similar temperament, go down upon your knees and devoutly pray the Great Giver that He will also favour him with an extra guardian angel to accompany him through life. There is a fiction of English law—a fiction, however, founded in justice—that a man shall not be tried but by his peers; whilst it is well known that no two men are constituted alike, and that the world around us is to everyone, according to his constitution, a different world. How then shall a human alp, starting up from surrounding molehills, with its majestic cranial dome rising into the highest heaven of thought, be rightly comprehended and estimated by such as *never can* be his peers? What chance would the royal harp of David itself have had in a competition with tin horns and kettle-drums; or how could the virtues of the most delicate watch-works be tested by the aid of coarse rasps and sledge-hammers? Yet somewhat analogous to this, among the crowd and in the time in which it was cast in this lower world, was the fate of the fine Æolian spirit of John Clare, distinguished from all others of his name as 'the Northamptonshire Peasant.'

The son of Parker Clare, of Helpstone, a little village on the border of the eastern Fens—in simple fact, son of the poorest man in the parish, who had been made prematurely decrepid by hard labour, low diet, and severe chronic rheumatism,—and with the scantiest elements of scholastic knowledge imaginable, John Clare started up in the great sea of life, as some of those volcanic isles one reads of start up where not expected, to the great bewilderment of the mariner, who finding no allusion to them in his accustomed chart, interprets their existence or gives them a name in accordance—not necessarily with what they really are, but with his own notion of them, in the circumstances. Hence it was that, with a head almost as noble to look at as that of Shakespere; with a heart as affectionate as that of a true woman, and a soul as sensitive as her tenderest babe, when by the strength of his innate fires he was forced up to public gaze, the poetical phenomenon was interpreted and gauged by everyone according to his own calibre and custom. The literary haberdasher naturally measured him with his wand; the literary sweep treated him to a professional brush; the literary mince-meat man and sausage-maker thought his verses very extraordinary 'links;' while the illiterate boor regarded him as a more unfortunate boor, for having more of lightning and less of the clod in his nature than himself. Not a greater mistake did Boswell make in his estimate of Goldsmith, than that made with regard to Clare, by some of those who glorified themselves as friends and patrons at the expense of his manliest feelings. His genius, instead of being regarded and *honoured* by them, as a beautiful gift from Heaven to his country, for the better opening of the mind of its rural population to the love and wisdom of God in the creation around them, and the conveying into urban life itself the very breath and bloom of nature, was merely referred to by the majority of his earlier critics and patrons as furnishing an apology for their noticing at all one whose original guise was so rustic and so poor; and that, not very seldom, in opposition to his own emphatic protest. Nor did his further and higher development, with a more polished style of composition, much reduce this tendency. It was a start on a wrong line at first; it had become *a custom*; and the critics of that day, who (when they were not tigers and fought with one another) were frequently like sheep, taking the same gap in the same manner as their leader, kept up the suit. No matter how beautifully, or even sublimely, he might write, the same apologetic string was nearly always fiddled upon to the same tune, till people got tired, and, shutting their ears to it for relief, unfortunately thereby shut their ears also to some of the most sweet and original song that had ever been poured forth in the English language—song which, had it been only regarded on its own merits first, would have made all such officious apology (and the not always ungrudged patronage it procured,) as ridiculous as superfluous. But do not let me here be misunderstood. My blessing—every man's blessing—and the blessing of Heaven, be upon everyone who has at once the heart and the purse to aid, in a right noble and generous spirit, the development of struggling genius! Thrice blessed be the memory of all such, from Virgil's Macænas down to Capel Lofft, who procured the printing of Bloomfield's 'Farmer's Boy' after it had been refused insertion in a common magazine. What I mean is, that conceited officiousness which uses the language of condescension in regard to what is at least seven heavens above *its* petty platform of action, and which while it was pretending to serve John Clare, was marring his destiny as much as it was rasping his nerves,—was causing him to be misunderstood by the world it pretended to be instructing respecting him, and finally with its rudeness (all the while flattering itself with the name of friendship) took on itself an air of indignation, when it found it had missed its aim and got no grateful response from the man whom it was driving into madness as a refuge from its persecutions! Of course there were not wanting some glorious exceptions to this rule—many, indeed,—but there is no disguising that they were exceptions, and that the rule in the case was one of the most inglorious that could have been; and the people, of whatever rank, with whom Clare was brought most in contact by such means, instead of delicately befriending him, regarded him too often with a vulgar curiosity not unlike that with which (though with less emolument to the object) they in turn regarded Tom Thumb and the Hippopotamus—whichever happened for the moment to be most in fashion. It was through such effete meddlers and the pompous boast they made of what they imagined themselves to be doing for him, that some of his more truly genuine and generous patrons were turned against him, and made to withhold succour to which they would otherwise, no doubt, gladly have made additions; while the world at large had been amused with the belief that he was rendered independent, when in truth, both he and his large family were sometimes so pinched, and his little debts—little in one sense, but great enough in their effect on him—so harassing, that he was kept for years together in a state of anxiety and gloom, just as it was with Robert Bloomfield before him. . . .

My personal acquaintance with Clare was but brief, and sad; my admiration of his genius and many of his writings commenced early and continues still. It is doubtful if the whole range of modern authorhood furnishes a more remarkable and interesting psychological study than this—not a second Bloomfield, as some have called him, nor the English Burns, as he has been designated by others—not an imitator or likeness of any other man—but a bard so true to her as he saw her, that, in reading his poetry, it is sometimes difficult to know where Nature ends and her interpreter begins. When he said that he

> *Found* his poems in the fields
> And only wrote them down,

words more true were perhaps never written, and yet those two lines were penned by him at a retreat for mental invalids.

It was on one of the quietest, sunniest of summer Sundays, after diving the week before into a deep work on natural philosophy, that I first took up some passages of this natural poetry. In the morning I had risen early and strolled far into the country, with 'Telemachus' for a companion, in a neighbourhood noted for its natural beauty; had attended my usual place of worship during the forenoon, and in the afternoon had strolled out again through scenes having such descriptive names as Colwick Grove, Carlton Fields, St. Ann's Well, and Bluebell Hill, to a friendly cottage at Forest-side, where, during tea, I chanced to lay my hand on a review of *The Village Minstrel and other Poems*, by John Clare, prefaced by the inevitable mendicant-memoir got up by his publishing friends. It was easy to see that no man who had ever written anything half as interesting had been favoured with less of normal education. There were here and there striking defects of grammar; but owing to the peculiarity of their connection with his descriptions, imaginings, and fancies, which had a beautiful idiosyncratic logic of their own, there was a charm even about *them* for that very reason: they gave a more picturesque individuality to the man and his mind, serving as foils to throw out his excellences in finer relief, to those unconventional readers and thinkers who, enjoying what was *not* faultless, could make a reasonable allowance for *such* faults. In those simple extracts (I wish there were room for them here) I seemed to find nearly all my own sabbath musings made more real and glowing, and in the course of the week read three of Clare's volumes through. . . .

[Biographical details]

After his second visit the Peasant Poet had little liking for London. As with all such men, the 'sight' having been seen and the novelty rubbed off,—when prestige could no longer be gained by entertaining him, he was left pretty much to take his chance. One fact is very remarkable: After his first rustic volume, every succeeding one contained something better and better. For its graphic, though homely beauty, and truth to nature, his 'Woodman' has been ranked next to Burns's 'Cottar's Saturday night;' and his 'Shepherd's Calendar' is a truthful and exquisite history of the seasons; his poem on 'Antiquity' has images and fancies so startling as to remind one of Byron and even of Shakspere; his 'Adventures of a Grasshopper' is one of the richest and shrewdest allegories ever written for the young, and his rural sonnets improve in beauty and polish, but without losing any of their freshness, to the last: yet singularly enough, each successive volume after the first, was less successful in 'the trade' than its predecessors; and *The Rural Muse*, with its accompaniments—the most chaste, and in some respects perhaps the most beautiful of them all—fell, as the phrase goes, 'nearly· still-born from the press.' I bought two or three, and could have bought any number of the neat, uncut volumes, at a bookseller's shop in Stamford, in 1849, at eighteenpence a copy! . . .

Taken for all in all, Clare's treatment at Northampton Asylum was the most genial he had ever for any long period together received. I saw him there, or taking his walks in the neighbourhood, several times —the first in May, 1843. He wrote much beautiful poetry there, as he had done at High Beech, (where Cyrus Redding visited him and gave some of it to the world.) At Northampton every member of the staff of management, and many of the poor inmates, as well as a number of the inhabitants of the town, delighted in showing him all possible consideration and kindness. It can do the rest no injustice—though they were all so good to him—to say that Mr. Knight, (who was at one time steward at the Northampton, and is now superintending an asylum near Birmingham,) showed him especial sympathy, and had his fullest confidence in return. But there had been a period of his life when he had brooded (like poor Haydon) on the neglect—and worse than neglect— he had sometimes to endure, and on the way in which even great prize-fighters were petted and nourished, until at length he wished he were one of them; and then imagined he was one; and at last fancied himself anything or anybody rather than poor John Clare. In my first conversation with him he was rather shy, but less so as we talked, and somewhat cordial before we parted. This took place in the Asylum-grounds; and instead of the spare, sensitive person he appears in the portrait of him from Hilton's painting, forming a frontispiece to *The Village Minstrel*, I found him rather burly, florid, with light hair and somewhat shaggy eyebrows, and dressed as a plain but respectable farmer, in drab or stone-coloured coat and smalls, with gaiters, and altogether as clean and neat as if he had just been fresh brushed up for market or fair. He had been to see a friend, and get some tobacco, in Northampton town. On my asking him how he was, he said 'Why, I'm very well, and stout, but I'm getting tired of waiting here so long, and want to be off home. They won't let me go, however; for, you see, they're feeding me up for a fight; but they can get nobody able to strip to me; so they might as well have done with it, and let me go.' 'But, Mr. Clare,' said I, 'are you not more proud of your fame as a poet than your prowess as a prize-fighter?' When, rather abstractedly, as if considering or trying to recollect something, he answered, 'Oh, poetry, ah, I know, I once had something to do with poetry, a long while ago: but it was no good. I wish, though, they could get a man with courage enough to fight me.' This was just after he had been writing a beautiful and logical poem for my friend Mr. Joseph Stenson, the iron-master; so faithful to him was the muse, so treacherous his ordinary reason.

Next I asked him if he remembered ever receiving from me at High Beech a copy of the *Sheffield Iris* and a letter I had sent him. 'Sheffield Iris!' he exclaimed: 'oh, of course, I know all about the "Iris". You know I was editor of it, and lived with the Misses Gales, and was sent to York Castle, where I wrote that "Address to the Robin"'—thus identifying himself with James Montgomery. On my saying that I was going to London, and would have a pleasure in doing anything I could for him there, he seemed for a moment a little uneasy, and then replied, 'Ah, London; I once was there, but don't like it. There is one good fellow there; if you happen to see him you may remember me to him very kindly—and that's Tom Spring!' Such was the talk of a man who would not have hurt a fly or bruised a flower, much less have been one of the fraternity of Tom Spring, the greatest bruiser, of his day, in England! Another time on my seeing him, after he had just returned from a long and favourite ramble in the fields, he described it all, up to a certain point, with great accuracy and apparent pleasure, in beautiful language, and then broke off into talk it would be wrong to repeat; but more than once saying he should like to go home. The last time I saw Clare was on our accidentally meeting in the street, near All Saints' Church, in Northampton. He seemed very pleased thus to meet me, and I was not less so to see him and find that he remembered me. His face was lit all over with one sunny smile, and I congratulated him on his looking so well; but before we parted he talked again of wanting to go home, as though all his thoughts centred there.

A few years had passed, and I had been staying with some friends at Market Deeping, only a short distance from the villages of Helpstone and Northborough. In the former village I visited the cottage where he was born (at this time used as an infant school), as well as the grave of his parents, Parker and Ann Clare, in the old church-yard. At North-borough, in the pretty cottage which he never loved half so well as the more humble one in which he was born, I spent a kindly hour with some of his family, and saw them again at a lecture I had to deliver, the evening following, at Deeping. Mrs. Clare, still a fine, matronly, blooming woman, and who must have been a very comely girl in her day, was pleased to see and talk with me about her husband. I told her that when I saw him, he alluded to his home in a way that proved his affection for her in spite of his aberration. There were tears in her eyes as I mentioned this; but Mr. Martin alludes regretfully to Patty not having been once to Northampton to see her husband in all the twenty-two years he was there; and to none of the family having been except the youngest son, and he but once. I think it was probably under advice they abstained, from a fear that such an interview might be in some way injurious to him, by tempting him to escape, as he had done from High Beech, when he got home nearly dead after five days and nights' exposure to cold and hunger. At all events one trusts that it was not from indifference; for whatever his temperament, whatever his trials, John Clare had always been an affectionate husband and a most loving father—even though in his aberration he did often talk of another imaginary wife, 'Mary,' and equally imaginary children—an hallucination arising probably from his having in younger days had a sweetheart of the name of Mary, but who had now long been dead. . . . That he bitterly felt his exile from home, and that it preyed upon his mind, notwithstanding all the kindness with which he was treated at Northampton, is proved in the following, which Frederick Martin says was his last, and he thinks the noblest poem that poor Clare ever wrote. He calls it 'Clare's Swan-song,' and 'fervently hopes it will live as long as the English language.' It was not his last; for I have a copy of it in manuscript written years before some others of which I have also copies. But it is not likely soon to die. To have been written by one who owed little of his education to any man—whose every faculty, or almost every faculty, except his poetical one, was now deranged, and who was bowing his head with its long, white, flowing hair, as if constantly 'looking for his grave'—ought alone, independently of its wonderful poetical power, to make it a treasure to the psychologist and philanthropist as long as there is suffering in the world:—

[Quotes 'I am']

110. A female audience for John Clare

1867

From an unsigned article, 'John Clare, the Northamptonshire Peasant', *Englishwoman's Domestic Magazine*, February 1867, ii, 39–43.

There is a great deal of nonsense talked about neglected genius. Poets like Burns, Bloomfield, and Clare are sad examples of men who, in despite of genius which had power of affording delight and the best instruction to the whole world, were suffered to live in debt and poverty and to eat our their hearts in sorrow, while thousands and thousands of fools and knaves lived around and about them in splendour and luxury, with no more right to their ease than the accident of birth or the result of successful fraud. It is very easy to state all this, and then to say that the lives and deaths of such men as those above mentioned are disgraces to their nation, but it is not easy for us who come after to judge of the amount of culpability to be attached to the people of the age in which they lived, nor is it even easy to know what remedy we ourselves would have proposed to meet such evils.

In the first place, men of genius such as these, men born among the lower orders, cannot, as a rule, help themselves out of the mire in which they were born, but for which it is presumed that their genius unsuits them; and in the second place they do not like (and rightly) to be helped, except in such a way as will not wound their proper pride. It is all very well to say that the public is to blame for not sufficiently appreciating their books as to enable them to gain a livelihood by them, but this is more their misfortune than their fault, and it would be very hard to say they ought to purchase books they do not care about reading, because other people assure them that they are works of genius, and that if they don't like them they ought to do so. If Robert Burns were alive now and could reclaim the copyright of his poems, he would obtain therefrom a royal revenue; but it is also true that if he were now first beginning to write under the same circumstances, his life would probably differ not very much from that which he actually lived.

It is only very occasionally that a poet is able to live by his writings. We may say never to begin with. Tennyson himself would have starved if he had had nothing else to depend upon, long before he wrote the *Idylls of the King* and *Enoch Arden*. And a pastoral poet, such as John Clare, cannot now and probably never will be able to live by his poems, to use an Irishism, until some half-century or so after he is dead, and probably not then. Under these circumstances, if the poet cannot support himself and his muse, and it is a 'national disgrace' if they are not both supported, we must look out for some artificial means of support for him. Henry Taylor we think recommends that there should be a fund for allowing distressed poets a certain income, and no doubt according to his theory it would be an admirable institution, but it would be the most difficult of all possible funds to administer judiciously. To many men such an allowance would be positive ruin; for men like John Clare we fancy it would be but questionable kindness, and in most cases would destroy that feeling of noble independence without which the soul poetic cannot grow.

Such men are, in fact, the most difficult of all to assist, and until the public have become literary, poetical, and critical enough to support poets by buying their books, they will be so still. Not to buy their books hurts them most in all ways, to help them pecuniarily has an unpleasant flavour of charity about it which not the most delicate hand that ever gave can prevent, and to provide them with lucrative and

honourable employment—the best way, to our mind, when practicable
—is often out of the question by reason of their want of business ability
and education. We agree with Mr. Taylor in thinking it a matter in
which the state is concerned, and we think it a national duty to prevent
such men from undue pressure of poverty and physical labour; but we
consider it a most difficult question to settle how the assistance can be
rendered, and are not disposed to be too severe upon our ancestors for
not solving a riddle which puzzles ourselves. . . .

Poetical temperament he had; he had just sufficient mechanical skill,
he had stores, though small ones, of poetic and legendary lore, but one
thing was wanted to complete what may be termed the skeleton of a
poet and fasten together the *disjecta membra*,[1] and that was to fall in love.
John Clare was to be a poet, and so he fell in love. He fell in love (for the
first time) at the age of fifteen with one Mary Joyce, and was allowed to
indulge in his dream for six months, and then the 'beggar boy' was
dismissed. Yet how little suffices for the true poet! This passion, so short
in its happiness, gave life to his poetry from first to last. He fell in love
many other times; indeed, his soul seems to have been inflammatory in
the extreme; but this early passion was never extinguished. Mary was,
poetically, his love to the end of his days; when his mind left him, and
his wife and children faded from his memory, this wife of his imagination still lived; she was the theme of his most elevated poems, and the
spiritual consolation of his lonely madness. Not Petrarch's Laura nor
Dante's Beatrice was more faithfully and fondly worshipped than the
Mary of John Clare. We have compared his love to two other extraordinary examples of poetic devotion, but to our mind no psychological
phenomenon of this kind was so remarkable and inexplicable as this
soul-worship of John Clare. It is alone, unique, *sui generis*.

[1] 'limbs of a dismembered poet', Horace, *Satires*, I, iv, 62.

111. An American view of a peasant poet

1869

From an unsigned article, 'John Clare, the Peasant Poet', *Harper's New Monthly Magazine*, November 1869, xxxix, 882–6.

There are two modes of measuring human power. The first and most common mode is by the value of the works it accomplishes; the second, and we think the most just, is by the difficulties it has overcome. The most ordinary observer who sees a steam-engine, and knows the uses to which it has been applied, the least imaginative man who witnesses the performance of Macbeth or Hamlet, or who reads our great epic, *Paradise Lost*, is ready to pay homage to Watt or Shakspeare, or Milton, as men possessed of great power. But a finer discernment is needed to acknowledge the power of one who, starting from a lower level, fought his way unaided, through obstacles that would have seemed to most men insuperable, not to the empyrean heights reached by these,

> The few, the immortal names
> That were not born to die,

yet to a position far above that from which he started, to a position to which he could have been elevated only by uncommon powers. To this last class belongs the hero of our story—a true story of triumphant genius and successful love; alas! for our world, that there are so few such to tell. . . .

The night was surely gone for John Clare. His path was now along the world's sunny side. The publishers found ready sale for the little volume of his poems, and, with a generosity not too common among publishers, invested one hundred pounds in his name. The Earl of Fitz-william and the Marquis of Exeter—the greatest landholders in the poet's neighborhood—added largely to this sum; other noblemen and gentlemen, in admiration of the man's faithful, patient, courageous life, sent donations for him to his publishers. Thus an annuity large enough for comfort, though not for luxury, was secured to him. The crown of all was the hour when, without violation of honor or conscience, with the harmonious assent of his whole being, he could unveil his heart to the girl he had loved so truly and so long. With what shame-faced pride she must have read the poems in which her charms were celebrated! Again we picture him straying through the flowery meadows and by the side of his favorite brook; but he is not now alone; his pretty, artless Patty is by his side. He recites his verses—some perhaps that the world has not yet heard—and he receives from her the reward that the poet most desires, praise from the lips he loves.

Perhaps it was under these circumstances that he composed the stanzas to Patty in which occur the following lines:

> Flow on, thou gently plashing stream,
>   O'er weed-beds wild and rank;
> Delighted I've enjoyed my dream
>   Upon thy mossy bank:
> Bemoistening many a weedy stem,
>   I've watched thee wind so clearly,
> And on thy banks I found the gem
>   That makes me love thee dearly.

The picture, in its minute noting of features that would have little charm for a common eye, recalls some of Tennyson's masterly paintings of scenes of the same character among the Lincolnshire fens, where,

> Through the marish green and still
> The tangled water-courses slept,
> Shot over with purple and green and yellow.

We have but one other scene to offer the reader. It is a scene of real life, drawn for us by one who was attracted to Helpston by his interest in the peasant poet. The humble cottage of the pauper Parker Clare had been enlarged and repaired, presenting the aspect of a comfortable English farmer's home, and there was the proud father, pauper no longer, the prouder mother, and the gentle, loving wife, sunning themselves in the glow of his prosperity who had thus won the crown of faithful endurance and steadfast working.

Here we rest. The end for him had not yet come. Life had other scenes to unfold for him. Were they dark?—were they bright? The sibyl is silent. What has been told is enough for her purpose, which was to sketch a suggestive picture for the young, who, conscious of some intellectual power, are shrinking from less pleasing forms of labor, and are in danger of falling into indolent, hopeless vacuity, or it may be into debasing dependence, rather than accept the work which they consider beneath their powers. Let them see in John Clare that the humblest labor does not degrade genius, nay, that its faithful performance elevates.

If the task assigned you be lowly, work in it diligently and steadily. In such work lies true heroism, the only heroism possible to most of us; and to the earnest worker, never to the idler, comes the call, 'Come up higher!'

112. The doomed poet

1873

J. L. Cherry, from *Life and Remains of John Clare*, 1873, pp. 129–30. See Introduction, pp. 15–16.

In looking back upon such a life as Clare's, so prominent are the human interests which confront us, that those of poetry, as one of the fine arts, are not unlikely to sink for a time completely out of sight. The long and painful strain upon our sympathy to which we are subject as we read the story is such perhaps as the life of no other English poet puts upon us. The spell of the great moral problems by which the lives of so many of our poets seem to have been more or less surrounded makes itself felt in every step of Clare's career. We are tempted to speak in almost fatalistic language of the disastrous gift of the poetic faculty, and to find in that the source of all Clare's woe. The well-known lines—

> We poets in our youth begin in gladness,
> But thereof come in the end despondency and
> madness—

ring in our ears, and we remember that these are the words of a poet endowed with a well-balanced mind, and who knew far less than Clare the experience of

Cold, pain, and labour, and all fleshly ills.

In Clare's case we are tempted to say that the Genius of Poetry laid her fearful hand upon a nature too weak to bear her gifts and at the same time to master the untoward circumstances in which his lot was cast. But too well does poor Clare's history illustrate that interpretation of the myth which pictures Great Pan secretly busy among the reeds and fashioning, with sinister thought, the fatal pipe which shall 'make a poet out of a man.'

And yet it may be doubted whether, on the whole, Clare's lot in life, and that of the wife and family who were dependent upon him, was aggravated by the poetic genius which we are thus trying to make the scapegoat for his misfortunes.

It may be that the publicity acquired by the Northamptonshire Peasant Poet simply brings to the surface the average life of the English agricultural labourer in the person of one who was more than usually sensitive to suffering. Unhappily there is too good reason to believe that the privations to which Clare and his household were subject cannot be looked upon as exceptional in the class of society to which both husband and wife belonged, although they naturally acquire a deeper shade from the prospect of competency and comfort which Clare's gifts seemed to promise. In this light, while the miseries of the poet are none the less real and claim none the less of our sympathy, the moral problem of Clare's woes belongs rather to humanity at large than to poets in particular. We are at liberty to hope, then, that the world is all the richer, and that Clare's lot was none the harder, by reason of that dispensation of Providence which has given to English literature such a volume as *The Rural Muse*. How many are there who not only fail, as Clare failed, to rise above their circumstances, but who, in addition, leave nothing behind them to enrich posterity! We are indeed the richer for Clare, but with what travail of soul to himself only true poets can know.

113. From some reviews of Cherry's *Life and Remains*

1873

Cherry's *Life* (No. 112) was widely noticed. For further comments, see Introduction, p. 16.

(a) *Nonconformist*, 19 February 1873, xxxiv, 193:

[Of the asylum poems] There is all the unaffected simplicity, the quiet love of nature, and the quaint use of local phrases, which gave such a peculiar colour to his earlier works. There is a clearness, a sanity, and now and then a perfection of expression, which could never suggest aberration of any kind. Clare was always sweet, with a sustained lingering intensity of tone. His poems only needed a quantum of strength to have claimed the title of great. But this is never found in Clare. He is a sweet singer, but a singer of the second or of the third order only—lacking wholly the robustness, the dash, which we so admire, say, in Burns or Beranger. He is pensive, he is glad, he can be merry; but he is never boisterous in any mood, and he rather lacks strong humour, which above all gives richness and fulness of poetic character. In this, he is like Keats: he walked in a world of his own, and "watered" the impressions of other men, so far as he got hold of them, rather than dashed into the atmosphere which they coloured, identifying himself with wide variety of character and emotion. His harp was sweet, tenderly sweet, but it had few strings, and the ceaseless striking of them wore them through very soon; and thereafter they gave out only an echo amid disharmonies, and that at long intervals.

(b) *Sheffield Daily Telegraph*, 8 March 1873 (plagiarizing Cherry):

But too well does poor Clare's history illustrate that interpretation of the myth which pictures Great Pan secretly busy in fashioning with sinister thought the fatal pipe which shall 'make a poet out of a man'.

289

CLARE

(c) *Saturday Review*, 5 April 1873, 35, 461–2:

We doubt very much if the selection was worth making, much more whether it was worth publishing. At all events, if the poems of a lunatic are published, they should be given, if indeed with omissions, yet most certainly without corrections. But with one or two exceptions the poems seem to us poor . . . .

(c) *Antiquary*, 21 June 1873, iii, 312:

It is generally remarked that one of the saddest pages in the history of literature, is that which chronicles the biography of poets. Even if external circumstances be all that can be desired, the poetic tempera-ment, from its frequently morbid sensibility, is constantly in a state of excitement, and often of suffering; but when to the internal torments all the miseries of an uncertain existence are added, the picture presented by the life of one, we might almost say, thus *unhappily* gifted, is distress-ing and painful in the extreme. If, in order to be a poet, a susceptibility so highly developed as to cause almost continual pain to its possessor be requisite, then it must be confessed that the gift is dearly paid for. . . . To all literature-loving natives of his own country, the possession of these remains of the poet would seem almost indispensable. . . . In various of the poems, the influence of Burns is apparent. This is but natural, though Clare's individual genius had not by any means the same characteristics as that of the Ayrshire poet. Burns was all fire and impetuosity of feeling. The inspiration of the Northamptonshire singer took its rise from a calmer fount, and he seems most natural and most at home when pencilling the myriad tranquil beauties of field and forest, and this he does with a sweetness very individual and charming. His observation of nature was most minute and loving, and characterized by that sympathetic appreciation of colour and effect which marks and makes the artist—whether of pen or pencil.

(e) *Manchester Guardian*, 30 July 1873:

Although John Clare was certainly within his own field a poet, it is to be doubted whether any but his very best pieces will live. His minor poems are by far his best, but of these there are by far too many, and while they never fail in ease and spontaneous melody, they lack variety, lyric brevity, and that passionate glow which fires the volcanic heart of Burns. The more ambitious poems, 'The Village Minstrel' and 'The

Rural Muse', are now little read even by professed literateurs, and, though they show abundant proofs of poetic power, there is a certain strain and effort about them which detracts from the reader's pleasure. In elemental power of describing the grand or terrible, and in moralizing over the mortality of Kingdoms and 'the dreadful past' Clare never comes near Byron; in lyrical bursts he does not approach Burns. He belongs to the Kirke White, Ebenezer Elliott, David Gray, and Bloomfield class of poets—a small but rare band, whose noble rage, in spite of the poet's words, chill penury did not repress, and the genial current of whose soul was not frozen by their poverty. We place him above Bloomfield, but scarcely on a level with the others judged by their best pieces compared with his best, especially when we remember how short were the lives of two of them, while Clare lived out his span of three score years. The sonnets in the present volume cannot rank high. . . . Clare's real forte was pathos . . . [quotes 'The Dying Child']. We know nothing more simply pathetic than this in the English language. The poet has indeed entered with his own childlike heart into the heart of the little simple dying child, and interpreted every languid movement of the drooping eyelid and the enfeebled hand. . . .

114. Clare and the soul of the people

1873, 1884

Richard Heath, from *The English Peasant*, 1893, pp. 292–3, 317–19, 42–3.

The section on Clare ('Types of English Agricultural Life', ii), pp. 292–319, originally appeared in two instalments in *Golden Hours* (A Monthly Magazine for Family and General Reading), 1873, pp. 161–7, 231–9. The second article includes this revealing comment: 'If we think of the poet merely as the writer of pretty verses, one who has the power to utter fine sentiments in tuneful language, his life is not a whit more interesting than that of any other artist. But the true interest of the poet's life lies in something deeper than his art, in the fact that he is, in the most real sense, a man' (p. 238). The third extract is from the chapter entitled 'The English Via Dolorosa', section ix, 'How to Destroy a People's Soul', pp. 37–43. This originally appeared separately in 1884. Little is known of Richard Heath, author of a biography of Edgar Quinet, 1881, and several other books.

A little fair-haired boy, with bright, eager eyes, clad in well-patched smock and heavy clouted shoes, is running joyfully over a wild heath at early dawn. Every now and then he stops to take breath, and sometimes plucks a bluebell or a sprig of marjoram, yet he presses onwards, over common and field, through woodland and park, down into the valley and up the hill; at first singing, but after a time often sinking down wearily by the wayside, for the sun is getting fierce, and his strength is well-nigh gone.

Whither is the child bent? Yesternight and again this morning he saw hanging midway between heaven and earth a beautiful land. To reach it he set out breakfastless, but alas! the nearer he seems to get to it, the further off it appears; and now, as he gains the summit of the hill he has made such an effort to climb, a dark cloud has fallen, and the alluring vision is lost in dull, grey gloom.

Ready to faint from sheer exhaustion and distress of mind, some men working in the neighbourhood take pity upon him, give him a crust or two from their wallets, and set him out on his road home. Thither he returns at nightfall, to receive his punishment, and then to hide his sorrows in the dark, and to sob over the destruction of the bright illimitable hopes that delusive horizon had aroused in his imagination.

Just as the child is father to the man, so this early adventure of John Clare proved an omen of what his life would be. Again and again he realised the bitter experience of his 'Dream,' and learnt how

> Hopeless distance with a boundless stretch,
> Flashed on despair the joy it could not reach,
> A moment's mockery.

In Helpstone, an obscure village in Northamptonshire, not far from Peterborough Great Fen, dwelt, towards the close of the last century, one Parker Clare, 'a hind born to the flail and plough.' He was the child of sin and suffering; his mother a poor girl, misled by the audacious manners and glib tongue of a roving vagabond who had made the village his halting-place for a season.

Parker Clare solaced himself in the only way he could by taking a companion to share his woes. Those were days when wages in North-amptonshire, for able-bodied men, were only eight or nine shillings in summer, and about five or six shillings in winter; but since Parker Clare could never claim to be an able-bodied man, he went through life mainly as a pauper. Knowing what we do of agricultural homes, we may suppose that the dwelling of such a poverty-stricken wretch was just a little more miserable than those of his fellows. But, doubtless, even he felt its misery more acutely when, seven months after he had taken to himself a wife, he became the father of twins. Nevertheless, if he could have seen it, there was just at that time a ruddy glare on the social horizon, which betokened a bright to-morrow. The feudal sys-tem, of whose dregs he was a victim, was rapidly passing away. Its sun was setting in blood-red clouds, and all Europe stood aghast, as men who watch in silent horror some awful conflagration. John Clare was born in that 'Annus Terribilis,' 1793.

He was, as I have said, a twin child, much more sickly than his sister, who died; but, like so many sickly people, the very weakness of the body seemed to give the soul more play. The walls of sense were not so thick, the veil which hid the Invisible was not quite so dense; and if John Clare suffered more than his chubby companions, he was compensated by a power to perceive and enjoy glories which were hidden from them. (pp. 292–3)

John Clare is the poet of English peasant life. He, if any one can, may claim to be a representative man. Bloomfield has not depicted that life with more sympathy, nor Crabbe with a truer touch. Crabbe looked down upon it from above; Clare lived it, felt its joys, and endured all its woes.

I have tried to give some idea of the sordid suffering of his childhood and youth, but only those who have read his works can know how the iron entered into his soul. He was one with his brethren in that bitter, long-fought fight with grim Poverty; one with them in his content and discontent; contented to do as his fathers did, yet discontented, profoundly discontented with his lot.

With a love for his native scenes, capable of being developed into the intensest patriotism, with a love of old customs and old institutions— in fact, a Conservative by nature—he is driven to cry—

> O England! boasted land of liberty,
> With strangers still thou may'st the title own,
> But *thy poor slaves* the alteration see,
> With many a loss to them the truth is known.
>
> .   .   .   .   .   .
>
> And every village owns its tyrants now,
> And parish slaves must live as parish kings allow.

With the intensest love of home, with a capacity for the fullest, deepest human affection, he is driven at last by utter stress of woe to feel completely weaned from it, and to cry, as many an aged labourer, the inmate of a Union so distant that he is forgotten by kith and kin, might do, that

> Even those he loved best
> Are strange—nay, they are stranger than the rest.

And then his errors: are they not just those of the labouring man? And so too the deep yet melancholy piety which marks him all through life—so in harmony with what one reads everywhere in our village churchyards.

Life is a misery—an *ignis fatuus*,—death a freedom from misery—

something that will heal every wound, and enable him to lay his aching head to rest. He is resigned; 'God's will be done,' he says.

> Fate's decree,
> Doomed many evils should encompass thee.

He speaks of God as 'the Omnipotent,' thinking doubtless of Him a the poor labourer does in His awful character as 'the Almighty.' His simple theology is this:—God has mysteriously doomed us to pain and want here; if we bear it patiently and well now, we shall be rewarded hereafter. Thus, speaking of the dead who lie in the churchyard, he says—

> The bill's made out, the reck'ning paid,
> The book is crossed, the business done;
> On them the last demand is made,
> And heaven's eternal peace is won.

Who will deny that there is some truth in this view with our Lord's words before him? 'But Abraham said, Son, remember that thou in thy lifetime receivedst thy good things, and likewise Lazarus evil things; but now he is comforted, and thou art tormented.' But at best it is a view which can only help men to endure; it is utterly powerless to raise them from sin, from suffering, and woe.

Oh! when will the true light shine upon our poor *pagani*?[1] when will they learn that the God and Father of our Lord Jesus Christ is not a stern Fate, who dooms thousands of His creatures to want and misery? How could they, if they were truly taught His character from the Bible, and learnt there what pains the God of Moses took to prevent any of His people coming to utter poverty?

Only let the true gospel be preached, the good news that God himself is the Saviour, the Redeemer of man, and this melancholy religion which teaches men calmly to resign their children to want and dirt—in reality to disease and death—will pass away as a dark oppressive cloud from the minds and souls of our agricultural poor, and enable them to be, as they ought from their occupation to be, the most joyous, most independent inhabitants of our land. (pp. 317–19)

The truth, however, about the Revolution had not reached the majority of his [Pitt's] supporters, and their nerves being less sensitive, they judged the state of the country more correctly. As to the agricultural labourers, they knew them to be what we see them depicted in

[1] 'countrymen'.

the drawings of Morland, and in the writings of Crabbe, Blomfield, and Clare; an artless, patient, gregarious herd, who went on plodding from day to day, hopeless and aimless, with no other relief than an occasional burst of frantic merriment, of which horse-play and hard drinking were the chief features. Freed from all anxiety concerning the future, mostly ignorant of any higher good than the satisfaction of their senses, there was nothing to fear from such a people.

However, the soul of the Agricultural Poor was not quite dead. It fluttered still in the breasts of a few sufferers, and came out as such deep vague sorrows do in verse.

Blomfield and Clare, these poets of the people, have throughout the same undertone of melancholy, arising from the conviction that they belonged to a class which is day by day falling into a deeper, more abject state of poverty or crime. When the former, as he reflected on the distance the increasing wealth made between different ranks, cries out—

> Has Wealth done this?—then Wealth's a foe to me;
> Foe to our rights; that leaves a pow'rful few
> The paths of emulation to pursue:—
> For emulation stoops to us no more:
> The hope of humble industry is o'er—

we have, as it were, a throb from a slumbering volcano.

And the conviction that the sleeper might awake seems to have been the result of Mr. Pitt's bill, for though dropped, its main proposition, the making up out of the rates of the deficiency of a labourer's income, came to be the general practice throughout the country. This suggested the necessity of a scale, and the amount a labourer ought to have was fixed, from time to time, by the price of the quartern loaf, which might vary from 6d. to 2s.

By this system it was admitted that every man in the country had a right to an adequate maintenance, whether he was idle or industrious, honest or dishonest; and that he ought to receive public aid in proportion to the number of his family. English people are frightened at the word Socialism. Who ever conceived a worse type of Socialism than this?

When the Parliamentary Commission of 1833 inquired into the effect of this system, they could not find words strong enough to paint their dismay. They found the poor's rates in 1830 had reached an annual amount of six to seven millions sterling; that in some parts of the country, nearly all the labourers were paupers; that the rascally idler was better off than the honest and laborious; the latter, one after the other, being driven to the conviction that the man who worked hard was a fool; they found, however, that employers liked the system, because it enabled them to give low wages, knowing the deficiency would be made up by the parish.

Never, perhaps, in history has there been a state of things so ridiculously immoral. (pp. 42–3)

115. Some late nineteenth-century views of Clare

1887, 1893, 1897

(a) Leslie Stephen (1832–1904), from his article on Clare in the *Dictionary of National Biography*, 1887. For Lamb's advice, see No. 64. Edmund Blunden characterized this article as 'callous and spiritually grotesque' (*Athenaeum*, 5 March 1920, no. 4688, 299).

Clare's poetry is modelled upon that of the cultivated classes, instead of expressing the sentiments of his own class. Lamb advised him to avoid his rustic 'slang', and recommended Shenstone's 'Schoolmistress' in preference to 'Goody's own language'. Clare becomes less vernacular in his later poems, and the advice may have suited the man. The result is, however, that the want of culture is not compensated by vigour of local colouring. Though Clare shews fine natural taste, and has many exquisite descriptive touches, his poetry does not rise to a really high level and though extraordinary under the circumstances, requires for its appreciation that the circumstances should be remembered.

(b) Richard Henry Stoddard (1825–1903), an American poet, from 'John Clare', *Under the Evening Lamp*, 1893, pp. 120–34:

Poetry was not a mental acquisition and development with Bloomfield and Clare; it was an alms which Nature bestowed upon them in a generous mood, to lighten the dark road they were to travel, and to console them in their misfortunes and sufferings.　　　　(p. 121)

The poetry of Clare is what might have been expected from his long familiarity with rural scenery, and his intimate knowledge of country life. Simple as the song of a bird, it is best described by Milton's phrase, 'native wood-notes wild', for art it has none, and only such music as lingered in the memory of Clare from the few poets that he had read. It abounds with picturesque details, which declare the naturalist as well as the poet; it sparkles with happy epithets, and to those who delight in Nature for its own sake, and not for the human quality which the present race of poets are striving to infuse into it, it is winsome and charming. It is not the kind of poetry to criticize, for it is full of faults, but to read generously and tenderly, remembering the lowly life of Clare, his want of education, his temptations, his struggles, his sorrow and suffering, and his melancholy end. (p. 132)

(c) C. H. Herford (1853–1931), from *The Age of Wordsworth*, 1897, p. 186. Herford was Professor of English at Manchester from 1901 to 1921, and an influential critic.

Clare had a keen eye and a bright and tender descriptive touch; but his imaginative and intellectual qualities are slight, and where he passes beyond description he becomes insignificant.

116. Norman Gale, a rhapsodic view

1901

From the Introduction to Norman Gale's *Poems by John Clare*, Rugby 1901, pp. xlii–iv.

Norman Gale (1862–1942) was a poet of the countryside and the cricket field.

That some of CLARE's poems belong of right to the excellent things of this earth admits of no dispute. A worshipper of Nature, by whom he was surely appointed to be one of her chief historians, he revelled in her manifestations, whether they showed in the higher heaven of blue or in the lower heaven of green. He was, if the phrases may pass muster, a gossip of the rainbow, a crony of the flowers. His heart was not less slow than that of Wordsworth to leap up with joy when he beheld standing across the sky, its feet treading the horizon, the most splendid triumphal arch ever devised; and though it was not granted him to render homage to his mistress in such large accents as those which fell from the lips of his great brother in song, he paid for her love and favours in music far from perishable, as may be noted by all who will read the pieces that have been selected for this volume from *The Rural Muse*. Who passes by any one of these poems because he early finds a flaw, does so at his own danger, for each of them belongs, as I venture to assert, so indubitably to the particular treasures of pastoral poetry that I doubt whether the contradiction of our greatest critics could frighten me from the attitude of admiration. To influences other than those of the countryside, CLARE remained unimpressionable. To be in London was to long for Helpstone, the commons and pools of which were more precious to the poet than all the glories of Westminster Abbey, and the expanses of the artificial lakes. While he sojourned in the Metropolis the right spark would not fall from heaven, but as soon as he wandered once more among the scenes so long familiar to him, the Muse was his unfailing companion. Brooks glided in his songs; birds and clouds and leafage were foundations without which he had been well-nigh powerless. He understood, and was content with, his limits; and so perfectly did he accomplish his duty as Nature's cherished amanuensis, that it is no hard task for a man with an ounce of imagination in his being to hear the trickle of streams, and to fancy his study carpeted with grass, while reading JOHN CLARE'S poems within four walls. As this volume of selections is designed for the purpose of attracting readers to a poet whose appreciative receipts from his posterity are sadly deficient in quantity, the publisher has thought well to ask from me the tale of CLARE'S life, rather than my views of the poet's work and its effect upon his successors in the production of poetry dealing almost exclusively with the vowels and consonants in Nature's mighty alphabet. Enough has been said to prove the writer no half-hearted advocate; and if these few pages serve to increase the number of CLARE'S friends, he will be more than satisfied, happy in the thought that he has been the means of introducing readers to poetry as gentle as it is healing, as simple as it is sincere. Touching its wholesomeness, how could it fail to delight in this respect when the chief of its constituent parts were the large and lovely expressions of Nature's handicraft? JOHN CLARE'S gift fell upon him direct from the skies. It came clean; and clean he kept it from the beginning to the end of his stewardship.

117. Arthur Symons on Clare

1908

From the Introduction to *Poems by John Clare*, ed. Arthur Symons, 1908.

Arthur Symons (1865–1945) edited an extremely valuable selection of the poems; his Introduction puts the criticism of Clare on to a new footing (see Introduction, p. 18). Part of this Introduction was reprinted in his *The Romantic Movement in English Poetry*, 1909. Symons's most notable book was *The Symbolist Movement in Literature*, 1899.

We are told in the introduction to a volume of poems by John Clare, published in 1820, 'They are the genuine productions of a young peasant, a day-labourer in husbandry, who has had no advantages of education beyond others of his class; and though poets in this country have seldom been fortunate men, yet he is, perhaps, the least favoured by circumstances, and the most destitute of friends, of any that ever existed.' If the writer of the introduction had been able to look to the end of the career on whose outset he commented, he would have omitted the 'perhaps'. The son of a pauper farm-labourer, John Clare wrote his earlier poems in the intervals of hard manual labour in the fields, and his later poems in lucid intervals in a madhouse, to which ill health, over-work, and drink had brought him. In a poem written before he was seventeen he had asked that he might

> Find one hope true—to die at home at last,

and his last words, when he died in the madhouse, were, 'I want to go home.' In another early poem he had prayed, seeing a tree in autumn, that, when his time came, the trunk might die with the leaves. Even so reasonable a prayer was not answered.

In Clare's early work, which is more definitely the work of the peasant than perhaps any other peasant poetry, there is more reality than poetry.

I found the poems in the fields,
And only wrote them down,

as he says with truth, and it was with an acute sense of the precise thing
he was saying that Lamb complimented him in 1822 on the 'quantity'
of his observation. It is difficult to know how much of these early poems
were tinkered for publication by the too fastidious publisher Mr.
Taylor, and what is most smooth and traditional in them is certainly
not what is best. The ballads and love-songs have very little value, and
there is often a helplessness in the language, which passes from the over-
familiar to the over-elevated. Later on he would not have called the
glow-worm 'tasteful illumination of the night', nor required so large a
glossary of provincialisms. As it is, when he is not trying to write like
Burns, or in any way not quite natural to him, he gives us, in a personal
and unusual manner, a sense of the earth and living things, of the life of
the fields and farmyards, with a Dutch closeness, showing us himself,

Toiling in the naked fields,
Where no bush a shelter yields,

in his hard poverty, and with his sensitiveness to weather, not only as it
helps or hinders his labour. You see him looking up from it, looking
and listening, and noting down everything he has observed, sometimes
with this homely detail:

Now buzzing, with unwelcome din,
The heedless beetle bangs
Against the cow-boy's dinner-tin
That o'er his shoulder hangs.

No one before him had given such a sense of the village, for Bloomfield
does not count, not being really a poet; and no one has done it so well
again until a greater poet, Barnes, brought more poetry with him.
Clare's poetry begins by having something clogging in it; substance,
and poetical substance, is there, but the poetry has hardly worked its
way out to freedom.

That it should have got so far on the way there is one of the most
astonishing things in literature. . . .

It must not be assumed that because Clare is a peasant his poetry is in
every sense typically peasant poetry. He was gifted for poetry by those
very qualities which made him ineffectual as a peasant. The common
error about him is repeated by Mr. Lucas in his *Life of Lamb*: 'He was to

have been another Burns, but succeeded only in being a better Bloom-field.' The difference between Clare and Bloomfield is the difference between what is poetry and what is not, and neither is nearer to or farther from being a poet because he was also a peasant. The difference between Burns and Clare is the difference between two kinds and qualities of poetry. Burns was a great poet, filled with ideas, passions, and every sort of intoxication; but he had no such minute local lore as Clare, nor, indeed, so deep a love of the earth. He could create by naming, while Clare, who lived on the memory of his heart, had to enumerate, not leaving out one detail, because he loved every detail. Burns or Hogg, however, we can very well imagine at any period following the plough with skill or keeping cattle with care. But Clare was never a good labourer; he pottered in the fields feebly, he tried fruitless way after way of making his living. What was strangely sensitive in him might well have been hereditary if the wild and unproved story told by his biographer Martin is true: that his father was the illegitimate son of a nameless wanderer, who came to the village with his fiddle, saying he was a Scotchman or an Irishman, and taught in the village school, and disappeared one day as suddenly as he had come. The story is at least symbolic, if not true. That wandering and strange instinct was in his blood, and it spoiled the peasant in him and made the poet.

Clare is said to have been barely five feet in height, 'with keen, eager eyes, high forehead, long hair, falling down in wild and almost grotesque fashion over his shoulders.' He was generally dressed in very poor clothes, and was said by some woman to look 'like a nobleman in disguise'. His nerves were not the nerves of a peasant. Everything that touched him was a delight or an agony, and we hear continually of his bursting into tears. He was restless and loved wandering, but he came back always to the point from which he had started. He could not endure that anything he had once known should be changed. He writes to tell his publisher that the landlord is going to cut down two elm trees at the back of his hut, and he says: 'I have been several mornings to bid them farewell.' He kept his reason as long as he was left to starve and suffer in that hut, and when he was taken from it, though to a better dwelling, he lost all hold on himself. He was torn up by the roots, and the flower of his mind withered. What this transplanting did for him is enough to show how native to him was his own soil, and how his songs grew out of it. Yet the strange thing is that what killed him as a human mind exalted him as a poetic consciousness, and that the verse

303

written in the asylum is of a rarer and finer quality than any of the verse written while he was at liberty and at home.

Clare educated himself with rapidity, and I am inclined to doubt the stories of the illiterate condition of even his early manuscripts. His hand-writing, in a letter written in 1825, enclosing three sonnets on the death of Bloomfield, contained among the Bloomfield Papers in the British Museum, is clear, energetic, and fluent, very different from the painful and incompetent copy-book hand of Bloomfield; and the only oddity is that the sonnets are not punctuated (anticipating Mallarmé), and that the sign for 'and' is put, whimsically enough, at the beginning of a line. The pencil scribble on the back of a letter dated 1818 of a poem pub-lished in 1820, is in no sense illiterate. We know from Mrs. Emmerson's letters in the Clare Papers in the British Museum that by 1820 he was familiar with Percy's *Reliques*, and in the same year she sends him Coleridge's and Akenside's poems, and 'two volumes of miscellaneous poems, which contain specimens from most of our British bards'. In the same year, sending him a Walker's Dictionary, she reminds him of 'those authors you possess—Blair, Addison, Mason, Young'. In 1821 Taylor saw in his cupboard copies of Burns, Cowper, Wordsworth, Coleridge, Keats, and Crabbe. And in a printed letter of 1826, addressed to Mont-gomery, Clare says that he has 'long had a fondness for the poetry of the time of Elizabeth', which he knows from Ellis's *Specimens of Early Poets* and Ritson's *English Songs*. It was doubtless in Ellis that he found some of the metres in which we may well be surprised to find him writing as early as 1821; Villon's ballad metre, for instance, which he uses in a poem in *The Village Minstrel*, and which he might have found in poems of Henryson and other Scottish poets quoted in Ellis. Later on, among some poems which he wrote in deliberate imitation of Elizabethan poets, we shall find one in a Wyatt metre, which reads like an antici-pation of Bridges.

Thus it cannot be said in Clare's very earliest work we have an utterance which literary influences have not modified. The impulse and the subject-matter are alike his own, and are taken directly from what was about him. There is no closer attention to nature than in Clare's poems; but the observation begins by being literal; nature a part of his home, rather than his home a part of nature. The things about him are the whole of his material, he does not choose them by preference out of others equally available; all his poems are made out of the incidents and feelings of humble life and the actual fields and flowers of his particular part of England. He does not make pictures which would imply aloofness and selection; he enumerates, which means a friendly knowledge. It is enough for him, enough for his success in his own kind of poetry, to say them over, saying, 'Such they were, and I loved them because I had always seen them so.' He begins anywhere and stops anywhere. Some simple moralising, from the fall of leaves to the fading of man, rounds a landscape or a sensation of autumn. His words are chosen only to be exact, and he does not know when he is obvious or original in his epithets. When he begins to count over aspects, one by one, as upon his fingers, saying them over because he loves them, not one more than another, setting them down by heart, with exactly their characteristics, his words have the real sound of what they render, and can be as oddly impressive as this:

> And the little chumbling mouse
> Gnarls the dead weed for her house;

or, in a poem on 'The Wild-flower Nosegay', can make so eager and crowded a grouping of names:

> Crimp-filled daisy, bright bronze buttercup,
> Freckt cowslip peeps, gilt whins of morning's dew,
> And hooded arum early sprouting up
> Ere the white thorn bud half unfolds to view,
> And wan-hued lady-smocks, that love to spring
> 'Side the swamp margin of some plashy pond;
> And all the blooms that early Aprils bring,
> With eager joy each filled my playful hand.

His danger is to be too deliberate, unconscious that there can be choice in descriptive poetry, or that anything which runs naturally into the metre may not be the best material for a particular poem. Thus his longer poems, like *The Village Minstrel*, drop from poetry into realism, and might as well have been written in prose. He sets himself to write *Village Tales*, perhaps to show that it was possible to write of village life, not as he said Crabbe did, 'like a magistrate'. He fails equally when he sets himself (perhaps in competition with Byron's famous and over-rated 'Dream') to elaborate an imaginary horror in the poem which he too calls 'The Dream'; or, setting himself too deliberately to secure in verse the emphasis of an actual storm, loses all that poetry which comes to him naturally when he is content not to search for it.

To Clare childhood was the only time of happiness, and his complaint is that 'Poesy hath its youth forgot'. His feeling towards things was always that of a child, and as he lived so he wrote, by recollection.

When, in *The Shepherd's Calendar*, he writes the chronicle of the months, he writes best when he gives the child's mood rather than the grown-up person's, and always regrets that reason has come with years, because reason is disheartening. Yet still, as when he was a child, he is friends with all he sees, and he sometimes forgets that anything exists but birds, insects, and flowers. By this time he has a firmer hold on his material, and his lists turn now to pictures, as when he sees

> Bees stroke their little legs across their wings,
> And venture short flights where the snowdrop hings
> Its silver bell, and winter aconite
> Its buttercup-like flowers that shut at night;

or looks up to where,

> Far above, the solitary crane
> Wings lonely to unfrozen dykes again,
> Cranking a jarring, melancholy cry,
> Through the wild journey of the cheerless sky;

or, in May, sees in a quaint figure

> The stooping lilies of the valley,
> That love with shades and dews to dally,
> And bending droop on slender threads,
> With broad hood-leaves above their heads,
> Like white-robed maids, in summer hours,
> Beneath umbrellas shunning showers.

His epithets strengthen and sharpen; earlier he would not have thought of speaking of 'bright glib ice', or of the almanac's 'wisdom gossiped from the stars'. A new sense of appropriate melody has come into the verse, which has lost none of its definite substance, but which he now handles more delicately. One even realises that he has read Keats much more recently than Thomson.

Much of the verse contained in the last book published by Clare, *The Rural Muse*, of 1835, appeared in annuals of the time, and would seem to have been written for them. He repeats all his familiar notes, with a fluency which long practice and much reading have given him, and what he gains in ease he loses in personal directness. Others besides himself might have written his meditation on the nightingale and on the eternity of time, and when he questions the skull on Cowper's Green we remember with more pleasure the time when he could write of the same locality as he really knew it. Here and there, as in the coloured fragment on 'Insects', he is himself, and there are a few of the many sonnets which convey a sudden aspect of nature or comment aptly upon it. But it may be questioned whether the impression made on us by *The Rural Muse* is wholly the fault of Clare. Mr. Martin tells us that Messrs. Whittaker & Co., 'fearful of risking money in printing too large a quantity of rural verse, so much out of fashion for the time, had picked those short pieces from about five times as many poems, furnished by the author.' I have before me the original manuscript, in Clare's handwriting, from which his book was printed. It is written on 188 folio pages, often in double columns, in close handwriting, and contains, curiously enough, exactly 188 poems, though the average of length varies considerably. The choice made for publication may have been well calculated for the public of the day, though, as the book failed, perhaps it was not. A number of long tales in verse, some of the more trivial comic pieces, the poems written in series, like the 'Pewit's', the 'Pettichap's', the 'Yellow Wagtail's', the 'Yellowhammer's', and yet other birds' nests, were left out with little or no loss; but some of the rollicking and some of the quieter poems are, though a little rough and unfinished, more personal than anything in the published book. The best of these, seventeen sonnets and nine poems, I am printing here for the first time.

With *The Rural Muse* of 1835 ends the control of Clare over his work, and all the subsequent work which has been published since that time will be found in Mr. J. L. Cherry's invaluable *Life and Remains of John Clare*, brought out in Northampton in 1873. Mr. Cherry tells us that his selection has been made from the manuscripts of more than five hundred poems; and he adds: 'Of those which are printed, scarcely one was found in a state in which it could be submitted to the public without more or less of revision and correction.' I have tried in vain to find the original manuscripts, which I would have liked to have printed exactly as they were written, having convinced myself that for the most part what Clare actually wrote was better than what his editors made him write.

And I was the more anxious to get at the the real text because it is more worth getting at than that of any other of Clare's earlier poems. Here, for the first time, Clare's lyrical faculty gets free. Strangely enough, a new joy comes into his verse, as if at last he is at rest. It is only rarely, in this new contentment, this solitude even from himself, that recollection returns. Then he remembers

I am a sad lonely hind:
Trees tell me so, day after day,
As slowly they wave in the wind.

He seems to accept nature now more easily, because his mind is in a kind of oblivion of everything else; madness being, as it were, his security. He writes love songs that have an airy fancy, a liquid and thrilling note of song. They are mostly exultations of memory, which goes from Mary to Patty, and thence to a Gypsy girl and to vague Isabellas and Scotch maids. A new feeling for children comes in, sometimes in songs of childish humour, like 'Little Trotty Wagtail' or 'Clock-a-Clay', made out of bright, laughing sound; and once in a lovely poem, one of the most nearly perfect he ever wrote, called 'The Dying Child', which reminds one of beautiful things that have been done since, but of nothing done earlier. As we have them, and so subtle an essence could scarcely be extracted by any editor, there is no insanity; they have only dropped nearly all of the prose. A gentle hallucination comes in from time to time, and, no doubt, helps to make the poetry better.

118. The distinction between early and late Clare

1909

From an unsigned article, 'A Poet-Peasant', *T.P.'s Weekly*, 26 February 1909, xiii, 266.

Thomas Power O'Connor (1848–1929) started his weekly in 1902.

He is now linked, like Chatterton and Kirke White, with his own unhappy story, and it is impossible to read the poems . . . without remembering the character and fate of the poet. . . .

In at least the poems written before his mind lost half its consciousness there does not seem any definite distinctive quality. All that one can say is that there is an atmosphere of poetry—a breath and finer spirit of knowledge, diffused over them. It is, one realises, because Clare loves the object, and places which he describes or 'enumerates', and not chiefly because he writes about them that he is a poet.

To the asylum poems, however—as they are best known—and to one or two written before his mind finally lost itself in mirage, this criticism does not apply. . . . The fact is that the infirmity which overclouded the mind of Clare brought to the surface that feverish love and sensibility, 'almost too deep for tears', which had always been latent in the earlier descriptive 'prosings' or reveries. This new tremulous, half-tearful note is first heard distinctly in the poem written on leaving his 'own dear home of homes', entitled 'The Flitting', and there is, too, something suggesting the now disordered, sick, and feverish imagination of the poet, which is distinctly evident in the greater number of the verses written during his twenty-two years' residence in the Northampton Asylum.

119. Clare as a poet of greatness

1910

Hugh Walker, from *The Literature of the Victorian Era*, Cambridge 1910, pp. 241–5.

Walker (1855–1939), Professor of English at St David's College, Lampeter, is sure that Clare's best work dates from the asylum, and adduces Smart and Blake as the closest parallels. A similar point is made by Walker in 'The Enigma of Genius', *Yale Review*, October 1914, 4, 79–97, where he writes, 'I am very certain that Clare, in his days of sanity, was a better poet than Smart; I am not so certain . . . that, in his period of madness he was a worse one' (p. 87).

. . . there is one poet of these years, John Clare, who stands absolutely alone, a figure of singular interest, at once like and strangely unlike what a man of poetic gifts, in circumstances such as his, might be expected to be. He deserves careful consideration, not only for his pathetic story, but for the high poetic merit of his writings.   (p. 241)

Not the least remarkable point about Clare is that he bears triumphantly a test under which even Burns breaks down. In his early verse Clare used dialect with some freedom; in his later writings he confined himself almost wholly to the diction of classical English; yet his poems lost nothing in ease and naturalness. He even ventured on imitations of some of the older English poets; and, strange to say, he succeeded. The success proves that his poetic gift was something more and greater than a narrow compass of 'native wood-notes wild'; and the proof is clinched by the dignity, almost unsurpassed, of at least one of his pieces. Surely, if the over-burdening head portended disease, that head was also the home of a genius which needs no excuse from circumstance, but demands homage simply on the grounds of its own greatness. There are no better tests of a poet than the power to write a lyric, and the power to impress the reader with the sense of the dignity and greatness of the verse,—to write, in short, in 'the grand style'. The first of the two following quotations is a lyric of wonderful sweetness and charm; the second, for grandeur, would do honour to any poet of the nineteenth century . . . It is almost uncanny to find, in the poor poet of the asylum, a reminder of that most dauntless of souls, Emily Brontë.

[Quotes 'O the evening's for the fair, bonnie lassie O!' and 'I am']

(p. 243)

120. Edward Thomas on Clare

1906, 1910, 1917

Edward Thomas (1878–1917) shows in his poetry, as does Edmund Blunden, some affinity with Clare. The following extracts indicate something of his developing attitude to Clare.

(a) From a letter to Gordon Bottomley, 24 August 1906, *Letters from Edward Thomas to Gordon Bottomley*, ed. R. George Thomas, 1968, p. 117. James Hurdis (1763–1801), the author of *The Village Curate*, 1788, and *The Favorite Village*, 1800, was a poet whom Clare read and admired, but he is scarcely comparable with Clare.

I have an old friend still here and we usually rise at 4, fish until 9 and then walk, and in the intervals I edit and write letters and read a lot of 3rd rate old country poetry with sweet feeling in it, lent me by W. H. Hudson—Hurdis and the unhappy peasant John Clare.

(b) From chapter iv, 'Women, Nature and Poetry', *Feminine Influence on the English Poets*, 1910, pp. 65–90. The extract is from pp. 80–7.

Perhaps the most unanswerable testimony of all is to be found in the poetry which John Clare wrote during his twenty years' imprisonment in a madhouse. He had already in earlier days called his Muse a wild enchantress, and had wooed her on a bed of thyme, and had seen solitude as a woman with wild ringlets lying unbound over her lily shoulders. He had already written a poem on the 'Death of Beauty'—

> Now thou art gone, the fairy rose is fled,
> That erst gay Fancy's garden did adorn.
> Thine was the dew on which her folly fed,
> The sun by which she glittered in the morn. . . .

But he was to get far beyond this statement that with the death of the woman died Nature's beauty. These latest and finest poems leave personifications far behind. His native trees and fields, and the women he loved after they had died or vanished, haunted him in his prison. His mind seemed to shed all its mere intelligence and all its conventionality in the use of words. He was left free as a spirit in his ghastly solitude. Then to him his Mary became a part of the spring, a part inexplicably absent. He had talked to the flowers when a child, and when a man they had 'told the names of early love': now that he was alone, they decked 'the bier of spring.' But if one of the Marys came into his mind it was in as complete a harmony with Nature as one of Wordsworth's women, yet with little or nothing of his thin spiritual quality. The woman of 'The Invitation' is real:

> Come with thy maiden eye, lay silks and satins by;
> Come in thy russet or grey cotton gown;
> Come to the meads, dear, where flags, sedge, and
>   reeds appear,
> Rustling to soft winds and bowing low down.

If she is a spirit, she is a spirit of the English earth, not of the transparent air. Another 'Lover's Invitation' shows the same union of woman and earth and sky. So too such poems as 'Evening' with its—

> I walk with my true love adown the green vale,
> The light feathered grasses keep tapping her shoe.

In 'The Morning Walk' the country maid climbing the stile in the early summer morning is as much a flower as the rose that she crops—

> She cropt a flower, shook off the dew,
> And on her breast the wild rose grew;
> She blushed as fair, as lovely, too,
>   The living rose of morning.

He has a poem to the 'Maid of the Wilderness,' a nymph of place made of firm flesh. When primrose and celandine come in March, he says, 'The sun shines about me so sweet, I cannot help thinking of love.' In a poem on Evening that begins with a verse of description, he says:

> The evening comes in with the wishes of love

and

> For Nature is love, and finds haunts for true love,
>   Where nothing can hear or intrude;
> It hides from the eagle and joins with the dove,
>   In beautiful green solitude.

He breaks out into a wild cry for a 'bonny lassie O!' and it might be thought, so full of natural things is the poem, that she was a flower maid like the Welsh Blodeuwedd whom Math framed out of blossoms, but she is an English country girl notwithstanding and he wants her

> In a grassy nook hard by, with a little
>   patch of sky
> And a bush to keep us dry,
>   Bonny lassie O!

The gipsy lass in the smoky camp among the scented woodbine is a fellow to her. Perhaps the maddest and most perfect of the asylum poems, 'Love lives beyond the tomb,' is remarkable for nothing so much as for its eloquent but inexplicable expression of this harmony of nature and love.

[Quotes]

This and perhaps all of his best poems show Clare as one of those who have in them the natural spirit of poetry in its purity, so pure that perhaps he can never express it quite whole and perfect. They are songs of innocence, praising a world not realised, or, it is more reasonable to say, a world which most old and oldish people agree to regard as something different. For such a writer the usual obstacles and limits are temporary or do not exist at all, and as with children the dividing line between the real and the unreal, either shifts or has not yet been made. No man or woman is a poet who does not frequently, to the end of life, ignore these obstacles and limits, which are not just and absolute but represent the golden mean or average, and have less reality than the equator. Few, except idiots, can escape them altogether, since they are produced by weariness and compromise, which are produced by time and without effort. Some great men escape while seeming to accept them, but there is hardly a pleasure in the world equal to that of seeing one who is not a child and has yet escaped them so happily as Clare. He reminds us that words are alive, and not only alive but still half-wild and imperfectly domesticated. They are quiet and gentle in their ways, but are like cats—to whom night overthrows our civilisation and servi-tude—who seem to love us but will starve in the house which we have left, and thought to have emptied of all worth. Words never consent to correspond exactly to any object unless, like scientific terms, they are first killed. Hence the curious life of words in the hands of those who love all life so well that they do not kill even the slender words but let them play on; and such are poets. The magic of words is due to their living freely among things, and no man knows how they came together in just that order when a beautiful thing is made like 'Full fathom five.' And so it is that children often make phrases that are poetry, though they still more often produce it in their acts and half-suggested thoughts; and that grown men with dictionaries are as murderous of words as entomologists of butterflies.

Here, I think, in 'Love lives beyond the tomb,' in this unprejudiced singing voice that knows not what it sings, is some reason for us to believe that poets are not merely writing figuratively when they say, 'My love is like a red, red rose,' that they are to be taken more literally than they commonly are, that they do not invent or 'make things up' as grown people do when they condescend to a child's game. What they say is not chosen to represent what they feel or think, but is itself the very substance of what had before lain dark and unapparent, is itself all that survives of feeling and thought, and cannot be expanded or reduced without dulling or falsification. If this is not so, and if we do not believe it to be so, then poetry is of no greater importance than wallpaper, or a wayside drink to one who is not thirsty. But if it is so, then we are on the way to understand why poetry is mighty; for if what poets say is true and not feigning, then of how little account are our ordinary assumptions, our feigned interests, our playful and our serious pastimes spread out between birth and death. Poetry is and must always be ap-parently revolutionary if active, anarchic if passive. It is the utterance of the human spirit when it is in touch with a world to which the affairs of 'this world' are parochial. Hence the strangeness and thrill and painful delight of poetry at all times, and the deep response to it of youth and of love; and because love is wild, strange, and full of astonishment, is one reason why poetry deals so much in love, and why all poetry is in a sense love-poetry.

(c) From 'John Clare', *A Literary Pilgrim in England*, 1917, pp. 224–35.
The extract runs from p. 229.

It is hard to imagine a combination with more possibilities for wretchedness than that of poet and agricultural labourer. I mean a poet of any
known breed. Of course, it is easy to invent a poet suddenly making
poetry of all that dignity and beauty in the labourer's life which we are
so ready to believe in. But such a one has not yet appeared. It is doubtful
if he ever will, or if we ought to complain of the lack, since what we
want to see in some perhaps impossible peasant poetry has always been
an element in great poetry. If we knew their pedigrees, we should find
more than one peasant among the ancestors of the poets. In fact, every
man, poet or not, is a more or less harmonius combination of the peasant and the adventurer.

In no man have these two parts been more curiously combined than
in John Clare, a real poet, however small, and actually an agricultural
labourer out and out. He was far from being the kind of peasant poet
who would be invented in an armchair. Mortal man could hardly be
milder, more timid and drifting, than Clare. He heard voices from the
grave, not of rustic wisdom and endurance, but

> Murmuring o'er one's weary woe,
> Such as once 'twas theirs to know,
> They whisper to such slaves as me
> A buried tale of misery:—
> 'We once had life, ere life's decline,
> Flesh, blood, and bones the same as thine;
> We knew its pains, and shared its grief,
> Till death, long-wish'd-for, brought relief;
> We had our hopes, and like to thee,
> Hop'd morrow's better day to see,
> But like to thine, our hope the same,
> Tomorrow's kindness never came:
> We had our tyrants, e'en as thou;
> Our wants met many a scornful brow;
> But death laid low their wealthy powers,
> Their harmless ashes mix with ours:
> And this vain world, its pride, its form,
> That treads on thee as on a worm,
> Its mighty heirs—the time shall be
> When they as quiet sleep as thee!'

He looked back to childhood, asking:

315

> When shall I see such rest again?

Contact with the town—

> In crowded streets flowers never grew,
> But many there hath died away

—sharpened his nerves for natural beauty. The poet consumed the
labourer in him, or left only the dregs of one, while the conditions of
the labourer's life were as a millstone about his neck as poet. As a young
man, sometimes neither labouring nor poetry could satisfy him, and he
would escape to two brothers named Billings, men given to 'poaching,
hard drinking, and general rowdyism', whose ruinous cottage at Helpston was nicknamed 'Bachelor's Hall.' His biographer says that he was
'too deep a lover of all creatures that God had made' to become a
poacher, but that nevertheless, for all his ordinary shyness, 'he was at
these meetings the loudest of loud talkers and singers.' He seems to have
taken most of the opportunities of leaving his cottage and Helpston, and
most opportunities of coming back to them. Marriage meant crowding
into that fourth part of a cottage with parents, wife, and children.

For a short time he was a minor celebrity, meeting some of the great
men of his day, such as Coleridge and Lamb, after the publication of
Poems Descriptive of Rural Life and Scenery in 1820. But he was then no
more fitted for the literary life than at birth he was fitted for the life of
the fields. Delicate and passionate, he was early broken by under-
feeding and over-drinking, so that he could love only the incidents of
the country, the birds, the flowers, the young girl like a flower:

> Nor could I pull
> The blossoms that I thought divine
> As hurting beauty like to thine.

Unlike Burns, he had practically no help from the poetry and music of
his class. He was a peasant writing poetry, yet cannot be called a peasant
poet, because he had behind him no tradition of peasant literature, but
had to do what he could with the current forms of polite literature. The
mastering of these forms absorbed much of his energy, so that for so
singular a man he added little of his own, and the result was only thinly
tinged with his personality, hardly at all with the general characteristics
of his class.

His work is founded chiefly on literary models. Yet he lacked the
intellect and power of study to live by the pen as he lacked the grit to
live by hoe and pitchfork. A small income was subscribed for him, but

he failed to found even a moderately sound productive life on it. Never, except in fancy rhyme, had he the Plenty which he desired, or the cottage of his verses, 'After reading in a letter proposals for building a cottage.' His only lasting pleasure was in remembering happier things, with the reflection:

> Ah! sweet is all that I'm denied to share;
> Want's painful hindrance sticks me to her stall.

He said truly:

> No, not a friend on earth had I
> But mine own kin and poesy.

He never became any more docile to the fate of agricultural labourers than he had been when a young man. After walking home for the first time with the girl who was to be his wife, and saying good-bye, he waited about, watching the lights of her house, for an hour or two. He then set out homeward, but lost his way in the dark, and sat down contentedly when the moon rose, to write a love-song. In the morning he awoke by the brink of a canal where he had slept, exhausted at the end of a long night's wandering.

But it was in his power to do for his native district something like what Jefferies did for his. He possessed a similar fresh, sweet spirituality to that of Jefferies, a similar grasp and love of detail. Some of his plain descriptions anticipate and at least equal the 'Nature article' of to-day. His was a pedestrian Muse

> who sits her down
> Upon the molehill's little lap,
> Who feels no fear to stain her gown,
> And pauses by the hedgerow gap.

And he often wrote long formless pieces full of place-names and of field-lore charmingly expressed, songs uttering his love and his pathetic joy in retrospection, poems mingling the two elements. A thousand things which the ordinary country child, 'tracking wild searches through the meadow grass,' has to forget in order to live, Clare observed and noted—as, for example, how in July's drought

> E'en the dew is parched up
> From the teasel's jointed cup.

In putting down some of these things with a lowly fidelity, he often achieves a more rustic truth than other poets, as in—

317

> And rambling bramble-berries, pulpy and sweet,
>   Arching their prickly trails
>   Half o'er the narrow lane.

Sometimes he attains almost to magic, as in—

> For when the world first saw the sun,
>   These little flowers beheld him, too;
> And when his love for earth begun,
>   They were the first his smiles to woo.
> There little lambtoe bunches springs
>   In red-tinged and begolden dye,
> For ever, and like China kings
>   They come, but never seem to die.

He was something more and less than a peasant become articulate. For example, he had an unexpected love, not only of the wild, but of the waste places, the 'commons left free in the rude rags of Nature,' 'the old molehills of glad neglected pastures.' Though he did call the henbane 'stinking,' he half loved it for the places, like Cowper's Green, where he found it, with bramble, thistle, nettle, hemlock,

> And full many a nameless weed,
> Neglected, left to run to seed,
> Seen but with disgust by those
> Who judge a blossom by the nose.
> Wildness is my suiting scene,
> So I seek thee, Cowper Green.

To enumerate the flowers was a pleasure to him, and he did so in a manner which preserves them still dewy, or with summer dust, perhaps, on 'an antique mullein's flannel-leaves.' Can he ever have cultivated his garden? If he did, and then wrote—

> Hawkweed and groundsel's fanning downs
> Unruffled keep their seeded crowns,

he must have been a kind of saint; and, indeed, he had such a love for wild things as some saints have had, which he shows in the verses:

> I left the little birds
> And sweet lowing of the herds,
> And couldn't find out words,
>   Do you see,
> To say to them good-bye,
> Where the yellowcups do lie;
> So heaving a deep sigh
>   Took to sea.

318

When he lamented leaving his old home, he did not mention the building itself, but the neighbouring heath,

> its yellow furze,
> Molehills and rabbit tracks that lead
> Through beesom, ling, and teasel burrs . . .

the trees, the lanes, the stiles, the brook, the flowers, the shepherd's-
purse that grew in the old as well as the new garden;

> The very crow
> Croaked music in my native fields.

One of his Asylum Poems, first printed by Mr. Arthur Symons, is
full of place-names that were music to him, and become so to us—
'Langley Bush,' 'Eastwell's boiling spring,' 'old Lee Close oak,' 'old
Crossberry Way,' 'pleasant Swordy Well' again, 'Round Oak,' 'Sneap
Green,' 'Puddock's Nook,' 'Hilly Snow'—as he mourns:

> And Crossberry Way and old Round Oak's narrow lane
> With its hollow trees like pulpits I shall never see again.
> Enclosure like a Buonaparte let not a thing remain,
> It levelled every bush and tree and levelled every hill
> And hung the moles for traitors, though the brook is running still
> It runs a naked stream cold and chill.

But he had the farm life also by heart, and, along with blackbird and
robin and magpie, drew the dog chasing the cat, the cows tossing the
molehills in their play, the shepherd's dog daunted by the rolled-up
hedgehog, the maids singing ballads at milking or hanging out linen
around the elder-skirted croft, while

> The gladden'd swine bolt from the sty,
> And round the yard in freedom run,
> Or stretching in their slumbers lie
> Beside the cottage in the sun.
> The young horse whinneys to his mate,
> And, sickening from the thresher's door,
> Rubs at the straw-yard's banded gate,
> Longing for freedom on the moor.

No man ever came so near to putting the life of the farm, as it is lived,
not as it is seen over a five-barred gate, into poetry. He gives no broad
impressions—he saw the kite, but not the kite's landscape—yet his
details accumulate in the end, so that a loving reader, and no one reads
him but loves him, can grasp them, and see the lowlands of Northamptonshire as they were when the kite soared over them.

121. Alan Porter, a violent view

1920

From 'Unpublished writings of John Clare', *Oxford Outlook*, May 1920, ii, 202–9.

Alan Porter edited, with Edmund Blunden, *John Clare: Poems, Chiefly from Manuscript*, 1920. See Introduction, p. 19.

In his lifetime John Clare was forgotten, starved, and by his utter destitution driven mad: after his death a more complete oblivion obscured his name. In the four books he published there is a knowledge and love of rural life that makes our nature poets, Wordsworth, Hartley Coleridge, Crabbe, Thomson, Grahame, Tennyson, Bloomfield, seem paltering amateurs and jugglers with pretty sentiment; and it seems strange that the rich music and the clear imagination of his greatest poems are not everywhere familiar. Yet to this day his best and most personal work is unpublished. Two months ago the manuscripts lay for the greater part untouched in the ramshackle archive-cupboard of a provincial museum, black with dust, mouldered and worm-eaten, slowly fading beyond the power of man to decipher. Among his papers Clare has put a recipe for ink; and for six or seven years, it seems, he used ink made to his recipe. It hardly deserves transcription; the ink has spread and eaten like smouldering saltpetre along the paper. But with all these difficulties his manuscripts are for the moment easy to read; for he wrote a beautiful clear, and steady hand, and he duplicated most of his poems: were the labour herculean, still it would be pleasurable to open this treasure-cave of poetry.

It is as hard, however, to convince the reactionary, old high Tory party of literature-dabblers that Clare is great as if he were still living.

'Tennyson we know, and Matthew Arnold; but never a great writer has followed these.' It is impossible that any precursor should be great and have escaped their omniscience. It follows, therefore, that Clare is a minor poet; enthusiasm for him is pardonable, and lack of proportion is natural, in the young, but with age and experience come sanity and balance. What need to hear a line of Clare? He must be a minor poet. Thus they are deliberately deaf, and if you read them a poem, 'It has much merit,' they will say. 'A ploughman, wasn't he? Did he ever write a poem to which a regiment of soliders could march?' He did, he did; but, oh, one cannot argue with dunderheads like these.

And yes, ploughman he was; this circumstance has harmed his fame more than any other. Perpetually Clare asked that no allowance should be made for his poverty; and as persistently people counted a rung to heaven climbed when they pretended to patronship or spoke him well. In truth Clare needs no allowance, no compassion; merely a freedom from prejudice. To an open and sensitive mind his writing will prove him a major poet, compeer with Keats, and Shelley, and Blake. Yet among so many new poems all of so high an achievement, it is impossible for any man to select what is unquestionably the best, and I would ask only that Clare should not be judged by the errors of my opinions or the weakness of my advocacy.

Clare's first book was unequivocally a bad book. It had been selected by a good-natured publisher from an already huge mass of material; he chose the most conventional, dull, and moral poems. Their author being a ploughman, his publisher ventured to improve them and regularise them. There are, nevertheless, disturbing flashes of poetry. On the whole, the book should be read only by preconceived lovers of Clare.

We have good reason to hate this bookseller. He might have chosen poems like this:—

[Quotes 'Song's Eternity']

He might have issued a thin volume of great poetry. I weigh the word and do not speak in hyperbole. He published instead a book which had an immediate and staggering popularity. Clare's reputation was made and ruined. The really discriminate readers of verse saw that his book did not deserve success, and paid no attention to his later works. The wider public soon forgot their three-month wonder, or, if at any time they saw another of Clare's books in Taylor and Hessey's, opening the covers they were discouraged to find a so vastly superior beauty and vigour.

122. Samuel Looker on Clare's genius

1920

From 'The Life and Genius of John Clare', *Poetry Review*, September, October 1920, xi, 260–4.

S. J. Looker (with the pseudonyms 'Game Cock', and 'Thomas Wade') was an assiduous editor of the naturalist Richard Jefferies (1848–87) and John Lionel Tayler (1874–1930), Unitarian and social educationalist.

Of all the poets of the sweet English countryside (not excepting Wordsworth) John Clare is to my mind the truest and most delightful. His verse is full of unfeigned joy in the sights and sounds of the open air, redolent of the scents of spring, of bluebells in the woodlands.

The songs of birds, the vision of white clouds and blue skies speak through his poems directly to the heart. He writes with an unaffected grace and simplicity which after the hot-house scents of much recent verse is most refreshing to the mind. . . .

There is no sense of strain in Clare's poetry; it is natural and unforced, it seems to dribble from the fountain of his heart. That irritating sense of something manufactured and pieced together which is the bane, and so often present, in modern poetry is entirely absent in the lyrics of Clare. He wrote down what he felt, and felt what he wrote. The melody of his verse is at times extraordinary in its beauty and rhythm. The following wonderful lyric is the most finished and charming he ever wrote, and to my mind worthy to rank with the most splendid lyrics of the last century.

[Quotes 'I hid my love']

There is a simplicity, freshness and charm in these vivid transcripts from Nature. Clare was a true poet, and produced immortal poetry under conditions of the utmost difficulty. . . .

This poor peasant, born in obscurity and doomed to poverty and neglect from his youth up, wrote nature poems which are worthy to rank with the very highest of their class, and entitle the name of John Clare to be enscrolled for ever with those glorious English poets, the immortal sons of light.

123. J. C. Squire, with reservations

1921

From a review of *Poems, Chiefly from Manuscript, Observer,* 2 January 1921, no. 6762, 4. This review was reprinted in *Books Reviewed,* 1922, pp. 1–8.

John Collings Squire (1884–1958) founded the *London Mercury* in 1919, which he edited until 1934. His *Cambridge Book of Lesser Poets,* 1927, included poems by Clare.

In the nature and persistence of his love for, and zeal to record, the commonest incidents of the life of the country, he closely resembled the late Edward Thomas, though his pictures were less often tinged with the melancholy of his mind than were Thomas's. His descriptive poems continually remind one of the landscape painters of the time: sometimes of the water colourists, sometimes of Old Crome and Constable, but most often of George Morland, most rustic and most English of painters, a man who loved the thing he saw anywhere on any day, and was content to show it as it was. . . .

He does not tumble his details out without discrimination. There is always cunning in his arrangement, and he has a sound instinct for emotional significance. Take these two brief examples from poems on November and another on winter:

> Where dead leaves rustle sweet and give alarm
> To little birds that flirt and start away.

Moody crows beside the road forbear
To fly, though pelted by the passing swain.

Each of these phrases suggests far more than it says, and they are characteristic of him. But he was largely a poet of details, and it is for his details that one likes him. His best whole poems are too long to quote. But here is one of the short pieces discovered by his recent editors, 'The Stonepit':

[Quotes]

Such a style, as straightforward and simple as Wordsworth's at its barest leads inevitably to occasional weakness of expression. You get in Clare couplets such as:—

And all expected such a rosy face
Could be her ruin—as was just the case.

But if you like Clare you do not mind that any more than if you like Wordsworth you mind the excessively plain statements of fact that you sometimes find in him. . . .

We must keep our sense of proportion. We have enough of Clare's work to be certain that we shall never think him a great poet. Even a 'final' edition of him must be a selection. Clare was not a Keats or a Shelley that his feeblest fragments must be scoured for and perpetuated; an edition of him in ten volumes would be a monument not to his genius but to an admirer's folly. But he was a far better poet than has ever been realised; he had talents peculiar to himself; his best work is worth looking for industriously; and his character and career were sufficiently remarkable to justify a biography far more considerable than anything which has yet been done. A large volume of intelligently-chosen poems and a companion volume of life and letters would justify themselves, and would leave him securely established among the secondary English poets.

124. H. J. Massingham on Clare's uniqueness

1921

From a review of *Poems, Chiefly from Manuscript, Athenaeum*, 7 January 1921, no. 4732, 9–10.

Harold J. Massingham (1888–1952) was the son of Henry W. Massingham (1860–1924), editor of the *Nation*, 1907–23. Massingham takes a surprisingly forceful line on Clare.

The criticism of a poet who, like some sleeping seed planted by pious hands, first germinates in our own generation, is a knotty privilege. . . .

There are over 140 chosen poems in the book, and the first question to be asked of so ample and orderly a landscape is its topography. How does Clare fit into the map of his own poetic period? It is perfectly clear that he is on a divergent tack of poetic evolution from the Romantic Revivalists, proper or improper. There are bits out of the Preface to the 'Lyrical Ballads' which might be modelled into one for himself, but, granted a fragment or two, Clare and the Lake Poets part company. In the whole of this volume there are only four lines which suggest that Clare had ever read a line of Wordsworth's—from 'The Fallen Elm':

> Thou owned a language by which hearts are stirred
> Deeper than by a feeling clothed in word,
> And speakest now what's known of every tongue,
> Language of pity and the force of wrong.

In the same poem there is an angry reference to the enclosures, the only clear political impression (the sonnet to Buonaparte is a stiff and impersonal exercise) in the book. It cannot be too strongly stated that Clare is a poet of the spirit—a transparent spirit through which things filtered —and not of the mind; that his attitude to nature is less conscious, less formulated, less burdened (or elevated) by human or abstract preoccupations than any other poet's in the language. Clare's men and women and children are part of the landscape—they grow and shine like flowers

—part whether of the actual or the imaginative landscape, none too easy to disentangle, and not, as they are in Wordsworth, Shelley, Coleridge, Byron and Keats (in the second draft of 'Hyperion'), moralized beings in a purposed relationship with the universe. Clare does indeed moralize, and frequently, not in the manner of his contemporaries, nor of the eighteenth century, but, surprising as it sounds, of the seventeenth. There is very little positive imitation of any poet or period in Clare; but, dropping the metaphysics, there is more than a stray reminder of the lyrical quietism of Marvell and Bishop King, musing upon the vanishing shows of the world, extending even to turns of phrase.

It is needless to discuss the slander upon Clare as a 'better Bloomfield.' The only likeness between the two men is that neither of them was a 'peasant poet,' and for precisely opposite reasons. Whatever the facts of Bloomfield's career, he writes about nature as from a countryfied coffee-house, and it was doubtless through his facility in generalization and personifying qualities, and in a towny diction which conveys not a single sharp image nor particular impression, that his rural Muse made such a good thing out of her borrowed clout. But Clare, whether wandering in fancy or rarefied fact, is fastidiously concrete and precise, never the eloquent professionalist, exploiting the object to the phrase. The objective, the ordinary, the plain speaking in Clare, which makes even his flattest diarizing so vivid and so individual, has been indulgently smiled upon by the wiseacres of nearly a hundred years. But it is one of his greatest virtues, and places him in the van of the romantic liberators who destroyed the professional tricks of eighteenth-century poetry. 'Tasteful illumination of the night' (viz. the glowworm)—it is very rare indeed to find Clare cutting that kind of decorative figure. The one eighteenth-century poet with whom Clare is on any kind of poetic terms is Collins:

> Sweet Vision, with the wild dishevelled hair,
> And raiment shadowy of each wind's embrace,
>   Fain would I win thine harp
>   To one accordant theme;

or,

> But now the evening curdles dark and grey,
>   Changing her watchet hue for sombre weed;
> And creeping owls, to close the lids of day,
>   On drowsy wing proceed.

Both the long poems 'Autumn' and 'Summer Images' bear the Collins stamp, and beautiful phrases like 'Here poor integrity can sit at ease' and the swallow 'unsealing morning's eye' are Collins to a hair. The parallel must not be pressed too far, for Clare's experience of nature is richer, more intimate and varied than Collins's, while Collins stands more to pose; he is better balanced, and a greater master of his instrument, and his verse altogether more of a formal and symmetrical pattern. Yet Clare in his mood of elegiac repose joined to beguiling melody is the only nineteenth-century poet to take over the Collins tradition, reshape it, and bear it through all the distractions of a period abounding in poetic experiment and discovery.

Collins, of course, is an allegorical poet, and, lulled by the magic of his atmospheric effects, one is tempted to overlook his powers of detail and definition. His figures are not flesh and blood, but they perform distinct if ritual actions and gestures, and here Clare by his unforced absorption in nature surpassed his master, if master he was. It is a commonplace that Clare possessed a greater knowledge of earth and natural life than any other poet whose appeal is one of literature. Both as a man and a creator he was, I think, primarily a spiritual type, but he did not find the gift of the spirit inconsistent with a knowledge of its material works. Now a portion of his expression is quite patently nothing more than rhymed natural history, a quite literal picking of nature's pocket without, so to speak, any reinvesting of his gains in the poetic funds. But it has not been pointed out that this side of Clare is as much detached from his general poetic significance as Tennyson's bad biology is from his picture-writing.

The real question in an attempt at justly estimating an artist who cannot any longer be handled as a minor poet is whether the body of his work translated or transliterated its material; whether, in Coleridge's words, it trusted more to the memory than the imagination; whether it observes or creates, describes or sees; whether a radical defect in imaginative will confused truth to nature with truth to poetry. The great advantage of this volume is that it helps us to come to a decision by observing the continuous growth of the poet's mind—a growth not interrupted nor diverted into new channels of expression in the Asylum period, but strangely crowned. The majority of the poems in this period, with their quickened rhythm, airier music, finer sensibility and greater freedom not from but *in* nature, are unambiguously lived in the country of imagination. But it is wholly arbitrary to assume that madness was the mother of imagination. Clare lived all his life in verse: it was food, comfort, religion, happiness—his living—and the natural play of his spirit between nature and verse explains why the eternal odds against him so little affected his content and serenity. And the history, the internal conflict of a poetic achievement which bears so little outward sign of it was the accommodation he nearly always sought and often found between imagination and fact, and which, when found, leaves us with the conviction that he was not only a true but a unique poet. He was unique because he solved his own special problem in his own way, and he solved it partly because of his peculiar advantages in inheriting a racial tradition in pastoral poetry and in possessing a native genius in close relationship with the soil; partly because his approach to nature is not deliberate nor in any way philosophical; and partly because his own spiritual nature was endowed with a power of identifying himself with the dumb thought, the inner life of nature, not as a visionary, but simply as a lover. In this faculty Keats alone, I think, of all the Romantic poets, is kin with him. The best poems of the Middle Period are neither pure data nor pure imagination, but an individual blend of both which does express the music of his own soul and 'the inward stir of shadowed melody' in nature in one. In the Asylum period he was to become more imaginative, and at the same time more closely drawn into the truth behind the forms of nature; and when he was removed from his own place and wrote the pathetic verses about it, he might have said that he was uprooted and (with Swift) would wither at the top. But if his mind failed him, his poetic spirit did not, and what he lost in the acute sense of a particular locality, he gained in a wider interpretation.

Where Clare fell short has already been partly indicated, and his over-facility is obvious; his most serious lack, however, is in the quality of the blend between fact and imagination. It is too diffused, too seldom fused into a concentrated flame. His gentlest of spirits is as innocent of passion and intensity as of prophetic vision and of that profound nostalgia which is only content with a seventh heaven reconciling the ultimate end of human thought and feeling with the principles of all things. Nevertheless the final value of Clare is that he does not imitate, but creates his own world.

125. J. Middleton Murry, an enthusiastic view

1921

'The Poetry of John Clare', *The Times Literary Supplement*, 13 January 1921, no. 991, 17–18. This was reprinted in *Countries of the Mind*, 1922, pp. 103–19, and again in *John Clare and Other Studies*, 1950, pp. 7–17, from which this text is taken.

J. M. Murry (1889–1957) contributed frequently to *TLS*, and edited the *Athenaeum*, 1919–21. He founded the *Adelphi* in 1923. See also No. 131 and Introduction, p. 19.

In 1820 Messrs. Taylor & Hessey published two books whose immediate renown was in singular contrast with their after-fame. *Poems Descriptive of Rural Life and Scenery*, by John Clare, a Northamptonshire Peasant, ran into four editions within a year; the five hundred copies of the single edition of *Lamia, Isabella, and other Poems*, by John Keats, were not exhausted till the 'forties. Clare's popularity dwindled gradually into complete neglect; he had been all but forgotten by the time that Monckton Milnes assumed the practical task of impressing upon the world the conviction of the poets that Keats was among the greatest. Quickly the labours of piety were accomplished; within a few years Keats's poetical remains were gathered together, until nothing substantial remained to be added. Clare went on writing indefatigably in the exile of an asylum for nearly thirty years after he had been forgotten, and not till 1920 did Mr. Edmund Blunden set himself to the task of rescuing all that is valuable in his work.

It is not merely because the year and the publishers were the same that we are drawn to think of Keats and Clare together. The association of the great name and the small one has a curious congruity. Keats and Clare both suffered a vast shipwreck of their life's esteem, the one sudden and intolerably tragic, the other lingering and not without a sunset-haze of vaguely remembered happiness. There were elements common to their characters—they were both parvenus in the ranks of men of letters,

329

and they shared a resolution and an independence which became almost intolerant; Keats had an unusual, and Clare a unique knowledge of country sights and sounds; the most perfect poem of each is an *Ode to Autumn*.

We are inclined to lay stress on the points of resemblance in order that the cardinal point of difference may more plainly appear; for the eagerness with which we welcome this collection of Clare's poetry is likely to be so genuine and so justified as to disturb our sense of proportion. Into a generation of poets who flirt with nature suddenly descends a true nature-poet, one whose intimate and self-forgetful knowledge of the ways of birds and beasts and flowers rises like the scent of a hay-field from every page. Surely the only danger is that the enthusiasm of our recognition may be excessive; the relief overpowering with which we greet a poet who not only professes, but proves by the very words of his profession, that his dream of delight is

> To note on hedgerow baulks, in moisture sprent,
> The jetty snail creep from the mossy thorn,
> With earnest heed and tremulous intent,
> Frail brother of the morn,
> That from the tiny bents and misted leaves
> Withdraws his timid horn,
> And fearful vision weaves.

We have indeed almost to be on our guard against the sweet, cool shock of such a verse; the emotional quality is so assured and individual, the language so simple and inevitable, the posture of mind so unassuming and winning, that one is tempted for a moment to believe that while Wordsworth was engaged in putting the poetry of nature wrong by linking it to a doubtful metaphysic, John Clare was engaged in putting it right.

And so in a sense it was. As a poet of nature Clare was truer, more thoroughly subdued to that in which he worked than Wordsworth. Wordsworth called upon the poet to keep his eye upon the object; but his eye was hardly so penetrating and keen as Clare's. Yet Wordsworth was a great poet, and Keats, with whom Clare's kinship was really closer, was a great poet, and Clare was not; and it is important in the case of a poet whose gifts and qualities are so enchanting as Clare's are to bear in mind from the outset the vital difference between them. Wordsworth belongs to another sphere than Clare in virtue of the range of his imaginative apprehension: Keats in virtue not only of his imagination, but also of his art. In one respect Clare was a finer artist than Wordsworth, he had a truer ear and a more exquisite instinct for the visualizing word; but he had nothing of the principle of inward growth which gives to Wordsworth's most careless work a place within the unity of a great scheme. Wordsworth's incessant effort to comprehend experience would itself have been incomprehensible to Clare; Keats's consuming passion to make his poetry adequate not merely in content but also in the very mechanism of expression to an emotional experience more overwhelming even than Wordsworth's would have seemed to him like a problem of metaphysics to a ploughboy.

Clare was indeed a singer born. His nature was strangely simple, and his capacity for intense emotion appears at first sight to have been almost completely restricted to a response to nature. The intensity with which he adored the country that he knew is without a parallel in English literature; of him it seems hardly a metaphor to say he was an actual part of his countryside. Away from it he pined; he became queer and irresponsible. With his plants and birds and bees and fields he was among his own people. The spiked thistle, the firetail, the hare, the white-nosed and the grand-father bee were his friends. Yet he hardly huma-nized them; he seems rather to have lived on the same level of existence as they, and to have known them as they know each other. We feel that it is only by an effort that he manages to make himself conscious of his emotion towards them or of his own motive in singing of it. In those rare moments he conceives of the voice of Nature as something eternal, outlasting all generations of men, whispering to them to sing also. Thus, while he sits under the huge old elm which is the shepherd's tree, listen-ing to 'the laugh of summer leaves above',

> The wind of that eternal ditty sings,
> Humming of future things that burn the mind
> To leave some fragment of itself behind.

That is the most imaginative statement Clare ever made of his own poetic purpose. He, the poet, is one more of Nature's voices; and the same thought or the same instinct underlies the most exquisite of his earlier poems, *Song's Eternity*, a precious discovery of his present editors:

> Mighty songs that miss decay,
>   What are they?
> Crowds and cities pass away
>   Like a day.

Books are out and books are read;
  What are they?
Years will lay them with the dead—
  Sigh, sigh;
Trifles unto nothing wed,
  They die.

Dreamers, mark the honey bee,
  Mark the tree
Where the bluecap *tootle-tee*
  Sings a glee
Sung to Adam and to Eve—
  Here they be.
When floods covered every bough
  Noah's ark
Heard that ballad singing now;
  Hark, hark,

Tootle tootle tootle tee.
  Can it be
Pride and fame must shadows be?
  Come and see—
Every season owns her own;
  Bird and bee
Sing creation's music on;
  Nature's glee
Is in every mood and tone
  Eternity.

In many ways that is the most perfect of Clare's poems; it has a poetic unity of a kind that he attained but seldom, for in it are naturally combined the highest apprehension of which Clare was capable and the essential melody of his pre-eminent gift of song. It is at once an assertion and an emotional proof of the enduringness of the voice of Nature. Clare does not, like the modern poet who has chosen the same theme, adduce the times and the seasons and thereby challenge the evolutionary theory; his history is the history of myth. Not the Neanderthal man but Adam and Eve heard the bluecap's same immortal song; for it is not the fact, but the sense of song's eternity that the poet has to give us. Clare does it triumphantly. Moreover, in this poem, which we believe must henceforward take its place by right in every anthology of English poetry, Clare achieved that final perfection of form which was so often to elude him. The bird-note begins, rises, dies away: and the poem is finished.

Clare's music was a natural music; as with Shelley's skylark, his art was unpremeditated and his strains profuse. He was perhaps never to find a form which fitted his genius so intimately as that of *Song's Eternity*. His language was to become more coherent and more vivid; but the inward harmony that is essential to a great poem was too often to escape him. He was like a child so intoxicated with his wonderful gift for whistling and with his tune that he whistled it over and over again. The note is so pure, the tune so full of delight that we can never be tired; we listen to it as we listen to the drowsy enchantment of the monotony of sounds on a summer's afternoon, for it is as authentic and as sweet as they. The eternity of song was in Clare's blood; and when he recurs to the theme of enduring nature in simple stanzas,

> Some sing the pomps of chivalry
> As legends of the ancient time,
> Where gold and pearls and mystery
> Are shadows painted for sublime;
>
> But passions of sublimity
> Belong to plain and simpler things,
> And David underneath a tree
> Sought when a shepherd Salem's springs,
>
> Where moss did into cushions spring,
> Forming a seat of velvet hue,
> A small unnoticed trifling thing
> To all but heaven's hailing dew.
>
> And David's crown hath passed away,
> Yet poesy breathes his shepherd skill,
> His palace lost and to this day
> A little moss is blossoming still,

we feel that here, too, is a music that need never end.

Clare's difficulty as a poet, in fact, can and ought to be put baldly; he did not know when to stop. Why, indeed, should he stop? He was either a voice, one of the unending voices of Nature, or he was an eye, an unwearied eye watching the infinite process of Nature; perhaps never a poet consciously striving by means of art to arouse in men's minds an emotion like his own. All the art he had was that which he gained from his recollection of other poets' tunes; the structure of their harmony eluded him, he remembered only the melodies. Take, for instance, his extremely beautiful *Autumn*: the melody comes directly from Collins's famous *Ode*; yet how greatly Clare enriches it, as though with a material golden stain of autumn! The last leaf seems to be falling at our feet, the last bee zooming in our ears,

> Heart-sickening for the silence that is thine,
> Not broken inharmoniously as now
>   That lone and vagrant bee
>   Booms faint with weary chime.
>
> Now filtering winds thin winnow through the woods
> In tremulous noise that bids at every breath
>   Some sickly cankered leaf
>   Let go its hold, and die.

Not only these, but any one of a dozen other stanzas in the poem have a richer mellowness, reveal a finer sensitiveness than any in Collins's lovely *Ode*. For all that the melody derives from Collins, we are borne away from him to the neighbourhood of Keats's great poem. But Collins had a classical, almost Miltonic, sense of form; what he lacked in the richness of direct perception he supplied by his careful concentration of emotional effect: so that, despite the more splendid beauty of the elements of Clare's poem, we dare not say it is really as fine as Collins's *Ode*. Collins gathers up all his more exiguous perceptions into a single stimulus to emotion: Clare lets them fall one by one, careless of his amazing jewels. Set his *Autumn* against Keat's three strophes, where the imagination has come to crystallize perceptions not less rich in themselves than Clare's into a single symbol—the very spirit of Autumn.

> Who hath not seen thee oft amid thy store?
>   Sometimes whoever seeks abroad may find
> Thee sitting careless on a granary floor
>   Thy hair soft lifted by the winnowing wind;
> Or on a half-reaped furrow sound asleep
>   Drowsed with the fume of poppies, while thy hook
> Spares the next swathe and all its twined flowers;
> And sometimes like a gleaner thou dost keep
>   Steady thy laden head across a brook
>   Or by a cyder-press, with patient look,
> Thou watchest the last oozings hours by hours.

Clare could not do that; for Keats had Collins's art and Clare's richness of perception, and he had also that incomparable imaginative power which alone can create the perfect symbol of an overwhelming and intricate emotion.

Yet we need to invoke Keats to explain Clare, and to understand fully why his wealth of perception was refined into so few perfect poems. Collins himself is not sufficient for the purpose; one cannot well invoke the success of a poorer to explain the failure of a richer nature. Keats, the great poetic artist, however, subsumes Clare. Careless critics, confusing the life of every day with the life of the poetic mind, rebuke Keats for his lack of discipline. Yet where in English poetry shall we find a power of poetic discipline greater than his, a more determined and inevitable compulsion of the whole of a poet's emotional experience into the single symbol, the one organic and inevitable form? In him were combined miraculously the humanity that can reject no element of true experience and the artistic integrity to which less than a complete mastery and transformation of experience is intolerable. When, therefore, we invoke Keats to explain Clare, when we feel the need to merge Clare into Keats in thought in order that we may discover his own poetic fulfilment, by completing the great pattern of which he is a fragment, we are passing a judgment upon the value and quality of Clare's own work of which the implications are unescapable. It is a fragment, but it is a fragment of the Parthenon pediment, of intrinsic value, unique, and beyond price.

Clare's qualities were authentic and without alloy. It was the power to refine and shape his metal that was denied him; his workshop is littered not with dross but with veritable gold—of melody, of an intensity of perception (truly, his 'mind was burned'), and, more rarely, of flashes of that passion of the pure imagination which is the mysterious source of the magic of poetry. Let our partial quotation of *Song's Eternity* suffice to prove the quality of his spontaneous melody. For the intensity of perception we may choose at random any page in this book. Is not a picture such as this cast upon 'that inward eye'?

> Where squats the hare to terrors wide awake
> Like some brown clod the harrows failed to break.

Such things are scattered throughout Clare; they range from the quiet vision of the actual, focused by a single word, such as

> The old pond with its water-weed
> And danger-daring willow tree,
> Who leans, an ancient invalid,
> O'er spots where deepest waters be,

to the authentic fancy of

Here morning in the ploughman's songs is met
Ere yet one footstep shows in all the sky,
And twilight in the East, a doubt as yet,
Shows not her sleeve of gray to know her by.

How perfect is the image, as perfect to its context and emotion as the 'sovran eye' of Shakespeare's sun! And what of the intense compression of a phrase like 'ploughed lands thin travelled by half-hungry sheep', precise not merely to a fact, but to an emotion?

This unmistakable core of pure emotion lies close to the surface throughout Clare. His precision is the precision of a lover; he watches nature as a man might watch his mistress's eyes; his breath is bated, and we seem to hear the very thumping of his heart, and there are moments when the emotion seems to rise in a sudden fountain and change the thing he sees into a jewel. 'Frail brother of the morn' to a jetty snail is the tender cry of a passionate lover; there is a delicateness in the emotion expressed which not even Wordsworth could attain when he called upon the Lesser Celandine. It is love of this kind that gives true significance to the poetry of nature, for only by its alchemy can the thing seen become the symbol of the thing felt: washed by the magic tide of an overwhelming emotion, the object shines with a pure and lucid radiance, transformed from a cause to a symbol of delight, and thus no longer delighting the senses and the emotions alone, but the mind. This mysterious faculty is not indeed the highest kind of poetic imagination, in which the intellect plays a greater part in the creation of the symbol; this emotional creation leaps from particular to particular, it lacks that endorsement from a centre of disciplined experience which is the mark of the poetic imagination at its highest: but it is purely poetic and truly creative.

In this authentic kind Clare was all but a master, and it may even be suspected that his unique gift would have suffered if he had possessed that element of technical control which would have made him a master indeed. For when we come to define as narrowly as we can the distinctive, compelling quality of his emotion, we find that in addition to tenderness we need the word impulsive. Clare's most beautiful poetry is a gesture of impulsive tenderness. It has a curious suddenness, almost a catch in the voice.

The very darkness smiles to wear
The stars that show us God is there.

We find, too, a still more authentic mark of the tenderness of impulsive love in his way of seeing his birds and beasts as ever so little absurd. 'Absurd' has a peculiar and delightful meaning in the converse of lovers; Clare's firetail is 'absurd' in precisely the same sense.

> Of everything that stirs she dreameth wrong,
> And pipes her 'tweet-tut' fears the whole day long.

And so, too, are his bees—the 'grandfather bee', the wild bees who 'with their legs stroke slumber from their eyes', 'the little bees with coal-black faces, gathering sweets from little flowers like stars': even the riddle of the quail appears to be rather a delicate and loveable wayward-ness in the bird than a mere ignorance in the man.

> Among the stranger birds they feed,
>   Their summer flight is short and low:
> There's very few know where they breed
>   And scarcely any where they go.

A tenderness of this exquisite and impulsive kind might have been damaged as much as strengthened by a firmer technical control; a shiver of constraint might have crept into the gesture itself and chilled it; and perhaps we may touch the essential nature of Clare's emotion most closely in the mysterious and haunting Asylum poem, discovered by the present editors, and called by them *Secret Love*.

> I hid my love when young till I
> Couldn't bear the buzzing of a fly;
> I hid my love to my despite
> Till I could not bear to look at light:
> I dare not gaze upon her face
> But left her memory in each place;
> Where'er I saw a wild flower lie
> I kissed and bade my love good-bye.
>
> I met her in the greenest dells
> Where dewdrops pearl the wood blue bells.
> The lost breeze kissed her bright blue eye.
> The bee kissed and went singing by;
> A sunbeam found a passage there,
> A gold chain round her neck so fair;
> As secret as the wild bee's song
> She lay there all the summer long.
>
> I hid my love in field and town
> Till e'en the breeze would knock me down.

The bees seemed singing ballads o'er,
The fly's bass turned a lion's roar;
And even silence found a tongue
To haunt me all the summer long;
The riddle nature could not prove
Was nothing else but secret love.

Clare is invoking the memory of Mary Joyce, the girl lover whom he did not marry, and who, though long since dead, lived for him as his true wife when he was immured in the asylum. But the fact of this strange passion is less remarkable than its precise quality; it is an intolerable tenderness, an unbearable surge of emotion eager to burst forth and lavish itself upon an object. Whether it was his passion for Mary Joyce which first awakened him to an awareness of the troublous depths of emotion within we cannot tell, for this poem is in itself no evidence of fact. But it bears witness unmistakable to the quality of the emotion which underlay all that is characteristic and unforgettable in his poetry.

When we have touched the unique emotional core which consists throughout the work of a true poet, we have come perhaps as near as we can to his secret. We stand as it were at the very source of his creation. In the great poetic artist we may follow out the intricacies and ramifications of the intellectual structure by which he makes the expression of his central emotion complete, and the emotion itself permanent. In Clare the work is unnecessary. The emotion is hardly mediated at all. The poetic creation is instinctive and impulsive; the love is poured out, and the bird, the beast, the flower is made glorious. It is the very process which Stendahl described as *la cristallisation de l'amour*.

We may therefore most truly describe Clare as the love poet of nature; and we need not pause to explore the causes why nature and not a human being was not turned to crystal by the magical process of his love. Those who care to know may find the story woven in among the narrative of Mr. Blunden's sympathetic introduction; they can discover for themselves the reason why Clare appears in the world of grown men and women as a stranger and a changeling; why the woman of his dreams is disembodied; why, when he calls to her in his *Invitation to Eternity*, the present is 'marred with reason'—

The land of shadows wilt thou trace,
Nor look nor know each other's face;
The present marred with reason gone,
And past and present both as one?

Say, maiden, can thy life be led
To join the living and the dead?
Then trace thy footsteps on with me:
We are wed to one eternity.

In eternity perhaps a woman, but in the actual Nature was Clare's
mistress; her he served and cherished with a tenderness and faithful
knowledge unique in the poetry of nature. Like a true lover he stam-
mered in long speeches, but he spoke to her the divinest and most
intimate things. Assuredly his lines were cast so that he had no need of
woman even in eternity, and perhaps the truest words he ever wrote of
himself are those of the poem by which he is most generally known:

I long for scenes where man has never trod;
    A place where woman never smiled nor wept;
There to abide with my creator, God,
    And sleep as I in childhood sweetly slept:
Untroubling and untroubled where I lie;
    The grass below—above the vaulted sky.

126. Robert Lynd on Clare and Mr Hudson

1921

From an unsigned review of *Poems, Chiefly from Manuscript*, *Nation*, 22 January 1921, xxviii, 581–2. This was reprinted in Robert Lynd, *Books and Authors*, 1922, as chapter x, 'John Clare', pp. 94–102.

Robert Lynd (1879–1949) was a regular essayist for the *New Statesman*, and literary editor of the *Daily News* (later the *News Chronicle*). W. H. Hudson (1841–1922) was a popular naturalist and writer.

It is obvious that if we are asked to appreciate Clare as a poet in the same company as Keats and Shelley, our minds will be preoccupied with the sense that he is an intruder, and we shall only be able to listen to him with all our attention when he has ceased to challenge such ruinous comparisons. We do not know whether the critics of 1820 gave more praise to Clare than to Keats. But the public did. The public blew a bubble, and the bubble burst. Had Clare, instead of making a sensation, merely made the quiet reputation he deserved, he would not have collapsed so soon into one of the most unjustly neglected poets of the nineteenth century.

In order to appreciate Clare, we have to begin by admitting that he never wrote either a great or a perfect poem. He never wrote a 'Tintern Abbey' or a 'Skylark' or a 'Grecian Urn' or a 'Tiger' or a 'Red, Red Rose' or an 'Ode to Evening.' He was not a great artist uttering the final rhythms and the final sentences—rhythms and sentences so perfect that they seem like existences that have escaped out of eternity. His place in literature is nearer that of Gilbert White or Mr. W. H. Hudson than that of Shelley. His poetry is a mirror of things rather than a window of the imagination. It belongs to a borderland where naturalism and literature meet. He brings things seen before our eyes: the record of his senses is more important than the record of his imagination or his

thoughts. He was an observer whose consuming delight was to watch—
to watch a grasshopper or a snail, a thistle or a yellow-hammer. The
things that a Wordsworth or a Shelley sees or hears open the door, as it
were, to still more wonderful things that he has not seen or heard.
Shelley hears a skylark, and it becomes not only a skylark, but a flight
of images, illumining the mysteries of life as they pass. Wordsworth
hears a Highland girl singing, and her song becomes not only a girl's
song, but the secret music of far times and far places, brimming over and
filling the world. To Clare the skylark was most wonderful as a thing
seen and noticed: it was the end, not the beginning, of wonders. He
may be led by real things to a train of reflections: he is never, we think,
at his best led to a train of images. His realism, however, is often
steeped in the pathos of memory, and it is largely this that changes his
naturalism into poetry. One of the most beautiful of his poems is
called 'Remembrances,' and who that has read it can ever forget the
moving verse in which Clare calls up the play of his boyhood and
compares it with a world in which men have begun to hang dead moles
on trees?

> When from school o'er Little Field with its brook and wooden brig,
> Where I swaggered like a man though I was not half so big,
> While I held my little plough though 'twas but a willow twig,
> And drove my team along made of nothing but a name,
> 'Gee hep' and 'hoit' and 'woi'—O I never call to mind
> These pleasant names of places but I leave a sigh behind,
> While I see little mouldiwarps hang sweeing to the wind
> On the only aged willow that in all the field remains,
> And nature hides her face while they're sweeing in their chains
> And in a silent murmuring complains.

The pity that we find in this poem is, perhaps, the dominant emotion
in Clare's work. Helpless living things made a special appeal to him,
and he honored the spear-thistle, as it had never been honored in poetry
before, chiefly because of the protection it gave to the nesting partridge
and the lark. . . .

We have only to compare the detail of Clare's work with the
sonorous generalizations in, say, Thomson's *Seasons*—which he admired
—to realize the immense gulf that divides Clare from his eighteenth-
century predecessors. Clare, indeed, is more like a twentieth-century
than an eighteenth-century poet. He is almost more like a twentieth-
century than a nineteenth-century poet. He is neo-Georgian in his
preference for the fact in itself rather than the image or the phrase. The

thing itself is all the image he asks, and Mr. W. H. Davies in his simplest mood might have made the same confession of faith as Clare:—

> I love the verse that mild and bland
>   Breathes of green fields and open sky,
> I love the muse that in her hand
>   Bears flowers of native poesy;
> Who walks nor skips the pasture brook
>   In scorn, but by the drinking horse
> Leans o'er its little brig to look
>   How far the sallows lean across.

There is no poet, we fancy, in whose work the phrase, 'I love,' recurs oftener. His poetry is largely a list of the things he loves:—

[Quotes 'Autumn': 'I love at early morn . . .' to 'And fearful vision weaves']

As we read Clare we discover that it is almost always the little things that catch his eye—and his heart:—

> Grasshoppers go in many a thrumming spring,
> And now to stalks of tasselled sow-grass cling,
> That shakes and swees awhile, but still keeps straight;
> While arching ox-eye doubles with his weight.
> Next on the cat-tail grass with farther bound
> He springs, that bends until they touch the ground.

He is never weary of describing the bees. He praises the ants. Of the birds, he seems to love the small ones best. How beautifully he writes of the hedge-sparrow's little song!:—

> While in a quiet mood hedge-sparrows try
> An inward stir of shadowed melody.

There is the genius of a lover in this description. Here is something finally said. Clare continually labors to make the report of his eye and ear accurate. He even begins one of his 'Asylum Poems' with the line:—

> Sweet chestnuts brown like soling leather turn;

and, in another, pursues realism in describing an April evening to the point of writing:—

> Sheep ointment seems to daub the dead-hued sky.

His countryman's attempt at an echo of the blue-tit's song makes the success of one of his good poems tremble for a moment in the balance:—

[Quotes 'Song s Eternity', stanzas 4 and 5]

Obviously, Clare was more intensely concerned about the bird than about the eternity on which it set him thinking. He does come nearer an imaginative vision of life in this than in most of his poems. But, where Shelley would have given us an image, Clare is content to set down 'Tootle, tootle, tootle tee.' . . .

. . . Knowing the events of his life, we read Clare's poetry with all the more intense curiosity. And, if we do not expect to find a Blake or a Wordsworth, we shall not be disappointed. Certainly this is a book that must go on the shelf near the works of Mr. Hudson.

127. Edmund Gosse, a dissentient view

1921

From a review of Poems, Chiefly from Manuscript, Sunday Times, 23 January 1921, no. 5102, 5.

Sir Edmund Gosse (1849–1928), a frequent book reviewer, was famous for his Father and Son, 1907. He succeeded Leslie Stephen as a lecturer in English at Trinity College, Cambridge, 1884–90. See No. 134, and Introduction, p. 19.

One hundred years ago Keats was dying, and Shelley was unconsciously approaching his end, but these now illustrious names were not attracting any public attention in England. 'Prometheus Bound' and 'Lamia' had just been received with neglect and derision by the reviewers, who reserved their assiduous respect for two new poets, Bernard Barton and John Clare, the Northamptonshire ploughman. The Quarterly Review, so 'savage and tartarly' to the great singers, was enthusiastic in welcoming the descriptive poems of a village minstrel. There raged a fashion for the verse of peasants, and Southey wrote an entire volume of eulogies on our 'Uneducated Poets', a group who were really satellites of the vast Scotch planet, Burns.

There were threshers and shoemakers, washerwomen and brick-layers, among these humble bards, of whom Clare is the only one who retains any longer even a shadowy existence. We have outlined the patronising folly which valued the lisping of a muse not in spite but because of its lack of training. Yet, even to-day, when the elements of knowledge should be universally dispersed, there survives a senti-mentality which finds reason to admire a painting or a poem because a postman or a policeman has produced it.

The position of Clare in English literature is curiously undetermined, after more than a century. Criticism has never unanimously accepted him. . . .

[Biographical details]

He had no gifts except his dreamy sweetness of character, his child-like simplicity, and his redundant flow of verses. Let us not blame Society for the 'national disgrace' of not helping Clare, since Clare could not be helped. In these our days, there are organizations which may be, and should be, appealed to. Yet, even now, if there be a man who drinks, and has a tendency to insanity, and can ply no useful trade, such a case is heart-breaking, and does not call for a burst of indignation against 'Society'.

Clare wrote verse with inexhaustible fluency. Even in the asylum, he scribbled off enormous quantities of it, and well may his present editors speak of his 'incredible facility'. The great interest of the volume before us lies in the fact that with a small but very judicious selection of his published work, it gives a majority of pieces hitherto unknown. There were still left of these, I believe, more than a thousand, and rumour has it that within the last few weeks another huge store of hidden MSS. has been unearthed. However, it is very improbable that these would add to our gratification, if they were printed. They would rather add to the sense of dispersion, of dilution, which the work of Clare already awakens. His range was extremely limited, and he repeated his effects over and over again. His poetry is like honey and water; the water is pure and the honey Hymettan, but the brew is desperately thin. There is not one startling felicity, one concentrated ray, in the whole body of his work. It is clean and delicate, but tiresomely monotonous, and, above all, the spirit in it is diluted.

Leslie Stephen justly said of Clare's poetry that it shows how 'want of culture is not compensated by vigour of local colouring'. There are certain men of untaught genius who have been independent of scholastic training. No one regrets its absence in Blake or Burns, nor would Shakespeare be improved by more Latin and much Greek. But Clare is not on the level of these great spirits, and the gifts of nature were starved in him by lack of intellectual nourishment; his own mental resources were insufficient for the development of his talent, and it remained stunted and ineffective.

If we look at the beautiful head of Clare which Hilton painted, now one of the treasures of the National Portrait Gallery, we realise the tragedy of his life. These delicately-carven features, this dome of forehead surrounded by a profusion of silken curls, these ardent, uplifted eyes, this small, weak mouth, what were they doing in the cottage of a day-labourer? If ever there was born into the world a talent which demanded protection and indulgence, bodily comfort and intellectual sustenance, it was that of Clare, and to him all these things were permanently denied. Hence, the only mental accomplishment which he secured in any fullness was that which needed no cultivation but the activity of his own eyes.

He noted with extraordinary keenness and accuracy the animals and birds and plants which lived around him in Northamptonshire. Nothing escaped him in the fields, and he set everything down in verse: 'I dwell in trifles like a child', he said, but he gave these trifles a beautiful setting, especially in his sonnets, where the form obliged him to effect some condensation. 'Summer Images' is an example of his less concentrated manner, where the attention finds itself gratified, but at last wearied by dwelling on 'the jetty snail' and 'the green-swathed grasshopper' through a poem of two hundred lines. The observation is exquisite, but it is prolonged beyond measure, and is relieved by no reflection.

The new poems here printed exhibit the metrical skill of Clare in a fresh light. A long piece, called 'Song's Eternity', is written in a charming stanza, of which this is an example:—

> Dreamers, mark the honey bee;
>   Mark the tree
> Where the bluecap, 'tootle tee',
>   Sings a glee
> Sung to Adam and to Eve—
>   Here they be.

When floods covered every bough,
    Noah's ark
Heard that ballad singing now;
    Hark, hark.

We seem to be walking along a Northamptonshire lane, and suddenly, through the silence, there comes to us the sound of someone who is playing the flute in a field behind the hedge. We pause in rapture; we smell the beans in blossom; 'dear brother robin', just above us, listens and emulates the song; the sky begins to assume a 'watchet hue'; and still the flute shrills on. 'Tootle, tootle, tootle, tee!' in a softly-coloured Fenland landscape—that is the sum of John Clare's poetry from boyhood to the grave.

128. Clare and Keats

1921

Thomas Moult, from 'The Poetry of the Green Man', *English Review*, February 1921, 32, 186–9.

Thomas Moult was president of the Poetry Society, 1952–61, and edited *Poetry Review* during that period.

Sir Sidney Colvin once wrote a passage in which he speaks of 'John Clare, the distressed peasant poet, in whom many kindly people fancied they had discerned an English Burns.' When we consider that this disparaging tone was widely adopted notwithstanding that two of Clare's finest pieces, 'Autumn' and 'Summer Images', were to be read in the volumes issued during his lifetime, we are set wondering whether the neglect that fell on the poet was due to some other reason than lack of discernment. For the quality of these pieces is obvious enough—and especially so after we are set in a receptive and sympathetic attitude by the excellent biographical introduction.

. . . And oft as morning from her lattice peeps
To beckon up the sun, I seek with thee
　　To drink the dewy breath
　　Of fields left fragrant then,

In solitudes, where no frequented paths
But what thy own foot makes betray thy home,
　　Stealing obtrusive there
　　To meditate thy end:

There is something of the Keats influence, perhaps, as well as that of Collins, in this fine opening to the ode to 'Autumn', but no one would be justified in belittling or overlooking the poem on that account, any more than we could pass by 'La Belle Dame Sans Merci' because Keats remembered William Browne and Wordsworth while he wrote two of its most effective lines, or Dryden at a passage in 'Isabella'. But take this from 'Summer Images':

There the gay river, laughing as it goes,
　　Plashes with easy wave its flaggy sides,
And, to the calm of heart, in calmness shows
　　What pleasure there abides
To trace its sedgy banks, from trouble free;

and (because we need to break off at the foregoing point before an imperfection), a stanza even more beautifully sustained:—

To note on hedgerow baulks, in moisture sprent,
　　The jetty snail creep from the mossy thorn,
With earnest heed and tremulous intent,
　　Frail brother of the morn,
That from the tiny bents and misted leaves
　　Withdraws his timid horn,
　　　And fearful vision weaves.

In each of these, just as we have already detected his influence, we recognise something of the quality of Keats himself—but with a difference. We are almost forced, for once, into forgetfulness of the psychological distinction it is necessary to make, as regards the bulk of their poetry, between the fancy that characterises Clare's work and the imagination of the work of Keats. The distinction is a vital one, and probably accounts for the neglect of Clare, which appears to have increased in direct ratio to the growth of appreciation in the case of Keats. We might almost declare his fault to be that he observed too

347

much. Amongst the externals he wandered his life through. His interest lay with attractive anomalies rather than with their destiny and relation to the universal scheme.

> The maple with its tassel flowers of green,
> That turns to red a staghorn-shaped seed,
> Just spreading out its scolloped leaves is seen,
> Of yellowish hue, yet beautifully green;

Passages of this kind recall Richard Jefferies at his most descriptive—and his worst. 'Here and there upon the bank wild gooseberry and currant bushes may be found, planted by birds carrying off ripe fruit from the garden. A wild gooseberry may sometimes be seen growing out of the decaying "touchwood" on the top of a hollow withy-pollard. Wild apple-trees, too, are not uncommon in the hedges. . . .' Just as Jefferies rarely forgot that he was the gamekeeper and naturalist conspiring together within him to prevent his writing any other book to compare with his own *Story of My Heart*.

A poet of the higher order, whose vision is of such intensity as to be always imaginative, regards natural objects merely as the symbols by which he expresses his æsthetic conception; never using them in his poetry for their own sake. When Wordsworth wrote his sonnet on Westminster Bridge he forgot that there was any such bridge as that named specifically in his title, any such place as London. And Keats, in his ode 'To Autumn', gets right away from the season's physical facts— *as* physical facts. The gathering together and presentation of John Clare's poems in this worthy form has enriched English poetry of another order than Wordsworth's, another order than Keats'. More and more as his strangely happy, strangely sad, life went on, Clare was leaving the world of the second order for theirs, and had those who forgot the man possessed the advantage, as we now have it, of studying his later production, they would have revived their interest in him no longer as a peasant, but, probably for the first time, as a poet. The difference in the position to-day of Clare and of Keats is that the author of *Poems Descriptive of Rural Life* remembered too long his own green smock and gaiters, while the poet of 'Isabella' forgot, early enough, even that he was John Keats.

129. Maurice Hewlett on Clare's derivations

1921

'Clare's Derivations', *Cornhill Magazine*, March 1921, n.s.l, 274–81. This article was reprinted in *Wiltshire Essays*, 1921, pp. 58–68.

Maurice Hewlett (1861–1923), novelist, poet and essayist, lectured in mediaeval art and was an authority on heraldry. His approach to Clare was new and potentially fruitful (see No. 130).

It is now possible to learn what sort of a poet this peasant, son of peasants, was. I emphasize his degree in life because, to the best of my knowledge, he is the only genuine peasant-poet we have. He was not only the son of a farm-labourer, but brought up to the calling himself, with all the hindrance to the ripening of genius which such an upbringing involves, and for the whole of his life at liberty, whenever he was not trying to live by poetry he was making shift to do so by farm labour. That sets him apart from such a man as Robert Bloomfield, as the quality of his verse does also. Bloomfield was a bad poet, Clare was a good one; but Bloomfield at twelve years old was apprenticed to a shoe-maker in London, and seems never to have lived in the country again. It sets him apart also from Mr. Hardy, who may have been of peasant origin, but scarcely served the ordinary calling of his class, and received an education which rapidly trained him, and fostered, not impeded, his genius. Clare's schooling was of the scantiest, his life days were never prosperous, his work was exhausting, his lodging as poor as you please. Yet he became the lion of a season; his first volume went into three editions in a year; he was patronized by peers, met and was familiar with Lamb and Hazlitt, Haydon, and probably Keats. He was able somehow to collect books about him, and to read at large. The editors of the new Selection tell us he 'reverenced' Keats, that he admired Wordsworth, was critical of Scott. He must then have read Coleridge and Byron, perhaps even Shelley. There are indeed signs that he had read much. And from his reading, as may be guessed, he derived much.

But he had tunes of his own to sing, and was rarely an echo of other men. Here, from his early period, which the editors put at before 1824, is the opening of a ballad, which is like nobody else:

> A faithless shepherd courted me,
> He stole away my liberty.
> When my poor heart was strange to men,
> He came and smiled and took it then.
>
> When my apron would hang low,
> Me he sought through frost and snow.
> When it puckered up with shame,
> And I sought him, he never came.

If I don't mistake the matter, that is the peasant vocal of his tribe. And so is the song which follows it:

> Mary, leave thy lowly cot
> When thy thickest jobs are done;
> When thy friends will miss thee not,
> Mary, to the pastures run.

But how far Clare was indeed that rare creature, a peasant articulate, can be seen best in 'The Flitting', a poem which shows his love of his birthplace fast like roots in the soil. As a tree might cry when torn from the bank, so the peasant cries in his heart; and so cried Clare in his verse:

> I've left my own old home of homes,
> Green fields and every pleasant place;
> The summer like a stranger comes,
> I pause and hardly know her face.

He was moving from a hovel to a house found for him by Lord Milton; as his editors say, 'Out of a small and crowded cottage in a village street to a roomy, romantic farm-house standing in its own grounds.' Yes, but he was rooted in Helpston, and must be dragged out.

> I lean upon the window-sill,
> The trees and summer happy seem;
> Green, sunny green they shine, but still
> My heart goes far away to dream
> Of happiness, and thoughts arise
> With home-bred pictures many a one,
> Green lanes that shut out burning skies
> And old crookt stiles to rest upon.

'Nos patriae fines, et dulcia linquimus arva!'[1] There speaks the peasant.

'The Flitting' is a good poem, and very near to the bone; but Clare's particular excellence—that of close description—does not shine in it, and may have been dulled by his tears. 'Summer Evening' shows him at his best, a longish lyric in rhymed couplets of eight, interspersed with lines of seven, which may have been inspired by speeches in *Comus*, or by *L'Allegro*—as I think probable—but possesses what those works have not, an eye on the object without losing an ear upon the tune:

> The sinking sun is taking leave,
> And sweetly gilds the edge of eve,
> While huddling clouds of purple dye
> Gloomy hang the Western sky.*
> Crows crowd croaking overhead,
> Hastening to the woods to bed.
> Cooing sits the lonely dove,
> Calling home her absent love,
> With 'Kirchup! Kirchup!' 'mong the wheats
> Partridge distant partridge greets. . . .

and so on: a catalogue, if you will; but how closely observed, how fresh and happy!

Here he gets closer still: the plough-horse—

> Eager blundering from the plough,
> Wants no whip to drive him now;
> At the stable-door he stands,
> Looking round for friendly hands
> To loose the door its fastening pin,
> And let him with his corn begin. . . .

The geese:

> From the rest, a blest release,
> Gabbling home, the quarrelling geese
> Seek their warm straw-littered shed,
> And waddling, prate away to bed. . . .

Excellent. He runs thus through the farmyard, down to the very cat at the door, the sparrows in the eaves, and the boys below waiting till they tuck themselves in.

---

1 'I am leaving my native countryside with its delightful fields', Virgil, *Eclogues*, i, 3.
* Unless I hugely mistake, the *Shropshire Lad* has a reminiscence of these lines.

As he settled into his stride he grew stronger and better along his first line of minute observation and accurate phrasing. Best sign of any, he threw his description into his verbs. Take his so-called sonnet, 'Signs of Winter', and mark the verbs in it:

> The cat runs races with her tail. The dog
> Leaps o'er the orchard hedge and *knarls* the grass.
> The swine run round, and grunt, and play with straw,
> Snatching out hasty mouthfuls from the stack.
> Sudden upon the elm tree *tops* the crow,
> Unceremonious visit pays and croaks,
> Then *swops* away. From mossy barn the owl
> *Bobs* hasty out. . . .

Not one of those but does its work. 'Knarl', as used in Northamptonshire, has the meaning of querulous complaint: its use here is onomatopœic, probably from 'gnaw'. 'Swops away' is Northamptonshire dialect for 'swoops'.

Here are some more verbs, beautifully used:

> The nuthatch *noises* loud in wood and wild,
> Like women turning *skreeking* to a child.
> The schoolboy hears and brushes thro' the trees,
> And runs about till *drabbled* to the knees.
> The old hawk *winnows* round the old crow's nest . . . .

Wrens, according to Clare, 'chitter', peewits 'flop' in flight; the woodpecker 'bounces,' and

> Holloas as he buzzes by, 'Kew kew'.

But I had intended to write about his derivations, and will turn to them now.

Oddly, perhaps, he did not begin with Thomson's *Seasons*, as Bloomfield did, to his undoing, because he never left it as long as he went on writing. The vague idyllism, the obviousness and persistent generality of Thomson, are not to be found in Clare. On the other hand, in his 1820 volume, you have Burns:

> Ay, little Larky! what's the reason,
> Singing thus in winter season?
> Nothing, surely, can be pleasing
>   To make thee sing;
> For I see nought but cold and freezing,
>   And feel its sting.

That is rather feeble, and though it improves as it goes on, never for a moment catches the unapproachable sauciness and raciness combined of its original. Clare had very little humour—which that stanza demands.

He imitates Crabbe freely—in poems like 'The Gypsies' and 'The Parish: a Satire'—but lacks the antithesis of Crabbe, and the sententiousness too. Crabbe must always be moralizing. Clare, like a true peasant, is a fatalist to the core. Let things be as they may, because they needs must. That is the philosophy of the peasant—Sancho Panza's philosophy. One of his boldest derivations is from the lovely 'Ode to Evening' of Collins. Clare's is addressed to 'Autumn':

> Sweet vision, with the wild dishevelled hair,
> And raiment shadowy of each wind's embrace,
> Fain would I wind thine harp
> To one accordant theme;
> Now not inaptly craved, communing thus,
> Beneath the curdled arms of this stunt oak,
> While pillowed in the grass,
> We fondly ruminate
> O'er the disordered scenes of woods and fields,
> *Ploughed lands, thin-travelled with half-hungry sheep,*
> *Pastures tracked deep with cows,*
> *Where small birds seek for seeds. . . .*

The voice is the voice of Collins, but the eye is Clare's. I have spoken of his verbs. Certainly he did not get those from Collins. Observe them here:

> See! from the *rustling* scythe the *haunted* hare
> Scampers circuitous, with *startled* ears
> Prickt up, then squat, as by
> She *brushes* to the woods.

And once more:

> And now the *bickering* storm, with sudden start,
> In *flirting* fits of anger *carps* aloud,
> Thee urging to thine end,
> Sore wept by troubled skies.

I suspect that distich to be fruit of Clare's 'reverence' for Keats.

There are traces of Wordsworth, as in the following 'Impromptu':

> 'Where art thou wandering, little child?'
> I said to one I met to-day.
> She pushed her bonnet up and smiled,

353

> 'I'm going upon the green to play.
> Folks tell me that the May's in flower,
> That cowslip-peeps are fit to pull,
> And I've got leave to spend an hour
> To get this little basket full!' . . .

and there are others to be found; but he did not apprehend anything more than the wrappings of the great poet, did not touch his sudden and starry magic—those chance gleams of unearthly light, unearthly insight which, in Wordsworth, make us catch our breath. But there was another Wordsworth who could make Dutch pictures, from whom Clare could more happily borrow. I think he gets near to that one in 'The Wood-cutter's Night Song', which begins:

> Welcome, red and roundy sun,
> Dropping lowly in the west;
> Now my hard day's work is done,
> I'm as happy as the best. . . .

and ends:

> Joyful are the thoughts of home,
> Now I'm ready for my chair,
> So, till morrow-morning's come,
> Bill and mittens, lie ye there!

The whole is a sweet and happy fireside picture.

The most curious derivation remains, rather more than a derivation. The editors print (or, in this case, reprint) a ballad called 'The Maid of Ocram, or Lord Gregory', which at first blush is not only remarkable as a poem, but even more so as an imitation of a real folk-ballad. It imitates not more the garb than the spirit of that beautiful thing. This is the opening verse:

> Fair was the maid of Ocram
> And shining like the sun,
> *Ere her bower key was turned on two*
> *Where bride bed lay for none.*

If that is not a terse and graphic opening, I don't know one. Then the tale begins.

Now it is proper to say here that the tale is exactly the subject of a ballad called 'The Lass of Roch Royall', published for the first time in Child's great book 'from a manuscript of the first half of the eighteenth century'. It is there called 'Fair Isabell of Roch Royall'; but there is a variant, 'The Lass of Ocram', which derived itself in turn from an Irish version called 'The Lass of Aughrim'. That is only half the story. Where did Clare find the poem which, until it was printed in the *Roxburghe Ballads*, only existed in the British Museum? There can be little doubt of the answer. When he was a boy, cow-tending on Helpston Common, his present editors tell us, 'he made friends with a curious old lady called Granny Baines, who taught him old songs and ballads'. That is the answer; but other questions arise. What did Clare do with 'The Lass of Ocram' when he had it? The quatrain just quoted, at any rate, is not in it. It will be found also that he has added an ending. The tale shortly is that the lass was betrayed by Lord Gregory, and found herself with child and forsaken. She went to plead with her lover, who was asleep. His mother answered for him and denied her the entry, failing proof. Three 'tokens' are demanded, which the lass supplies. Finally, the mother drives her away, and at her despairing cry Lord Gregory wakes. He has dreamed of the lass, and questions his mother:

> Lie still, my dearest son,
> And take thy sweet rest;
> It is not half an hour ago
> The maid passed this place.

The ballad ends with Lord Gregory's remorse and lamentation. Clare, after his masterly opening, plunges into the tale:

> And late at night she sought her love;
> The snow slept on her skin:
> Get up, she cried, thou false young man,
> And let thy true love in.

That is new, except for the matter of the second line, which Clare has lifted and, I think, not improved. The original has:

> It rains upon my yellow locks,
> And the dew falls on my skin.

He uses that also, but, since he was bothered by the snow which he had invented, is forced to change it for:

> The wind disturbs my yellow locks,
> The snow sleeps on my skin.

In the revelation of the tokens he is not so simple as the ballad, but his additions are to the good. The second token:

> O know you not, O know you not
> 'Twas in my father's park,
> You led me out a mile too far,
> And courted in the dark.

That is both original, and observed—from many a rustic wooing. The third token was the betrayal, where, as he cannot possibly better his model, he wisely conveys it. The ending, which is Clare's own, is artless and rather comic:

> And then he took and burnt his will
> Before his mother's face,
> And tore his patents all in two,
> While tears fell down apace.

Finally, 'He laid him on the bed, And ne'er got up again.'

While we may be satisfied how much of 'The Maid of Ocram' is Clare's, we shall never know how much was Granny Baines's. That is one of the secrets of folk-song which is insoluble. The 'rain upon her yellow hair', 'the dew sleeping on her skin', are beautiful additions of some unknown English minstrel to 'The Lass of Roch Royall'. A close collation of the two would be interesting, if not fruitful. Clare's 'lay-out' of the tragedy, in his two opening octaves, is his only serious contribution. I do not find that he did anything else of the kind. He has plenty of narrative, but no other dramatic narrative, and of his many tales in verse none approaches this one either for terseness or the real ballad touch of magic.

The present editors have done a real service to literature as well as to Clare's memory by their new Selection; and it may be that they are not at the end of their discoveries. By what they have put forward so far they have shown Clare to be a considerable poet, more considerable than we could possibly have supposed by the work published in his life-time. It is very much to me that the peasantry should have produced a poet of such power and charm, who interprets so faithfully the life of a race so old upon our earth, and so close to it.

130. Maurice Hewlett on Clare as peasant poet (again)

1924

From 'Peasant Poets', *Last Essays*, 1924, pp. 82–7.

The peasant is a shy bird, by nature wild, by habit as secret as a creature of the night. If he is ever vocal you and I are the last to hear of it. He is as nearly inarticulate as anyone living in civilisation may be. Consequently a peasant sufficiently moved, or when moved, sufficiently armed with vocables to become a poet, even a bad poet, has always been rare. When you need to add genius to sensibility and equipment, as you must to get a good poet, you may judge of the rarity. Indeed, to put a name to him, *exceptis excipiendis*, I can only find John Clare. Other names occur, but for various reasons have to be cut out. There was a postman poet in Devonshire, a policeman poet in Yorkshire; and there was a footman poet. One of those certainly had merit, even genius, and any one of them may have been a peasant in origin. But by the time they began to make poetry they had ceased to be peasants; and that rules them out, as it does Robert Blomfield and Thomas Hardy. Then there is Burns. But Burns was not a peasant. We in England should have called him a yeoman. Besides, his is one of those cases of transcendent genius where origin goes for nothing, but all seems the grace of God. At that rate the corn-chandlers might claim Shakespeare, or the chemists' assistants Keats.

But there's no doubt about Clare, a Northamptonshire peasant, son of peasants, brought up at a dame-school, and at farm labour all his working life. It is true that he was 'discovered' by Taylor and Hessey, published, sold; that his first book ran into three editions in a year; that he was lionised, became one of the Lamb-Hazlitt-Haydon circle, and thus inevitably sophisticated with the speculations not of his own world. But roughly speaking, from start to close, his merits were the merits of the peasantry, and his faults as pardonable as theirs. He was never gross, as they never are; he was never common, as the pick of them are not; he was deeply rooted, as 'The Flitting', one of his best poems, will prove; he was exceedingly amorous, but a constant lover; nothing in nature escaped his eye; and lastly, in his technique he was a realist out and out. Of his quality take this from 'Summer Evening':

> In tall grass, by fountain head,
> Weary then he crops to bed.

'He' is the evening moth.

> From the haycocks' moistened heaps
> Startled frogs take sudden leaps;
> And along the shaven mead,
> Jumping travellers, they proceed:
> Quick the dewy grass divides,
> Moistening sweet their speckled sides;
> From the grass or flowret's cup
> Quick the dew-drop bounces up.
> Now the blue fog creeps along,
> And the bird's forgot his song:
> Flowers now sleep within their hoods;
> Daisies button into buds;
> From soiling dew the buttercup
> Shuts his golden jewels up;
> And the rose and woodbine they
> Wait again the smiles of day.

The poem runs to length, as most of Clare's do, but the amount of exact, close and loving observation in it may be gauged from my extract. It is remarkable, and worthy of memory for the sake of what is to follow. You may say that such microscopic work may be outmatched by gentle poets; you may tell me of sandblind Tennyson, who missed nothing, of Cockney Keats and the 'Ode to Autumn,' and say that it is a matter of the passion which drives the poet. There is, I think, this difference to be noted. Observation induces emotion in the peasant-poet, whereas the gentle or scholar poet will not observe intensely, if at all, until he is deeply stirred. I don't say that that will account for everybody: it will not dispose of Tennyson, nor of Wordsworth—but it is true of the great majority.

131. J. Middleton Murry on Clare and Wordsworth

1924

'Clare and Wordsworth', *The Times Literary Supplement*, 21 August 1924, no. 1179, 511. This review, of *Madrigals and Chronicles*, was later reprinted, as 'The Case of John Clare', in *John Clare and Other Studies*, 1950, pp. 19–24, from which this text is taken.

See No. 125 and Introduction, p. 19.

Not many poets justify and repay editorial piety more bountifully than John Clare. Though comparatively few of his poems achieve the beauty of form which is the evidence of completely mastered and related perceptions, scarce one of them is without a strange intrinsic beauty of the perception itself. Clare's sensibility was of the finest and most delicate, and his emotional reponse to nature almost inhumanly sweet and pure. His weakness lay in his power of poetic thought. Inevitably, in reading the precious additions made by Mr. Blunden to his previous collection of Clare's poetry, we are reminded once more, as we were reminded at the time of the first collection, of Wordsworth. Even more than then the comparison of Clare with Wordsworth seems necessary if we are to gain that precise sensation of Clare's individuality, without which it is scarcely possible to know a poet fully. And not only does Wordsworth appear necessary to a criticism of Clare, but Clare to a criticism of Wordsworth. The reference is reciprocal: it is also quite unavoidable. We doubt whether anyone could read, without thinking immediately of Wordsworth, Clare's beautiful poem in this volume on 'The Primrose Bank':

> With its little brimming eye
> And its crimp and curdled leaf
> Who can pass its beauties by?

For here evidently was someone to whom a primrose by the river's brim was in a sense, just a primrose: but it was wholly a primrose, not 'something more' indeed, but altogether itself. 'Its little brimming eye,' 'its crimp and curdled leaf,' are phrases which almost make us hold our breath in order not to disturb the exquisite perfection of their truth. And this truth is of such a kind that it is complete: there is nothing more to be said, and perhaps nothing more to be thought. At least it is hard to imagine that the poet to whose vision a primrose thus appeared, who could express what he saw with an ease and naturalness such that the expression strikes as part of the very act of seeing, in whose eyes (it is obvious) 'Solomon in all his glory was not arrayed like one of these,' should ever have thought, or ever have had the impulse to think, about what he saw. The particularity of the created universe was sufficient for him; he saw each several thing in itself as sovereign and beautiful. What more did he need, what more can we ask?

Clare's faculty of sheer vision is unique in English poetry; not only is it far purer than Wordsworth's, it is purer even than Shakespeare's. Or, it might be wiser to say, Shakespeare passed so quickly beyond this stage of pure vision that only traces of it remain. And yet we feel there is an intrinsic impossibility that vision of this kind, so effortless and unparading, should ever pass beyond itself; we feel it must demand so complete an engagement and submission of the whole man that it leaves no margin for other faculties. Clare's vision, we might say paradoxically, is too perfect. Shakespeare had as much of it as a man can have if he is to develop into a full maturity; Wordsworth had some of it. Wordsworth's vision came to him in flashes, therefore it seemed to him an abnormal and extraordinary visitation which needed to be related by thought and meditation to ordinary experience. We may put it in this way: if Wordsworth had seen a primrose as Clare saw it—and he did occasionally see things thus—he would have felt that he was seeing 'into the heart of things,' whereas Clare—who seems always to have seen in this way—felt that he was merely seeing things. It is dangerous to be made after so unusual a pattern, and Clare was locked up.

The penalty was monstrous, an indescribable refinement of torture for this child-man whose very life was seeing things. But it was a cruel approximation made by half knowledge to the truth that Clare was not really a man. Those thoughts, for which his seeing left no room to grow, are necessary to the condition of manhood, and therefore necessary also to the writing of the finest poetry. Wordsworth, in his preface to the second *Lyrical Ballads*, was essentially right.

All good poetry is the spontaneous overflow of powerful feelings: and though this be true, poems to which any value can be attached were never produced on any variety of subjects but by a man who, being possessed of more than usual organic sensibility, has also thought long and deeply.

Never were the primary conditions of poetry, as Wordsworth defined them, more exactly satisfied than by Clare. He was possessed of infinitely more than 'usual organic sensibility,' and all his poetry is 'the spontaneous overflow of powerful feelings.' Wordsworth's general definition is a precise description of Clare's work: the epithets, 'organic' of his sensibility and 'spontaneous' of his emotion, fit Clare more happily than any other poet who comes to mind. And the reason is that the poetic natures of Clare and Wordsworth were closely allied. The difference between them is that Clare could not, while Wordsworth could, think long and deeply.

This inability of Clare's was a defect of his quality; and it was because Wordsworth's sensibility was not so pure or so uninterrupted as Clare's that he had the opportunity and the need for thought. But even for him thought was something almost unnatural, so that he was extremely conscious of himself thinking and of himself as a thinker. His thought is not always spontaneous as Shakespeare's is always spontaneous and as Keats's thought promised to be spontaneous; we are often aware of it as an element that is not really fused with his perception, but super-imposed upon it, and Wordsworth's poetry then takes on that slightly didactic, slightly distasteful tone of which Keats (who belonged to the Shakespearian order) was so acutely conscious when he wrote about Wordsworth:

We hate poetry that has a palpable design upon us, and if we do not agree, seems to put its hand into its breeches pocket. Poetry should be great and unobtrusive, a thing which enters into one's soul, and does not startle or amaze it with itself, but with its subject. How beautiful are the retired flowers! How they would lose their beauty were they to throng to the highway, crying out, 'Admire me, I am a violet! Dote upon me, I am a primrose!'

In this criticism of Wordsworth by a still finer poetic mind than his own, the ground is, as it were, once more cleared for a just approach to Clare. Again the very words are apt to him. His poetry is 'unobtrusive.' 'How beautiful are the retired flowers!' is true of him perhaps more than any other poet. His poetry has no 'palpable design upon us'; it has no design upon us at all.

The cause of Clare's so curiously fitting into these utterances of his great poetic contemporaries, is, first, that he was in the essential as authentic a poet as they and, secondly, that he was allied to Wordsworth by the nature of his 'organic sensibility' and to Keats by his wonderful spontaneity. Wordsworth would have denied poetic 'greatness' to Clare because of his lack of thought, but Keats would have denied poetic 'greatness' to much of Wordsworth's work because of its lack of spontaneity and unobtrusiveness. These criticisms, in their ascending order, are just and profound, and they establish the real precedence of these three true poets. Moreover, this conclusion follows: in order that Clare should have been as great a poet as he was a true one, the quality of his thought would have needed to be equal to the quality of his perception, equally spontaneous, equally organic. Then he would have been, in Keats's phrase, both 'great and unobtrusive,' and a very great poet indeed. As it is, he is unobtrusive and true, not a great poet, but assuredly not a little one—a child, on whom the rarest and most divine gift of vision had so abundantly descended that he could not become a man.

The quality in Clare which most enthrals us, the general quality of which the quintessence is manifest in the beauty of his seeing, is one which we can only describe as a kind of *naïveté*. If we use a similitude, we might say it was an abiding sense of a quite simple fraternity with all the creatures of the world save self-conscious man. Man, the thinker, the calculator, the schemer, falls outside this universe of simple comprehension, and is the inhabitant of an alien world. He will not enter, he has no wedding garment. And the reality of Clare's vision and its power over our hearts is such that there are moments when our conviction that this is a limitation of Clare's understanding suddenly abandons us and we have a secret fear that his may be the true and unattainable wisdom. 'Except ye become as little children . . .' That fear does not remain with us; we know that the word is not thus literally to be understood. Our childhood must come to us as the achievement of our manhood. We cannot divest ourselves of our birthright. But Clare's *naïveté* reinforces the admonition of the word, that unless we can achieve, out of all our wisdom and despair, a comprehension as pure as was his vision, we shall have lost the day.

For in Clare's vision is indubitable truth, not comprehensive, not final, but because it strikes our hearts as truth, and is truth, it is prophetic of the final and comprehensive truth. It is melody, not harmony:

> Yes, night is happy night,
> The sky is full of stars,

> Like worlds in peace they lie
> Enjoying one delight.

But true melody, as this is, is separated from false harmony by a whole universe of error. If it has not been troubled by thought, it has also not been corrupted by the temptation to turn stones into bread. The spontaneous feeling of

> [He] felt that lovely mood
> As a birthright God had given
> To muse in the green wood
> And meet the smiles of heaven,

though it does not itself achieve it, would at least never be satisfied by thought that was not as spontaneous as itself; it would have no room for the speculations of mere intellectual pride. And Clare's nascent thoughts, as far as they go, are as true as his feelings; indeed they *are* feelings:

> I thought o'er all life's sweetest things
> Made dreary as a broken charm,
> Wood-ridings where the thrush still sings
> And love went leaning on my arm.

Experience, the organic knowledge from which organic thought is born, was for Clare the dreary breaking of a charm. The phrase is beautifully, agonisingly true. Up to the extreme verge of his capacity Clare never betrayed himself. On the one side his world of his vision, on the other side broken charms and mystery; he did not, he could not, try to reconcile them. When he was shut out by destiny and the hand of man from his own world, he lived within the memory of it. In *Mary*, a poem to his child-love, the memory is heart-breaking even to us:

> Mary, or sweet spirit of thee,
>   As the bright sun shines to-morrow
> Thy dark eyes these flowers shall see
>   Gathered by me in sorrow,
> In the still hour when my mind was free
> To walk alone—yet wish I walked with thee.

Something terrible has been done to this child-man that he is forced to wander in an alien world alone. It was intolerable to him, and it is intolerable to us who hear the voice of his suffering. Yet, though the charm was broken and he was outcast from his world, he was loyal to it. He did not betray his knowledge. The evidence of his triumphant loyalty is in the last, and the greatest of the poems in this book. It is obscure, because Clare was struggling with an order of thought to which he was not born, but in spite of the obscurity, its purity and truth and justice are manifest. He had indeed 'kept his spirit with the free.'

Quotes 'I lost the love of heaven above . . .']

132. Alan Porter on a book of the moment

1924

From a review of *Madrigals and Chronicles*, *Spectator*, 23 August 1924, no. 5017, 260–1.

For Alan Porter, see No. 121.

It is the early Clare who wins our affection, Clare who was in love with the 'shy-come nightingale,' the yellowhammer, 'fluttering in short fears,' the white-nosed bee and its 'never absent couzen, black as coal,' the 'little fish that nimble by,' every spot in the cowslip, every streak in the bindweed. We are in the Age of Innocence when we read the detail of nature so transfigured by love, and by wonder, too:—

> Aye, as I live! her secret nest is here,
> Upon this white-thorn stump. I've searched about
> For hours in vain. There! put that bramble by—
> Nay, trample on its branches and get near.
> How subtle is the bird!

We can picture him well at this time: short and thin and pale, with a great head too large for his elfish body; country-dressed, in a green smock and hob-nailed boots; with rough hands and a shameless Northamptonshire accent, but bearing himself with such grace that strangers took him for 'a nobleman in disguise,' and Lamb used to refer

to him as 'Princely Clare.' We have absurd anecdotes of him that
increase our affection. We know, for example, how frightened he was
when he first visited London, the wicked city. His fellow-labourers had
warned him, in the tap-room of the 'Bell,' that everyone there was on
the look-out to pick your purse or to murder you. And so, when his
publishers sent their porter to meet him on his arrival, and when the
porter asked him 'Are you Mr. Clare?' he firmly and finally answered
'No!' It is Clare 'gentle and simple,' as Hood called him, whom many
love as the whole Clare.

There is another Clare, an old man. The tranquillity and the regular
diet of the Northampton Public Asylum have benefited him physically;
he looks quite prosperous and fat. The large head seems even larger; he
is bald at the front and at the back his hair hangs down long and white;
his brow seems incredibly high. His eyes are more piercing and wilder.
No one has come to see him for years except a journalist or two. His
wife and children are too miserably poor to afford a journey of thirty
miles; and, besides, if they came, they might find him in one of his
worst moods—he might be too deeply sunk in despair to recognize
them, he might manage to forget, as everyone else seems to have forgotten, that he was John Clare, a once-famous poet. He has nothing to
do but read the newspaper, play dominoes with the other inmates, or sit
in the porch and smoke. He is allowed a good deal of freedom, for he is
classified in the books as 'harmless.' There is not much wrong with him;
he sometimes pretends that he is Lord Byron, or a prize fighter, or a
cavalier; he talks to himself about a certain John Clare, who is happily
settled in his old cottage; once he saw figures moving from the floor of
a room to the ceiling; once he pointed to a molehill and said 'Look at
that mountain'; he has fits of bitter melancholy and incoherent speech:
there is the sum total of his madness. He still writes poems on any scrap
of paper he can obtain. Some of them are inconsequent jingles; some
have flashes of genius; some are the most vivid, the most passionate, the
most visionary, the most delicate of all his poems. He experiments in
metres that no one has used before; he writes in free verse and he writes
in complicated stanzas. His range of subject has widened; he has had
time enough, the twenty years he has been in the madhouse, to dig into
his own soul. He still writes of Nature, and of Nature in detail. He goes
over the memories of his early years, the things that were so dear come
back to him, but he sees them more at distance, more golden. The
tragedy of his first love occupies him still, and in a hundred different
settings, under a hundred different names, he writes lyrics in praise of

Mary Joyce. Now and then he imagines himself with his passions fulfilled:—

> In every language upon earth,
> On every shore, o'er every sea,
> I gave my name immortal birth,
> And kept my spirit with the free.

More often he sees himself as he is, rejected and forgotten. In his moments of greatest sanity he petitions God for the gift of death. Here, then, is another Clare, who wins our pity and amazement.

Between these two there is a third Clare, the strangest and, to me, the greatest of all: unfortunately we know little of him. He is not yet mad, but those blows which are to drive him mad are battering in upon him. He is in ill-health and poverty: he has a small income, thirty-six pounds a year, but he has a wife and seven children to keep. No farmer will take him on as a labourer; he is too frail, and anyhow they look upon him with suspicion—he has left the station to which God called him and has been seen talking to the nobility and to gentlemen from London. Those gentlemen from London haven't done him much good; they lionized him and fêted him at first; a peasant poet was a most amusing figure; but now they never think of him. Certainly they never buy his poetry. He can't make a penny by writing. When nobody thinks anything of Clare, is it any wonder that Patty, his wife, a hard-working matron, gets rather short with him at times? Someone has done a kind action, to be sure; Lord Milton built him a cottage at his own expense in a village a few miles from Clare's home—from the cottage where he was born, where he had lived for forty years. But the last thing in the world that Clare desired was to leave the place where every inch of ground was passionately loved. If anyone felled a tree near his home he was plunged into sorrow. How could he bear to have every field and every stream, every bird's nest, every rabbit track taken from him? They told him how ungrateful he would be if he insisted on staying where he was; they half persuaded, half dragged him away. He reached this new home in tears, and he was to take no joy in living for the rest of his days.

His friends had forsaken him, his fame was gone. He believed that he despised 'the glory and the nothing of a name'; but it is those who possess that nothing who despise it. He was sick and almost starving. He scarcely dared go beyond his door; for everything he saw in the fields and woods reminded him so bitterly of those dearer fields and dearer woods. He lived in his study and brooded over life. It was the treachery of men that distressed him most:—

> I hate the very noise of troublous man,
> Who did and does me all the harm he can.
> Free from the world, I would a prisoner be,
> And my own shadow all my company;
> And lonely see the shooting stars appear,
> Worlds rushing into judgement all the year . . .

Well, he was to be free from the world, and a prisoner, too, in a short space of time. 'O take this world away from me,' he cries again:—

> Its very praises hurt me more
> Than even its coldness did before,
> Its hollow ways torment me now,
> And start a cold sweat on my brow.

He was not mad yet, but he turned Methodist—and that could be a gloomy religion in the first half of the nineteenth century. He wrote down on the edges of newspapers vivid and stern paraphrases of the Psalms and the Book of Job. He found comfort in one who was

> An outcast thrown in sorrow's way,
> A fugitive that knew no sin,
> Yet in lone places forced to stray—
> They would not let the stranger in.
> Yet peace, though much himself he mourned,
> Was all to others he returned.

But his religion for the most part was more desperate and more lurid.

His nature poems were still his best poems. Something odd had happened to him, though: he did not now so often irradiate Nature with love. One of the strangest and most terrible moods that I have heard of captured him from time to time. His observation was as close as ever: read, for example, his description of the marten:—

> The marten cat, long shagged, of courage good,
> Of weazel shape, a dweller in the wood,
> With badger hair, long shagged, and darting eyes,
> And lower than the common cat in size,
> Small head, and ever-running on the stoop,
> Snuffing the ground, and hindparts shouldered up . . .

But how does Clare, tender-hearted, whose fiercest complaint against men was roused by the smallest show of cruelty, write so many poems at this time in which cruelty of the most brutal kind is faithfully recorded, with utter impartiality, it would seem, without praise or blame? If we had not known Clare, if we had not known that cruelty set him shivering with anger and grief, we might almost, from the poems, have suspected him of enjoying the cruelty for its own sake. A badger is set loose in the street; men and boys set dogs at him, throw sticks and cudgels and stones at him, jump at him and kick him. He falls down as though dead:—

> Then starts and grins and drives the crowd again;
> Till kicked and torn and beaten out he lies,
> And leaves his hold and cackles, groans, and dies.

So the poem ends. We are given a picture of a ploughman beating an old dog fox, 'till his ribs would crack,' of boys running after a lame boy and jeering at him. This trait is most terrifying when we get it in half a line, apparently for no purpose, in the middle of a quite innocent poem:—

> The boy that stands and kills the black nosed bee.

The truth is that something had already snapped in Clare's mind. He was, in such moods, no longer a lover of Nature; he had become Nature itself. He felt as a wild animal felt, he suffered in sympathy, being hit and fighting back, without passing judgment. He had been obsessed and tormented with the thought of man's cruelty; he had seen so much of it, and at last his torture had become so wholly a part of him that it remained a horror pervading the depth of his mind but never working its way into speech. Cruelty, cruelty—he must set it down; but it comes out stark and monstrous. These are, I think, the most gruesome poems in the English language.

Another habit goes to prove that already his mind was weakening. In many of the sonnets—if we can call them sonnets—they were in a form invented by Clare himself—a few words echo themselves throughout the poem. It is as though Clare, in the first line, had set up a sound in his brain that could not exhaust itself until his poem was over. The poems in consequence, have often a *naïveté* of phrasing, a sort of lisp in sense, that is pleasing from its quaintness.

133. Percy Lubbock, a hesitant view

1924

From a review of *Madrigals and Chronicles, Nation and Athenaeum*, 6 September 1924, xxxv, 694.

Percy Lubbock (1879–1965), essayist and novelist, wrote *The Craft of Fiction* (1921).

A good editor must be a devoted one, and a devoted editor will always claim a little more for the object of his care than the first-comer, cool in detachment, will be willing to concede; and it may be that for Clare's fame fifty poems are better than many hundreds. It will be a pity if that which is large and true and fine in his work is swamped by that which is trite and careless; and there is enough of the latter in nearly every page of Clare's to raise the question. But the answer is with Mr. Blunden, and if he is devoted in care he is scrupulous in appraisement; and Clare has doubtless fallen into hands that will do the right thing by him at last. He has had to wait long for it in all conscience; it is sixty years since he died in the County Asylum at Northampton.

And what, as we know it at present, is the true value of Clare's poetry? It has little art, it has no great range of reflection, its hold upon life is uncertain, its passion runs easily to conventional pharses. Clare was no stammering genius, battling for expression in the face of the many difficulties that hampered him; it is impossible to believe that in happier circumstances, with all the opportunities of freedom and ease that he never had, his poetry would have been any deeper or wider or fuller than it is—though with a taste more leisurely trained it might have been better made. It does not seem that his nature was cramped, only that his mind was worn and vexed to madness, by poverty and toil and anxiety. His long years of insanity appear as the result of fretted nerves and exhausted patience, not as the downfall of genius overwrought and overdriven by itself. He evidently poured out his poems with great facility and fluency—tunefully, songfully, with no troubled revolt against the narrowness of his village life. The change of the seasons around the farmstead, between the sparkle of romance in springtime and the comfort of the fireside on winter evenings—there was all the inspiration that he needed, his world was big enough for him. He wrote of the thoughts which it stirred in him, and they were not profound—of the love that he found and lost and found again, and the full and final expression of it was beyond him; and he also wrote of the country, of the fields, and the weather and the birds and the folk of the good, plain, laborious countryside in which he lived, and when he wrote of these he was a poet.

An 'unparalleled intimacy' with the nature of the English landscape—so Mr. Blunden puts the leading characteristic of Clare's poetry. If the word is to be strictly scrutinized it will have to be said that this intimacy is unparalleled only among poets, and that with that qualification the claim is considerably reduced. Sensitive to nature, absorbed in nature, in love with nature many and most of our poets have been, with Chaucer at that end and Mr. Blunden himself at this. But intimacy, if it implies a real and close acquaintance, is another matter, and it is intimacy in this sense that is ascribed to Clare, and from his poetry it would seem that the claim may be easily exaggerated. The knowledge of the life of nature that is revealed in his poems is not extraordinary; anyone who has lived in the country and used his eyes may soon have matched it. But Clare had an exquisite gift, by far his greatest, for rendering in small pictures the sight of what he saw in the country; and after so much that is unreal and conventional in most 'nature-poetry' the freshness and sharpness and directness of his vision are admirable. Sometimes there is also a singing joy in the vision which gives such a poem as 'The Primrose Bank' (in this volume) a beautiful radiance. Unfortunately, Clare could never write more than a few lines without betraying the uncertainty of his hand in form and phrasing; so that it is difficult to find a single complete poem that is perfectly apt for quotation. But here perhaps is one—'Sunrise in Summer':—

> The summer's morning sun creeps up the blue
> O'er the flat meadows most remotest view:
> A bit at first peeps from the splendid ball,
> Then more, and more, until we see it all.
> And then so ruddy and so cool it lies,
> The gazer views it with unwatering eyes,
> And cattle opposite its kindly shine
> Seem something feeding in a land divine:

Ruddy at first, yet ere a minute's told
Its burning red keeps glowing into gold,
And o'er the fenny level richly flows,
Till seeded dock in shade a giant grows;
Then blazing bright with undefined day
He turns the morning's earnest gaze away.

That is a picture drawn and left without a moral, and it was in simple impressions like this that Clare showed the best of his quality. Did he not? His editor attributes to him a wider imaginative reach and a rarer music, than the effect of these fifty poems would seem to warrant. Perhaps after all the effect will be more convincing in many hundreds.

134. Edmund Gosse, again

1924

From 'Nature in Poetry', *Sunday Times*, 5 October 1924, no. 5295, 8. This article, a review of *Madrigals and Chronicles*, was reprinted, under the same title, in *Silhouettes*, 1925, pp. 103–9.

Gosse (see No. 127) refers in his preface to 'the little sermons which I preach every week out of the pulpit of the *Sunday Times*.' Gosse also had a brief word on Clare in *More Books on the Table*, 1923, in an article on 'Georgian Poetry', pp. 229–35, where he referred to the fact that Edmund Blunden wrote under Clare's spell: 'Mr. Blunden will grow out of this, when he perceives that why Clare was not a poet of the first rank was that his attention was hampered by incessant beauties, and that he lacked the gift of selective apprehension' (p. 232).

The double publication has greatly augmented the importance of Clare as a figure on our crowded Parnassus, and has made it certain that he can never again be overlooked, as he was between 1820 and 1920. He will take his place as one of the authentic English poets, and the only danger now to be apprehended is that he will be exalted unwisely. It is a natural weakness in those who have had the good fortune to find hidden treasure to exaggerate the value of what has so romantically been unearthed. The poetry of Clare is charming, his approach to Nature genuine and sincere, but when the claim is put forward that he was a great artist, for the sake of his own reputation we must be on our guard. When a responsible reviewer declares that Clare's faculty was 'far purer than Wordsworth's,' and 'purer even than Shakespeare's,' it is time to weigh our standards of merit.

Although Clare is his discovery, Mr. Blunden is not betrayed into this riot of hyperbole. He does not rank Clare above Wordsworth and Shakespeare as a poet of Nature. His definition of the theme is not injured by depreciation of other writers to the advantage of his Northamptonshire labourer, and yet it calls for a certain further discrimination. Mr. Blunden says:—

> The characteristics of Clare's Poetry are an unparalled intimacy with the English countryside: a rare power of transfusing himself into the life of everything beneath the sky, save certain ardours and purposes of men; a natural ease of diction, well suited to hold the mirror up to Nature; a sense of the God in the Fly and the Cataract; a haunting sense of an Ethereal Love, Woman *in excelsis*, and, as the charm for his casual hearer, a delicate and elemental music.

This is well said—although I am afraid I cannot follow the fling about God and the Fly and the Cataract—and I think that each clause is *nearly* true, calculated, that is, to prepare the reader for what he will find in Clare, without mentioning what he will not find. Let us now take an example from the poet himself, the very characteristic sonnet called 'The Foddering Boy,' and see how far it justifies Mr. Blunden's definition:—

> The foddering boy along the crumping snows
>   With straw-band-belted legs and folded arm
> Hastens, and on the blast that keenly blows
>   Oft turns for breath, and beats his fingers warm,
> And shakes the lodging snows from off his clothes,
>   Buttoning his doublet closer from the storm
> And slouching his brown beaver o'er his nose—
> Then faces it again, and seeks the stack
>   Within its circling fence where hungry lows
> Expecting cattle, making many a track
>   About the snow, impatient for the sound
> When in huge forkfulls trailing at his back
> He litters the sweet hay about the ground
> And brawls to call the staring cattle round.

Here, to a wonderful degree, we find the 'unparalleled intimacy with the country-side,' and an exactitude of observation which nowadays we call 'photographic,' but where is the 'transfusion' which Mr. Blunden promised us? Every detail which photography can seize is precisely rendered, but all is exterior; there is not a phrase that shows the poet 'transfusing' himself into the life of the Foddering Boy. Clare's is sheer descriptive poetry, painted with a wonderful delicacy and conscientiousness, but all from the outside. He concentrates his attention on the stray path rambling through the furze, on the patter of squirrels over the green moss, on the shaggy marten startling the great brown hornèd owl, and always has at his command the just phrase, the faultless vision, the economy and daring of epithet. His notes of birds and flowers are those of a naturalist, and it is, perhaps, ungracious to remark that this was a fashion of his time, as we may still see in such pieces as the botanical sonnets of Charlotte Smith. Clare does the pictorial and half-scientific business much better, of course, than Charlotte Smith did it, but surely we are far indeed in his watercolour drawings from the exaltation of 'Tintern Abbey,' from the human poignancy of 'A Poet's Epitaph'? Clare hung over 'the meanest flower that blows' with the rapture of a miniaturist, but it never gave him 'thoughts that do often lie too deep for tears.'

In the generation which preceded Clare's, Canning had pointed out that observation without reflection is of secondary value in imaginative literature. This is a remark which is too often forgotten in the criticism of descriptive poetry. To bring vividly before us the 'oval leaves' of waterweed in the deep dyke among the rushes, to note the 'marble' clouds of spring, to paint the wet blackbird cowering down on the whitethorn bush, requires a rare and beautiful talent which the North-amptonshire labourer possessed in a very remarkable degree. No one must dream of denying or belittling so precious a gift. But to excel in such clear painting is to be William Hunt or de Wint, not Titian or Velasquez. It is to be a Little Master of high accomplishment, but not a Great Master in Poetry.

What is lacking is the intellectual element, the 'organic sensibility' which Wordsworth demanded, and which he himself enjoyed in a superlative fullness. It is, to quote another Great Master, to be able to create out of the phenomena of Nature 'forms more real than living man.' This Clare could not do. He saw the tattered gold of the ragwort with perfect sincerity, and he makes us see it, but the sight suggests nothing to him beyond its own fresh beauty. It does not induce in him a train of thoughts, as the sight of the celandine did in Wordsworth. The admirers of Clare lay great stress on the stanza in which he describes the primrose

> With its little brimming eye,
> And its yellow rims so pale,
> And its crimp and curdled leaf—
> Who can pass its beauties by?

The accuracy of the picture is wonderful, but it is too much like a coloured plate in a botanical treatise. Here is nothing that transcends unreflecting observation, nothing that speaks to the spirit of Man. Indeed, without carping, we are bound to admit that here one is speaking to whom a primrose on a river's bank was just a primrose, and 'nothing more.' But the highest poetry requires more. So, too, let any unprejudiced lover of verse compare Clare's ode to the Skylark with either Shelley's or Wordsworth's, and he must confess that the Northamptonshire stanzas, charming as they are, belong to a lower order of inspiration.

It was the misfortune of Clare that, with unsurpassed exactitude of vision and delicate skill in stating fact, he was devoid of all reflective power. I am surprised that Mr. Blunden, whose introduction displays candour as well as sympathy, does not admit this defect. Clare had no thoughts. He wandered through the country, storing up images and sounds, but he wove his reproductions of these upon no intellectual basis. His was a camera, not a mind; and while we must admit that he showed a praiseworthy reserve in not pretending to find any philosophical relation between his negatives and the human spirit, still, the fact cannot be ignored that the philosophy was absent.

Connected with the absence of thought is the imperfection of form, which Mr. Blunden acknowledges, but is a little too indulgently disposed to slur over. His attributes it, perhaps justly, to Clare's lack of primary education, yet it seems more likely, in one who had read all the best English verse, to have been an inherent defect. Clare had a bad ear; he was satisfied to rhyme 'alone' with 'return,' 'crow' with 'haw,' and 'season' with 'peas in.' His metrical structure is often loose, and his grammar not above reproach. Yet on these technical trifles I would not insist.

Let it not be thought that though I hint a fault I hesitate dislike. On the contrary, the verses of Clare give me great pleasure, and those not least which are contained in this collection of 'Madrigals.' His poetry is English in the extreme; not a phrase, not an epithet takes us out of our country, and hardly out of Clare's own county. As the habits of local life become modified by time, his record of Northamptonshire ways and scenes will increase in value. His 'word-painting,' to use a Victorian phrase now much fallen into disfavour, will keep alive his simple lyrics, and will remind successive generations how

> The little violets blue and white,
> Refreshed with dews of sable night,
> Come shining in the morning-light
> In thorn-enclosed grounds;

And whether winds be cold or chill,
When their rich smells delight instil,
The young lamb blaas beside the hill
And young spring happy sounds.

135. Edmund Blunden on Clare

1929, 1931

Edmund Blunden (b. 1896), poet and critic, edited, with Alan Porter (see No. 121) *John Clare: Poems Chiefly from Manuscript*, 1920. He has also edited *Madrigals and Chronicles*, 1924, and *Sketches in the Life of John Clare, written by Himself*, 1931. Blunden's work on Clare and the circle in which he moved has always been sensitive.

(a) From chapter ii, 'The Spirit Wooed: Collins, Keats, Clare', *Nature in English Literature*, 1929, pp. 50–9.

A third nature-poem now calls for our regard, one which is on the subject of Keats's Ode and in the unrhymed stanza of Collins. This is the 'Autumn' of John Clare, in some lights the best poet of Nature that this country and for all I know any other country ever produced. Clare was known in his time as the Northamptonshire Peasant Poet, and is, I am afraid, still looked upon as such by many of those who have heard of him. Simple as he may at a hasty reckoning appear, he is not so when he is known better: Clare is a rustic, but imaginative enough to see the meaning of that; he is an exact naturalist, but a poet of the mystical temper as well; he is not learned, but makes considerable excursions into learning by which he is enabled not to stand still between naivety and great art, and can be at home in both. There is extraordinary development in his poetry between the early clownish scrawl of alehouse ballads and the later work of which the Dantesque 'I am! but what I am none cares or knows!' is the most generally reprinted. However, this is not the place for attempting an analysis of Clare's work; my eyes are on the poem 'Autumn,' written at the time of his maturest and least distracted powers, and certainly one of the most sustained and creative of his pieces. It first appeared, a little battered, in Cunningham's *Anniversary* for 1829, and was collected in *The Rural Muse*, 1835:

> Syren of sullen moods and fading hues,
> Yet haply not incapable of joy,
> Sweet Autumn! I thee hail
> With welcome all unfeigned;
>
> And oft as morning from her lattice peeps
> To beckon up the sun, I seek with thee
> To drink the dewy breath
> Of fields left fragrant then . . .

So Clare begins. His invocation of a spirit stranger in mien and characteristics than those of the other poets just mentioned is not long; in the third stanza it closes, and it is, he says, the end of Autumn that he intends to meditate. Then comes a succession of pictures of solitude, such as he has particularly frequented in autumn; he pauses from these, and seems to confess that none of these will capture his desired supreme vision. He again utters his desire—he invokes the answer of Nature:

> Sweet Vision, with the wild dishevelled hair,
> And raiment shadowy of each wind's embrace,
> Fain would I win thine harp
> To one accordant theme.

If only the mystery will take his verse as she takes the forest for her instrument! This is Clare's 'Make me thy lyre.' He fancies her under the oak, a lover beside him, with him, looking out on

> the disorder'd scenes of woods and fields,
> Ploughed lands, thin travelled with half-hungry sheep,
> Pastures tracked deep with cows,
> Where small birds seek for seed;

on the herdboy pulling down the berries from the thorn, and the hedger red-cheeked and hardy in the dykeside, the mower with his stubbling-scythe, the thatchers on barn and rick, and the 'haunted hare' started and scared into the woods. Then he suddenly looks for his 'wild sorceress' beside him, and blesses her for her 'restless mood,' and 'the silence that is thine' in all this minor unrest; the enigmatic moments when the din of joy is past, and the storm is not come. But a change in the note of the wind in the midst of this true and beautiful melancholy warns him; even this dark-glorious presence is doomed.

> Now filtering winds thin winnow through the woods
> In tremulous noise, that bids, at every breath,
>> Some sickly cankered leaf
>> Let go its hold and die.

> And now the bickering storm, with sudden start,
> In flirting fits of anger carps aloud,
>> Thee urging to thine end,
>> Sore wept by troubled skies.

Autumn, 'disorderly divine,' is going; the gold on the leaf is the sign of her death—those dyes 'prepare her shroud.' The queen of the winds, she droops beside him, and the dirge is low; the lark alone arises with his inexhaustible heart of music and goodwill, but then comes silence, and Autumn's grave. 'That time is past.' And yet, if the mystery has escaped, next year there will be a chance again for a song in her honour and to her liking: when she

> from her ivied trance
> Awakes to glories new.

The associations of Clare's 'Autumn' with previous poetry are soon summed up; Collins has taught him a means of rendering a difficult music in Nature without rhyme, and given him a word or two, as 'the willing lark' and the 'faint and sullen brawl' of the stream. Shelley, of whom he knows a little, is with him in the 'unpremeditated' song not of the lark but the child, and Keats in the 'winnowing' wind. But the larger effect is that of a dweller in the woods, who is in love with what may or may not have been regarded as a symbol. Even Clare's 'votaress' or 'season' is a vision uncertain as those far-projected fluttering forms which some are said to see on the wind.

> The earth hath bubbles,

and she may be of them; it is not with him as with Collins, who changes his picture of Evening with all the design of a mythological painter, or with Keats, who similarly enriches the canvas with a masque of gleaners, reapers, cider-makers. It is a direct though a pale passion, and can have at the end only one aim and expectation—a vision, apart from the creations of our normal affection and thought. Perhaps it will be reckoned fantastic to interpret Clare's 'Autumn' in this almost psychic way, but a great part of his verse is a history of the transference of love in him from woman to Nature. He describes the poet as 'a secret thing, a man in love none knoweth where'; he sums up his autobiography in lyrics of which the correct text has not been found, but which even in their injured state reveal the thrilling enigma of his heart. 'I hid my love when young'—and then, the companionship of woman became more beautiful and immutable in a wood-change:

> I met her in the greenest dells
> Where dewdrops pearl the wood bluebells;
> The lost breeze kissed her bright blue eye,
> The bee kissed, and went singing by.
> A sunbeam found a passage there,
> A gold chain round her neck so fair;
> As secret as the wild bee's song
> She lay there all the summer long.

Having this Grace, this Dryad always in hope and almost in ocular proof, Clare wrote his poems as if for her; not all of them, but the later kind, when his old friends in London had died or drifted from him. He did not fail at times to regard verse as an art for the use of mankind, and indeed accomplished such examples of his intellectual eagerness as a series of poems in the manner of Elizabethan writers; but more and more he conceived his chief singing to be an offering to that mystery whom he loved, a repetition of all her endowments, her lineaments, her devotions and delights. So hastening on and giving her 'his posies, all cropt in a sunny hour' with childlike haste and ecstasy, he did not shape his compositions in the intense school of Collins and Keats. They lose, in the arbitration of our criticism, for that reason, and the splendid 'Autumn' which we are considering now is as a whole, as a marshalling of idea and circumstance, inferior to the other two Odes. But we can, by a sympathy of the imagination, approach Clare's poem in the light of his wooing of the 'fair Flora,' the wind-spirit, the music-maker, the shepherdess, and accept his unpremeditated and disunited perfections so. No one has surpassed these perfections in themselves, these tokens of his secret love. They may be classed as 'observation' but only true passion can observe in Clare's way,

> By overshadowed ponds, in woody nooks,
> With ramping sallows lined, and crowding sedge,

Which woo the winds to play,
And with them dance for joy;

And meadow pools, torn wide by lawless floods,
Where water-lilies spread their oily leaves,
    On which, as wont, the fly
    Oft battens in the sun;

Where leans the mossy willow half way o'er,
On which the shepherd crawls astride to throw
    His angle clear of weeds
    That crowd the water's brim;

Or crispy hills, and hollows scant of sward,
Where step by step the patient lonely boy
    Hath cut rude flights of stairs
    To climb their steepy sides;

Then track along their feet, grown hoarse with noise,
The crawling brook, that ekes its weary speed,
    And struggles through the weeds
    With faint and sudden brawl.

You cannot reply 'Notebook, notebook' to this exactitude, this close inventory of little things, of which Clare's work presents an infinity; it is the eye of a lover that feasts on such glances, gestures, and adornings of his mistress. Through all, her life gives life, her wonder gives wonder. The fly on the lily-leaf might have little meaning, did not that 'sorceress' set him there, and what she does is to Clare touched with hieroglyphic eternity.

Hence, too, this happiness of animation, this familiar characterising of what are called 'objects of landscape.' All are equal here in the universal fancy of autumn. The sedge and the winds have their pastime apart like a group of children; the floods were common trespassers; the lonely boy and weary brook alike are patient in their labours of indolence. In the poem too there is another lonely boy, who exactly like the sedge 'woos the winds' with his song. The lark springs up 'to cheer the bankrupt pomp' of the time, and it is when the wind 'bids' that the cankered leaf 'lets got its hold'; in short, it is all one whether a ploughman passes or a bee. They bear the impress of the strange siren Autumn, and play their part without distinction of power and glory. I must not deaden this vitality of Clare's nature-vision with too much talking. He has commented on it himself in several poems, giving 'every weed and blossom' an equality with whatever this world contains:

All tenants of an ancient place
   And heirs of noble heritage,
Coeval they with Adam's race
   And blest with more substantial age.
For when the world first saw the sun
   These little flowers beheld him too,
And when his love for earth begun
   They were the first his smiles to woo.

It is that last word, if one word can be, which is the keyword to John Clare's long life of unselfish, uncopied nature-poetry.

(b) From 'On Childhood in Poetry', *Votive Tablets*, 1931, pp. 338–9.

To Clare, childhood was all that was actual; it remained, while the world of men faded like dew. His writings are nothing else but the record of a strife with circumstance for the privilege of the child's clarity through years that obscure it. Without the companionship of what he remembered from a boy John Clare would have welcomed death. Rather than unsee the vision of his child love he 'went to his cell' in the madhouse. As a youth he had turned his look on the glories to come—the mirage vanished, and he made no second mistake, dreaming on to recapture if he might, no matter what the cost, 'the green happiness of love's young dreams'.

THE PERIOD 1935-64

136. Clare's dream

1935

From an unsigned review of *Poems of John Clare*, ed. J. W. Tibble, *The Times Literary Supplement*, 21 February 1935, no. 1725, 97-8.

John Clare's place is secure among the poets. Quality is not overwhelmed in the quantity of these crowded volumes. 'Peasant poet', 'pathetic and forlorn figure' were the customary epithets used even after the brave effort—and abortive so far as the general public were touched—made by Mr. Arthur Symons in 1908 to resuscitate his fame. Mr. Blunden's devotional insistences and extended researches have borne fruit. The sensational interest which draws attention to one who 'hummed his lowly dreams far in the shade where poverty retires,' and for that reason alone, is misdirected. Clare was a poet by his right, and a poor peasant by the world's mischance. Even his sufferings are above the pathetic order; like Keats's, they loom as tragic rather than pitiable. 'Tears are for lighter griefs.' We suffer, not weep, when Lear is betrayed to the storm. The tragedy of Clare has a terrible beauty. Overthrown and in bondage, he still kept the vision and the dream, and conquered amid the collapse of hope. That agony was his triumph.

In the final exile in Northampton Asylum Clare might tell visitors he was Byron or Tom Spring, whichever hero, poet or pugilist, was uppermost in his disorder that day; but often, pen in hand, his mind rewon its intellectual alacrity and he would recover the reality of his inner life without deformity of knowledge or derangement of poetry. Indeed, many of his asylum pieces had a lyrical perfection his earlier work had not attained. There was a perfect confluence of observation, expression, passion and music. The sweet bells sometimes jangled out of tune, but even when they did some kind of logic, though not entirely explicable, is heard in the sound. Nature's moods and aspects were always within the call of memory. The phantom of his lost love, Mary Joyce, from being part of the loveliness of Nature became its symbol, till at last in hymning the woman of his dream he is hymning his Nature-love. In one place identification is direct and no mystical guesswork is called for. Mary was

> Nature's self, and still my song
> Is her, through sun and shade, through right and wrong.

. . . It would be setting too high, or too low, a value on the quality of his thought to speak of his philosophy, a word which implies some kind of system, whereas the poet is concerned with his reactions to life's experiences; but it is an exciting adventure to trace the development of Clare's decisions. His hints of immortality were made in a quiet utterance, often a primitiveness, in accord with Wordsworth's aesthetic, but held meanings as deep as those in the other's structural magnificences. Thought long brooded over cannot be denied to this poignant expression of experience:—

> I lost the love of heaven above,
>   I spurned the lust of earth below,
> I felt the sweets of fancied love
>   And hell itself my only foe. . . .
>
> I loved, but woman fell away;
>   I hid me from her faded flame.
> I snatched the sun's eternal ray
>   And wrote till earth was but a name.
>
> In every language upon earth,
>   On every shore, o'er every sea,
> I gave my name immortal birth
>   And kept my spirit with the free.

In seeing so acutely the life before us he sees a life beyond, and conveys convincing senses of it by melody if not always by words. He was one with Nature by an intuitive identification of himself with all things that live; yet he insisted on the preciousness of individuality. Harmony and love were the quest; and, until at the end, when he seemed to have resolved the question, he was disturbed by the contest of life with the spirit and of the spirit with life. At the last

there is no room for fears
Where death would bring me happiness; his shears
Kill cares that hiss to poison many a vein;
The thought to be extinct my fate endears;
Pale death, the grand physician, cures all pain;
The dead rest well who lived for joys in vain.

The mind flies to Keats and his intenser 'Death is Life's high mead.' The perilous journey is beautiful to the traveller who holds fast to his identity and keeps his natural dignity and compassion; and its reward is death, which also is beautiful.

137. John Speirs on Clare's limitations

1935

A review of *Poems of John Clare*, ed. J. W. Tibble, 1935, *Scrutiny*, June 1935, iv, 84–6.

John Speirs (b. 1906) is the author of several books, including *The Scots Literary Tradition* (1940), *Chaucer The Maker* (1951), and *Poetry Towards Novel* (1971).

The exhaustive collection of Clare's poems now for the first time published is intended to complete the work of restoration with which Mr. Edmund Blunden, appropriately, has been associated. But whether it will add anything actual to the reputation the 1920 selection established is doubtful. It may well have the contrary effect of reinforcing the reader's sense of Clare's limitations. There is certainly here an overwhelming quantity of genuine stuff, but a stuff that is all of the same sort, so that the ultimate effect of it in such bulk is to emphasize its own sameness. We may find, it is true, a number of precious things in it which might well have replaced some of the things in the selection. The selection was not simply a selection, but was, we are reminded by Mr. Tibble, a *representative* selection. This suggests that the criterion was not solely one of intrinsic value. It seems to have been part of the purpose to represent different phases of Clare's development. Actually what is of value in Clare's work seems to develop singularly little, and this is a radically adverse criticism to make of any poet. Certain of the Asylum poems have been seen as something different, marking a final phase, and have even been regarded as Clare's finest work. There is in these an ecstatic note and occasionally a hint that Victorian influences have filtered through, but only the fact that they are nearer to what the nineteenth century had learnt to think poetry ought to be like could have blinded readers to their unsatisfactoriness in comparison with Clare's characteristic work, which remains essentially eighteenth century in quality.

What an edition of the collected poems does facilitate is a study of the particular influences which formed and later informed Clare's work. In his earlier work the influences of Thomson, Shenstone, Collins, Gray, Cowper and Crabbe separately are explicit, and the 'literary' eighteenth century remains implicit throughout his work. The following lines come comparatively late:

> From every nook the smile of plenty calls,
> And reasty flitches decorate the walls,
> Moore's Almanack where wonders never cease—
> All smeared with candle-snuff and bacon-grease.

It would be impossible to mistake these lines for Pope, but it is equally impossible not to recognize that but for Pope they would not have existed as what they are. This relationship between Clare's characteristic (which is also his valuable) work and the 'literary' eighteenth century is what distinguishes him from Burns, with whom, as a 'peasant poet,' he has often been compared, and whose work provoked him to one or two imitations. Clare's very revealing autobiographical fragment* helps to explain the difference. His parents he tells us were illiterate, except that his father could read a little in the Bible, but his father was 'fond of Ballads, and I have heard him make a boast of it over his horn of ale, with his merry companions, that he could sing or recite above a hundred.' At the age of thirteen (he thinks it was) a fragment of Thomson's *Seasons* fell into his hands. From that time he educated himself as a poet solely through frequentation of the 'literary' poets of the eighteenth

* *Sketches in the Life of John Clare by Himself*, edited by Edmund Blunden.

century, and even learnt rather to despise as 'trash' the Ballads of his father. At the same time, though he thus became a 'literary' poet, he continued to share even as such a poet the traditional life of the country-side. Also he is notably free at his best from the Miltonic inversions and diction of his 'literary' masters, though there are traces in his work of the 'L'Allegro' Milton as well as of the blank verse Milton who so tyrannized over the later eighteenth century. He even draws consider-ably upon the vocabulary of peasant speech. To this extent he has indeed a certain affinity with Burns. But I notice that Mr. Adrian Bell deals with this aspect of Clare's work in his review in the *Spectator*.[1]

It is easier to see why Clare is a poet than why he is not a great poet. His poetry, and that considering his facility is a surprisingly large pro-portion of his work, is the product of an extraordinary intimacy with the nature that surrounded him, particularly with the *minutiæ*, insects, blossoms, of the inexhaustible meadow-life. He is a nature-poet as Wordsworth is not, for Wordsworth is a psychologist interested funda-mentally in the workings of his mind. What Clare's poetry evidences is a complete absorption with that other life, not felt as another life. It consists of perceptions crystallized richly and presented with a particu-larity and concreteness which are a warrant of their absolute authenticity. Yet it is a profusion that is spilt, almost one is tempted to say let run to waste. Clare has no hard core of individuality compelling his perceptions to serve an inner purpose. He has no inner purpose. He is scarcely even conscious of himself. It is this which distinguishes him from Mr. Blunden as a poet. Mr. Blunden's is a poetical world specially created with the aid of the 'literary' eighteenth century from memories of a world known in boyhood but more than half passed away; it suggests a poet who is extremely self-conscious, but sure neither of himself nor of the world he now lives in. It is what distinguishes Clare also from the great poets* Wordsworth and Keats (Clare's poetry is often just as rich in sensation as the 'Ode to Autumn' of Keats) who begin from particular observa-tion whereas Clare both begins and ends there.

[1] *Spectator*, 8 March 1935, no. 5567,399.
* Even from the Coleridge of *This Lime-Tree Bower* and *Frost at Midnight*.

138. H. J. Massingham on the labourer poets

1942

From chapter iv, 'The Labourer', *The English Countryman*, 1942, pp. 72–3.

For Massingham, see No. 124.

The nature of the farm-labourer is still more directly disclosed by the labourer poets, Duck, Bloomfield and the great Clare. These men are persistently classified as 'peasant poets', when it is perfectly clear that they are nothing of the kind. First, they were all wage-earners on the land before taking up smallholdings on Parnassus. Next, they were all writing when the Enclosures were in full swing (Stephen Duck rather earlier). Thirdly, and omitting Clare for the moment, they expressed themselves in the literary language of the period, penned into formal couplets, lessoned by the Horatian muse, generalized and as Ben Jonson sang, 'still to be neat, still to be drest'. The anonymous peasant poets no more wrote like this than Blake himself, not only because they belonged to a different age but because they were communal singers, as their villages were co-operative farms. Is it conceivable that even John Clare could have written *The Nut-Brown Maid* or *The Ballad of Chevy Chase*? No, *he* did not write it but his old villager sang it:

> And many a moving tale in antique rhymes
> He has for Christmas and such merry times.
> When 'Chevy Chase', his masterpiece of song,
> Is said so earnest none can think it long.

The only post-peasant poet who wrote peasant poetry was William Barnes. . . .

139. W. K. Richmond on Clare

1947

From chapter vi, 'The Peasants' Revolt', *Poetry and the People*, 1947, pp. 150–80.

Kenneth Richmond (b. 1910), an educationalist, is the author of a number of books, chiefly on education. *Poetry and the People* is a passionate and often persuasive work. See Introduction, p. 20.

Clare's tragedy is so significant, indeed, that his case is worth examining in detail. As peasant-poet he had gifts, attitudes of which the Romantics were scarcely aware: and in its humble way the quality which he wished to contribute was something more enduring than any which they possessed.

Circumstances prevented that contribution being made. Socially, the poet fell between two stools. For the sake of his art he had become an outcast among his own kind: and the city intellectuals regarded him as an interesting freak, or when the novelty of his first acquaintance was done, discarded him. Though the accounts which Clare has left of his conversations with Lamb, Hazlitt, Coleridge, Hood and the rest of the Londoners show that he could more than hold his own with them, it is clear that he could never have been really at home in company of this kind. Gradually he came to feel that he had been betrayed, lured on by flattering hopes and then neglected, left to his fate. Thus abandoned, he turned moody, fell into a sadness, thence to a watch, thence into a weakness, and so into the madness in which he raged at last. By little and little that happy impersonality which had been his at the outset—that objectivity which was to have been the folk-poet's contribution to literature—was taken from him. Put crudely, Clare was forced into Romanticism.

(The same fate had almost overtaken Burns. Study his life. Unable to make farming pay, unable to make more than a precarious living by his pen, he, too, ended his days among strange faces, other minds. . . . The Dumfries port authorities were hostile: he had lost the natural social setting without which he was helpless; and so, as far as writing went, his last nine years were largely unproductive. But then Burns was lucky—he died young, before an empty melancholy had time to cheat him out of his first attitude. At his best, even when he seems to be most individual, as in 'My luve is like a red, red rose', his emotion is not of the subjective order: it is only later, and with some surprise, that we discover that it is an adaptation of an old, popular song. It is this impersonal sense which makes him so universal, preserves him from himself. Keats is never anything but Keats, Shelley remains Shelley, but Burns speaks for Everyman.)

For poor John Clare it was not to be. Success was just not in his stars. From his boyhood he was afflicted with the personal canker. His unfortunate love-affair with Mary Joyce (—unfortunate simply because, as a labourer, he was deemed unworthy), aggravated by his awareness of social inferiority, contributed largely to the blight which perverted him. Disappointment following on disappointment the way it did, he was forced in upon himself, became the self-consumer of his woes. He took refuge first, however, in the observation and recording of the common delights of Nature (the only solace left remaining): 'snatches of sunshine and scraps of spring that I have gathered like an insect while wandering in the fields'.* For a time it seemed that these were riches enough: how often and valiantly did he protest that he was quite content to be the solitary singer; but all the while he suffered from a host of repressions like a linnet in a cage. Black melancholy was eating his heart away. He took refuge in his verse, then in a pseudomysticism, next in wishful hallucination (forcing himself to believe that Mary, his rustic Beatrice, was at his side—with such uncanny success that he ceased to regard Patty, who had borne his children, as his 'real' wife), finally in the most doting of lunacies. His attempt to *realize* had become swallowed up in the effort to idealize (the same 'ideal fallacy' which had dogged all post-Renaissance verse); and as a consequence he suffered an acute attack of split-personality. The inroads made by literary convention upon poetic tradition, by individualism upon communalism, cannot be more clearly demonstrated than by an examination of Clare's case-history. As peasant he was utterly defenceless against the virus of modernism and the ravages which it made upon his health and sanity are plain to see. He was a survival of what had once been a common figure in every community—*The Village Minstrel* he called his second book of poems—now become a heart for daws to peck at. Once away

* From an unpublished MS.

from the shelter of his village he was exposed to all the vicissitudes which poetry had suffered since the breakup of the mediaeval world. The accumulated weight of history, concentrated into a few short years of his lifetime, bore him down. For a time he resisted bravely but it was too much . . . he never had a chance.

In his lucid intervals (—for twenty-one years he dragged out a life-in-death imprisonment in Northampton Asylum, 'the land of Sodom where all the people's brains are turned the wrong way'*) Clare understood only too well the essential ghastliness of his failure:

> . . . And yet I Am, and live with shadows, tost
> Into the nothingness of scorn and noise,
> Into the living sea of waking dreams
> Where there is neither sense of life nor joys
> But the vast shipwreck of my life's esteems.

Even this was not the worst: before the end came he was reduced to such pitiful metaphysics as this:

> Is nothing less than nought?
> Nothing *is* nought.
> And there is nothing less.
> But something is, though next to nothing
> That a trifle seems: and such am I.†

Even in his last senilities he could not drown himself in commiseration as Cowper had done—though he had moments of such haunting poignancy (expressed in second-childhood language) as have rarely been surpassed:

> I left the little birds
> And sweet lowing of the herds
> And couldn't find out words
> Do you see? . . .

But by that time Clare had become a cypher. As a folk-poet he was constitutionally unfitted to be a romantic, for romanticism implied individualism, idealism . . . therefore for him there was only one way out—cruellest idiocy. He could only have expressed himself fully through contacts with people like himself and with the earth by which he lived: only in them could he know himself more perfectly as a man and as a poet. Without this necessary environment his major instincts

---

* Letter to his wife, 19th July, 1848.

† From Clare's unprinted (mostly unprintable) Northampton transcripts. Perhaps it is not fair to the poet to salvage such details: if so, I have endeavoured to make amends later in the chapter, by quoting some of his finer work, much of which has still to find a publisher.

were denied. For one poet at least, the Tower had become terrifyingly real; and the pity of it was that he knew it . . . for more than twenty years.

There are, then, two Clares: the Seeker and the Lost. The first is solid, real: the second, for all its eldritch, latter-day prophecy, is hollow, unreal. The poetry of the one is gloriously visual—the peasant's eye: the other is visionary, the same eye in an inward frenzy rolling. His experience belied the truth of the adage, *sub cruce veritas*—for though his ultimate darkness was not entirely unrelieved, pierced here and there by squinting gleams—the light had been taken away from him. His best work, as his first reviewer was quick to point out, was 'composed altogether from the impulses of the writer's mind, *as excited by external objects*'.* The peasant finds his meaning in the soil. Remove that and he is like a fish out of water.

It is rather surprising to find so eminent an authority on country matters as Mr. H. J. Massingham declaring that Clare was, in fact, not a peasant.† He classes him as a labourer-poet. Surely the worst of quibbles. Certainly Clare was never allowed to be anything better than a wage-earner, though it was his cherished ambition to have his own farm (an ambition which might easily have been realized had it not been for the niggardliness of his 'trustees and benefactors'). But we have already shown that as a class the English peasantry had ceased to exist. After the middle of the eighteenth century the title is a courtesy; and to-day, in the absence of any better definition, the *Oxford English Dictionary* assures us that it signifies 'one who lives in the country and works on the land, either as a small farmer or labourer; the name is applied to any rustic of the working classes'. No doubt the term has lost its definitive meaning, but in so far as it may be used at all it would be truer to assert not only that Clare is a peasant-poet but that he is (at any rate in the modern period) the only peasant-poet that this country has produced.

Massingham claims that dubious honour for Dorset's William Barnes, chiefly on the grounds that whereas Clare 'muses and dreams alone', Barnes partakes in and expresses the life of the village community. Which is true enough—up to a point. We have already admitted that Clare was driven to play the recluse and we have sought to show how it went against his better nature; but by breeding, work and wish he was of the soil. Barnes was not. To be sure, he loved his parishioners, but however sincerely he may have tried to live with them he

---

* *Quarterly Review*, 1820.
† *The English Countryman.*

was never of them. The community-sense was not bred in him: his friend Thomas Hardy says of him merely that though Barnes 'was not averse to social intercourse, his friendship extended over but a small area of society',*—which certainly does not suggest the born folk-poet.

The fact remains that of all these so-called peasant writers Clare was the only one who achieved that peculiar balance of brain and body, the tireless uncomplaining patience of the landserf. The peasant's shrewdness, self-reliance (*and* self-effacement), natural piety, steady dignity, composure, good taste (*and* execrableness) were his: he did not have to assume them. His was the essential modesty of one accustomed to zero status, not the affected humility of one who wished to associate himself with country-folk because, in doing so, he believed himself to be committing an act of faith: Clare could never have been anything other than the cottager. . . .

As a sustained and serious effort to state the countrymen's fundamental point of view in universal terms, Clare's attempt stands alone. It broke him, but he made it.

In order to understand something of that point of view it is necessary to read his first *Poems descriptive of Rural Life and Scenery*, the volume which ran into three editions in 1820 and made the 'Northamptonshire peasant' for a brief interval the lion of the literary world; not that it contains his best work, but because it shows us the Clare that could have been. Necessary, too, to know of his intensely happy childhood to which he was ever afterwards referring, elysian days spent in a countryside which was, even at that time, beginning to be encroached upon: and of his parents who, to while away the winter evenings, sang the traditional folk-ballads, 'Peggy Band', 'Lord Randal', 'Barbara Allen' and all the rest of them. The father, Parker Clare, one-time wrestler, labourer, now parish-pauper, was a born teller of tales, a man with a picturesque turn of phrase and speech, one who was always in great demand as an entertainer at the village feasts. One of his proudest boasts was that he could sing or recite more than a hundred popular rhymes (—not by any means a remarkable claim when we consider that Cecil Sharp, not so very long ago, came upon an old lady of ninety who could remember 10,000 lines of folk-poetry). Though the poet's father was quite ignorant (—he could read a little, his wife not a word), he was, in his rough way, possessed of certain hereditary graces and attributes. Education and culture, remember, are not convertible terms. In his degenerate way, old Parker Clare seems to have been another of those unacknowledged

* The Rev. Wm. Barnes, B.D. *Life and Art.* p. 55.

singers of whom we have so frequently tried to make so much; nurse not unmeet for his poetic child. Sitting at his knees, young John caught the habit of listening, the love of speaking in rhyme. To be sure he had schooling of another sort, but the primary education of his genius was of the time-honoured variety—oral. In that cottage home there was a natural feeling for poetry of a kind which we can scarcely understand, such as survives to-day only in Wales and those remoter districts where 'people' are still 'folk'.

There was, too, that ancient sybil of Helpston Heath, Granny Bains: as a boy he met with her while tending sheep or crow-scaring. Another Meg Merrilees, she taught him tales in verse, and more ballads. And then the fiddling gipsies—to the end of his life their way of life had a strange fascination for the poet.

Such the original Clare. His real authorship derived from the un-written poetry of the commonalty, that remnant of a tradition which had so long conducted an underground struggle for survival. Literature of this kind had always been spontaneous, social, necessary only to the occasion which evoked it and which it served. Its composition seems amorphous to us only because our conventionally 'superior' attitude prevents our understanding, or partaking in it: its essence lay entirely in the exercise of the human voice. Clare himself confesses, 'I made a many things before I ventured to commit them to writing . . . imitations of some popular songs *floating among the vulgar at the markets and fairs till they were common to all*'*. True, it was not long before he was reading and imitating models more dignified, Thomson, Cowper and 'old Tusser'; but these were secondary influences.

(All this may seem unnecessarily tedious in detail. But the original tradition so rarely appears on the surface that when it does we must not fail to insist upon its vital importance. In spite of every misfortune and neglect, folk-poetry *had* contrived to remain a force in the land, and without some appreciation of this continuity we shall not be able to account for Clare's uniqueness. It made him the peculiar blend of weak-ness and strength that he was—indigent and indigene. It explains his many faults of style, diffuseness, formlessness, repetitiveness, his careless-ness of grammar or sense, the too-obviousness of his sentiment, his inability to state an argument: explains, too, his unpredictableness, the sudden glories, the concise, intermittent phrase that hits the ear and mind unawares, taking the winds of poetry with beauty.)

---

* Tibble: *Life of John Clare.*

One of the first poems in the 1820 volume was 'The Maid of Ocram, or, Lord Gregory', beginning:

> Gay was the Maid of Ocram
> As lady e'er may be
> Ere she did venture past a maid
> To love Lord Gregory.
>
> Fair was the Maid of Ocram
> And shining like the sun
> Ere her bower key was turned on two
> Where bride bed lay for none. . . .

Nothing could be less pretentious, yet in its terse, unaffected way it carries us straight back to the sixteenth century and beyond. It is, in fact, an adaptation of one of those 'popular songs floating among the vulgar'. The original (in so far as a ballad may be said to have one) is traceable to Ireland, where a song 'The Lass of Aughrim' had long been popular. A version of this latter was printed for the first time in William Chappell's *Roxburghe Ballads*, 1871, more than half a century after Clare's publication. Another, inevitably, is to be found in Child's compendious collection. As with Hogg, so here: the inference is obvious.

Not to the 1820 critics, however. 'Here are no tawdry and feeble paraphrases of former poets', said the *Quarterly* reviewer but he could not resist a patronizing afterthought: 'some of his ballad stanzas rival the native simplicity of Tickell or Mallett.' Faint praise, though doubtless it was well intended, typical of the complete misunderstanding which greeted Clare from the outset.

> I wish, I wish, but all in vain
> I wish I was a maid again.
> A maid again I cannot be
> O when will green grass cover me?

—you do not have to search Child's tomes to know whence that came. You will certainly not find it in Tickell. In its maturity, Clare's genius was peculiarly descriptive: later still it turned contemplative; but from start to finish all he wrote was shaped by the loose ballad-pattern, every verse underlined by a vocal influence. Even in his last asylum drivellings it was the same:

> And then they closed the shutters up
> And then they closed the door.

One of his fellow inmates has recorded how the poet '*always sang with a* *repeat . . . with a degree of emphasis that seemed to be rather elevating and somewhat touching'.* Precisely.*

But the state of literature would not allow it. Had there been a more substantial corpus of folk-poetry 'floating among the vulgar' his career might have been different. The communal tradition, unfortunately, had lost its cumulative effect: its hoary antiquity debased by social and economic evils. Such authentic scraps as came to hand he used, but most of the material left was by that time all but worthless. Here again Clare was far less fortunate than Burns. He was largely without precedents.

Nor was this the only disability under which he laboured. The process by which folk-poetry had been dissociated from the printed page merely reflected the persistent tendency of literature to keep aloof of the language of common speech. Not only that, either, for common speech had itself suffered a change for the worse. The Industrial Revolution, education (of sorts), newspapers—everything tended to reduce the beauty of right speaking to utility standards: and in the process language somehow lost grace, immediacy . . . mystery. Instead of communities there were institutions: rural customs had been replaced by urban regulations, the singing voice by the hum of printing-machines. At the opening of the nineteenth century any farmer's lad might still have spoken of 'a plume of trees on the far hills' without the phrase being thought in any way unusual or picturesque. This lack of affectation in the use of words was rapidly becoming a thing of the past. So was pride in one's own language. Language suffered the same inflation as finance: its gold was exchanged away for paper currency.

True common speech was fast becoming localized, a curious survival. As urbanization and intellectualism took to themselves an ever-increasing measure of control, the breach between artisan and artist was widened. The two no longer shared a common consciousness: they had ceased to speak the same language.

Certainly Clare was never clearly conscious of the whole unfortunate issue. He could only see it in its more patent manifestations in his everyday life, in the ploughing up of his boyhood haunts—the felling of his old favourite Lea Close Oak, the desecration of Swordy Well, the suspicion of his neighbours, the steady deterioration in his relations with his publishers, royalties dwindling, family increasing. . . .

The jostling world was not long in losing interest. The Londoners, for all their early kindness, soon tired of him, found him tedious, out of place, a bit of an oddity. From time to time he took holiday trips to

* Northampton Asylum MSS.

town to seek the stimulus of their company; but the heady conversations upset him, he was aware of their ill-hid condescension and fled back to his troubled household. There was no refuge in society: he just *had* to get away from it all!

This was getting 'back to Nature' with a vengeance. Previously poets had returned thither more because they felt themselves in need of a change of air, for fresh imagery, fresh inspiration. In Nature Crabbe found copious matter for new description. Wordsworth distilled from it his philosophy of dead things. The painters took it to irradiate their canvases, Constable for freshness, Turner for atmosphere, Danby in hopes to catch the light that never was on sea or land . . . but for Clare Nature was the all-in-all. He did his best to believe that it was enough, to be grateful for nothing:

> Summer is prodigal of joy. The grass
> Swarms with delighted insects as I pass.
> And crowds of grasshoppers at every stride
> Jump out all ways, with happiness their guide;
> And from my brushing feet moths flit away
> In safer places to pursue their play.
> In crowds they start!,—I marvel: well I may
> —And more,—to see each thing however small
> Sharing Joy's bounty that belongs to all.
> And here I gather, by the world forgot,
> Harvests of comfort from their happy mood,
> Feeling God's blessing dwells in every spot
> And nothing lives but owes Him gratitude.*

Yet even God's blessing was only given to be taken away, it seemed. Hateful Enclosure came creeping closer on every side, threatening his little world. It made him mad to see how

> Freedom's cottage soon was thrust aside
> And workhouse prisons raised upon the site.
> E'en Nature's dwellings far away from men,
> The common heath, became the spoiler's prey;
> The rabbit had not where to make his den . . .

—nor the poet his.

The story of Clare's gradual encirclement and the futility of his lonely struggle, makes bitter-sweet reading: but one which will always be worth retelling. The quick success of his first book was scarcely main-

* From the Peterborough Museum MSS. (as are most of the Clare quotations in this chapter).

tained by *The Village Minstrel* of 1821. Of his *Shepherd's Calendar* (1827), barely 500 copies were sold, despite the fact that it contained poetry far in advance of anything he had done before. Thereafter Taylor and Hessey were chary of venturing good money on further publications. Tastes had changed; and now that its novelty had worn off, Clare's style no longer had any market value. It was not alluring, not sufficiently 'romantic'. In spite of all his pleadings and protestations he could not gain a hearing for what he had to say. Meanwhile his financial position was becoming desperate and he had a large and growing family to support. He had to fall back on footling contributions to second-rate periodicals in order to earn a few shillings. Conditions on the land were as bad as they could have been and to make matters worse illness now prevented him from earning anything like an adequate living. The general discontent of the lower agricultural classes revealed itself in the riots of 1831. Days of exasperation, nights lurid with rick-fires: but Clare's mind was darkening with more than material troubles. After heartbreaking delays and niggardly prevarications Taylor at last consented to risk a further publication. *The Rural Muse*, which appeared in 1835, had a modified success and helped somewhat to defer the ultimate disaster. Thereafter the poet was quietly but firmly cold-shouldered.

The circumstances in which *The Rural Muse* finally appeared were galling in the extreme. Disgusted by the indifferent treatment he had received at the hands of his publishers. Clare had long tried to get his poems into print by private initiative (—he was already reduced to peddling copies of his previous volumes from door to door), but the hundred subscribers necessary for the promotion of the new venture were not forthcoming. Of all his acquaintances there were not a dozen willing to back him to the extent of purchasing a copy (price 7s. 6d.) of his 'proposals' for the projected 'Midsummer Cushion'. To-day his carefully prepared manuscript lies fading in a glass case in the Peterborough Museum. Yet it was chock-full of good things and could have been a crowning achievement. Much of it was used in the 1835 volume, but in the end the poet was compelled to submit to all manner of supervision from Taylor: otherwise not a word would have seen the light of day. It was Taylor who decided what must go in, what be left out; Taylor who corrected the errors of spelling, inserted all punctuation marks, altered as he thought fit—and all in such a take-it-or-leave-it attitude that Clare was left as helpless as a baby.

It would be wrong to picture Taylor as the unscrupulous rascal. On the balance, his dealings with Clare were honest enough. Even when the poet had been put away Taylor seems to have had spasms of remorseful kindness. As to the rough-handling of texts, *some* sort of editing was essential—as anyone who has seen Clare's manuscripts will have realized. (Even Keats had to accept the same treatment. 'My dear Taylor,' he wrote, 'your alteration strikes me as being a great improvement. And now I will attend to the punctuations you speak of' (Letter XLII.)— Evidently Keats was not so stoutly independent as a Clare.)

Nothing, in fact, could more clearly illustrate the growing difference between country and town than a study of this strange relationship between the poet and his publisher. In a strained and distant way each respected—and utterly failed to understand—the other. How could it have been otherwise? Their private worlds were worlds apart. Clare was the earthborn child, lover of simple things, intuitive: Taylor the suave, shrewd intellectual. Picture Clare out in a shower, sheltering by Langley Bush to scribble verses on the back of a sugar-bag or an election bill:* picture Taylor in his out-of-office hours studying Egyptology, or his favourite author, Locke, exposing Junius, writing on problems of finance. Clare in his cottage, with lunacy already nattering at his ear, writing that he is half-convinced his mind is bewitched: Taylor in his town-house (too busy to allow himself to be much concerned) writing back a reasoned argument that the poet's superstitions were groundless, cold reassurance. One was a survivor from an England that was dead or dying. The other was a typical representative of the newer spirit of progress. The one dealt in *things* for idealist ends; the other thought in terms of ideas for materialist ends. Their outlooks were opposed.

If Spenser erred in commending himself to the scholars for protection, Clare was compelled to submit to far worse masters. He was at the mercy of those who insisted on treating him not as a child only, but as a problem-child. Everything he wrote had to be submitted to *their* censorship. With inherent fatalism he resigned himself to their ceaseless interferings, knowing himself to be at a permanent disadvantage, but there were times when it went against the grain. As a peasant there was always a certain amount of stiff-necked independence about him. Personal vanity he did not know, but he felt the craftsman's solicitude for his work. Sending off a first draft of a midnight-oil poem hastily done 'when the headache was very mortifying and the bed very enticing' he suddenly recalls a previous effort which has been returned with Taylor's suggested emendations, and adds, sourly, 'I can't say I much like the two first lines of the alteration . . . I shall give my reasons as a critical

* Still preserved.

Bard (not as a critical wolf who mangles to murder)'. Clearly he was not always at their service, their obedient John Clare.

But though he might kick against the pricks like this there was no real measure of freedom left to him. When he determined to go his own way, regardless alike of publishers, critics and friendly advisers, the results were ignominious. Such a venture was his 'Pleasures of Spring'. Written in 1828, it was intended to be a sort of *magnum opus*: certainly his correspondence suggests that Clare was considering writing a long poem which would be after his own heart, irrespective of the modes and moods then prevailing among the poetry-reading public. Both Cary and Darley, his unofficial literary executors, did their best to dissuade him from proceeding with it, possibly because they felt his genius was not fitted for a major flight. They were all against it—the poem would never *sell*—but he persisted.

The consequence? 'Pleasures of Spring', which was to have been the *pièce de résistance* of the ill-fated 'Midsummer Cushion', was so persistently ignored that even to-day it is left languishing in its original notebook. Symonds, Blunden and Tibble, who have done so much to salvage Clare's unpublished work, saw it there but evidently thought fit to pass by on the other side. Yet despite a host of faults it contains the real Clare. Rambling, shapeless, gratuitous as it is, it is nevertheless more than worthy of being resurrected—and not merely for its occasional beauties, either. It reveals the peasant-poet in all his strength and weakness. It alternates between bathos and sublimity in most unaccountable fashion: irritates, disappoints, bores . . . and suddenly delights. As a whole it is very far from satisfactory and yet (paradoxically) on the whole it satisfies. It would have been strange, indeed, had Clare succeeded where Shelley, Keats, Byron and even Wordsworth had failed— in mastering the long poem. Matthew Arnold was not far from it when he wrote 'English poetry of the first quarter of this nineteenth century; with plenty of energy, plenty of creative energy, *did not know enough*'.*
Certainly there was a deal of things on which poor Clare was uninformed.

If the characteristic faults of the oral tradition in English verse are to be diffuse, to be un-self-critical, to lack art, then the 'Pleasures of Spring' has them all in full measure.

> The blackthorn deepens in a darker stain
> And *brighter freckles* hazle shoots regain;

---

* *The Function of Criticism at the Present Time.*

The woodland rose in bright aray is seen
Whose bark receives, like leaves, a vivid green;
And *foulroyce twigs as red as stock doves' claws*
Shines in the woods, to gain the bard's applause.*

Gaucheness and felicity. One line reflects all the hackneyed abstractions and conventional diction of the worser kind of the eighteenth-century verse: the next comes up as fresh as a daisy. Was ever poetry quite so consistently, so aggravatingly uneven? Yet these are but minor undulations: as with Cædmon or Langland there is no effort to maintain more than a minimum-standard style, to achieve any *personal* success. The poet is content to wind about and in and out: there is plenty of time; and like the true Englishman he knows he will muddle through in the end. So the 'Pleasures' pursues the even tenor of its way, aiming nowhere, getting nowhere . . . admiring trees and flowers by the wayside, noticing countrymen at work in the fields, pausing now to indulge in idle thoughts (all vague), telling now of children's games, geese on the green, village superstitions, now the celandine,

Like a bright star Spring-tempted from the sky
Reflecting on its leaves the sun's bright rays
That sets its pointed glories in a blaze
—So bright that children's fancys it decieves
Who think that sunshine settles in its leaves. . . .

So Clare strays. His Milkmaid 'loiters along': his Shepherd 'guesses on': his Husbandman 'muses in pleasure on his homeward way': his Boy 'soodles on'. So does the poem. It is written as a labourer might hoe a field of turnips, with no eye on the ending, no thought of what is to come next, but with a massive, unquestioning patience which sustains the work and makes it not ignoble. It has a heavy and leisurely dignity such as only the born landworker can achieve—dignity which is none the less real for being so little acknowledged.

Judged by usual standards of heroic-couplet criticism most of the 'Pleasures of Spring' is pedestrian, a clumsy attempt to copy a style that Crabbe had already written far better, Goldsmith best of all. Compare it with 'The Deserted Village' and it is a thing of clay. Both grammar and spelling are atrocious, the rhymes almost invariably obvious, the sentiment commonplace: and when it comes to expressing even the most elementary thought Clare tends to be muddle-headed or, worse,

* Italics mine: I give it here as Clare wrote it, with all its imperfections on its head.

loose-mouthed. The language is an unhappy mixture: one moment birds are 'left mourning in their sad despair' (stuffed, no doubt)—the next a live Northamptonshire Lapwing comes 'whewing' overhead, a Kite 'swees' in the wind and a Partridge goes 'nimbling' through the stubbles. There is much that might well be omitted. Clare was nothing if not prolific. As the scop had sung, so he wrote—for the sheer pleasure of 'unlocking the word horde'—and when it came to erasure or revision he was too indolent or else too indifferent. Words came, he put them down and was content to leave them at that. Like the hoer in the field, it never occurred to him to consider—certainly not to reconsider—his work, nor did he deem it necessary to smooth off raw edges. Whatever other infinite capacities his genius possessed, that of taking pains was certainly not one: the poem remained a draft. Even when he came to recopy—and there are at least three versions of 'Pleasures of Spring' in his own hand—he altered and removed nothing: all the original errors are allowed to stand. In the whole of his enormous output there are not more than one or two manuscripts ('The Thrush's Nest' is one) which show any signs of retouching: the rest came straight off the reel and were given no second thought.

From the critical point of view it would, no doubt, have been better otherwise, but there it is: the peasant-poet remains a poet *and* a peasant. We must take him for what he is, accept the rough with the smooth, remembering the disabilities which so offset the abilities. Only when we think of poetry in terms of a national culture rather than in terms of intellectual, individual achievement, shall we begin to appreciate the importance of Clare—as a symptom. We need a lower as well as a higher criticism.

Regarded thus, the 'Pleasures of Spring' has genuine worth, more, perhaps, than many of the published poems. No accident, either, that it should never have been printed. Its tempo is that of a time now past. Its movement is genial, unhurried, bespeaking an idle reflectiveness and an openness of mind quite alien to the intenser focus of the modern mood. To most of us it must seem lax, redundant, slow: but, then, so is 'Piers Plowman', so are the ballads with their interminable refrains. To the land-serf time is of no account: as often as not, it is his sole luxury. Day by day, talking and singing to himself, he becomes *at length* identified with the unfeeling earth; but the effect is not that of a blank torpor. Though his thought grows vague his outlook gains in clarity: he is educated in a wise passiveness. *Some* communion occurs. Meaning emerges. *His* is a synthesis of mind, body and spirit which *we* lack: not materialist nor idealist but (in ways that we can only guess at) a blend of both.

For the 'peasant-poet', then, poetry does need to be emotion re-collected in tranquillity. For him poetry and emotion are one: tranquillity is all. He must not, as the intellectual must, be for ever analysing the nature of his own experience, striving to pinpoint

> the experience
> In a different form, beyond any meaning
> We can assign to happiness.*

He does not strive for anything: the moment of insight comes without his expecting it—satisfies—and leaves no need for him to question its authenticity. He is content to *wait*.

'Pleasures of Spring' reflects this firm assurance of the peasant mind. Its childlike serenity may be too simple for the problematical needs of the twentieth century, its texture too earthy; but it has its occasional felicities:

> The clouds of Heaven, scaled in many a dream . . .
> Now long and green grows every laughing day . . .

it delights *in* things without troubling to think too much *about* them: the corncrake—

> fairey left by night
> To wander, blinded by the sunny light,

the little streams,

> Loud laughing on their errands watering flowers

and the lanes

> All carpeted anew with young silk-grass.

From it all there appears, not a personal philosophy such as Wordsworth pursued, but the rudiments of a country faith: Nature the All-giver, Nature the Leveller. If the poem has any real aim it is only to prove that

> Spring's joys are universal and they fall
> From an unsparing bounty blessing all:
> The meanest thing that lives to crawl or flye
> Has equal claims in her impartial eye,

—which to us, no doubt, is a truism.

---

* Eliot may protest as much as he likes—he is as much a romantic as any of them. So are we all. Francis Scarfe is right; whether we like it or not 'we are in it up to the neck' (*Auden and After.* p. 184).

Nature is all very fine but human nature is finer, as Keats very rightly realized. The more Clare took refuge in the country the more was he forced into a position of isolation from society—the distant, disgruntled spectator. When every prospect pleases and only Man is vile, what other home is there for the poet if not in Bedlam? And so in his last despair he wrote, still thinking of Mary,

> Had we ne'er been together
> We'd ne'er ha' slighted ane anither
> Never loved and never hated
> Had we never been created. . . .

The Peasants' Revolt had failed. Yet as an attempt to emancipate poetry from literature it was not without deep significance. The trouble was that each of these men was so isolated as to be without influence; they were so cut off from all the original sources of their strength. In an age of hardheaded empiricism, of Benthamism, there was no place for the peasant: his still small voice was drowned by the juggernaut clangour of industry. As social entities they were complete misfits. Folk-poetry was no longer of general interest: *there was no folk*. Robbed of his audience, the rural minstrel had to content himself with alternatives. Either he could knuckle under, as Duck or Bloomfield did; in which case the best he could hope for was a third-rate performance. Or he could remain true to his original premises, the soil, in which case he remained localized (the 'dialect poet') or was ignored. Clare alone made a major effort to break through, but he was driven back slowly and surely into that individuality so fateful for all of us, for him fatal. He could *not* pretend—as Barnes and Hawker pretended. Always he kept his feet firmly implanted on the earth; and when that was taken from him what else was there for it but

> To realise his glowing dreams and flye
> To the soft bosom of the sunny sky.

—the old Spenserian velleity?

140. Geoffrey Grigson on Clare

1950

From the Introduction to *Selected Poems of John Clare*, ed. Geoffrey Grigson, 1950, pp. 7–20.

Geoffrey Grigson (b. 1905), poet and critic, editor of *New Verse* (1933–9), has been the most consistent and balanced advocate of Clare's poetry in recent years. His *Poems of John Clare's Madness*, 1949, with its carefully exciting Introduction, must still be regarded as a crucial document, in spite of textual inadequacies (see Introduction, p. 21.

If one were to draw up a syllabus and a recipe for the making of a poet at this time, Clare's early life would supply them: a freedom akin to Wordsworth's in the country; a knowledge of folksong and ballad and of the elegant pastoral poets strengthened with a knowledge of those Golcondas of romanticism, *Paradise Lost, Pilgrim's Progress*, and *The Seasons*; a knowledge of the Bible with a leaning toward its deeper and darker portions; and added to them all the delicate sensibility of a schizophrenic. Lack of a formal education was less of a drawback than the lack of the country, Milton, Thomson, and folksong would have been. Clare learnt to read and write, but gained little else from his schooling, which was diluted by hard work alongside his father. He went out threshing, for example, taking a light flail which was made specially for him. He drew geometrical figures and letters in the dust on the sides of the barn. There were times when he 'could muster three farthings for a sheet of writing paper', and when in learning to read he 'devour'd for these purposes every morsel of brown or blue paper' in which his mother brought back the tea and sugar. His education never gave his mind, it is true, exercise and skill; his mind lacked the breadth of co-ordinating knowledge, just as it lacked such stimulus, later on (since Clare was twenty-seven when his first book was published and he began to meet other poets), as Wordsworth had derived from Coleridge,

from his sister, his brothers and his other undergraduate friends. Isolation interfered with him intellectually, retarded and weakened the
development of his ideas, and made his eventual madness more certain;
but it also meant his sensibility—his vision and his ability to *hear*—were
less contaminated. It is curious to contrast Clare with Crabbe. Crabbe
was rather more fortunate in his emancipation from poverty. It had not
been a peasant's poverty, leading towards parish help and the workhouse.
His father had had some education. He had read 'the graver classics' to
his children, and had seen to Crabbe's education. Like Clare, Crabbe
did not reach London until he was well on in the twenties; but before
he met Burke, Reynolds and Johnson, he had moved in a wider and
more stimilating variety of experience and acquaintance than Clare ever
knew between the fields, the garden, the threshing-floor and the lime-
kiln; and he had contrived to get his *Inebriety* printed and published. By
contrast, Clare at Helpston, in his parents' small cottage, in the gloom
of the fens, was a wingless insect knowing only two inches around
himself in a vast desert. He was a yokel, a whop-straw, when he took
the coach to London in 1819, not a medical student with something of
a classical education who would soon, and reasonably, be directed into
Holy Orders and become a ducal chaplain. The nearest his patrons came
to conferring a new livelihood upon Clare was his publisher's offer to
educate him as a teacher in a National School. He added, knowing
Clare's liking for women and for drink, that teaching would demand
'the strictest moral conduct': the scheme was abandoned. Always,
when he could write at all, Clare was able to summon up the existence
of a childhood of delight in poems which are either joyful or regrets for
joy. Crabbe calls up, on the whole, an autumnal gloom of childhood,
contrasts the things which delighted him with the gloom by which the
delights were impaired, and was incapable of writing

> The flowers join lips below, the leaves above;
> And every sound that meets the air is Love

as Clare, even in his most melancholic depressions, was incapable of
conceiving a poem in Crabbe's mournful, stern and downward sloping
rhythms. Crabbe's attitude is one of having always been in chains and
making by a moral effort, by a masterly effort, the best of their chafing
and drag; Clare's is one of celebrating freedom in the chains put upon
him by life. One is the attitude of grim realism, lit by sparkles of pure
apprehension, sparkles of a scarcely attained delight, the other the
attitude of lyricism. A different Crabbe (both men, in their different

ways, died in madness. So, practically, did Wordsworth) may be visible here and there in these sparkles, but though he matured, he had to fight against an ugly childhood and a mainly sombre personality. Clare's childhood made him, despite his miseries and his madness, almost automatically resilient. And he matured rather more than it has been the custom to allow.

All of Clare's childhood was spent at Helpston. John Taylor, the publisher he shared with Keats, who had sent him up like a rocket from his Northamptonshire obscurity, paid him a visit in 1821. He was surprised by the contrast between the scenery of Helpston in fact and the vision of the scene in Clare's poetry. 'A flatter country than the immediate neighbourhood can scarcely be imagined.' He had just published Clare's second book, *The Village Ministrel*, which contained a poem 'The Last of March—written at Lolham Brigs':

> Here 'neath the shelving bank's retreat
>   The horse-blob swells its golden ball;
> Nor fear the lady-smocks to meet
>   The snows that round their blossoms fall:
> Here by the arch's ancient wall
> The antique elder buds anew;
>   Again the bulrush sprouting tall
> The water wrinkles, rippling through. . . .

Taylor remembered the poem and looked in astonishment at Clare when the two of them had reached the scene, for 'with your own eyes you see nothing but a dull line of ponds, or rather one continued marsh, over which a succession of arches carries the narrow highway: look again, into the poem in your mind, and the wand of a necromancer seems to have been employed in conjuring up a host of beautiful accompaniments, making the whole waste populous with life and shedding all round the rich lustre of a grand and appropriate sentiment.' In fact, Clare had projected his own sense of happiness and love into an unremarkable landscape. Wordsworth and Coleridge searched for landscape imagery appropriate to their thought, in Dorset, North Devon, the Quantocks, Wales, and the Lakes. Clare with his restriction of thought had neither such need nor such opportunities. There was ample reciprocity—as far as he dealt with landscape and not nature in details—between himself and the only landscape he knew, enough in fact for his life as a poet. No one will find it very rewarding to visit 'John Clare's Country' instead of visiting and revisiting John Clare's poetry. Here, in a scene mediocre in itself, he accomplished that business of learning nature by heart, as a child and as a young labourer. Indeed the bulk of his poems (including many too highly praised in the spirit which informed much of the appreciation of poetry in England before Mr. T. S. Eliot's tart incursion into English affairs) recite that learning in all its minutiae. No one, so great is the quantity of his manuscripts, will ever publish a complete edition of Clare. He versified rather than put down in prose what might have filled the note-books of another poet. Much of it is poetry humdrum and flat, though lit very often with precise and pure observation. Observation and description are not poetry, or at least cannot be poetry of the higher order; and no 'nature poet', if such an imagined phenomenon has ever appeared, can have been more than one of the lesser poets. But we have so long confused nature with art that we speak of Clare and even of Wordsworth as 'nature poets'. All appreciation of Clare, so far, has attended too much to Clare in this sense, to Clare's innocence of perception, that 'faculty of sheer vision', which the acutest of his critics, Mr. Middleton Murry, has maintained is not only 'far purer than Wordsworth's' but is even purer than Shakespeare's. Clare's vision intensifies the selected reality of most things it describes:

> From dark green clumps among the dripping grain
>   The lark with sudden impulse starts and sings
> And mid the smoking rain
>   Quivers her russet wings

The comparison of such vision with Wordsworth's or Shakespeare's may be completely just. But Mr. Murry quickly explains that Clare's vision was 'too perfect', that Shakespeare (thinking of Shakespeare and Clare, one should think of Ophelia's songs) had as much vision 'as a man can have if he is to develop into a full maturity'. And then Mr. Murry quotes Wordsworth on good poetry as 'the spontaneous overflow of powerful feelings', with Wordsworth's rider that 'poems to which any value can be attached were never produced on any variety of subjects but by a man who, being possessed of more than usual organic sensibility, had also thought long and deeply'. The answer to Clare was that he had not thought long and deeply. The difference between Clare and Wordsworth was that Wordsworth could think, while Clare could not. The one produced harmony, the other melody.

Elsewhere Mr. Murry argued that an object would evoke Clare's feelings, and that the feelings could only be passed on by describing the object, which is certainly true of many of Clare's poems, as it would be true of the sketches of his exact contemporary, John Constable. But the claims of the limitation of Clare's thought and the restriction of his poems to the transmission of innocent feeling and of his perpetual child-ishness, in a good sense, his perpetual immaturity, are too absolute; and so are the parallel claims that Clare learnt nothing of aesthetic economy and form. Clare thought more at length and more deeply than has been allowed; or indeed than it was possible for Mr. Murry to realize in 1924 when the two large volumes of Clare's poetry edited by Professor Tibble had not been published. As Constable thought of painting as an art by which he was able to pass on his feeling, so Clare, it is true, held that poetry was another name for feeling. He tells us so again and again. His 'feelings grew into song'. His own poetry grew from learning and loving the material of nature, from vision, into meditated vision. From feeling, he came to meditate upon feeling, upon himself and so upon man, and so at last he reached out into a poetry of ideas or at any rate of ideas limited. Keats admired Clare's poetry, so far as he knew it, and rightly observed that the 'description too much prevailed over the sentiment' (Clare had his say in return about Keats, that he was 'a child of nature warm and wild', but that *Endymion* was too stuffed with Dryads, Fauns, and Satyrs, that as a Cockney 'he often described Nature as she had appeared to his fancies, and not as he would have described her had he witnessed the things he described'). Yet when Keats knew his poetry, he had scarcely moved from description to idea and he was incapable of writing with such metaphysical intimations as came into his work between 1830 and 1844; he was incapable of such lines as

> When dead and living shall be void and null
> And nature's pillow be at last a human skull.

An increasing series of deprivations threatened Clare's mind, indeed unbalanced him from the delicate thread of his life, but increased his self-knowledge and made him look more and more for meanings in that nature in which like Hölderlin and so many artists of his spiritual type he found a consolation which he did not discover, after the happi-ness of childhood, in the society of men. In the end, Clare's deeper perceptions had to race against his psychosis. With ups and downs the psychosis gained upon him. But before his mind lost its power com-pletely, his ideas of nature, love, creative joy, freedom, and eternity had developed and had informed that small number of poems which raise him so far above the mere 'naturalist' of his common reputation. More-over with this development there came, as chaotic notions cleared into certain ideas, an increased rhythmical subtlety combined with an improved economy of form.

The experiences were his own, but the clue for ordering them and harmonising them he found in Wordsworth mainly, and in Coleridge. He had much to find a meaning for. His poetic life, after childhood, is a history of deprivations. He is deprived of the happiness of childhood; he is deprived, by enclosure, of the actual scenery and objects of that happiness, and so deprived of the freedom of the commons. He is deprived of love and freedom by a marriage which on the whole he did not desire, and against which he developed the fantasy of his ideal wife, Mary Joyce. He emerges from the penury, the thick obscurity, and hopelessness of his life as a labouring whopstraw into the success and the hope which attended the publication of his first book in 1820. He comes to know poets and patrons and friends; to be deprived of them, and the hope and the success, bit by bit, as his later books successively failed, and as mental illness was increased by the waxing of his difficulties. Deprived of the scenery of happiness by the enclosures around Helpston, he was, by his removal across the stream to the village of Northborough in 1832, deprived of Helpston itself. When the keeper arrived at Northborough in 1836 and took him to the asylum in Epping Forest, he was deprived of his home, his family and his freedom. He regained his freedom by escape; but regained it, for what the freedom was worth in a cold world, only to discover that his 'poetic fancy', Mary Joyce, was indeed a fancy. She was long dead.

The asylum reached out for him again. The keepers arrived, and Clare entered the alien world at Northampton, in which he was to die after a final deprivation lasting just over twenty-three years.

His ideas, out of the interaction of suffering and delight, of life, love, freedom, creative joy and eternity, ripened on the withered tree of his mind round about 1844, at Northampton. But they had begun to shape themselves in 1824 after visiting London for treatment in his distress of mind and body. Happiness in nature he had discovered to be unreliable. He had wanted love and he had wanted hope, and he began feeling 'a relish for eternity'. On the one side he had dismal dreams of Hell, and read *Macbeth* for about the twentieth time, and was anguished by thinking of the 'dark porch of eternity whence none returns to tell the tale of his reception'. On the other, eternity obsessed him as desirable and as the attainment of victory over the world. 'Mind alone', he put down, 'is the sun of the earth—it lives on when the clouds and paraphernalia of pretentions are forgotten'. It was a seedling of that final poem, 'A Vision', in which in the asylum in 1844 Clare wrote himself into immortality and freedom and release from woman and the lost mortal joys with the appropriate pen, an eternal ray taken from the sun. Indeed if there is one image around which his poetry circled and grew, from the beginning to the end, it is the image of the blinking, coppery immensity of the sun burning through the clouds of confusion or shining through the trees above the flats of the world.

He had known the poems of Wordsworth and Coleridge for a good many years, since 1820 at the least, and he had found in them, no doubt in 'Resolution and Independence' and certainly in Coleridge's 'Pains of Sleep', the last two lines of which remained long in his mind, evidence of situations like his own. He may have read Wordsworth to begin with for his vision of nature, impatient at first with what he held to be Wordsworth's affectation of simplicity and with their depths. He recorded in his diary of the 'White Roe of Rylstone' that it contained 'some of the sweetest poetry' he had ever met with, though it was 'full of his mysteries'. The mysteries gained on him. The notion of creative joy took hold of him, as he puzzled over Coleridge's 'Dejection', and over the 'Intimations' ode. Moved by these two poems as well as by 'Tintern Abbey', he wrote not long after that curious extract of Wordsworth, Coleridge, and Clare called *Pastoral Poesy*, to celebrate 'the dower of self-creating joy'. Many more of his poems on love, immortality, and the immortality of nature, and hope are obviously affined to the 'mysteries' of Wordsworth and Coleridge.

> To be beloved is all I need
> And whom I love, I love indeed—

Coleridge's two lines were, so to say, answered by Clare, if there was no one else to love and be loved in that fullness, through the creation of the ideal of Mary Joyce. Twice, with a length of time in between, he worked the lines into poems calling on Mary.*

If Wordsworth and Coleridge helped him to meaning, relation and harmony, it was help received and not plagiarism committed. In many ways the cases of all three poets (and the case of John Constable) were much alike. All three and Constable were contemporaries caught up in the exaltations and the preordination of their peculiar time, only Clare, however much his limits closed him in, was blessed with that resilience by which he never lost the shaping power of his imagination. In 'The

---

* 'The Progress of Rhyme', and 'O Mary, sing thy Songs to Me', written after his escape from Epping Forest.

Progress of Rhyme' in the twenties, Clare defined poetry as hope, love and joy. He wrote later of tramps who 'dally with the wind and laugh at hell'. He was another such tramp on the long roads, but one driven down them by thoughts desperately acquired; and when he came to 'A Vision' in August 1844, for a while at least he was the victor and not the victim. Love and joy, of the earth and even of heaven, had been found out by him, or had left him. Hope he had surpassed and he proclaimed his penetration to eternity:

[Quotes 'I lost the love of heaven above . . .']

However much Blake might have visited upon Clare that reproof of allowing the natural man to rise up against the spiritual man which he applied to Wordsworth, he would have applauded 'A Vision' as repentance, as an immortal moment reached after and attained.

Sensibility is the denominator, in literature, in painting, in music, of the period in which Clare lived, a sensibility directed towards nature, from which, Schiller maintained, civilized men were already feeling divorced. 'Nature is for us nothing but existence in all its freedom', and therefore sensibility was directed with emphasis and exaggeration to-wards nature, so that all but the most intellectually endowed artists plunged into nature, floated for a while in nature, and tended to drown themselves in nature. The personality of artists such as Clare drive them anyway to this refuge; and the individual drive was made more compelling by the general situation of men. Civilized men were in, so to say, a schizophrenic period of history, from which they have not yet emerged and which seems to have brought them now to the advanced melancholic stage of the psychosis. The marvel is that Clare developed so far, and acquired such insight into the sweet and bitter harvest of his senses. The sad thing, perhaps, is that the harvest was, so much of it, left as sensation and nothing else. A superabundance of sensation, that pouring into loose poems of the note-book material of poems, becomes unbearable, just as it would be hard to bear with an endless journal of Dorothy Wordsworth. When Clare could publish no more, when he was both exiled and safeguarded in the protective arrest of the asylum, his genuine compulsion to write, to spill himself out into poems, was not at first weakened or destroyed. 'I became,' he said, 'an author by accident,' which is the proper beginning. 'I wrote because it pleased me in sorrow, and when happy it makes me happier.' The making of poems was part of him, like laughing, feeling sad or feeling elated, like waking and sleeping. Indeed it was most of him. And this is worth saying, obvious as it may be, because so much poetry is always so diseased by being, not a willed product, but a willed product outside the nature of the poet.

If there is too little of will, too much of flow about Clare's writing, will can only be applied to refine what is given, and to create the circumstances by which more is given. Clare did labour, nevertheless, upon what he received, only the flow from him was enormously incessant through his life like the flow of a river breaking up through flowers out of limestone. It might have defied the labour of a poet far better equipped by the formalities of education. But he was rather more than the lyric poet writing in answer to an intermittency of impulse.

There are 'classic' poets who contrive something at least of shape either because they avoid, or because they are not forced by the exigency of their nature very far into, the bubbling of life. And there are classics forced into that bubbling and greater in themselves than the confusion, which they are able to subdue. Such a romantic as Clare is stationed between them. He goes further than the one class and as far as the other, but his power to cut and shape what is solid out of what is chaotic is certainly limited and was reached expensively and late; yet he makes and endures the right exploration. One may remember Mr. T. S. Eliot's remark, the more forcible as it comes from a romantic who has attempted to become classic by self-mutilation, that the business of romantic is to prepare for the classic. And beyond the delight that comes of reading Clare selectively, even so romantic and fluent a writer has something to teach. Not only is he an exemplar of the pure life of the artist, a purity founded upon an unevasive appetite, but he is a poet who employs a language unsoiled in his strongest work, which he is able to shape into the most emotive of melodic rhythms. He was unique. His uniqueness and stature cannot be diminished by talk of his origins or his shortcomings, or by talk of the peculiarity of the romantic decadence in human affairs. There is a universal element even in the extreme romantic posture. The relationship between man and nature varies, but since man is conscious, it can never be an equilibrium. Clare is a poet who became homeless at home, naturally and tragically conscious of exclusion from nature. Wriggle as we may, that, many times worse, is still our own position. Clare's asylum foretells our need for an asylum, his deprivation foretells our deprivation. Our modern selves have to eat (if we admit to any) our own sins. Clare, as he exclaimed in 'I Am', was the self-consumer of his woes. We could be pardoned, then, for seeing our own case in Clare's. Yet not quite our case, for in Clare there was no failure of nerve, no concealment of such failure under the rhetoric of a false heroism.

What then we have in Clare is a poet in defeat entirely undefeated.

141. Robert Graves on Clare as a true poet

1955

From 'Peasant Poet', *Hudson Review*, spring 1955, viii, 99–105.

Robert Graves (b. 1895), poet and writer, includes an almost identical passage on Clare in his important book, *The Crowning Privilege*, 1955, pp. 46–51.

Since the sixteenth century in England poetry has been a dangerous trade for those without any other resources but the poetic gift. They soon come up against the paradox that a poet cannot keep this gift if he caters for contemporary taste but that, unless he does so, or unless he dies tragically young, his poems are likely to take at least thirty years before they reach any but the most limited and uninfluential public.

If poetry were not so exacting in its demands on a poet's time and energy, the case would be different. But once a poem forms in his mind and demands to be taken through the necessary stages until its completion, he must obey. And if he has neither inherited means, nor a patron, nor a sinecure, how is his allegiance to poetry reconcileable with his bread and butter job? Ideally, he feels, a poet should be his own master, of sacrosanct person, and privileged to expect hospitality and maintenance wherever he goes. But since ours is not that sort of world, what is he to do? Should he die young and offer promise for performance? It is remarkable how many poets succeed in dying young, even when they have not deliberately pressed the trigger or swallowed poison. Or force himself upon the public by a manifesto or some even more sensational means? That would be undignified, and the public is hard to fool. Or postpone the completion of his poetic career until the statutory thirty years have elapsed? That would mean smothering the poetic impulse meanwhile. Or marry a rich wife? Difficult; rich women tend to marry men who are already worldly successes. Or somehow contrive to keep bread in his mouth by finding a negligent employer, or by doing hack jobs at home? But thirty years is a long stretch.

John Clare found the dilemma more than usually cruel. He was mouse-poor, quite without influence or connexions, and though his first book of poems (1820) proved immediately successful, it sold well only because Taylor, his publisher, who had come across his work by accident, was billing him truthfully enough as an 'English peasant poet'. . . .

How good was Clare? At his best he was very good indeed, with a natural simplicity supported by a remarkable sense of language; meant what he said, considered it well before he wrote it down, and wrote with love. When he was not good, he was no worse than any other not-good poet of his time: most of his poems were about Nature because, after all, he had never been anything but a countryman and described only what he knew. Few things bore me more than the Countryman's Diary featured in the London press today:

Now the triangular seedpods of the great meazle ripen autumn-brown under the mellow Martinmas sun and great companies of Turton's Wendletrap—which the countryman readily distinguishes from the Common Wendletrap by its ecstatic *weet-woot* and its long prehensile toe—perch on the haulms and crack the scarlet seeds with a noise like fairy artillery; while from a neighbouring coppice . . .

Clare wrote a great deal of descriptive verse about the nesting habits of particular birds, about wild animals and insects, and about country people as part of the landscape. But he never bores me: he is always precise and technically admirable. And he had acquired the most unusual faculty of knowing exactly how and when to end a poem. His obsession with Nature made him think of a poem as a living thing, rather than an artifact, or a slice cut from the cake of literature. Take these essays on the vixen and the hedgehog:

> Among the taller wood with ivy hung,
> The old fox plays and dances round her young.
> She snuffs and barks if any passes by
> And swings her tail and turns prepared to fly.

The horseman hurries by, she bolts to see,
And turns agen, from danger never free.
If any stands she runs among the poles
And barks and snaps and drives them in the holes.
The shepherd sees them and the boy goes by
And gets a stick and prongs the hole to try.
They get all still and lie in safety sure,
And out again when everything's secure,
And start and snap at blackbirds bouncing by
To fight and catch the great white butterfly.

. . . He makes a nest and fills it full of fruit,
On the hedge bottom hunts for crabs and sloes
And whistles like a cricket as he goes.
It rolls up like a ball or shapeless hog [log?]
When gipsies hunt it with their noisy dog;
I've seen it in their camps—they call it sweet,
Though black and bitter and unsavoury meat.

I find myself repeating whole poems of Clare's without having made a conscious effort to memorize them. And though it was taken as a symptom of madness that he one day confided in a visitor: 'I know Gray—I know him well,' I shall risk saying here, with equal affection: 'I know Clare; I know him well. We have often wept together.'

142. Clare as an intruder into the canon

1956

From an unsigned review of *Life and Poetry*, *The Times Literary Supplement*, 27 April 1956, no. 2826, 252.

The canon of English poetry seemed until recent years fairly settled, fairly complete. There might be shifts of interest and concern, an occasional dethronement (likely to be followed by a quick restoration) might occur, a few minor figures might slip their way in; but it did seem, after adding up the decisions of Johnson, Coleridge, Arnold and latterly Mr. Eliot, after the selectors from Palgrave onwards (Palgrave aided by Tennyson), after the editors, the historians and the university scholiasts, that we could be fairly sure who was who; who, at any rate, was in the lists, up to, let us say, Hardy and Kipling and Yeats.

There have been intruders. Since 1918 a major intruder, of course, has been Gerard Manley Hopkins, whose claims are now generally allowed, backed by the wonderful clarity and acuity of his own criticism, which completes our grasp of his powers and his poetic personality. Hopkins is certainly a more dangerous intruder than we are yet willing to realize; he threatens by practice and precept and the exciting demonstration of poetic essences, a great deal of nineteenth-century verse.

But what are we to say of another intruder into the canon—John Clare? No one seems absolutely sure. In 1908 Arthur Symons edited a new selection of Clare and said that in the poems he composed in madness his lyrical faculty freed itself for the first time; he declared also that his lyrics (though Symons's phrase would not pass now—quite rightly —in Cambridge or in Redbrick) are in fact distinguished by 'a liquid and thrilling note of song.'

The novelty of this lead was followed and not followed—not always followed by historians, for example. It was hard to shake off a settled judgment that while 'Clare's descriptions of rural scenes show a keen and loving appreciation of nature, and his love-songs and ballads charm by their genuine feeling,' his vogue 'was no doubt largely due to the interest aroused by his humble position in life.' Before Symons, one historian called him insignificant when he passed beyond description; after Symons, another put him among poets of an 'inferior order,' with some 'individual accent' and some 'occasional flash of personality' to save him from oblivion.

Those who felt for Clare could also be hesitant. Mr. Edmund Blunden, for all his love, fused or confused Clare with his own poetic circumference. After denying him at any time a deep knowledge of the dictatorial art of poetry, he concluded that his best poetry grew 'from the incident and secrecy of wild life.' Brave Mr. Middleton Murry in 1924 took a deeper breath, and jumped, and awarded Clare (on new evidence, new poems, brought to light by Mr. Blunden) a visionary faculty unique in English poetry, purer, he argued, than Wordsworth's, purer even than Shakespeare's. That was generous, it was a revolution; yet, added Mr. Middleton Murry, this faculty of vision was so pure, was so perfect, that it kept him a poetic child.

However, bit by bit, volume by volume, more of Clare's poems emerged from the mountain of his manuscripts, and more of Clare's prose, along with more exact knowledge of his life, aims and thoughts, Professor Tibble editing at last, in 1935, a full, fat two volumes of his poems. Clare was creeping up. In 1940, in the *Cambridge Bibliography of English Literature* (which showed how skimpy Clare exegesis remained) he was actually promoted. Mr. Bateson included him not among the minor versifiers of the early nineteenth century but in its group of major poets.

Since 1940 it is true that the revelation of Clare has not slackened. In 1949, for example, more than one hundred poems of the asylum period, a few of them very remarkable, could still be published for the first time, and there is evidence that we go on being touched by Clare either as a man or as a poet. Yet are we agreed? Do we really allow his place inside the canon in an unreluctantly granted relationship to Giant Keats, Giant Coleridge or Giant Wordsworth?

Consider the opinions of Professor and Mrs. Tibble, who have devoted so much labour and love to raising Clare from the dead, and have now revised and re-written the life of Clare they gave us first in 1932, making it both Life and estimate, and dedicating it, with a gesture the poets may not all appreciate, 'to the living poets of England.' In 1932 Professor and Mrs. Tibble were Georgian about Clare. That has to be admitted. Clare, to his young biographers, was still too much of a leafy 'nature poet': he found 'a star in the petals of a flower,' he had 'a secret of melody known to birds'—put on tape no doubt by Mr. Ludwig Koch—'but rarely to man.'

Their biography, to be critical, was quite obviously uncritical, transcripts were altogether unreliable, and Clare had to survive (which he was well able to do) a confusion of himself with Miss Patience Strong.

Professor Tibble made some amends in the *Poems* of 1935. The choice of poems, though, was still vitiated by pastoral preconceptions, many extraordinary poems went unrecognized and were left out, the texts were still unreliable and were now and again even 'improved.' In the new Life the authors catch hold of the firmness of poetry a little more firmly, they abjure more of Patience Strong, they show more respect for accuracy in transcription, yet they still treat us to more than is necessary of the 'Clare Country,' and still, in estimating the final victories of Clare, neglect altogether to point to such poems as 'Death,' 'Hesperus,' 'It is the Evening Hour,' 'First Love,' or 'Solitude.'

It is true that for all their faults these two investigators had seen from the first, in a muddled way, that Clare by keeping his spirit with the free, had passed a great distance 'beyond description'; it is true that the grounds of their respect for Clare became, stage by stage, more recognizable to themselves; it is also true that the full excellence, the full human relevance of Clare can still escape these scholars of increasing conscience and decreasing sentimentality.

This is an interesting failure. Does it reflect only Professor and Mrs. Tibble's critical deficiencies, only that they matured in a tradition of poetry too weak, too restricted and too ungenerous to contain, shall one say, John Donne and John Clare at extremes, with Hopkins in the middle? Or shall we always argue and vacillate about Clare, always remember his 'humble position in life,' always group him with Crabbe, and a few more, among 'doubtfuls' of literature, who should not really be doubted at all?

The last is the important question. Since unwilling duchesses have so long ago been forced to lick stamps, and since we have long been surrounded with poets proclaiming their humble origin, Clare's origin would hardly seem to matter or cause concern any more. When other poets (Hopkins, for one) wrote down for themselves Clare's wonderful and terrible poem 'I am: yet what I am none cares or knows' (much as poets have so often written out for comfort Wordsworth's 'Resolution and Independence'), they asked themselves no questions about Clare's education, Clare's syntax and grammar, Clare's single subjects and plural verbs or the other way round. They were moved instead by Clare's admission that he as well was forced to be the 'self-consumer of his woes'; and no doubt they admired his refusal, even then, to admit wreck in shipwreck.

But is it Clare's destiny or Clare's poetry we find so touching, or both in one? That, too, is a question to answer. We all know, at last, how poignantly Clare lived, failed and triumphed. Would no genuine power be left, or would his poems be drained of an adventitious content, supposing that we knew nothing at all of Clare's history?

Long ago Professor Tibble suggested—a little too frowardly—that Clare 'was not interested in words as words': Clare focused himself upon an image, the image found its words, its phrasing, and so poems were built up. It is true that Clare hardly reshapes his language to a characteristic degree; he hardly produces a Clare language, as, for example, there is a Christopher Smart language, a very particular impression having been given to his words, as Smart said ,'by punching, that when the reader casts his eye upon 'em, he takes up the image from the mould which I have made.' Just as that punched impression can be good or bad (Hopkins or Dylan Thomas; Hardy or Francis Thompson), so a good or a bad poetry can exist in a language fined, simply, as a Spanish vintner fines his sherry with whites of egg, but not greatly transformed; in that way, Clare's language, for all his less perfect, less educated command of it, is not so different, after all, from Wordsworth's or Byron's or Blake's; and no more than faulty syntax or grammar does this imply that our knowledge of Clare's history is the mere liquid which is spilt into the poems to make them alive and active. We need know nothing of Clare's biography to accept melodious statements of the human predicament when Clare asks:

> Is love's bed always snow

or when he says that:

> Flowers shall hang upon the palls
> Brighter than patterns upon shawls.

Faced with Clare's imperfections, we still have to ask who is perfect. In fact, we should do well to remember Hopkins answering Bridges, when Bridges complained that the poetry of William Barnes, that 'perfect artist,' as Hopkins called him, lacked fire. It might be so: 'but who is perfect all round?' said Hopkins. 'If one defect is fatal what writer could we read?'

Is Clare also the arrested child of vision? When Mr. Middleton Murry said so in 1924, there were not poems enough, there was not an ordered enough history of Clare's poetry to show him wrong. We must not be too much misled by Clare's own statements. He certainly said that Nature would be his widow, that he found his poems in the fields and only wrote them down; and he did not feel with an especial subtlety or sophistication of mind. But to his own melodic exploration, his own experience of the human dilemma, he did apply thoughts about which his biographers should have been more emphatic—thoughts he had borrowed from Coleridge, and also from Wordsworth. His notion of 'self-creating joy,' which he mentioned, for example, in *Pastoral Poesy* and which was one of the names of his Mary Joyce, was never forgotten, and was pondered, and developed, by Clare. Coleridge's 'Dejection' and Wordsworth's 'Intimations' ode, it seems quite obvious, enabled Clare to recognize 'joy' in himself; and Clare was luckier than Coleridge (or Wordsworth), not losing so quickly or completely this joy he had to project and so receive.

Also one may search the new Life, or the old one, for a single, particular word, for the single image of the sun; in which the development of Clare's poetry—Clare's life indeed—can also be traced from beginning to end. The sun is the king-image of Clare's poetry, much as it is of Turner's painting. It is the red and roundy, red-complexioned sun of early poems and early experience, which rose over the fens as Clare went to work, winter or summer. It gives a glitter to cesspools (in 'The Mouse's Nest'). It is, or it was—'A splendid sun hath set!'— Clare's *alter ego*, Lord Byron. The sun, indeed, is hope, nature, love ('sun of undying light'), eternity; proffering at last to Clare the 'eternal ray' he snatched to write himself into freedom and immortality in his deepest and most clinching poem.

So far in the exegesis of Clare, it is that sun-filled, nearly sun-worshipping sense of the whole of him, that pondered development, of joy and love and eternity and freedom, that metamorphosis from time into timelessness, which needs still to be comprehended, without little-lambish deflections. It needs to be shown—and is not shown starkly enough, unequivocally enough, by his biographers—that in a dozen or two dozen poems, in which imagination does its melodic and verbal shaping with unusual energy and completeness, Clare does become a momentous poet—momentous at least to those readers whose experiences have matured their sensibility, their power, and their need, to respond. If in one way Hopkins is a dangerous intruder into the canon, so in another way is Clare, since he strips away certain current pretensions about verse-reading as an intellectual exercise and not a central experience, and since he demands discernment, in a situation not already mapped out and signposted.

143. Clare as a lyric poet

1956

Naomi Lewis, from 'The Green Man' (a review of J. W. and Anne Tibble, *John Clare: His Life and Poetry*, 1956), *New Statesman*, 5 May 1956, n.s. 51, 492–3. This was reprinted in *A Visit to Mrs. Wilcox*, 1957, pp. 56–62.

The last thirty years of Clare's life were spent in mental asylums, first in Epping, then at Northampton—enlightened places enough for their time—but still a forced uprooting from his home. Yet the shift in focus was to turn him from an innocently charming pastoral poet into a haunting and sometimes a brilliant one. The poetry of external nature had flashed into what we might now call the poetry of impressionism.

In the asylum years Clare identified himself with figures of social power and physical authority—Byron, Nelson, certain prize-fighters. Yet in his poetic life he never claimed to be anything but the countryman he was. The grass-green coat that was his choice in those few bright years of London fame and friends, the coat that Hood described as 'shining verdantly out from the grave-coloured suits of the literati', has, as we look back, a symbolic air. Unlike Wordsworth, unlike Edward Thomas even, Clare, the Green Man of poetry, was always the servant of the land and not its guest; he knew it at its coarsest and most harsh. Yet his love of nature never fell short of passion. Even the simplest descriptive poems have a touch of this fever—once the reader accepts that it is the observation itself that holds the intensity. His note on

Keats's over-literary vision of nature—a Greek goddess behind every bush—is shrewd and intelligent. Clare was no landscape poet. He did not perceive the unremarkable local scene in vistas but in miniature detail. As Dickens saw people, Clare seems always to have viewed his rural world from a child's level, each object slightly more insistent than in life. A flat Northampton field would thus be a paradise of little plants, fragile insects, snail shells, grasses, weeds, 'the heaving grasshopper in his delicate green bouncing from stub to stub' or, overhead, 'the wild geese skudding along and making all the letters of the alphabet as they flew'.

But there were further reasons why Clare should be imaginatively rooted in his past, why he could write:

> Were all people to feel as I do, the world could not be carried on—a green would not be ploughed—a bush or tree would not be cut for firing or furniture, and everything they found when boys would remain in that state till they died.

In that time he had known the pre-Enclosure landscape; he had been free then, and only then, from heavy responsibilities; he had walked on equal terms with Mary Joyce, too far above him in later years to marry —the Glinton girl who became the symbol of all loss and all desire, his dream wife and spiritual companion in his years of madness.

Clare's gifts were at their height during the Epping sojourn—a time both of shock and release. (Is there a comparison here with the war years of Edward Thomas, and the sudden flowering of his poetry?) And there was a sudden miraculous year at Northampton (1844) in which he wrote the great and haunting poems 'I am', 'A Vision' and 'An Invite to Eternity'. But his control was fitful, harder and harder to keep during the second asylum banishment. The power of writing a long, sustained, intricate poem like 'Child Harold' certainly did not return. And though there is no doubt that Clare was well used and had some liberty, the impact of direct experience was weakening all the time. Without the stimulus of affection given or taken, with fewer visits and letters as his old friends died, he turned to memory, to recollections of his childhood and of early sweethearts; but memory, too, thins out and needs renewing. His prose and conversation were the first to go: his verse, in which his all-important 'identity' lay, held out longer against the dissolution. Indeed, through most of the Northampton poems the natural music remains—'In bed she like a lily lay' . . . 'My love is as sweet as a beanfield in blossom'—and even where the thought rambles into confusion there are striking passages:

Lay bare those twin roses
That hide in thy hair,
Thy eye's light discloses
The sweetness hid there,
For thy dark curls lie on them
Like night in the air.

'A green delight the wounded mind endears,' Clare wrote in a poem praising Solitude; and in his later and stranger works, compounds of love and joy, separation and loss, nature is still the image and the theme. Through nature he betrays his changing mood. A poem beginning 'How beautiful the morning' turns from a water-colour into an angry Van Gogh:

A ball o' fire, he blazes high
Till bulging clouds succeeds.
The coal black snails that fear to fry
Now creep among the weeds.

The familiar poem 'I Hid My Love' is one of the most impressive examples of this intensified perception.

It would be a mistake to assume too much *naïveté* in Clare's achievement. Simple his vision may have been before the asylum years—but writing itself is a sophisticated matter. The rural poet, no less than any other kind, must come to literature through literature, and pass through an almost artificial stage before he can reach his own kind of simplicity. Clare (who worked his way through Thomson, Collins, Byron, Burns and lesser models) was cannily aware that nature alone does not make a countryman into an articulate poet. Education, he once said, 'would put human life . . . into the dull and obstinate class whence I struggled into light like one struggling from nightmare in his sleep'. Once he had established his manner, he was by no means clogged in his time. What marks his metrical variety is its seeming effortlessness; greater poets appear formal and over-deliberate in comparison.

Now is past, is changed agen,
    The woods and fields are painted new.
Wild strawberries which both gathered then
    None know now where they grew
        The sky's o'ercast.
Wood strawberries faded from wood-sides,
    Green leaves have all turned yellow;
No Adelaide walks the wood rides,
    True love has no bed-fellow.
        Now is past.

423

or from 'It is the Evening Hour':

> Spirit of her I love,
>   Whispering to me,
> Stories of sweet visions, as I rove,
>   Here stop and crop with me
> Sweet flowers that in the still hour grew,
> We'll take them home, nor shake off the bright dew.
>
> Mary, or sweet spirit of thee,
>   As the bright sun shines tomorrow,
> Thy dark eyes these flowers shall see,
>   Gathered by me in sorrow,
> In the still hour when my mind was free
> To walk alone—yet wish I walk'd with thee.

If a poet is to be judged by his best, a half-dozen, at least, of Clare's shorter poems are among the peaks of English lyrical poetry. In spite of its borrowed title and its passages of madness, his long 'Child Harold' contains some of the most notable lyrical writing in the language. Even his minor work has an unfailingly living quality because of its extraordinarily close relation to life as Clare experienced it. Has time yet made its amends? Today we have grief for his long years of exile, shame for the dole he received in the servants' halls of the gentry. But it would be disingenuous for unacclaimed young poets today to see their own image in this story. It is not merely that the circumstances would be almost impossible, now, to find. The fact is that the lesson, if any, is a rather uncomfortable one. It may be left for the reader of Clare's disturbing life and remarkable poems to discover.

144. More doubts about Clare

1958

J. W. R. Purser, a review of J. W. and Anne Tibble, *John Clare: His Life and Poetry*, 1956, *Review of English Studies*, 1958, n.s. ix, 97–8.

The subject of this work, though his story makes an interesting and moving biography, is a difficult one from a critical point of view, and the aims of Professor and Mrs. Tibble, as the title indicates, are critical as well as biographical. Clare is a simple poet, but the merits and defects of simplicity are perhaps the hardest of all to gauge. He depended very much on impulse for his inspiration, and felt impatient at being asked to correct. His work can be original and imitative by turns, unconsciously borrowed words, images, and phrases being found side by side with novel and even daring ones almost everywhere in his verse. He can be apparently deaf to some major defect of music, such as ending three or four lines running with exactly the same rhythm, or leaving an un-assimilable extra syllable or foot in a line (though it is hard to believe that he wrote 'Where there's neither light nor life to see', as Mr. and Mrs. Tibble have it, in the midst of the octosyllabics of 'Invite to Eternity') while at the same time commanding a subtle sweetness of tone in the individual phrases. He can go astray in elementary rules of grammar and yet express himself in a neighbouring sentence with the acumen of someone apparently well practised in the handling of words. So too he can pass from a platitude to a prophecy, from a naïve wise saw or profession of good feeling to a humorous or pathetic remark that 'makes one's heart turn over'. His critics are therefore to be sympathized with if there is a certain haziness about their approach. Their apparent reluctance, too, to feel, as some contemporary taste would have it, that the striking quality of Clare's prophetic work quite rules out the merits of his earlier nature verse is understandable; for the prophetic work, in spite of its greatness, is scanty and often obscure, while the nature verse surely betrays, if ever poetry did, a deep reverence for the works of God on earth, which is in its own way a prophecy. Mr. and Mrs. Tibble, however, do rather markedly fail in such things as their analyses of changes of style and outlook, and their elucidation of particular poems. For example, their effort to explain the impressive but obscure poem 'A Vision' is surely most unsatisfactory. Of the most difficult phrase, the opening one, they only say that it is 'clear enough', and if Clare's words 'I felt the sweets of fancied love' have the sense that Mr. and Mrs. Tibble say they have, the first phrase and the whole poem would seem to want some very recondite interpretation indeed. Again, in a verse such as

> This love, wrong understood,
>   Oft turned my joy to pain;
> I tried to throw away the bud,
>   But the blossom would remain.

we are indeed reminded of Blake (one would like to know, by the way, if the information were available, what knowledge of Blake Clare had) yet suspect that Clare is using 'bud' and 'blossom' negligently for the same thing, as Blake would not have done. If Mr. and Mrs. Tibble have faith that this is not so, they should have gone into such points in support of their faith. Perhaps it is too much to ask for a complete explanation of these difficult poems, and perhaps an overall caution is excusable in Clare's case, but in places the authors seem purposely to avoid plain statements. Though Clare comes out of an inspection of his life and poetry with the reader's deep affection and esteem, it cannot be said that Mr. and Mrs. Tibble have cleared away much of the 'brushwood' from the criticism of his work, or have really established him as 'one of the truly great English poets' which their publishers claim him to be.

Defect of critical power, however, is the only big defect of Mr. and Mrs. Tibble's work; their instinct for what is poetry and what is not seems mainly true, their treatment of the biography is sympathetic and painstaking, and they succeed in passing on some of their own obviously genuine enthusiasm for their subject. Clare's personality, and the story of his happy early years, his exasperating and unsuccessful bid for fame and a living, and his final pathetic collapse make a strong impact on the reader, while well-chosen quotations from his verse and prose assure us all along that we are giving our attention to someone who deserves it, at the same time as providing us with a good general survey of his literary output. The desire to reinstate simplicity and the 'singing voice' as estimable qualities in poetry is no doubt responsible for the renewed —indeed the almost entirely new—interest in Clare and his work. It would be desirable if his defenders could speak out more loud and bold, and 'place' him and his merits more precisely than do Mr. and Mrs. Tibble, but when all is said and done, poetry is more for appreciation than for judgement, and we must be grateful to them for their labours in editing Clare's poems, letters, and prose works, and for compiling his biography in (originally) *John Clare, a Life* and (its revised form) the book under review.

145. Harold Bloom on Clare

1962

From chapter vii, 'Beddoes, Clare, Darley and Others', *The Visionary Company*, 1962, pp. 428–50.[1] This extract is from the section entitled 'John Clare: The Wordsworthian Shadow', pp. 434–45 (pp. 444–56 of the revised edition, 1971).

Harold Bloom (b. 1930), Professor of English at Yale, provides the only serious treatment of Clare by modern American academic criticism.

Clare is a poet who became homeless at home, naturally and tragically conscious of exclusion from nature.

—GEOFFREY GRIGSON

> And Memory mocked me, like a haunting ghost.
> With light and life and pleasures that were lost.
> As dreams turn night to day, and day to night,
> So Memory flashed her shadows of that light
> That once bade morning suns in glory rise,
> To bless green fields and trees and purple skies,
> And wakened life its pleasures to behold;—
> That light flashed on me, like a story told.
> —CLARE, *The Dream* (1821)

Clare is the most genuine of poets, and yet it does not lessen him to say that much of his poetry is a postscript to Wordsworth's, even as Beddoes, Darley, and Thomas Hood are *epigoni* in their poetry to Shelley and Keats. It is not that Clare is just a Hartley Coleridge, writing, however well, out of greater men's visions. Clare's vision is as unique as Grigson has insisted it is. But the mode of that vision, the kind of that poetry, is Wordsworth's and Coleridge's. Clare's relation to Words-

[1] Reprinted from Harold Bloom: *The Visionary Company: A Reading of English Romantic Poetry*. Copyright 1961 by Harold Bloom. Copyright 1971 by Cornell University. Used by permission of Cornell University Press.

worth is closer even than Shelley's in *Alastor* or Keats's in *Sleep and Poetry*. Clare does not imitate Wordsworth and Coleridge. He either borrows directly, or else works on exactly parallel lines, intersected by the huge Wordsworthian shadow.

Clare's dialectic begins as Wordsworth's, passes into a creative opposition resembling that in Coleridge's *Dejection: An Ode*, and climaxes, in a handful of great poems, remarkably close to Blake's. Here is a Song of Experience Blake would have joyed to read, written perhaps twenty years after Blake's death, and in probable ignorance of the greater visionary:

> I hid my love when young till I
> Couldn't bear the buzzing of a fly;
> I hid my love to my despite
> Till I could not bear to look at light:
> I dare not gaze upon her face
> But left her memory in each place;
> Where'er I saw a wild flower lie
> I kissed and bade my love goodbye.

It is terrifying, altogether beautiful, and thoroughly Blakean. The language itself is almost Blake's: it lacks only the terminology. He had put his emanation away from him, in Blake's terms, and he suffered the intolerable consequences. With the total form of all he created and loved put aside, he could not bear the minutest of natural particulars, for he had concealed his vision behind nature. Averted from light, like the protagonist in Blake's *Mad Song*, he peopled nature with 'her memory,' substituting that treacherous faculty for the direct imaginative apprehension of a human face. And so, necessarily, his bondage to nature is completed.

> I met her in the greenest dells,
> Where dewdrops pearl the wood bluebells;
> The lost breeze kissed her bright blue eye,
> The bee kissed and went singing by,
> A sunbeam found a passage there,
> A gold chain round her neck so fair;
> As secret as the wild bee's song
> She lay there all the summer long.

Amid so much magnificence, it is the word 'secret' that takes the stanza's burden of meaning. The fly's buzzing of the first stanza is reinforced here by the bee's song; the entire second stanza is an intensification of the last couplet of the first. His imaginings are reduced to illusions, the deceptions of fancy: the sunbeam as gold chain, the dew-drops on bluebells as her eyes. What remains is the madness of destroyed vision:

> I hid my love in field and town
> Till e'en the breeze would knock me down;
> The bees seemed singing ballads o'er,
> The fly's bass turned a lion's roar;
> And even silence found a tongue,
> To haunt me all the summer long;
> The riddle nature could not prove
> Was nothing else but secret love.

Part of the sudden increase in rhetorical power here is due to skillful repetition, augmenting the increased weakness of the protagonist and the growth in power of the hostile Spectre he has created in nature. The breeze, the fly's roar, the bee's cyclic repetitiveness in song are the lengthening external shadow of the Selfhood within, which comes entirely to dominate the speaker, confining him in solipsistic isolation from his beloved nature itself. Like all solipsists, he must subside in tautology, which is almost a definition of Blake's state of Ulro. So even silence finds a tongue to haunt him. The final couplet is difficult. Nature could not 'prove' the riddle of secret love in any sense, test or demonstrate or solve. Nature, either before or after the hiding of his love, was inadequate to conceal or retain or even identify her. He has lost both, nature and love.

In this poem, and in 'I Am!,' 'A Vision', and 'An Invite to Eternity', Clare wrote as Blake wrote, against the natural man (Grigson notes this for 'A Vision'). These poems are palinodes; they need to be set against some of Clare's best Wordsworthian poems: 'Pastoral Poesy', 'To the Rural Muse', 'To the Snipe', 'The Eternity of Nature', and the late poems, 'The Sleep of Spring' and 'Poets Love Nature', which belong to the so-called asylum poems written during Clare's confinement in an insane asylum. Taking these together, we will still not have considered all of Clare, even in modest representation. Nothing in either group of poems resembles the grim and meticulous power of 'Badger', a poem prophesying Edward Thomas and Frost, or the Shakespearean purity of a song like 'Clock-a-clay'. But these two groups of poems, which contain some of his most characteristic (and best) work do show the Romantic Clare, as a Wordsworthian and as a final independent visionary, equal at his most intense to Smart and Blake. And a consideration of them should further illuminate the varieties of Romantic dialectic, in its endless interplay between nature and imagination.

In 'Joys of Childhood' (no certain date) Clare is closest to Wordsworth. Here, in eight Spenserian stanzas, the 'Intimations' ode is recalled in two of its aspects, the child's glory and the sense of loss, but not in its dialectic of saving memory. As in Wordsworth, the child, knowing no mortality, *is* immortal:

> Their home is bliss, and should they dream of heaven
> 'Tis but to be as they before have been;
> The dark grave's gulf is naught, nor thrusts its shade between.

But, unlike Wordsworth, this initial consciousness of immortality has no apocalyptic overtones:

> Oh, I do love the simple theme that tries
> To lead us back to happiness agen
> And make our cares awhile forget that we are men.

In his madness, Clare came again to overt celebration of his love for that 'simple theme':

> Wordsworth I love, his books are like the fields,
> Not filled with flowers, but works of human kind.

This sonnet, 'To Wordsworth', is perceptive both in analyzing the master and in implying the disciple's affinity:

> A finer flower than gardens e'er gave birth,
> The aged huntsman grubbing up the root—
> I love them all as tenants of the earth:
> Where genius is, there often die the seeds.

Partially, this is the tribute of the man who could say:

> I found the poems in the fields
> And only wrote them down.

But it is more than that, for it records also the death of the *seeds* of genius, not the flowers. Clare's desire was the desire of Wordsworth, to find the unfallen Eden in nature, to read in her a more human face. But Clare ended with a tragic awareness of apocalyptic defeat, akin to Coleridge's, and hinting, in the very last poems, at Blake's and Shelley's rejection of nature. Clare's sensibility was more acute than Wordsworth's, and Clare, as a poet and as a man, died old.

Grigson has remarked that Clare's involvement in the visionary complex of the 'Intimations' and 'Dejection' odes is most clearly indicated in the radiance of 'Pastoral Poesy':

> But poesy is a language meet,
>   And fields are every one's employ
> The wild flower 'neath the shepherd's feet
>   Looks up and gives him joy.

So far Wordsworth, but the burden is darker:

> An image to the mind is brought,
>   Where happiness enjoys
> An easy thoughtlessness of thought
>   And meets excess of joys.
>
> And such is poesy; its power
>   May varied lights employ,
> Yet to all minds it gives the dower
>   Of self-creating joy.

'Self-creating joy': without arguing, but by a mysterious synthesis, Clare has passed to Coleridge. As in Wordsworth, the resolution is in a particular silence, from which the varied autumnal music emerges:

> And whether it be hill or moor,
>   I feel where'er I go
> A silence that discourses more
>   Than any tongue can do.
>
> Unruffled quietness hath made
>   A peace in every place
> And woods are resting in their shade
>   Of social loneliness.
>
> The storm, from which the shepherd turns
>   To pull his beaver down,
> While he upon the heath sojourns,
>   Which autumn pleaches brown,
>
> Is music, ay, and more indeed
>   To those of musing mind
> Who through the yellow woods proceed
>   And listen to the wind.

Listening to the wind is an honored mode of summoning the Muse, and the wind is the music of reality to those of musing mind when they yield themselves to the 'social loneliness' of nature. Without the strife of contraries, Clare passes from this 'Tintern Abbey' vision to the 'Dejection' climax:

The poet in his fitful glee
　　And fancy's many moods
Meets it as some strange melody,
　　A poem of the woods,

And now a harp that flings around
　　The music of the wind;
The poet often hears the sound
　　When beauty fills the mind.

So would I my own mind employ
　　And my own heart impress,
That poesy's self's a dwelling joy
　　Of humble quietness.

Whether the simplicity here is deliberate or not, we cannot say; in either case it is only *apparent* simplicity. When Blake employs an apparent simplicity in the *Songs of Innocence*, he takes care to hint, however subtly, that he is deliberate. Clare sets no traps; his 'organized innocence' is straightforward, but not naïve. Clare's resolution in 'Pastoral Poesy' of the Wordsworth-Coleridge visionary conflict is as 'modern' as Rimbaud or Hart Crane; the *Poem itself* is more than the therapy, as it was for Wordsworth and Coleridge, if less than the apocalyptic act it was for Blake. For Clare his poem is not a second nature but a kindly nurse or foster mother, and yet not a nurse who would have us forget the primal joy:

That poesy's self's a dwelling joy
　　Of humble quietness.

This goes beyond 'a timely utterance gave that thought relief.' Clare's desperation is still clearer in 'The Progress of Rhyme':

O soul-enchanting poesy,
Thou'st long been all the world with me;
When poor, thy presence grows my wealth,
When sick, thy visions give me health,
When sad, thy sunny smile is joy
And was from e'en a tiny boy.
When trouble came, and toiling care
Seemed almost more than I could bear,
While threshing in the dusty barn
Or squashing in the ditch to earn
A pittance that would scarce allow
One joy to smooth my sweating brow

Where drop by drop would chase and fall,
Thy presence triumphed over all.

The point of 'The Progress of Rhyme' is to develop this early dependence until the chant's conclusion is inevitable for all of its breadth of identification:

And hope, love, joy, are poesy.

In some of the asylum poems, this Wordsworthian vision attains a final authority. The perfect sonnet of Romanticism may be the 'Bright Star' of Keats, or Wordsworth on Westminster bridge or the Calais sands, or it may be this:

Poets love nature and themselves are love,
The scorn of fools, and mock of idle pride.
The vile in nature worthless deeds approve,
They court the vile and spurn all good beside.
Poets love nature; like the calm of heaven,
Her gifts like heaven's love spread far and wide:
In all her works there are no signs of leaven,
Sorrow abashes from her simple pride.
Her flowers, like pleasures, have their season's birth,
And bloom through regions here below;
They are her very scriptures upon earth,
And teach us simple mirth where'er we go.
Even in prison they can solace me,
For where they bloom God is, and I am free.

The concern for liberty here is not just the obsessional desire of an asylum-pent countryman; the liberty is freedom from Self, the mocking of the Spectre. The flowers are nature's scriptures *because* they teach mirth, and mirth endows Clare with the greater joy of liberty.

The most poignant of the asylum poems that look backward to Clare's early vision is 'The Sleep of Spring', a hymn of home yearnings, remarkable alike for its clear identification of Nature as a loving mother and its chilled recognition that there is no way back to her love:

I loved the winds when I was young,
    When life was dear to me;
I loved the song which Nature sung,
    Endearing liberty;
I loved the wood, the vale, the stream,
For there my boyhood used to dream.

In a few of the asylum poems, the sense of loss is transformed into a rejection of nature for a humanistic eternity, an apocalypse akin, as has been remarked, to Blake's. 'Secret Love' is such a poem. But if one had to present only the best of Clare, the poems that are indisputably an absolute poetry, I would suggest a trilogy of 'An Invite to Eternity', 'I Am', and, most perfectly, 'A Vision'. These are 'Songs of Experience,' as the aged Blake might have written, had he not by then gone on to a stage that he alone, finally, can demonstrate to be perhaps beyond the reach of a lyrical art.

Clare's invitation to eternity presents a problem in tone: how are these lines to be read?

> Wilt thou go with me, sweet maid
> Say, maiden, wilt thou go with me
> Through the valley depths of shade,
> Of night and dark obscurity,
> Where the path has lost its way,
> Where the sun forgets the day,—
> Where there's nor light nor life to see,
> Sweet maiden, wilt thou go with me?

Is it merely a Hades, nature projected in its worst aspects? Rather, a displacement of nature is involved, when the path 'loses its way' and the sun 'forgets,' in a land:

> Where stones will turn to flooding streams,
> Where plains will rise like ocean waves,
> Where life will fade like visioned dreams
> And mountains darken into caves,
> Say, maiden, wilt thou go with me
> Through this sad non-identity,
> Where parents live and are forgot,
> And sisters live and know us not.

More terrifying than Hades and the eternities of Dante, this vision is of a state of changed natural identities and human non-identity. What is the moral and spiritual meaning, the trope and the anagoge, of a vision so hopeless, especially when it is presented as an invitation to a maiden?

> Say, maiden, wilt thou go with me
> In this strange death of life to be,
> To live in death and be the same
> Without this life, or home, or name,

> At once to be and not to be—
> That was and is not—yet to see
> Things pass like shadows, and the sky
> Above, below, around us lie?

This is, at its close, something like a vertigo of vision, necessary to sustain the paradox of simultaneously affirming both of Hamlet's contraries. Clare is attacking, as Blake did, the most rugged of the 'cloven fictions,' the dichotomy of being and non-being, a discursive antithesis alien to the imagination. But is *this* enough for a symbolic eternity?

> The land of shadows wilt thou trace,
> And look—nor know each other's face;
> The present mixed with reason gone,
> And past and present all as one?
> Say, maiden, can thy life be led
> To join the living with the dead?
> Then trace thy footsteps on with me;
> We're wed to one eternity.

This is more than enigmatic and yet less than obscure. Perhaps dark with excessive light, again like so much of Blake. What meaning can the poem's last line have if eternity is a state merely of non-identity? Why 'wed' rather than 'bound'? The poem seems to be an appeal for love and courage, and the close has a tone of something like triumph. Why, then, the striking 'the present mixed with *reason gone*'? Last, and most crucial, if this *is* an invitation, where is the voluntary element in the vision; what lies in the will of the maiden?

The same questions, in kind, are evoked by the more powerful 'I Am', a poem on the nature of Coleridge's 'great I Am,' the Primary Imagination:

> I am: yet what I am none cares, or knows,
>   My friends forsake me like a memory lost,
> I am the self-consumer of my woes—
>   They rise and vanish in oblivious host,
> Like shadows in love's frenzied, stifled throes:—
> And yet I am, and live—like vapours tost
>
> Into the nothingness of scorn and noise,
>   Into the living sea of waking dreams,
> Where there is neither sense of life or joys,
>   But the vast shipwreck of my life's esteems;
> Even the dearest, that I love the best,
> Are strange—nay, rather stranger than the rest.

I long for scenes, where man hath never trod,
  A place where woman never smiled or wept—
There to abide with my Creator, God,
  And sleep as I in childhood sweetly slept,
  Untroubling, and untroubled where I lie,
  The grass below—above the vaulted sky.

'I am,' God's *ehyeh asher ehyeh* reply to the questioning of His Name, is Coleridge's universal creative word, the primal imaginative act. The force of Clare's 'I Am' is negative—I am, but what I am is uncared for and unknown, consumes its own woes, is as a vapor tossed into a sea of chaos, an infinity of nothingness. Memory is only a forsaking; it is necessarily lost. The yearning is apocalyptic—not for childhood but for scenes 'where man hath never trod'—the break with Wordsworth is complete. For Clare the Fortunate Fields *are* 'a history only of departed things.' There is no goodly universe to be wedded to man in a saving marriage. The dower of a new heaven and a new earth, given by joy when we take nature as bride, is not to be paid. And Clare is looking for a place beyond the possibility of any marriage—'where woman never smiled or wept.' This final yearning, to be free of nature and woman alike, is the informing principle of Clare's most perfect poem, the absolutely Blakean 'A Vision':

I lost the love of heaven above,
  I spurned the lust of earth below,
I felt the sweets of fancied love,
  And hell itself my only foe.

I lost earth's joys, but felt the glow
  Of heaven's flame abound in me.
Till loveliness and I did grow
  The bard of immortality.

I loved but woman fell away,
  I hid me from her faded fame,
I snatch'd the sun's eternal ray
  And wrote till earth was but a name.

In every language upon earth,
  On every shore, o'er every sea,
I gave my name immortal birth
  And kept my spirit with the free.

Grigson applies to 'A Vision' Blake's version of the Pauline distinction between the natural and the spiritual man, that is, the natural and

437

the imaginative, seeing it as 'repentance, an immortal moment reached after and attained.' The best analogue in Blake is 'To Tirzah', where Blake's rejection of nature as the mother of his imagination is fitted into Jesus' denial of Mary as mother of more than his mortal part:

> Whate'er is Born of Mortal Birth
> Must be consumed with the Earth
> To rise from Generation free:
> Then what have I to do with thee?

Free from Generation and rejecting the changing earthly paradise of Beulah (Wordsworthian Nature), Clare and Blake elect the creative paradise of Eden, in which the poet's pen is an eternal ray of the sun and the poem reduces earth to but a name. Clare's rejection of the earth is not merely orthodox, for, like Blake, he has lost the love of the heaven that is above. The crucial process of imaginative incarnation is in:

> Till loveliness and I did grow
> The bard of immortality.

This is not Platonic loveliness, in simple contrast to 'earth's joys,' but a loveliness of vision. Clare himself, by this mutual interpenetration of growth with loveliness, grows into a world he helps create, the world of the Blakean visionary, where the earth as 'hindrance, not action' is kicked away and the poet sees through the eye, not with it. 'A Vision' is a lucid moment of immortality attained on August 2, 1844. Clare lived another twenty years without expressing such a moment so lucidly again. But the poems of those years are more serene; another Wordsworthian rose in Clare, remote without coldness. The very last poem, written in 1863, can be taken as an emblem of these last decades. The beauty of the verse here is more than its pathos; it stems from a perfect equilibrium between nature and a poet who has learned its limitations for the imagination, but yearns after it still. 'Birds' Nests' is a simple pastoral description, but the arrangement, in its alternation of descriptive detail, is meaningful. Spring; the chaffinch nesting; the poet charmed by the bird's song, are succeeded by the bleakness of the wind over the open fen, hinting at the essential inadvertence of nature. But the picture is quietly resolved in warmth and leisure:

> 'Tis spring, warm glows the south,
> Chaffinch carries the moss in his mouth
> To filbert hedges all day long,
> And charms the poet with his beautiful song;

The wind blows bleak o'er the sedgy fen,
But warm the sun shines by the little wood,
Where the old cow at her leisure chews her cud.

146. Some centenary comments

1964

(a) Robert Shaw (b. 1933), poet and critic, from 'John Clare's "Paradise
Lost"—and Regained', *Northamptonshire Past and Present*, 1964, iii, 201–2:

. . . however firmly placed in the landscape and social pattern of
Helpston and its neighbourhood is Clare's early and middle work, the
poems in this edition [*Later Poems*, ed. Eric Robinson and Geoffrey
Summerfield, Manchester 1964] are as delocalized as *Paradise Lost*, with
which it shares a preoccupation with the themes of Eden and the Fall.
Thus the Asylum is not just an Asylum or even the Bastille, but a
Purgatorial Hell, symbolizing the Fall and loss of freedom, while the
people and landscape of his childhood came to stand for the innocence
he had lost. Contemporary events, such as the visit of Queen Victoria
to Northampton, and people are mere grist to the symbolizing mill.
(Significantly, it is not known whether the names of many of the
women figuring in these later poems are those of real people or of
fantasy-products.) The sine qua non of Clare's being able to carry on
writing poetry and, perhaps, living, in the confinement of the Asylum
was that he escape its painful reality. It is his achievement that he did
better than to escape it: he transcended it.

Beginning as an Augustan pasticheur, maturing as a classicist—of a
peculiarly original turn but still a classical one, Clare's final art was
Romantic. There was method and aptness in the madness of Clare's
delusion in these years that he was Byron, a choice of persona that was
significant not so much because of shared sympathies regarding sexual
licence or radical politics or because Byron won with his poetry the

financial rewards Clare so desperately once sought, but because Byron reconciled Augustan disciplines and satirical modes with contemporary Romantic attitudes. *The Later Poems* confirms not that Clare was a major poet, which he was not, but that his talent was an immensely and rewardingly varied one. The final irony is surely that as a poet he found 'freedom' from limiting material and from the distractions of poverty and emotional disturbance in a provincial lunatic asylum. . . .

(b) Edmund Blunden, from 'Poet of Common Objects', *Daily Telegraph*, 11 June 1964, p. 20:

He is still too little known, and perhaps is one of the English writers whom it is singularly difficult to estimate. To label him as one of the best nature poets is easy but incomplete; to regard his work in an artistic sense, or in its intellectual or philosophical light, as of the very highest order, is to invite storms.

Keats just had time, as his illness grew serious, to praise one of Clare's early descriptive sketches and to hint that the description prevailed too much over the sentiment. Perhaps that judgment is one of the nearest to the truth concerning Clare, but Keats never read Clare's 'Asylum Poems' (for example); and some of those are as 'inevitable' as any lyrics we have.

One thing is certain; nobody in prose or verse has ever lived with wild or free nature more continually or lovingly than Clare of Northamptonshire.

(c) Donald Davie, 'John Clare', *New Statesman*, 19 June 1964, lxvii, 964. Donald Davie (b. 1922), Professor of Literature at Essex, 1964–8, became Professor of English at Stanford University, California, in 1968. A poet as well as critic, he is the author of *Purity of Diction in English Verse*, 1952.

There will always be sophisticated philistines who prefer, for diagnostic or more dubious reasons, the poems which poets write when out of their wits to the ones they write with their wits about them. Poets nowadays know that it helps their reputations and sales if they can manage a spell in the psychiatric ward. But anyone who goes to poems for poetry and not another thing will prefer the sane Clare of *The Shepherd's Calendar* to the lunatic Clare whose late poetry can be painfully deciphered from pathetic manuscripts in Northampton, the Bodleian and Peterborough.

Not that the late poems aren't worth the trouble. Every so often they come up with

> I love to see the shaking twig
> Dance till shut of eve.

And even in a scrap like that one can isolate Clare's peculiar purity, in the prosaic word 'shaking', so honestly and unfussily Clare's name for what a twig does. It strikes against and qualifies and thereby validates the much less straightforward and yet more commonplace 'dance' which follows. 'Dance' for what a twig does is a word with a metaphor inside it, an analogy or many analogies; 'shaking' stays stubbornly close to the thing it names, and won't let us look away or beyond to anything analogous.

And this is the virtue of earlier Clare also. It is the reason behind his use of dialect, which is not for him a valuable resource, an artful freaking of language. He says that robins 'tutle' because this is his and his neighbours' name for what robins do, not a *mot juste* sought for and triumphantly found; not the one exquisitely right word, just the one right one. It is not so far from what Pound applauded in Johnson's *Vanity of Human Wishes*, 'the merits of the lexicographer', for whom one thing has one name, and only one name.

This shows up in Clare in the conspicuous absence of 'elegant variation'. If things have fixed names, then the same words will and must recur as often as the same things are spoken of. And so in *The Shepherd's Calendar* 'crackling stubbles' is not embarrassed by the proximity of 'crackling stubs', 'sliving' does not mind being jostled by 'they slive', 'splashy fields' naturally provide 'splashing sports'; and in the later poems, the poems of madness.

> The rushbeds touched the boiling spring
> And dipped and bowed and dipped again
> The nodding flower would wabbling hing

becomes a few lines later

> The rush tufts touched the boiling sand
> Then wabbling nodded up anew.

This comes from a poem about Robert Bloomfield, whom Clare called 'our English Theocritus', and extolled as a better poet than himself. To compare Clare with Bloomfield, a proletarian poet of the previous generation, was commonplace in Clare's lifetime; now they are seldom read together. Indeed Bloomfield is seldom read at all, though he's well worth it. Apart from anything else, readers of Bloomfield are likely to be cautious about seeing Clare as *engagé*, as a socially committed poet: the June eclogue from *The Shepherd's Calendar*, which speaks of

> the old freedom that was living then
> When masters made them merry wi their men,

and deplores how

> proud distinction makes a wider space
> Between the genteel and the vulgar race,

is not a direct response to the consequences of agricultural enclosures, but weaves together a series of allusions to the same topic in one of Bloomfield's verse-tales.

And in a more narrowly literary perspective Bloomfield's name is still important. His *Farmer's Boy* of 1800 is an unabashed and very attractive descendant of Thomson's *Seasons*; and Thomson was, so the tradition runs (and nothing is more likely), the poet who first inspired Clare. It's true that when Clare uses decasyllabic couplets, as he does in the best parts of *The Shepherd's Week* [sic] (though some of the octosyllabics are also fine), he escapes the characteristically Augustan or post-Popian cadences, as Bloomfield in his verse-tales doesn't. Nevertheless, Clare almost certainly regarded himself as writing in a tradition stemming from Thomson through Bloomfield, as competing therefore for the neo-classical laurels of 'English Theocritus', stakes that Wordsworth and Coleridge, Keats and Shelley, were not entered for. Accordingly Clare can use the personification, for instance, with Augustan aplomb and wit:

> The ploping guns sharp momentary shock
> Which eccho bustles from her cave to mock.

And when in his madness he identified himself with Byron, and tried to write a *Childe Harold* and a *Don Juan*, the manoeuvre was not altogether senseless: Byron's special and Augustan kind of Romanticism is the only kind that can be invoked to make Clare any sort of Romantic poet, and indeed the poet who exhorted the 'deep and dark blue Ocean' to 'roll' shared Clare's attitude to words as names—there are no metaphors hidden in Byron's 'deep' and 'dark' and 'blue', any more than in Clare's 'shaking' or his 'wabbling'.

Equally, it did not have to be a Romantic generation which in 1820 made Clare's first book of poems, and its author, a 'Northamptonshire peasant', the literary sensation of the season. The 18th century had had its thresher-poets and milkmaid-poetesses, though Bloomfield the shoe-maker was the only one before Clare who had enduring talent. (Burns is in another category, though neither Clare nor Clare's generation realised it.) In fact, the Clare of that first book, of *The Village Minstrel* which followed it in 1821, and of *The Shepherd's Week* (1827), was not 'Romantic' enough.

The insensitive officiousness of Clare's first publisher, Taylor, whose emasculating revisions the new editors have removed, tells its own tale of what the taste of the 1820s wanted. And Clare's first biographer, Frederick Martin in 1865, thought that it wasn't until 1830 that Clare became 'a writer of perfect melodious verse'. It was only then, says Martin, that 'the outward form came to be mastered by the inward spirit, as clay in the hands of the sculptor.' And Martin was no fool, nor anything but a whole-hearted champion of Clare. His *Life of John Clare*, which is now very properly reissued, has been superseded as scholarship by the Tibbles' *John Clare* of 1932. But Martin wasn't writing a scholarly book, he was uncovering a scandal, the scandal of Clare's destitution which drove him to the madhouse; and for the sake of Martin's indigna-tion and his resolute naming of names, it's worth putting up with his confident fictionalisings about what no one can know, how Clare felt when he wasn't writing poems. As for the feelings that got into the poems, one can see that from Martin's Victorian-Romantic standpoint, which prized melodiousness and plasticity and subjectivity, Clare's *Shepherd's Week* was disconcertingly too faithful to the various angulari-ties of a social and physical world irreducibly outside the mind which registered it.

This is not the mistake which modern taste will make. But when we praise Clare for his 'observation', we do hardly any better. For as Walter De La Mare said, 'mere observation will detect the salient sharply enough' but, in Tennyson for instance, it often 'crystallises what should be free and fluent with a too precise, an overburdened epithet.' Clare never does this. His words are like the words of Edward Thomas, of which De La Mare said:

They are there for their own sake, of course, but chiefly because the things they represent have been lived with and loved so long that their names are themselves.

This describes not a naive or limited kind of minor poetry, but one kind of great poetry, sane, robust and astringent.

Bibliography

BLUNDEN, E., and PORTER, A., eds, *John Clare: Poems Chiefly from Manuscript*, 1920: includes a fairly comprehensive list of nineteenth-century periodical criticism.

GALE, N., ed., *Poems by John Clare*, 1901: includes a short bibliography compiled by C. Ernest Smith (see Introduction, p. 17), mentioning some critical works and early reviews.

POWELL, D., *A Bibliography of the Writings of John Clare with a Selection of Critical Material after 1893*: prepared for the London University Diploma in Librarianship. This unpublished dissertation gives a detailed account of the publishing history of Clare's poems, and includes a wide survey of books, essays, and articles on Clare.

TIBBLE, J. W. and A., *John Clare: His Life and Poetry*, 1956: contains a useful bibliography.

Index

The index is divided into three sections: I. Clare's writings; II. Clare: topics and characteristics; III. General, including people and periodicals.

II. CLARE: TOPICS AND CHARACTERISTICS

III. GENERAL